Out of the Garden

First published in the UK and USA by Verso 1993
Paperback edition first published by Verso 1995
© Stephen Kline 1993
All rights reserved

Verso
UK: 6 Meard Street, London W1V 3HR
USA: 180 Varick Street, New York NY 10014–4606

Verso is the imprint of New Left Books

ISBN 1 85984 059 0

British Library Cataloguing in Publication Data
A catalogue record for this book is available from the British Library

Library of Congress Cataloging-in-Publication Data
A catalogue record for this book is available from the Library of Congress

Typeset by Solidus (Bristol) Limited
Printed and bound in Great Britain by
Biddles Limited, Guildford and King's Lynn

Out of the Garden

Toys, TV, and Children's Culture
in the Age of Marketing

◆———————

STEPHEN KLINE

VERSO

London · New York

1993

Contents

Acknowledgements

A civilized society is one which struggles to make the world better for its children. Collectively, we in the industrialized world can feel proud that scientific progress and material affluence have helped to reduce the deprivation, neglect and abuse of our children. But as current events make clear, after several generations of affluence we still have no right to be complacent or arrogant about what has been achieved in the interests of our children; many children in the industrialized West continue to be partially educated, poorly fed and physically abused and neglected.

Similarly, we often forget that cultural progress has failed to keep pace with our science and our affluence. New media and expanding leisure time have not necessarily produced enlightened, fulfilled and creative children. Indeed, there is an overriding sense of dismay among the current commentaries on children's media that so much freedom and affluence should have produced so few products of cultural and artistic excellence. It was my attempt to understand why this should be the case that inspired the writing of this book.

Raising children can be a radicalizing experience. The two children in my life – Daniel Sennen and Meghan Sarah – have insured that this inquiry into children's culture was no abstract matter for me. From the start my son Daniel made a major contribution by first inspiring and then informing the critical argument which is forwarded in this book. It was his fascination with Voltron and Transformers which first alerted our family to the real 'power' of children's toy-marketing and helped us to recognize not only the importance of toys in children's lives, but the need to understand and criticize what was happening in children's cultural industries.

As Jill and I watched Daniel construct endless imaginary battles from bedclothes, chairs and those character toys promoted on

Acknowledgements

television we got a vague impression that his imaginative play was being framed by television: the battle arrays and formations, the language and voices, the endless ritual line-up of forces and motorized sounds, laser attacks and battle cries, which all parents must now endure, began to create in us a general discomfort with what the market offered children. We were both enthusiastic about Daniel's imaginative play and wanted to encourage it, but as we watched, listened and played with him, we began to worry about the repetitive and aggressive ideas that underwrote that play. Like many other parents who thought in this way, we attempted to counteract this influence by limiting television, banning violent toys and talking to our children constantly. But being an academic interested in the criticism of culture, my instinctive response was also to try to understand why parents were being backed into a position where they were forced to resist the pressure of television.

It was because we were raising children during an unprecedented boom in children's cultural industries that we were forced on a daily basis to confront the fact that expanding scale of marketing to children represents a powerful but ambiguous vector in our children's lives. I have focused my inquiry, therefore, on the growth of children's cultural industries in order to think more broadly about the particular malaise within market-industrial society that arises when the privileged position we give to marketing within media begins to undermine and threaten our aspirations for a more civilized society which would promote the full development of children.

My partner and friend, Jill Ineson, was naturally very much a part of this inquiry. She helped me to resist simplistic and abstract critiques in the same way that her commitment to quality and creativity in children's learning has always challenged the complacency that can descend on our family life. I am deeply indebted to her, not only for the support she has given to my work, but because she has helped me to understand in a personal way that human self-expression matters throughout our growth and development.

Anyone who has tried, knows that researching young children's thoughts and feelings is both a delight and an agenda for frustration. It's not that hard to talk to kids about some of their favourite things but it is another matter to make sense of what kids are really telling us. In this respect I think I was especially lucky to have Daniel not only as an inspiration but as an informant. He, and a number of his friends, talked openly with me about their fascinations, their experiences, and the pressures of playing with their peers, often saying things so clearly and directly that I couldn't obscure these statements with higher-level abstractions. I point out this special source of help because while I researched this book I was also negotiating my theories with Daniel. He listened patiently, he corrected me regularly, and often showed me ways to avoid intellectual closure or forced logic. And for those moments of graceless intrusion into his play I extend to him my appreciation for his tolerance.

Many of the fundamental arguments about marketing and the critiques of consumer culture explored in this book are in fact extensions of ideas which I worked on during the last ten years through my collaboration with Bill Leiss and Sut Jhally. I am sure it is a relief to them not have to take the blame for some of my arguments, yet I happily acknowledge that my friendship with both of them has not only been an inspiration but has had a profound impact on my own thinking about how to analyse contemporary cultural industries.

Although I have never been able to convince myself of the methodological and moral righteousness of scientism, I see no merit in substituting rhetoric and theoretical elegance for evidence. I have tried not to clutter this book with long reviews of scientific studies; but the book did emerge from a review of relevant literature and a three-year research project funded by the Social Sciences and Humanities Research Council of Canada's Strategic Grants Committee which enabled us to undertake five studies of different aspects of children's culture. I am indebted to those students in my workshop on children's cultural environments (ES 7458), which during the spring of 1986 began this foray with a series of exploratory studies carried out while I taught in the Faculty of Environmental studies, and indebted to York University which supported me on my sabbatical so that I could continue to work on this project. Although the research designs and results are not discussed in detail in this book, the arguments herein emerged directly from the research observations made. The SSHRC grant enabled our research team to undertake quite a varied and unusual research programme exploring separately the trends in toy-marketing, children's advertisements, television programming and play. These same funds allowed us to consult with many friends, teachers and parents in order to solicit their thoughts on the state of children's culture, and finally to observe and interview several hundred children. To the schools who allowed us to work with their students, to the teachers who allowed us to work with their classes, and to all these anonymous sources, I can only express my thanks for assisting with this project.

Leesa Fawcett was the research co-ordinator on the Technicians of the Imagination project who nobly sacrificed many hours in arranging and managing our working group's affairs and keeping us all on track. Leesa helped to conceive this project's framework at the outset, and her ideas and concerns guided the research throughout. Her sensitive work interviewing children was a major asset to our group. My friend and colleague Dian Marino was not only a great support and sounding board, but provided 'mega' assistance all through the study. Neil Evernden, another colleague at Environmental Studies also helped to launch the project and helped provide the analysis of the bio-technical dimension of children's television. Craig Neherniak and Jackie Pearce were a vital part of the research team too. They had a special responsibility in developing the content analysis of television programmes and their knowledge of children's television shows was staggering by the end of the study. Bruce Pierce took on responsibility for writing to all children's industries and collating material on children's marketing.

Debra Pentecost not only helped design and carry out the study of toy-advertising but has continued to be a valuable support and source of ideas throughout the preparation of this book. Without Deb's help I would never have gotten over some of those major hurdles of revision. Robyn Hall and Terry Van Quickenborne also helped with the preparation of the manuscript. In addition, my colleague at Simon Fraser University Rick Gruneau has not only maintained his faith but has helped enormously by giving the manuscript a serious reading and making excellent suggestions for its improvement. Peter Saunders of Garamond Press has been crucial supporting the preparation of the manuscript throughout and has ensured that it saw the light of day. Robert Clarke was the editor from Garamond who worked on the original manuscript and his thoughtful attention to language and detail has been a great asset to this work. Lucy Morton at Verso then co-ordinated the final preparation of the manuscript: her skill in managing the final edit and production of this book was crucial to its seeing the light of day. To the many others who have offered their help, support, advice and tolerance while this book went through its many stages I offer my thanks and hope they find some aspect of this book useful.

Stephen Kline
Vancouver, BC

Introduction

The Sovereignty of

Consumerism: Children in the

Age of Marketing

> [the merchant] generally, indeed, neither intends to promote
> the public interest, nor knows how much he is promoting it. By
> preferring the support of domestic to that of foreign industry, he
> intends only his own security; and by directing that industry in
> such a manner as its produce may be of the greatest value, he
> intends only his own gain, and he is in this, as in many other
> cases, led by an invisible hand to promote an end which was no
> part of his intention. I have never known much good done by
> those who affected to trade for the public good.[1]

With this image of an invisible hand, Adam Smith (1723–90) helped
to inaugurate a powerful, almost mystical belief in the marketplace as
the guiding institution for a modernizing society. Smith saw in the
market a force for economic rationality, a force that could shape and
inspire the pattern of social development independent of the
oligarchies of eighteenth-century Europe. The idea that an autonomous and unregulated 'marketplace' could adjudicate social purpose
helped to challenge the agrarian power of feudal aristocracy, but it
has also proved durable enough to shatter many ideological boundaries since: in the late twentieth century, fascination with the market
economy is busy reorientating the socialist world's agenda, just as it
once did for the capitalist world. The invisible hand of the market
now seems poised with the whole earth in its grasp.

Faith in the market as a progressive institution has been zealously
promoted by the cult of economists whose arcane science now has
an unusual sway both in the public mind and in our public policy
decisions. These are the double promises associated with the autono-

1

mous marketplace: that consumers will be sovereign because their choice determines what will be produced for that market; and that an invisible hand of market competition will ensure that these self-serving individual choices ultimately will be a benefit to us all in the form of endless growth in the economy. And so we hear repeatedly these days the 'affectations' of businesspeople declaring the necessity of competition in the market and their solidarity with the aspiration of growth. Their belief in the 'market's rationality' and in its ability to ensure 'consumer sovereignty' is currently becoming the theological dogma of the global economy.[2]

These twinned economic metaphors of a 'consumer king' backed by an 'invisible hand' are truly an example of inspired promotional prose. Indeed, the strength of the popular belief in the market's efficiency provides clear evidence of the power that abstractions can have in modern life. But why do we put so much faith in these unseen powers? These ideas originated with classical economists who were seeking to explain hypothetical behaviour in a 'perfect' theoretical market: where all consumers are assumed rational and adequately informed, where competition is real, and where merchants' persuasions have little influence on consumer choice. But economists so often revise their own predictions that their science now seems to be nothing more than an extrapolation based on unproven assumptions and hopeful prognostications; there appear to be no rules, mechanisms or laws of human economic behaviour. The contemporary language of economic explanations ('putting on the brakes' or 'runaway inflation') continues to reveal a depth of uncertainty that still lies at the core of economists' explanations of how the marketplace works. Betting on the trends of economic indicators is itself now a major dynamic of many financial and commodity markets. Occasionally an unguarded renegade from the economic priesthood admits that the greatest uncertainty in their science concerns human psychology in the form of the attitudes, confidence and motivation of consumers, business leaders and workers.

The Social Limits of the Market

An eighteenth-century commentator like Adam Smith can be forgiven for believing that it was possible to separate the social and economic dimensions of the market's dynamic. Smith's thinking was based on the exchange of simple staples and necessities. Indeed, aside from the sale of his own book, Smith probably had little experience of market transactions for 'cultural' goods. Even his daily newspaper would have been bought by his local coffee house and shared and discussed by the many patrons. Newspaper publishing, like so many other cultural goods, did not originate in the market sector.[3] Culture, including the arts, religion, education and literature, was buffered from the whims of merchants until the end of the nineteenth century. It is hard to imagine what Adam Smith would have to say about the contemporary market, where so many of the 'goods' are either cultural products (movies, TV programmes, art, books) or have a social value (prestige, power, style, personal identity, ceremonial display) related to their ownership and use.[4]

Potent though the classical economist's conception of the perfect marketplace has been, it is hard to ignore, too, the various limitations that economic theorists have identified in this model of the market's social activity, which include imperfect competition, excessive competition, anti-competitive conduct, imperfect information, internal and external side effects, public goods and income maldistribution.[5] Quick flips, profit-taking, insider trading, price-fixing, market positioning, monopolies, political bribery, tax write-offs and subsidies are just a few of the deviations that have left the public suspicious of a totally unfettered market. Perceiving the market's failures, many nations that profess faith in the free play of market forces choose mixed economies with stringent regulations of some market transactions. No one really believes that there should be no limitations placed on the way the marketplace works, and most industrialized nations have from 40 to 60 per cent of their Gross National Product (GNP) accounted for in the public sector and maintain stringent regulation of some marketplace transactions.

Indeed, as we are now learning, a concern with market failures must go beyond corporate crime and corruption to the heart of what former British Tory prime minister Edward Heath called the 'unacceptable face of capitalism'. The pursuit of business profits engenders activities that ignore and sometimes work against the long-term public good and confront deeply held cultural mores. This is why the Canadian Government was forced to declare, as it entered into a 'free trade' agreement with the United States, that culture would not be undermined by economic arrangements. The cultural life of the Canadian nation was a matter of 'sacred trust' that could be preserved from predations of short-term greed and exercises of bully-boy trade tactics, they ingenuously promised.

Yet in many cases it is the 'externalities' – by which economists mean the unintended social consequences of complex business decisions – that keep the dealings of the merchants in the public eye. Recent history has proved that independent businesses, especially transnational corporations following complex strategies to achieve market power, do not always act in the national or even broader public interest.[6] As factories close and welfare costs go up, the public is becoming increasingly alarmed about the seeming autonomy of the business sector. Even those governments that maintain faith in market economics are having to reassess the social impact of corporate investment, location, positioning, and marketing strategies – all of which have social consequences beyond that of growth in domestic GNP.[7] For this reason, most governments have national, sectoral and regional development policies, enter restrictive trading relationships, control the growth of monopolies, and regulate many aspects of their domestic market to maintain fair business practices. Moreover, since urban and regional growth, unemployment, education and social welfare are among the many factors that influence and are influenced by business decisions, the modern state has been forced to intervene in market processes where corporate decisions impinge on those critical social domains of environment, transportation, housing, interest and exchange rates, health, social welfare, education and communications.

So how much longer can we continue to assume that issues of culture and business will be separated in a market-driven economy? This question is becoming ever more relevant in the 1990s: Britain confronts the prospect of social integration into the European Community and the United States wrestles with mushrooming imports from Japan. The unfettered global market presents us with a paradoxical cultural effect. It erodes national boundaries in terms of the flow of goods and at the same time confronts national sensibilities and values as the consequences of market competition with other societies play themselves out. In the face of recession and deindustrialization, some of the leading industrialized nations are having to rethink their over-hasty commitments to the free-market mania of the eighties on sociocultural grounds. There is a growing tension between the ideology of an expanding free market and the desire for regional cultural autonomy.[8] It may be time to recognize the cultural impact of the global marketplace.

One difficulty for policies that attempt to separate matters of culture and economy lies in the changing structure of post-industrial economies, where the service or 'information sector' increasingly accounts for growth in the GNP.[9] In the industrializing economy, consumable staples (food, clothing, power, gas) and consumer durables (cars, stoves, fridges) account for the majority of market transactions and growth. In the post-industrial marketplace, the majority of goods exchanged in the market are of an essentially cultural nature, including the expanding market for cultural technologies (stereos, VCRs, telephones, computers), cultural goods (games, theatre, music videos, toys, sports equipment) and social services (restaurants, theatres, personal advice and welfare services, information processing, management services), which account for over 50 per cent of market transactions.[10] Yet there is little discussion of how this new form of market economy differs from its predecessors or whether we can continue to expect public welfare to grow through the same unfettered market mechanism. Should we believe that free markets in 'informational goods' contribute to 'social well-being' through mechanisms created for the exchange of staples?

The Social Analysis of Consumption

Taking up a theme first articulated by the US economist Thorstein Veblen, a number of anthropologists and social theorists have recently challenged the classical account of market exchange by noting that all goods have a cultural component that shapes and expresses their 'use-value'. Veblen was one of the first social theorists to see that the social nature of consumption presented serious difficulties for classical economics. His innovative analysis of the household economy was offered as a critique of the economic theories of the late eighteenth century, which focused on the value of goods but failed to consider the use to which those goods were put. In *The Theory of the Leisure Class* Veblen depicts the leisure and dining mannerisms of the US middle class as a ceremonial economy. He calls the social process in which goods are ritually displayed and consumed 'conspicuous consumption'. Veblen also points out that the deployment of conspicuous leisure parallels the demonstration of taste, wealth and power through consumption because it too can denote standing in middle-class society. He points to the conspicuous role of servants and the subtle arrangements, rules, spacing and timing of ceremonial dining as examples of the kind of customary practices in which sumptuary communication takes place. These

5

rituals, he argues, are based on 'invidious distinctions' that serve to reinforce subtle demarcations of social positioning between and within classes in the east-coast industrial bourgeoisie.[11] The possession and display of goods therefore were important elements in the consolidation of social groups and maintenance of class relations. For this reason, Veblen proposes that the social use of goods is an important component of consumer behaviour and therefore of economic demand.

The consumer roles and the implicit attitudes experienced in the course of our constant interaction with the marketplace inevitably supplement, shape and sometimes conflict with those we learn in the course of working, family, and community life. John Kenneth Galbraith's inquiry into the sociocultural basis of affluence in the 1950s was the first to recognize that the growth of marketing communication constituted a serious challenge to earlier social values and also to the assumption of market autonomy.[12] The sheer abundance of goods, and the temporal demands of choosing them, served to marginalize the reward that could be achieved in consumption. We need to consume more and more goods and to shop for longer periods to achieve the same levels of relative satisfaction. Galbraith observed that affluence also embodied its own psychology and ideology, which was necessary to make sense of that profusion of goods made available by mass production. Galbraith felt that the social emphasis granted to leisure and personal gratification in an affluent society might even subvert the traditional motivations, social relations and pride established in the industrial workplace. The growing emphasis on impulse buying and consumer credit might similarly lessen the social values of self-control and restraint so that the work ethic was transformed into an instrumental rather than ultimate value. Galbraith pointed out that the traditional basis of our whole industrial economy and the economists' understanding of it were being undermined by the intensification of marketing-for-consumption.

The picture of human exchange painted in Mary Douglas and Baron Isherwood's *The World of Goods* urged a more anthropological perspective on market exchanges. They argued that neo-classical economic theory was particularly blind to consumers' experience of the economy. Economic theory could never comprehend the social significance of the marketplace by conceptualizing products 'objectively' in terms of their potential for monetary exchange alone. Products, Douglas and Isherwood argue, are not simply 'exchange-values' but 'goods' – things that have taken on social meaning and value within the cultural flux.[13] Nor are goods understood solely as bundles of utilities. Because they are social symbols they can articulate social aspirations, define the experience of festivities and celebrations or convey complex social relations in gift-giving. Goods situate everyday life within a broader cultural universe; their use conveys the achievements of the individual, the special felt quality of the moment or the inviolability of certain timeless abstractions and values like truth and beauty. Goods also locate daily acts of consumption within the continuities of personal and family history, group and national styles, the cross-cutting tensions of work and leisure, or the wayward quest for knowing oneself. The classical economists' main mistake, Douglas and Isherwood argue, lies in their inability to comprehend the dual nature of commodities – as both objects and symbols.

In his *Limits to Satisfaction*, William Leiss notes that the structure of the contemporary marketplace, although wrought in the forge of town markets, now bears little resemblance to the original.[14] In his view, the intensification of marketing in the most recent stage of industrialization is an important social innovation because it expands the potential for blending the perception of symbolic (or psychological) and material (or utilitarian) benefits to be derived from things in their use.

Goods, as anthropologist Marshall Sahlins notes, have been a means within all cultures for articulating social occasions and demarcating social structures and relations.[15] Many aspects of preindustrial society's use, display and exchange of goods were defined around seasonal fluctuations, religious ceremonies or life-cycle transitions. In circumstances of both subsistence and abundance there exist prestige economies in which scarce goods serve as indicators of honour and social standing. Food and clothes, tools and decorations can all be employed within possession, display and consumption rituals as tokens and signs signifying categories within a broader cosmology of affiliation, power and social judgement. Consumer culture is different from earlier patterns of consumption primarily in terms of the scale and content of our consumption rituals.

Using an empirical questionnaire methodology, Mihaly Csikszentmihalyi and Eugene Rochberg-Halton documented the tremendous range of meanings associated with domestic life in the contemporary United States. They state: 'It is extremely difficult to disentangle the use-related function from the symbolic meanings in even the most practical objects. Even purely functional things serve to socialize a person to a certain habit or way of life and are representative signs of that way of life.'[16] Their study reiterates the familiar observation that commercially produced goods are intimately bound up with people's sense of their own status or standing in the modern social order. They also stress the development of consumption styles that express familial dynamics and choices, and they particularly note the importance of a sense of personal belonging and subjective identification for defining the meaning of our 'most cherished goods'.

Following a similar line of argument, Grant McCracken provides an interesting historical analysis of the roots of modern social consumption, noting that the way clothing signified social standing began to change in Elizabethan England.[17] McCracken argues that the rigid social hierarchies of the sumptuary laws connecting personal status with conventions of dress were challenged by the notion of fashion. He contrasts a 'patina' orientation (a kind of traditionalism in which the visible ageing of goods speaks of family solidarity and power) to the 'fashion' system (a more fluid system that began to emerge in the Elizabethan court, in which the judgement of social stature began to depend upon personal consumption styles and timely display). McCracken suggests that the constant pressures of consumerism may contribute to the passing of a 'curatorial' attitude to goods, in which the objects act as mementoes or talismans of personal and family history – the means by which the family interprets and preserves its past and transmits its percepts to succeeding generations in the form of treasured objects. A consumer culture may be one in which people establish fewer stable or lasting relationships with objects, as all goods become disposable in the maelstrom of fashion and style.

Unfortunately, the use of the common terms 'fashion' or 'culture' to describe the broadest patterns in a society can obscure key differences in consumption within the social classes or ethnic groups. Moreover, the continuous presence of some elements of fashion in earlier social practices of courtly consumption and in our own social practices can obscure real differences in the context, scale and qualities of the relations of consumption. Much of preindustrial consumption arises from the rural social fabric of small communities and family groups engaged in production for their own consumption; the consumption patterns of the contemporary social order are a result of the enormous trade in goods produced by others and offered in the marketplace for money. The fact that all goods are symbolic should not restrict us from inquiring into the ways that the marketplace mediates the particular social relations of consumption.

The marketplace, as an institution, ensures that all goods are valued primarily through their exchange. In our society, this is as true of cultural products – our literature, arts, music, drama and dance – as it is of staples. Noting the equivalence created between all goods by the 'commodity form', Sut Jhally argues in *The Codes of Advertising* that the significance of increasing commercial transactions in the cultural market itself should not be overlooked or trivialized. He sees the commercial media as imposing a double exchange in the cultural industries.[18] On one hand, marketers use the media to sell their products to consumers; on the other, the media audience is a 'commodity' regularly exchanged between media organizations and merchants. Jhally sees this double exchange as the key to a broader critical theory of consumer culture because it reveals the factors that bind industrial and cultural interests together in their orientation to promotion.

The Voice of the Market

Modern marketing practices did not emerge unbidden from the social milieu of personal selling by local merchants in small-town stores. The new emphasis on promotional communication began to gain force with the emergence of national brands distributed widely across urban centres through department stores.[19] During the last century the market expanded simultaneously as a system of distribution and sale of goods and as a technique of selling. In the process, our whole urban landscape has been transformed by merchants who sought to ensure that we can buy anything we want at our convenience. Likewise the expansion of our media systems has increasingly granted merchants the opportunity to speak to us about their wares.

But manufacturers and merchants have not always had such a privileged position in public planning or such ready access to the means of public communication. In the eighteenth century, marketing technique consisted simply of polished fruit, a few street cries, and occasional published announcements. Merchants felt little need to elaborate publicly on the promise of their products or the nature of their contribution to society, because both of these were assumed. The rapid expansion of production that took place in the nineteenth

9

century was fuelled primarily by new technology, competitive pricing, better product design and improved distribution. Only during the second half of the nineteenth century did the opportunities afforded by the press and magazines make advertising a valued instrument of merchandising. Merchants had to make a difficult decision – to take money that might otherwise go towards improving production technology or the product and allocate it to communicating with potential consumers. Many of these early promotional efforts were awkward and wordy affairs. Yet over time, merchants and manufacturers gradually learned to innovate in their communications, and in so doing they recognized that investment in promotion could be a basic principle of market growth.

The merchants' investment in promotion and advertising is what we experience as the 'persuasive' force of the contemporary marketplace. The reason our modern environment resonates with commercial themes and promotional motifs is because merchandisers strive to use all available channels to stimulate interest in their products. An average North American sees twenty thousand different TV commercials in one year. In the course of a lifetime he or she will also receive many millions of 'exposures' from the marketplace – in circulars and junk mail, on billboards and posters, in magazines and newspapers. Because of recent innovations in public relations and marketing strategy, consumers also experience the imprint of marketing strategy projected through the design and packaging of goods and on T-shirts, bus shelters, rink hoardings, and televisions in stores – on any surface that can bear a promotional imprint. Very few of these communications are conceived by the executives, engineers or managers of factories that make the goods; rather, they are developed by specialists in marketing departments and advertising agencies. Even the public statements of business executives have been contoured by public relations specialists whose job it is to orchestrate the public affectations of business.[20] Contemporary marketing practice subsumes a fantastic panoply of merchandising and communication techniques. The practical knowledge of persuasion they accumulate constitutes, to borrow a phrase from Canadian political economist Harold Innis, an 'oligopoly of knowledge'.[21] In the way that the medieval priesthood consolidated its position through control of the written word so today the marketplace appears to underscore the bias in contemporary communication systems.

Although Adam Smith could not have suspected that the 'affectations' of merchants might become the pre-eminent organ of social communication, there is no reason why contemporary economists should continue to misjudge the potential impact of the market's voice on contemporary life. Businesses of all types have learned to utilize the expanding information infrastructure to promote their point of view and plan the entry of goods into our lives with ever more clever and sophisticated means of communication. Merchants now employ every modern communication device and management technique to remind us of the availability and the desirability of goods, corroborating the ideology of market society by demonstrating the growth in our collective production: the full shops remind us daily of the marketplace's contribution to material progress; and the international news affirms our relative wealth compared to less competitive non-market societies. Our ideas about the market's social role therefore have become seamlessly linked with our belief that consumption is the best way to achieve success, happiness and well-being.

Indeed, we live in an era when it seems obvious that we should always be thinking about goods. Because we produce for ourselves very few of the things we need, we must shop continuously, searching out, examining and choosing among the thousands of products available to us at malls, supermarkets and corner stores. Yet because we are so little acquainted with the production and qualities of most of these goods, our surveillance of the marketplace demands that we spend considerable time and effort. We must constantly respond to and interpret masses of information about goods from the catalogues, want ads, salespersons, friends and electronic media that surround us. If we pause and think about it, the scope and scale of the market may seem daunting. Though the task of optimizing happiness through thoughtful purchase seems simple enough, when confronted by the myriad of individual goods, each with its own price, promise of satisfaction and purported benefits, some consumers become emotional – anxious, confused, distracted or overwhelmed. Happiness does not always characterize the experience of the harried consumer.

However confusing and uncertain our world, the promotional messages that cascade ceaselessly from the media at least adopt a consistent position on the ultimate purpose of a consumer society – that we can always find meaning, comfort and solace in our relationship with goods. In their relentless pursuit of social communication marketers have woven all the threads of daily life into the fabric of our world of goods. Indeed, for many people consumption

11

is definitional to the modern way of life. Our use of goods is no longer just a matter of the conspicuous display of wealth and social standing but an end in itself – a complex theatrical entertainment wherein the play of social values, fashions and lifestyles articulated through the choice of goods also expresses the essence of our highest cultural achievements.

In a consumer society we use goods extensively to construct and articulate the social relations of the family. And yet the consumerist vector in our society can sometimes appear disturbing when we see it reflected and expressed in children's behaviour. Children can become obsessed with wanting particular video games or toys and exceptionally persistent in their demands for them. On the other hand, they can treat very expensive or special gifts with total disrespect or disdain. If a particular article of clothing, a toy, or even a pencil is not designed with the right motifs accepted by their peers, children will refuse adamantly to use them. Parents often feel that their children simply don't know the 'value of their things', in part because they have too much. As parents confront their children's cluttered and messy rooms they may mutter to themselves that the traditional values, discipline and parsimonious sensibilities in which they had been brought up to believe should not have been abandoned. In a society where youths are swarmed in our schools for a 'Bulls' jacket; where it is vital for peer survival to wear the right running shoes; and where wealthy kids display their designer labels (and ghetto kids their price tags) as status symbols, consumerism may not always be seen as a good thing. It is, in fact, easiest to recognize the deeper paradoxes of our consumer culture when it is refracted back to us through the mirror of childhood.

A tone of foreboding particularly underscores popular commentaries on young children's leisure or cultural goods because the rise of electronic media seems to have undermined the traditional healthy preoccupations of street play, peer conversation and just wandering in the garden long associated with a happy childhood. If left to their own devices, most young children, it seems, would choose to play with their plastic toys, their video games, or watch TV. However limited and banal these activities seem, everyone acknowledges that they do at least absorb children's attention – so much so that it may be difficult to persuade a child watching the television or playing a video game to go outside and skip, build sandcastles, draw or sing songs. It is to counter the compelling quality of these technologies that middle-class parents whisk their children to alternative venues to 'civilize' them with dancing lessons, art classes and soccer matches.

With this in mind, critics have argued that the market's goods substitute for and 'displace' the traditional patterns of family relations constructed through goods. Moreover, many of these popular leisure activities offered in the market for children seem to lack the depth, authenticity and social richness of older non-commercialized forms. Something is missing from childhood, the critics argue, when we give a child a musical tape of children's songs because we don't have time to sing to or with them; when we give them a My Little Pony colouring book as a substitute for drawing; when we let them watch fantasies on TV, without reading to them or exposing them to the intimacy of personal story-telling; when we give them Nintendo, but fail to teach them the finger games or craft skills (knitting, carpentry, gardening) that have been traditions within our families.

As we listen to children's conversations we can't help but notice that the market touches their lives more directly than ever before. Whether it is two children agreeing on their admiration for Barbie's hairstyle or a group of boys debating the fire power of G.I. Joe, there is little mistaking the growing impact of marketing on the everyday expressions of our children.[22] Girls of three can be heard in shops insisting on brand-name shoes, and young 'dudes' wave Mutant Ninja Turtle swords at each other while whistling the tunes or reciting the slogans of advertisements. Boys of eight avidly debate the merits of video games or the future value of their hockey card collections. Given that merchants' attentions are increasingly focused on child-hood, it is reasonable to expect that this nascent concern with children's consumerism will grow stronger. Yet the academic and journalistic commentaries on childhood seldom acknowledge the marketplace as a part of the matrix of contemporary socialization or devote serious attention to how children learn those roles, attitudes and sentiments that reinforce the consumer culture. It is to redress this situation that I have made the evolution of children's marketing the central theme of this book.

The Matrix of Socialization: From Staples to Toys

The need to reassess the market as a growing force within the matrix of socialization goes against the grain of a vast academic and popular literature that has described and theorized about these processes. Pointing to progressive changes in the way modern families and schools 'civilize' the young (such as the decrease in physical abuse and the enlargement of children's freedom and choice), some prominent accounts of socialization maintain a hopeful prognosis for the future of childhood.[23] Some psychologists have pictured the family as the primary source of both developmental dynamics and socio-emotional disturbance, advocating progressive parenting and modernized teaching methods as the cure to childhood's ills. Others have called for more radical reforms to these institutions. But all bear the stamp of a common belief that family and schools are the main agencies of socialization.

Following this assumption, many psychologists have directed their research towards strengthening the traditional family and enhancing children's ability to develop through literacy and numeracy. Modern psychology is 'cognitivist', which reinforces the continuing importance of literacy in contemporary culture by revering knowledge acquisition as the basis of maturation. Even in fields of research such as the study of play or developmental social psychology, the tendency is to assume that cognition is the dominant modality of experience. This assumption drastically narrows understanding of children's culture experience and cultural learning, making it difficult to appreciate the part played by things acquired in the market in shaping children's experience.

Educational psychology's narrow perspective has ensured that academic research into children's normal everyday social attitudes, interactions and cultural practices conducted outside the school system has been limited; we have, therefore, only a vague outline of the social and emotional learning engaged in on a day-to-day basis as children interact with the formative environment of peers, family and media. Psychologists have shown limited appreciation of the part that mental processes associated with shopping, toys, television, stories, music, clothing or the economy have in children's development. This is not to say that developmental research has not provided useful insight into the conceptual sequences through which children mature. But our ethnographic picture of the child must remain incomplete if we view children only through the lens of a state-run education system and judge them against the standards valued by that system.

It is impossible to deny that family, school and community life have all been transformed by the successive pressures of industrialization and commercial media. Csikszentmihalyi and Rochberg-Halton's study of attitudes to household objects, for example, found generational differences in the meanings that children attached to, and the quality of their involvement with, their own range of goods, which hints at a separate order of youth consumption. Children generally reported that toys, stereos, and television were highest on their list of valued domestic objects. Moreover they referred to the ideas of personal 'experience' and 'self' to explain the felt relationships with these objects as opposed to functions, social judgement, cost or utility. Children's most cherished objects invoked a strong emotional response or attachment associated with their inner world of reference. As parents know, children's preferences in toys and computer games and their access to television guides most of their free-time activities and these activities are profoundly linked to their sense of happiness.

Although psychoanalysis has long maintained that the earliest patterns of consumption (breast-feeding, for instance) play a role in the formation of the personality,[24] commentators have tended to overlook the subsequent impact that the things given to children have on their growing awareness of their society. Books, for instance, have long been given to children to establish a love of reading, a moral code and a sense of their literary heritage. We know that families that read to their children and encourage reading support literacy, yet we know very little about what the ideas encountered in books mean for children. Similarly, children are provided with musical instruments, computers and sports equipment to induct them into the mysteries of these other fields of endeavour. Some children are dressed in designer fashions and fitted out for parties. All these goods contribute to and reinforce particular patterns of socialization because they acquaint children with socially sanctioned roles, skills, ideas and sentiments. Yet there is surprisingly little recognition among contemporary psychologists of the mediating role that any of these cultural objects play in children's development and generally no understanding of why possessions come to form such an important part of the contemporary child's life.[25]

Of all the cultural objects given to young children, argues Brian Sutton-Smith, toys are the most culturally salient because they provide a flexible and engaging tool of socialization. Middle-class children are given an enormous number of toys (tool sets, mini-kitchens, baseballs, dolls) because they are 'models of things' that invoke in play the behaviours or skills required in later life. Children often establish profound attachments to particular toys, which they remember throughout their lives. Though they are given to the young child with parental purpose in mind – to comfort and express love, to reward, to encourage social play, to help them learn skills, or simply to acquaint them with the behavioural templates of later life – the child also exercises some agency in their use. Agency is possible because, although any object (a stick, a box, a rag) can invoke children's play instincts, toys are also cultural symbols (a sword, a house, a friend) that can be manipulated and interpreted. Toys engage children, argues Sutton-Smith, because they invoke such a diverse and rich range of meanings that carry profound significance – love, friendship, power, mastery, skilfulness, achievement, fun.[26]

Lita Furby similarly argues that within the contemporary matrix of consumerism, toys are a child's prototypical possessions – the first things that children learn they can use, control and derive pleasure from. During the first three years of life a child's most fundamental attitudes are thus formed in the use of toys. The toys help children define the meaning of both 'the world' and 'themselves' providing them with a unique way of exploring, on their own, the relationship between these broad fields of experience. What the child learns through toys is then transferred to other objects. Contemporary parents actually sanction a progression of cultural objects for the child, starting with toys and extending through books, clothes, television, records or tapes and films. These objects are often given to help children adjust progressively to changing aspects of their social world.

Toys are just the first consumer goods given to children. It now seems evident that the matrix of socialization is undergoing transition in terms of a sequence of objects that we use as the implements of socialization. Teachers are quick to witness the fact that the play activities and learning styles of children outside the school are of a different kind, but certainly no less important to children than those sanctioned by the education system.[27] They often either ban particular toys from their classrooms or conversely try to employ toys and television, and the images from children's culture, to aid in-class learning. The schools must adjust to the fact that the attitudes and values of parents to the goals and means of childrearing are themselves similarly in flux as children become rewarded with toys and are baby-sat by television sets.[28] Moreover, it is becoming apparent that the modern parent has little time to devote to traditional family activities, and many urban neighbourhoods seem too intimidating to allow 'free-ranging' street life, so the interactions of children's peer culture are also changing. This menacing spectre of childhood out of control is now portrayed in daily stories of drugs, street gangs and weapons in schools.[29]

The Medium Is the Message

Although toys may establish the templates, the beacon that has been demanding a major rethinking of the modern matrix of socialization sits in most living-rooms. Since the early studies of television by Wilbur Schramm in the United States and Hilde Himmelweit in England, social theory has been concerned about television's ominous potential to attract and influence the young.[30] It has since become harder to ignore the much-repeated fact that by graduation from high school the average child will have spent over 20,000 hours watching television and only 11,000 in the classroom. A child will be exposed each year to 18,000–21,000 commercial messages. Heavy-viewing preschoolers may spend up to one-third of their waking days in front of the tube. They will forget many of the facts they learn in this TV-watching but will retain vague impressions from the thousands of stories they see. Because of this incidental cultural learning, they will also accumulate an encyclopedic knowledge of the preferred patterns of speech behaviour and social interaction in our popular culture. Meanwhile the act of family viewing, if it occurs at all, remains a passive ritual. Much of children's television viewing is done alone, or with siblings and friends. The rest of the young child's free time is spent playing alone or with peers. One discouraging US study estimated that the average parent spends only thirty seconds a day in 'meaningful' conversation with the child.[31]

Given television as a fact of life, during the 1970s a massive research effort helped to focus public interest and discussion on the relationship between television and childhood aggression.[32] Little wonder then that television has been the main villain, too, in the debates about the failing literacy and growing ignorance of North American children. Forceful proponents like Neil Postman have prognosticated the inherent demise of literate culture because of the rise of this medium.[33] Others, observing the fascination that children have with television, express their concerns about society's failure to use this medium for education and enlightenment. Television is a vast wasteland, it is argued, because private media businesses have no goals beyond profit and make no public commitment to educational or quality goals.[34]

Although we lack definitive information about the independent effects of television on children's schooling, attitudes and violent behaviour, advocates of public television are recognizing that the specific inadequacies of television may arise from the social purpose to which it has been put.[35] Contemporary social policy sanctions television not as the hoped-for independent educational technology, but as an entertainment market and communication channel for business. It is surprising, therefore, that so few of the commentaries about the fate of childhood have paid attention to the market dynamics of children's television. One exception to this is Cy Schneider's account in his book, *Children's Television*. His main point is simple: children's television is a business that thrives only in so far as it consolidates a children's market.

It is worth noting that the thinking and research discussed by Schneider in making his case have not been conducted by academics and teachers, but by market research firms and media business strategists. These interests have been taking the changes in household activities seriously, including family relations, free time and leisure, because these aspects of children's culture are the basis of their profitability. The perspective of their research is both pragmatic and proprietary, but that in itself hasn't prevented the cultural industries from gaining insight into contemporary children's everyday experiences of play, fiction and leisure.[36] Some of the most incisive accounts of how kids think and respond to the daily flux of modern communication systems are written in the pursuit of new ways of selling more chocolates and dolls.

The merchants and marketers of children's goods have always paid more diligent attention than educationists to children's active imaginations and incidental cultural interests. These researchers don't bother to observe comatose children in the classroom being battered with literacy; they study them at play, at home watching television or in groups on the streets and in shops. They have talked to kids about why they like playing Nintendo or trading sports cards. In their research they have used much more discursive methods that provide more insight into children's emotional and social perceptions.[37] And they are not discouraged when they discover that peer perceptions, the love of stories, strong attachments to goods, vivid imaginations and a lively fantasy life lie at the heart of children's conversations and leisure preoccupations. Marketing's ethnography of childhood has validated children's emotional and fantasy experience, which the educational researchers have by and large avoided and derided. The marketers didn't have to assume that children's daydreams, hero worship, absurdist humour and keen sense of group identity were meaningless distractions or artefacts of immaturity. Rather, they recognized that these attributes were the deep roots of children's culture, which could be employed as effective tools for communicating with them. Identifying the basis of children's daily experience provided the means for transforming them into a market segment.

The marketers' willingness to think about and research children's responses to the things in their lives was an essential step in the development of the children's cultural industries. Merchandisers first began to contemplate the unique position of children in the nineteenth-century book market, when publishers began to produce books especially for children. This same willingness to explore the roots of children's imagination has underscored the progressive commercialization of all children's media – especially comics, films and television. Because the foundation of children's media now rests upon the marketplace, it is not surprising that the themes and ideas articulated therein are governed by a marketing dynamic. What is surprising is the reluctance of educators and academic commentators to recognize that commercial media and the toy industries are vital agencies of socialization.

I offer the following account of the history of children's cultural industries in the hope of challenging the popular view that socialization rests primarily in the hands of schools and parents. There is also an invisible hand in the market, which influences childhood by shaping the things children use and the media through which they learn about them. Moreover, given the enormous promotional apparatus directed at influencing parents and children's preferences in the market, I also find it difficult to maintain that contemporary children's culture expresses children's autonomous choices and preserves their innocence. I am convinced that the strategies of the market influence the qualities of children's culture. Indeed, autonomy and innocence seem antithetical to the current practices of our cultural industries as they struggle ceaselessly to increase their hold over our children's imaginations. We cannot lose sight of the question of quality when the cultural products delivered by the market are ultimately motivated not by an interest in the desire to enlighten, integrate, or even educate the child, but by economic considerations. Finally, in view of the dramatic changes that took place in children's cultural industries during the 1980s, I shall argue that it is time to limit the sway that marketing strategists have gained over the key instruments of children's culture – toys and television.

Notes

1. Smith, Adam, *An Inquiry into the Nature and Causes of the Wealth of Nations*, ed. Edwin Cannan, New York, Modern Library, 1937, p. 423.

2. Penz, Peter, *Consumer Sovereignty and Human Interests*, Cambridge, Mass.: Harvard University Press, 1986.

3. Smith, Anthony, *The Newspaper: An International History*, London: Thames & Hudson, 1979.

4. John K. Galbraith, 'Who's Afraid of Adam Smith?', *Observer*, 15 July 1990.

5. Harris, R. and Carman, J.M., 'Public Regulation of Marketing Activity, *Journal of Macromarketing*, vol. 3(1), 1983.

6. Mittelstaedt, Martin, 'The Billion-Dollar Cure', *Report on Business*, June 1989, pp. 19–21.

7. See Leiss, William, *C.B. MacPherson: Dilemmas of Liberalism and Socialism*, Montreal, New World Perspectives, 1988, pp. 112–34.

8. Kline, Stephen, 'The Theatre of Consumption: On Comparing Japanese and American Advertising', *Can. J. Social and Political Theory*, 4, 1988.

9. Bell, Daniel, *The Coming of the Post-Industrial Society: A Venture in Social Forecasting*, New York, Basic Books, 1973.

10. Williams, Frederick, *The Communications Revolution*, New York, Mentor, 1983.

11. Veblen, Thorstein, *The Theory of the Leisure Class*, New York, New American Library, 1953.

12. Galbraith, John Kenneth, *The Affluent Society*, Boston, Houghton Mifflin, 1958.

13. Douglas, Mary and Isherwood, Baron, *The World of Goods*, Harmondsworth, Penguin, 1978.

14. Leiss, William, *The Limits to Satisfaction*, Toronto, University of Toronto Press, 1976.

15. Sahlins, Marshall, *Culture and Practical Reason*, Chicago, University of Chicago Press, 1976.

16. Csikszentmihalyi, Mihaly, and Rochberg-Halton, Eugene, *The Meaning of Things: Domestic Symbols and the Self*, Cambridge, Cambridge University Press, 1981, p. 21.

17. McCracken, Grant, *The Culture of Consumption*, Illinois, University of Illinois Press, 1988.

18. Sut Jhally, *The Codes of Advertising*, New York, St Martin's Press, 1987.

19. Leiss, W., S. Kline and S. Jhally, *Social Communication in Advertising*, Toronto, Nelson, 1990.

20. Nelson, Joyce, *Sultans of Sleaze*, Toronto, Garamond, 1989.

21. Innis, Harold Adams, *The Bias of Communication*, Toronto, University of Toronto Press, 1964.

22. Reid, L.N. and Charles Frazer, 'Children's Use of Television Commercials to Initiate Social Interaction in Family Viewing Situations', *Journal of Broadcasting*, 24, 1980, pp. 149–58; Sheikh, Anees and L. Moleski, 'Conflict in the Family over Commercials', *Journal of Communication*, Winter, 1977, pp. 152–7.

23. DeMause, Lloyd, ed., *The History of Childhood*, New York, Harper Torchbooks, 1974.

24. Most forcefully argued by Winnicott, D.W., *The Child, the Family and the Outside World*, Harmondsworth, Penguin, 1969.

25. Furby, Lita, 'The Origins and Early Development of Possessive Behavior', *Political Psychology*, vol 2(1), 1980; pp. 3–42 and 'Possessions in Humans: An Exploratory Study of its Meaning and Motivation', *Social Behaviour and Personality*, 6(1), 1978, pp. 49–65.

26. Sutton-Smith, B., *Toys as Culture*, New York, Gardner Press, 1986.

27. See G.E. Davie, et. al., *The Young Child at Home*, London, NFER-London, 1984; also Barbara Tizard, J. Philips, I. Plewis, 'Play in Pre-School Centres – The Effects on Play of the Child's Social Class and of the Educational Orientation of the Centre', *Child Psychology Psychiatry*, 17, 1976, pp. 265–74.

28. Van der Kooij, Rimmert and Wilma Slaats-van den Hurk, 'Relations between Parental Opinions and Attitudes about Child Rearing and Play', *Play and Culture*, 4, 1991, pp. 108–23.

29. Ordovensky, P., 'Parents Must Restrict TV, Aid Studying', *USA Today*, 24–26 February, 1989; Smith, Vivian, 'Laissez-Faire Parenting Concerns Psychologists', *Globe and Mail*, 8 May, 1990, pp. 1, 9.

30. Himmelweit, Hilde T., *Television and the Child: An Empirical Study of the Effect of Television on the Young*, London and New York, Oxford University Press, 1958; Wilbur Lang Schramm, *Television in the Lives of our Children*, Stanford, Stanford University Press, 1961.

31. Fortino, Michael, in a BBC Radio 4 report on the modern American family, 23 June 1988.

32. Rubenstein, E.A., G.A. Comstock and J.P. Murray, eds, *Television and Social Behavior*, vol. 4, *Television in Day-to-Day Life: Patterns of Use*, Washington DC, US Printing Office.

33. Postman, Neil, *The Disappearance of Childhood*, New York, Dell Publishing, 1982.

34. Kunkel, Dale, 'Child and Family Television Regulatory Policy', in J. Bryant, ed., *Television and the American Family*, Hillsdale, NJ, Lawrence Erlbaum, 1990.

35. Palmer, Edward, *Television and America's Children: A Crisis of Neglect*, New York, Oxford University Press, 1988.

36. Stern, Sydney Ladensohn and Ted Schoenhaus, *Toyland: The High-Stakes Game of the Toy Industry*, Chicago, Contemporary Books, 1990.

37. Rust, Langbourne, 'Children's Advertising: How It Works, How to Do It, How to Know If It Works', in *Everything You Should Know About Children's Research* (Proceedings of ARF Key Issues Workshop), New York, April, 1986.

1

Communication Analysis for

the Age of Marketing

> The central concepts of cultural science – understanding, value-judgement, the involvement of the investigator – have thus been excluded or circumvented. This explains the consequent emphasis on 'effects' and the dissolution of causes into abstract notions of 'socialisation' or 'social function' or into the false particularisation of a self-directing technology. It explains also the orthodox description of such studies as the study of 'mass communications'. What is really involved in that descriptive word 'mass' is the whole contentious problem of the real social relations within which modern communications systems operate.[1]

It has become customary in academic circles to chastise contemporary society for the emptiness and banality that appear to be the malaise of late capitalist culture. To critics of 'postmodernism', popular and artistic sensibilities have converged in a polyglot form of artistic expression that appears fractionated and lacks focus or integrity. Fredric Jameson, for example, characterizes our consumer culture in terms of its aesthetic of pastiche – a conflagration of empty styles that have lost the origins of their historical reference and their optimism about the future. Jameson argues that this stylized commodity culture of the late industrial period expresses a lack of depth of personal experience and authenticity in social relations in the consumer culture at large.[2]

It is also common for critics to blame television for this pattern of cultural expression, as if the contemporary mood of easy pleasure and immediate gratification were inherent in the technology itself.[3] Yet as Raymond Williams warned in his thoughtful book *Television: Technology and Cultural Form*, it may be misleading to blame television alone for the limited social vision expressed throughout our cultural industries. Williams argues that before we examine the cultural effects 'of' television we should think about the cultural effects 'on' this medium. According to him, an emphasis on the effects of television 'reinforces tendencies to think of a given cultural system – the intentions and uses of a technology – in limited or misleading ways. That is to say, it studies the symptoms of the operation of an otherwise unexamined agency.'[4] Williams suggests that we must look to the commercial interests that fuelled and guided the expansion of all cultural industries if we seek to understand the reasons for contemporary culture's present form. His history of television reveals that the patterns or forms of cultural expression derive more from the narrow commercial purpose that directs our media. He notes that commercial television in Canada, the United States and Britain has been given no sense of its cultural mandate or misson: The cumulative weight of forty years of market-driven experimentation with programming has demonstrated that increasingly business interests, not cultural and artistic considerations, are this medium's main priority.[5]

The shadow that marketing casts upon our most cherished means of cultural expression is now too ominous to be viewed naively. Little of what we experience in the realm of commercial culture is serendipitous. If *Ms.* magazine folds due to a lack of advertisers' faith in the editorial content, or if *thirtysomething*'s loyal TV audience of millions is not sufficient to sustain it, then it is not difficult to imagine another invisible hand at work – the hand of marketing professionals massaging programming into an ever more efficient vehicle of promotion. Media, after all, are subject to the same market forces that have set our whole culture upon its commercial vector. The imagery of the good life in advertising is not simply a backdrop to the commercial programming: it is the very *raison d'être* and the central narrative of television.

In 1991 marketers throughout the United States invested $100 billion in the television, radio, newspaper and magazine industries to ensure that these media continued to deliver audiences that would see their promotions. For a media event like the Superbowl, advertisers may be asked to pay $850,000 just to have access to that audience for thirty seconds. Unaware of how they pay for their media through the 'promotional levy' included in the price of goods, viewers often assume that television and radio provides us with 'free' entertainment. Since it is all free, consumers are content to discard or appreciate the elaborate shop windows, the commercials and the constant influx of junk mail as a facet of our culture. Consumers rarely worry about the intrusiveness of advertising or how they underwrite the market's persistent callings. The purpose, authorship and consequences of this enormous apparatus of social communication recede from our awareness at those crucial moments of the exposure, purchase and consumption. For advertisers this state of affairs is perfect: the most important thing is that we continue to watch and shop and never get too upset, resistant to or critical of advertising.

Although commercials are expensive and elaborate, media critics rarely bother to analyse or comment on the advertising campaigns that punctuate postmodern culture. A television commercial that will show for thirty seconds may take months to produce and absorb millions of dollars in the research, planning and production stages – in many cases the commercial messages are the most carefully crafted and costly productions in the media. Talented and clever people in cultural disciplines ranging from theatre to make-up spend day after day dreaming up ways to make us buy. Yet without credits and award ceremonies their skills, strategies and creativity must go unrecognized. It is the ironic fate of these 'high artists' of the postmodern era that they can never get the praise and recognition that suits their talents. The commercial arts' contribution to our culture is rarely celebrated by highbrow critics, who examine paintings and novels but disdain the lowly commercials. To be fair, the popular media seem even more reluctant than the critics to reflect upon the mechanisms through which marketing criteria, values and strategies exert a subtle pressure on their programming and news operations. It is only when a popular show is dropped from the line-up that the market dynamics of scheduling, audience ratings, and production costing is referred to in the press. But marketers prefer this anonymity. They are generally happy to avoid careful scrutiny and have their dealings remain peripheral to the saga of stars and their affairs.

The public's lack of interest in marketing's impact on our culture contrasts with a school of academic analysis that is profoundly opposed to this 'propaganda of commodities'. Some social theorists are quick to conclude after only a cursory look at the advertising industry that marketing is a simple matter of the manipulation of individual consciousness by wily advertisers.[6] It is not uncommon for critics to conjure Manichean visions of marketers mustering a hidden army of cultural workers to the merchant's darker purposes as a wasteful diversion of artistic resources.[7] Such limited depictions of the mechanisms of commercial influence proves unhelpful in the long run, however, for conspiracy theories tend to misrepresent the way people internalize culture and so distract us from the institutions, policies, organizations, and repetitious merchandising practices that have transformed our public media into a system of consumer management.

Our society is much too complex for us to talk as if culture were a unified and autonomous realm or as if one set of interests could hold hegemonic sway over it. But the underlying unity of culture need not be the sole project of media analysis, and contemporary critics are beginning to abandon the notion of abstract structures arising from iron-clad laws of history. The critical analysis of communication, Raymond Williams explains, demands 'a consciousness of process, which will include the consciousness of intentions and methods'.[8] The plans and techniques of media and marketing managers are essential to any analysis of our cultural industries, for this brings human intention and policy back into our account of the patterns of culture.

Plans and designs emerge from human judgements and creativity directed towards (not always well understood or socially useful) goals and objectives.[9] Media and marketing managers both use the term strategy to describe a goal-directed exercise of judgement in turbulent and uncertain circumstances. It is important for critics, too, to acknowledge the confusion and uncertainty that underwrites decision-making in the commercial media. The term 'strategy', while not implying conspiratorial manipulation, does imply repetition in the 'method' and 'design processes' that imbue our culture with regularities of form and patterns of meaning. Raymond Williams thus envisaged a type of cultural analysis that could uncover these regularities in practice as the best explanation of the forms of cultural expression.

Marketing as Method: The Development of Promotional Strategies

Most people have only a vague awareness of the scale of planning, concentrated resources and creativity that are directed at consolidating our beliefs, values and consumption patterns; and few actually feel influenced by them. Unfortunately, the marketer's body of craft knowledge remains invisible unless we happen to work in a marketing department or have developed the habit of reviewing the trade periodicals. Most of us remain unaware even of the basic ideas that guide product managers in their attempts to maximize purchases or of the techniques advertisers employ when they identify and appeal to specific market segments. Yet on a basic level marketing is not mysterious. Marketing strategies emerge from rather straightforward, practical selling guidelines referred to by those fond of alliteration as the 'four P's': Product, Price, Place and Promotion. In a popular marketing communication text, Michael Ray writes:

> In virtually all marketing situations, whether they be product or service, consumer or industrial, private or public sector, there are four components to the marketing mix – product, price, distribution and communication. The first three components are typically developed very carefully not only by the brand manager but also by many other top executives within the organization.

Indeed, price, product and distribution are the givens of marketing. But because product, price and distribution systems are seldom changed, 'the kind of communication mix required will be determined by these stable parts of the mix'.[10] Still, practitioners' views on the right balance in the marketing mix varies with their position in the firm.

Marketing is defined in most contemporary texts as a unified management technique – a decision model that uses the means of modern communications to sell all products, including services and ideas. Sales do depend on having a good product that is well designed and useful, on making it conveniently and attractively available to consumers at a time and price that will bring them to buy it. But promotion and advertising are also more than notifications of a product's availability in the market. As Ray notes, the modern context of marketing is one where production processes and competition lead to products that are comparable in price, design and performance – they must therefore be differentiated by promotion or lose market share. Ray portrays marketing communication as the heart of marketing strategy – a craft that blends economic purposiveness with communication craft. He notes a tendency in contemporary approaches to place greater emphasis on communication, because it is the one 'controllable' factor within a marketing strategy; although price, product design, and distribution are fixed, 'the communication mix ... is what the brand or campaign manager controls, the relatively flexible part of the marketing mix, for which one year or even shorter-term campaigns are developed.' Ray's position is that marketing must be understood as strategic communication. The tools of communication are varied, including packaging, personal selling, public relations and advertising through all media. The management task is complex because an effective marketing demands the alignment of the givens, the means and the ends around persuasion opportunities, bringing communication to the foreground in marketing practice.

Of all the persuasive techniques developed by marketers, advertising has revealed itself as the most innovative and durable. Several excellent histories of marketing and advertising have recently granted us a detailed picture of the evolution of these promotional techniques.[11] Advertising as we know it is a twentieth-century phenomenon, but its roots lie in the earlier industrial era. By the 1850s the streets of London were so jammed with advertising carts that civic authorities passed a law restricting their grouped passage to ten in a row. The stations and wall hoardings were plastered with posters and the pavements were filled with walking billboards. By the close of the nineteenth century the daily newspapers were fattening themselves to over a hundred pages. More than half the pages were taken up by the new illustrated display advertisements of the commercial press, which helped the advertising agencies demonstrate the power of advertising.

Most historians of advertising rightly see that the development of agencies was critical in the evolution of marketing because these organizations quickly gained leverage with merchants by developing an expertise in media buying, then later in writing and design.[12] The agencies encouraged merchants to worry less about direct and personal selling in stores or at doorsteps, encouraging them to practise 'salesmanship in print'. The agencies thus became the points of access between the merchants and the media channels through which promotional strategies flowed. Afloat the rising tide of billboards, newspapers and consumer magazines, advertising agencies gathered both marketing savvy and self-assurance in their new craft, often bragging about their services and their accomplishments. As each media opportunity developed, the agencies helped their clients adjust their methods of social influence to take advantage of the characteristics of each new channel – adapting music and a conversational tone from radio, the narrative from comics and films and the slice-of-life drama from television.

In the radio years, the direct sponsorship of programmes actually gave agency personnel considerable scope to influence programming and also learn from the broadcasters. Advertisers sometimes devised and wrote the programmes they sponsored, finding ways to work the hosts and themes into the product commentaries and programme orientation. Cosmetic manufacturers sponsored beauty programmes and *Amos 'n' Andy* provided smiles for toothpaste makers. The advertisers' control and influence over radio programming (and later television) were in fact so palpable and direct that they also appeared too apparent and intrusive. In the wake of public dissatisfaction with overt commercial control of the airwaves (galvanized by several TV scandals during the 1950s), spot advertising became the negotiated means for achieving a more arms-length relationship between the advertiser and the networks.

Since they could no longer develop and sponsor shows directly, the agencies demanded a more flexible and scientific approach to media buying. The escalating cost of television time and the spot-buying schedules made everyone more interested in the 'numbers' from audience research. Rate cards were critical as agencies tried to budget different combinations of reach and frequency in their campaign plans. Although circulation audits and audience surveys have a long history, the complex data gathered through polls, diaries and audience-measurement techniques came to include wired-city test sites, people meters and electronic focus groups. Marketing teams included research and statistical expertise as well as creative designers. This growth in audience-measurement services cannot be minimized as a factor that helped reshape the designs of ads as well as the hidden dynamics of programming in our cultural industries.[13]

Augmented by research, advertising is now a highly refined practice of persuasion. Contemporary practitioners must organize the broad spectrum of social communication about their products. A strategic approach to marketing therefore also implies fundamental realignment in the classical marketing decisions of price, design and distribution systems as these factors were rethought for selling through communications: branding, store design and display, shopping centre location, packaging, brand imagery, logo design, corporate image, segmentation, and population targeting all had to be harmonized because of the exigencies of image created by a promotion. A quality product could not be sold below a quality price; a friendly bank could not be represented by grumpy tellers. Indeed, in current marketing practice, all aspects of the firm's strategy are adjusted to the demands of communication.

Towards a Theory of the Consumer

Merchants have long known that the mood they establish in their shops and malls, and the subjective meanings with which goods are imbued, are essential to their promotion of consumption. Cultural theorists are only now discovering what marketing managers have known for some time: that consumers' orientation to goods goes far beyond price and product comparisons. Marketing pragmatists see advertising not as manipulation but as a vehicle for situating their brands within established cultural patterns and ideas.[14] Advertising is not, after all, just a matter of sizzles and steaks: a frivolous activity of making goods more exciting, interesting, and attractive. Marketers know there is nothing trivial about a consumer's attachment to goods. Consumers are involved and engaged in their purchases – they show devotion, loyalty and pride in their possessions. They envy others who have what they want. They care about what the products 'say' about who they are as well as what the products will 'do' for them. Marketing's task has been simply to communicate this experiential order within which goods take on personal meanings – through which products become embedded in social attitudes, sentiments and judgements of our culture.

Consumerism as a way of life demands a social imagination – an ability to project how we will look and feel once we own and use those goods, or what our families and friends will think of us once we do. Many people find this social tapestry woven of goods and fantasies an engaging problem and venue for self-expression. The marketplace is not merely the institution upon which we hang our economic survival, but a major source of meaning. The task of managing one's personal place within the constant flux of fashion and personal styles can be a demanding yet enjoyable preoccupation. Like a fish in water, an individual's personal and social identity is so bound up with the consumer culture that it becomes difficult to reflect on the broader question of how we came to be in this aquarium.

The ordinary consumer has little sense of how the activities of marketing research and planning, shop layout, product design, packaging, public relations and advertising exert a constant pressure on contemporary social experience. And though merchants hail and address them at every turn, consumers rarely pause to think critically about why this constant barrage of intentional communication is necessary. In part this is because modern merchants conduct their persuasion in a rhetorically disguised 'marketing speak' which is designed to make persuasive intent transparent at the moment of communication. Indeed, the language of the market has become so blended with the vernacular that it feels like normal discourse. The ideas promoted by merchants permeate the daily conversations of citizens who repeat these same themes and aspirations in words like 'cocooning' and 'yuppies'. Whether we are busy saving for a new car that seems appropriate for our new 'lifestyle' or 'comparison shopping' at a supermarket, the ideas and criteria promoted by marketers ('Volvo is safest for the family', 'Tide cleans whiter') are like a shadow cast in the background of our thoughts.

Marketing communication is a form of expression tuned through research and communicative artistry to strike what Tony Shwartz called a 'responsive chord'.[15] It is designed to speak directly to our innermost experiences of the cycle of desire and consumption, to our sense of personal satisfaction, to our quest for meaningful social identities and relations, to our daydreams and fantasies about ourselves, to our aspirations, ideals and social values. The world of goods promised by the contemporary market, therefore, does not appear to us as a vast array of objective things-in-isolation but rather clues to self-knowledge, to well-being, to personal and social identity, to modes of entertainment and pleasure.

Observing these elaborate distribution and sales practices that evolved with the market's most recent cycle of market expansion, William Leiss adopted an approach that highlighted the communication dimension of marketing.[16] He argued that like the state, the corporation, the family and the school system, the marketplace is now a social institution that forcefully communicates about the nature of modern social relations and ultimately asserts its place in shaping those relations. He points out that industrialists didn't have to invent the consumer attitudes, product anxieties and sumptuary rituals that became associated with the objects they promoted, because this way of life was already part of our cultural repertoire. But marketers did learn to match these socially accepted ideas with particular categories of goods, and communicate these associations forcefully. This tremendous growth in marketing endeavour, Leiss suggests, has helped make the marketplace the primary arena of acculturation in 'market-intensive' society.

Advertising grew swiftly from nineteenth-century printed declarations about a product's unique features and utility into a full-blown 'theatre of consumption'. This is advertising's agenda-setting role: to reinterpret the whole gamut of social life from the point of view of promoting consumption. Contemporary advertising consequently gives the clearest and most forceful expression to the merchants' perspective on consumer lifestyles and sentiments. By amplifying, augmenting, recycling and reinterpreting established social mores, values, attitudes and customs, marketing communication legitimates, guides and sets priorities for particular relations of consumption – and, of course, overlooks many others. In the course of this reinterpretation, marketers have added many new fictional motifs to the contemporary repertoire including 'the ecstasy of taking a shower' and 'the family fragmented over a choice of breakfast cereal'. Lest such examples seem trivial, it is worth remembering that it was precisely marketers' ability to embed products in familiar and seemingly natural social narratives that has enabled them to portray the connection between products and specific social situations, moods, lifestyles, aesthetics and feelings. For this reason, though marketing has undoubtedly influenced our social beliefs and consumer practices, it has not always done so in ways that can be neatly isolated from other cross-cutting social trends.

Marketing as Communication

To understand the impact of marketing we must analyse its communication practices. Michael Ray's definition stresses that marketing implies a systematic approach to communication that creatively unifies all the means and channels of contact with consumers:

> Within this ordered approach the student and manager can begin to be concerned with and understand the main target of communication: the individual members of the audience. It is obvious that meaningful communication occurs when there is understanding of the audience on the part of the manager. Understanding can be achieved first by introspection and then by dealing with each individual communication situation with creativity. The goal is as the communication theorists put it to create overlapping fields of experience.[17]

Marketing managers cannot simply pump out any amusing promotional idea about their products. Creative design must be supplemented with sophisticated market analysis infused with an appreciation of the consumers and what they bring to the market. Strategic communication implies that the cultural knowledge, percepts and orientations of the consumer must be fully accounted for in each campaign plan.

To create 'overlapping fields of experience', advertising managers incorporate insights from consumer and audience research into the marketing plan. Research guides the marketing manager throughout the developmental cycle of market identification, product design, copy-testing and evaluation. A massive and diverse spectrum of research techniques now get employed by marketing managers which are intended to help assess market niches, make decisions about targets, assess the positioning and evaluate the consumers' responses. The persuasion directed from the advertising agencies is derived from managing the iterative 'two-way' flow of information – from consumer to merchant and from merchant to consumer.

Simplistic models of manipulation clearly cannot account for the complex judgements that marketers make in their attempts to influence purchase in a highly competitive marketplace. Given the fluid and uncertain nature of what they must do to create overlapping fields of experience, marketers know there is no simple cause and effect relationship between message and effect that allows them to navigate through the turbulent waters of a competitive marketplace. Marketers are more likely to be concerned about the media weight and cost per thousand exposures, than with promises of creative writers claiming they know how to make consumers need their products.[18]

But marketing pragmatics did demand that advertisers systematize and research the consumer's social behaviour and attitudes to goods. Armed with this evidence, marketers abandoned or revised their economistic conceptions of autonomous decision makers: consumers identified themselves as belonging to groups or segments of the market. Many knowingly followed trends, life-cycle expectations and fashions: some are pioneers experimenting with new products, others are fashion-conscious trendsetters, while still others are traditionalists whose tastes and needs rarely fluctuate. Research also revealed that the consumer was persuasible. Neither calculating nor utilitarian in their thinking, consumers could be motivated to allocate disposable income to particular kinds of purchases if the right ideas were evoked. To do so was not easy. Each product needed an image that positioned it relative to its competitors; the price-point had to be appropriate to the target consumer who, in turn, had to be able and willing to buy; the display needed to be at the right level, in the right light, on a convenient store shelf; and the consumer must have entered the shop already disposed to a particular brand. The consumers' attention has, therefore, to be drawn to the specific brand through advertising. The advertisements had to be repeated at least three to five times in order to ensure that the consumer could remember the product's name and a few of its motivating attributes. Consumers were subject to moods and cycles of indulgence and restraint in their consumption; they might choose to try a product simply because of the feelings they had about it that day. If attracted to an advertisement, therefore, the image and emotion it conveys could be very important in changing their orientation to the product. Although consumers exhibit loyalty to certain brand names, they also choose products on whim and impulse. All this and more makes marketing a very uncertain influence.

Marketers claim that advertising reflects rather than leads social change. Through their cultural sensitivity and research, the advertising agencies must become adept at working with cultural 'givens'. And it is not unfair to say that advertisers have demonstrated an uncanny ability to anticipate and mediate social contradictions, to highlight and strengthen emerging social trends (1980s business-culture ethics, for example) while adapting their pleas to others (for example gender and ethnic attitudes). This adaptability makes advertising a telling weather vane of social trends. It also makes the broader assessment of the social role and impact of advertising a difficult task.[19]

Subtle argumentation about causation often misses an essential point about the contemporary context of advertising: the practices and methods of marketing communication have taken on a life of their own as the modern paradigm of social influence. These innovations in merchandising tactics have grown into a privileged method for all persuasion in contemporary society. And yet we have very little idea of the cultural impact of this system of marketing communication – not only on consumption, but on all sorts of social activities. Who has the right to advertise and how it may be done are two critical questions for a society where the primary products exchanged are knowledge, attitudes and human experience, and the primary means of promoting their acceptance is advertising.

Marketing communication now offers a uniform solution to all social problems. A common way of thinking that shapes the business news permeates film production, sports and corporate public relations. The criteria and polls that guide the performance of candidates at election time, the way government departments influence the discussion of health problems, the images broadcast by the army from the war zone – all these strategically target our thoughts and feelings through the same framework and techniques developed for marketing communication management. Indeed, we live in a time when the job of managing politicians at election time can be compared without irony to the task of shifting soap flakes off store shelves and when the political campaign manager for George Bush can declare: 'Feelings win elections. What I strive for is an emotion, not a position.'[20] The diffusion of the marketing model is the most compelling reason for seeking a broader understanding of the social impact of marketing.

Culture, Consumption and Critiques of Marketing

As the marketing approach became the model of all modern persuasion efforts, the questions that academics began to ask about its social impact were revised. Should the state promote its political programmes through social marketing and public propaganda? Does political advertising violate or enhance the democratic process? Are producers of goods that have high social risks and associated health costs (alcohol, tobacco) to enjoy the rights of commercial free speech? Should doctors and lawyers be allowed to advertise their esoteric services to the public? And not least, should children be buffered from the socializing forces inherent in advertising? Indeed, many social critics now realize that the foundations laid down in the nineteenth-century system of production-for-distribution entailed traumatic and far-reaching realignments in the social relations of the sphere of consumption.

Though advertising has emerged as an independent force for social change, the significance of these events has been minimized because social theory has trivialized the critical study of marketing communications with implausible theories of manipulation and subliminal seduction. It is easy to attribute to marketing, as many true liberals do, the most important benefits of modern life: the profusion of goods, enhanced productivity, democracy and social consensus. It is equally easy for critics of modern capitalism to launch attacks on marketing for all manner of manipulation, deception and irrationality without much detailed analysis of its actual practices, strategies, methods or social impact.

It was not until Vance Packard's book *The Hidden Persuaders* exposed the new 'depth' techniques of marketing research that critics' attention became refocused during the 1950s on marketing methods. Packard sounded this alarm when he discovered that certain marketers were reading Freudian psychology and applying its concepts to the task of selling. In motivation researchers' 'abuse' of psychoanalytic principles, Packard saw a means by which advertisers could sway unsuspecting customers. Packard was not the only social commentator to become concerned about the growing power of Madison Avenue but his argument that business should not be allowed to 'manipulate' consumers through subtle communication techniques became the most widely known critique of advertising. Madison Avenue's popular image as an unscrupulous but effective manipulator of pliable human minds owes much to this single work. Although Packard examined the whole panoply of marketing methods, his main concern was that the unconscious nature of these 'hidden' persuasions could violate freedom-of-choice conditions for rational market determinations.[21] In other words, his yardstick was the economists' model of autonomous rational consumers. In response to these accusations of hidden manipulation, the advertisers reiterated their feeble homily that all advertising does is provide product information to aid consumers express previously established preferences. This debate about the 'information' and 'persuasion' roles of advertising, which launched Packard's career, continues unresolved even in current marketing journals.[22] Clearly, neither account of the part played by advertising in determining consumer choices is adequate because the basic model of human consciousness which frames it is so flawed.

It is worth noting that Packard never criticized advertising as a system of promotion; rather, he focused on particular techniques used by a few marketers. In spite of his misplaced concern with the control of unconscious processes, Packard's unique contribution was to focus attention on criticism of marketing techniques and their consequences. He was among the first to turn a critical eye to the research and communication design activities employed by the postwar cohort of marketing and advertising experts who were exceptionally innovative in their marketing practice. The importance of Packard's book, therefore, is not that it proved manipulation (clearly, it did not), but that it forced others to recognize the procedurally sophisticated, pragmatic and coherent communication designs upon which advertising is based. Before Packard's research, very little attention had been directed to the social consequences of product and store design, marketing research, advertising styles – the whole array of marketing techniques shaping the contemporary merchandising system.

Stuart Ewen's study of the roots of consumerism, *Captains of Consciousness*, laid the groundwork for a more systemic critique of marketing's role. Ewen views the growth of marketing communication and promotion as directly related to the problems of industrial management faced by mass manufacturers in the 1920s: 'The development of an ideology of consumption,' he wrote, 'responded both to the issue of social control and the need for goods distribution' recognized by industrialists of the period.[23] Elaborating on the view that consumerism can be traced back to the ideology of industrial planning and scientific management expounded by the corporate barons of the nineteenth century, Ewen comments:

> With the development of an apparatus for the stimulation and creation of mass consumption, business assumed an expansionist and manipulative approach to the problem of popular consciousness. While much of the thinking in the American industrial 'war rooms' maintained an adherence to traditional 'democratic' rhetoric, the basic impulse in advertising was one of control, of activity channeling social impulses toward a support of corporation capitalism and its productive and distributive priorities.[24]

Even though Ewen's insistence on corporate domination seems overstated, his work shows that if the goals of business managers are economic, the techniques of management and marketing they use are typically psychological and social. Advertising was conceived as more than a simple technique for organizing distribution and sales; it was an organizational technique directed towards managing the whole system of capitalist production through promoting consumerism. Marketing is a pivotal social invention, primarily, as Ewen argues, because it is such an effective technique for managing and solidifying the psychic structure of industrial society, for reorganizing the experience of desire, for channelling protest and subduing the alienation of the capitalist economy. Such arguments have helped other critical social commentators give credence to what marketers think and say about their own efforts.

Marketing thought, like marketing practices, has established many of the maxims of the consumer culture. Price-points, targeting and market segmentation, polling, psychographics, lifestyle and positioning are terms we all recognize as part of the normal operations of our social order. Yet, as Ewen shows, of all the marketers' pragmatic theories, none had such enormous consequence as the 'marketing concept', for it was this simple idea that helped industrial producers recognize that all goods were cultural artefacts and that selling them was mostly a matter of communication. Advertising provided the link with culture that helped persuade industrialists that to increase consumption of their goods they would have to become practitioners of the arts of social influence.

The marketing concept asserted that what mattered most in all marketing designs was the consumers' orientation to the product. A cheap, well-engineered or well-designed product displayed in a store did not guarantee sales. Consumers had to enter the store wanting the product. They had to imagine themselves owning it and using it. Marketers therefore had to understand consumers and the social motivations they brought to the marketplace as well as their changing attitudes about the use of goods in their everyday life. The marketing concept helped manufacturers think about their customers in new ways. Underpinning this shift were the twinned social techniques of researching consumers' habits and motivating them through advertising to buy the products. Marketing practitioners therefore became adept at thinking about how consumers experience goods, form preferences or loyalties, talk to one another about products, and make decisions about what to buy. Merchandising witnessed the rise of entirely new distribution and marketing networks as the marketing concept evolved into the complex strategic protocol which is duly described in contemporary texts. Sales could be built only on the firm empirical base of consumer psychology. The methods marketers employed in communication were based on experience in understanding audiences, in knowing what drew and held their attention, and the best available means of communicating with them.

Merchandisers were ushered to the media to maintain and manage their contact with consumers. The television networks in turn had to ensure that size and composition of the audience were appropriate for their clients' marketing needs – a relationship which became based upon exacting study of the reach and frequency of each advertising exposure within the audience. Reading volumes of statistics is now an essential component of marketing decision-making, as marketing managers must translate marketing data into message designs and media plans which will grab a target's attention, and ensure sufficient repetition to establish brand awareness. Marketing strategists, therefore, must become comprehensive and flexible managers to keep pace with the evolving environment of competitive media, each with its own audience characteristics, schedules and persuasive advantages. The complexity of the communications system was itself an impetus to strategic thinking.

The main limitation of the neo-classical accounts of marketing practices is, therefore, their narrow thinking about the social impact of strategic communication. Although marketing methods subsume cultural analysis and social communication, marketing communication is rarely spoken of as a cultural enterprise by its defenders.[25] Some like Michael Ray insist that because the intended goals of marketing campaigns are economic – to change market share or increase brand sales – the impact of communication will likewise be restricted to the economic sphere. For Ray it is the inefficiencies of marketing that draw the critics – that is, when marketing does not get the right message to the right person at the right time through the right medium. This argument is inadequate for two reasons. First, it does not acknowledge the many intermediary goals of marketing communication – sponsorship and media buying, product repositioning, targeting, image redefinition or brand renewal – that are the focus of so much of marketing's strategic activity. Second, it forecloses on any judgements passed upon the unintended effects of campaigns (condom ads and sexual behaviour, for instance), the long-term consequences of specific marketing tactics (such as targeting middle class or female consumers), or the whole issue of the social implications of the intensified consumerism resulting from the rise of advertising.

The important shifts in marketing thought and practice that follow from the acceptance of the marketing concept helped to propel the advertising agencies (with their knowledge of communication design and media) to the centre of the promotional planning. In *Social Communication in Advertising*, William Leiss and his co-authors provide a historical analysis of the emerging techniques of advertising design, arguing that to understand the cultural impact of marketing we must examine how advertising agencies cultivated and practised new approaches to communication. The advertising agencies managed to become the fulcrum of marketing because they forged organizational arrangements for bridging the gap between the spheres of production and consumption. Agencies not only innovated in ways of changing the disposition of the consumer; they also created new structural relations within the communication industry which enabled new approaches such as market segmentation and lifestyle advertising. Advertising can have a profound impact on our culture precisely because the agencies became situated at the vortex of communication's system which 'bridged' and mediated between the spheres of industrial production and cultural life. This creation of a systemic link between economy and communication may be the most lasting achievement of marketing communication, transcending any of the more particular sectoral or campaign effects.

In this privileged position the agencies could crystallize successful marketing tactics and repeat them until they inscribed new patterns of media practice. Their contribution to the modern communications systems is reflected not only in campaign designs but in a realignment of most marketing communications functions: agencies brought new approaches to the purchase of space and time in various media, to marketing and audience research, and to codes of self-regulation. Leiss and the others therefore postulate a vital cultural function to advertising:

> Our main point is a simple one: Advertising is not just a business expenditure undertaken in the hope of moving some merchandise off the store shelves, but is rather an integral part of modern culture. Its creations appropriate and transform a vast range of symbols and ideas; its unsurpassed communicative powers recycle cultural models and references back through the networks of social interactions.[26]

Their work examines the emergence of four 'cultural frames' for goods, which they trace from the agencies' organizational practices, models of the consumer, and strategies adopted for selling to them into the field of advertising design and media strategies. These cultural frames are simply the templates or patterns of cultural meaning articulated in the discursive practices of advertising which, through repetition, privileges four central percepts of consumer culture – namely, that goods are utilities, but they are also symbols of social standing, representations of personal characteristics of the owner, and ultimately reflections of the person's choices of lifestyle.

Whether or not it can be directly attributed to advertising, people do spend an increasing amount of their non-working lives both looking at and shopping for goods. Consumers have become so compulsive about shopping that psychiatrists consider it a treatable addiction. Christopher Lasch sees in the obsessions of the consumer culture an unhealthy narcissism:

> The propaganda of consumption turns alienation itself into a commodity. It addresses itself to the spiritual desolation of modern life and proposes consumption as a cure. It not only promises to palliate all the old unhappiness to which flesh is heir; it creates or exacerbates new forms of unhappiness – personal insecurity, status anxiety, anxiety in parents about their ability to satisfy the needs of the young.... Advertising institutionalizes envy and its attendant anxieties.[27]

Steffan Linder also slyly points out that as consumerism intensifies the amount of unpaid time consumers must spend in unpaid consumption labour (shopping, maintaining goods, processing information about goods as well as their actual use) additional stress and tensions arise which cannot be resolved by higher consumption levels. The paradox of consumerism is that it engenders growing stress as people struggle to keep up while marginalizing happiness.[28]

Given these drawbacks, Fred Hirsch argues in *The Social Limits to Growth* that our own consumer culture may have gone too far in granting so much cultural power to the 'commercial sector'. Hirsch suggests that by letting commercial interests dominate the discourse about goods we overemphasize the contribution that those goods can make to social well-being and lose sight of other factors that contribute to it. For Hirsch our culture is biased by commodity fetishism: 'The concept of a commodity bias therefore implies that an excessive proportion of individual activity is channeled through the market so that the commercialized sector of our lives is unduly large.' This condemnation is based on the way other (non-consumerist) social relations are diminished or replaced because of the commodity bias in society: 'A related concept which is suggested by this approach is a "commercialization effect" – meaning the effect on satisfaction from any activity or transaction being undertaken on a commercial basis through market exchange or its equivalent, as compared with its being undertaken in some other way.'[29] The commercialization effect implies that market-mediated culture not only has its own bias and vision, but that the cumulative weight of intensive marketing gradually displaces other social forms as marketers transform both our built and symbolic environments.

Should we be concerned about the market's privileged position within our cultural discourses? To some degree this depends on the kind of cultural vision provided by the marketplace. Some critics have argued for limits on the market's communicative power, because through advertising it supports a culture overly concerned with materialism. Advertising gives rise to a culture endlessly fascinated with things. Seeing a modern citizenry transfixed by this penetrating vision of goods the Jesuit Marxist John Kavanaugh opposes the market's visions of a consumerist paradise with the traditional 'spiritual' culture of Christianity. Consumerism is in his view a form of idolatry; a worship of things, he argues, shapes and penetrates contemporary consciousness:

> Marketing and consuming infiltrate every aspect of our lives and behavior. They filter all experience we have of ourselves. They become the standard of our final worth. Marketing and consuming ultimately reveal us to ourselves as things; and if we find ourselves revealed as things it will follow that our diverse capacities for knowing are reduced to the truncated conditions of thing-like commodity knowledge. I am not merely trying to point out here that knowledge itself has become a saleable commodity ... what I am speaking of is a more subtle collapsing of human knowing into models and patterns which are more appropriate to cognition of things or commodities.[30]

On this point Raymond Williams remarks that we may be mistaken in believing that intensification of advertising makes our culture 'too materialistic'.[31] On the contrary, he argues, the problem with advertising is that it is not materialistic enough. What is absent from modern advertising's discussion of consumption, Williams concludes, is a sense of the good's 'materiality' – that is, the processes and means by which commodities are produced, their composition, the way they function, or their utilities. To this observation, we can now add the environmental origins and costs of these goods too. In this view, advertising is more at fault for the window on to the world of goods it provides, and its biased and partial 'fictionalization of reality'. By lifting goods out of the material constraints exerted on production and consumption, it falsely perpetrates the hope that ever expanding consumption can continue without limit or consequence.

Williams talks about advertising as if it were a modern 'magic system' in which products do not represent things so much as the potential transformation of our experience. Marketing communication, he points out, is a form of social narrative whose primary task is to convey those fictional social relations which can only be fulfilled in and through product ownership and use. Advertisers choose not to discuss goods as material things, but rather as motivated social symbols nested in stories about everyday life. Williams realizes that the most important aspect of modern marketing techniques is that through advertising marketers bring objects to life by filling in the product's 'story'. Goods are not just symbols, but narratives that dramatize our existence and, in doing so, allow us to fantasize about our lives with them. To understand and criticize marketing's impact we must assess the cultural forms of consumption and the narratives advertising produces, which situate and explain the role of goods in our everyday lives.

Notes

1. Williams, Raymond, *Television: Technology and Cultural Form*, London, Fontana, 1974, p. 120.

2. Jameson, Fredric, 'Postmodernism, or, The Cultural Logic of Late Capitalism', *New Left Review* 3, 1984, pp. 53–92.

3. See Kroker, Arthur, 'Television and the Triumph of Culture: 3 Theses', *Can. J. of Social and Political Theory*, IX (3) (Fall 1985) pp. 37–47; and Postman, Neil, *Amusing Ourselves to Death: Public Discourse in the Age of Show Business*, New York, Viking Penguin, 1985.

4. Williams, Raymond, *Television: Technology and Cultural Form*, p. 126.

5. Ibid.

6. Schiller, Herbert, *The Mind Manager: How the Master Puppeteers of Politics, Advertising and Mass Communication Pull the Strings of Public Opinion*, Boston, Beacon Press, 1973.

7. Smythe, Dallas, 'Communication: The Blindspot of Western Marxism', *Canadian Journal of Political and Social Theory*, (3) (1977), pp. 1–27.

8. Williams, Raymond, *Television: Technology and Cultural Form*, p. 12.

9. See Brown, Les, *The Business Behind the Box*, New York, Harcourt Brace Jovanovich, 1972; Barnouw, E., *The Sponsor: Notes on a Modern Potentate*, New York, Oxford University Press, 1978.

10. Ray, Michael, *Advertising and Communication Management*, Englewood Cliffs, NJ, Prentice Hall, 1982, p. 10.

11. I have relied most heavily on the following sources: Roland Marchand, *Advertising and the American Dream* (1986); Stephen Fox, *The Mirror Makers* (1986); Daniel Pope, *The Making of Modern Advertising* (1983); Blankenship et al., *Marketing Research in Canada* (1985).

12. Stephen Fox, *The Mirror Makers: A History of American Advertising and its Creators*, New York, William Morrow, 1984.

13. Ång, Ien, *Desperately Seeking the Audience*, London, Routledge, 1991.

14. Levy, Sydney, 'Symbols by which We Buy', in *Advancing Marketing Efficiency*, L.H. Stockman, ed., Chicago, American Marketing Association, 1969.

15. Shwartz, Tony, *The Responsive Chord*, New York, Anchor, 1974.

16. Leiss, William, *The Limits to Satisfaction*, Toronto, University of Toronto Press, 1976.

17. Ray, *Advertising and Communication Management*, p. x.

18. Jones, John P., *What's in a Name? Advertising & the Concept of Brands*, Lexington, MA, Lexington Books, 1990.

19. For the debates see Schudson, Michael, *Advertising the Uneasy Persuasion*, New York, Basic Books, 1984.

20. Perry, J.M., 'To Raise a Politician to the Heights, Try a Helicopter and Music, *Wall Street Journal*, 24 July 1979.

21. Packard, Vance, *The Hidden Persuaders*, New York, D. Mackay, 1957.

22. Holbrook, Morris, 'Mirror, Mirror, on the Wall, What's Unfair in the Reflections on Advertising?', *Journal of Marketing*, 51 (July 1987) pp. 95–103; Pollay, Rick, 'On the Value of Reflections on the Values in the "Distorted Mirror"', *Journal of Marketing*, 51 (July 1989), pp. 104–9.

23. Ewen, Stuart, *Captains of Consciousness*. New York, McGraw-Hill, 1976.

24. Ibid. p. 81.

25. Holbrook, Morris, 'Mirror, Mirror, on the Wall'.

26. Leiss, W., S. Kline and S. Jhally, *Social Communication in Advertising*, Toronto, Methuen, 1986, p. 7.

27. Lasch, Cristopher, *The Culture of Narcissism*, New York, Norton, 1979, p. 138.

28. Linder, Steffan, *The Harried Leisure Class*, New York, Columbia University Press, 1970.

29. Hirsch, Fred, *The Social Limits to Growth*, Cambridge, Cambridge University Press, p. 84.

30. Kavanaugh, John F., *Following Christ in a Consumer Society: The Spirituality of Cultural Resistance*, Maryknoll, New York, Orbis Books, 1981, p. 27.

31. Williams, Raymond, 'Advertising: The Magic System', in *Problems in Materialism and Culture*, London, New Left Books, 1980.

2

The Making of Children's

Culture

Because psychic structure must always be passed from generation to generation through the narrow funnel of childhood, a
society's child-rearing practices are not just one item in a list of
cultural traits. They are the very condition for the transmission
and development of all other cultural elements, and place
definite limits on what can be achieved in all other spheres of
history.[1]

Children's culture in the West has a complex history. Even the most
cursory mapping would require an overview of the succession of
institutions – family, law courts, church, school, media – that have
had a stake in the matrix of socialization. This is because what might
be taken for children's culture has always been primarily a matter of
culture produced for and urged upon children. This appears to be as
true of the hunting games or planting tales of preindustrial life as of
the street games and nursery-school songs of modern children. The
earliest stages of maturation have always been the period in which the
young are most intensely subjected to cultural forms designed for
and directed at them. Childhood is a condition defined by powerlessness and dependence upon the adult community's directives and
guidance. Culture is, after all, as the repository of social learning and
socialization, the means by which societies preserve and strengthen
their position in the world.

The forms of children's cultural expression are therefore intimately bound up with the changing alignments that define a
community's social beliefs and practices of cultural transmission.
Whether it is participation in medieval festivals, or the nursery songs,
riddles and stories of nineteenth-century childhood, or more recent

playground games and jokes, the seemingly autonomous expressions take shape within a broader cultural framework. Medieval festivals needed to have church sanction, nursery rhymes presumed both nurseries and books, and games require both playgrounds and time to play. Children's culture is always highly inflected with societal purpose.

This is not to say that young children on their own, in their games, humour, songs, stories and interactions, do not create and express themselves authentically. No doubt, wherever children gather together and interact among themselves, spontaneous acts of self-expression occur. Indeed, the momentum of contemporary trends in childrearing is towards granting greater freedom and encouragement to young children's leisure. Through language, art, play, music and peer interaction contemporary childrearing practice privileges children's cultural activities, including 'playfulness' itself. At first glance it appears that children's humour and play may be the two authentic (emancipatory) regions of their culture. Yet, as a Dutch study of the relationship between family practice and play concluded, even 'children's play seems to become more and more a product of the educational and cultural orientation of parents'.[2] The emphasis on play also makes the contemporary framework for socialization confusing, because the very idea of play cloaks the momentum of socialization in a hoped-for perception of autonomy and freedom.

In a series of interviews, a number of parents from the Toronto area responded to questions about priorities for their children's development. Some 78 per cent of them said learning to read and write was the top priority. A tie for second priority went to learning moral behaviour and interacting with peer social groups (52 per cent each), while the parents considered fitting in with society (44 per cent) and becoming imaginative and self-expressive (43 per cent) to be relatively less important. In other words, although parents recognize the importance of children's imagination and self-expression, that recognition exists within the context of a very directive concept of socializing purpose. Indeed, the results of this survey indicated some very confused and conflicted reasons for buying children toys and encouraging their 'free and expressive play'. Although the parents believed that these activities gave their children great pleasure, 38 per cent of the sample also expressed serious concerns about the way children play, especially with toys promoted on television. To some degree we must look back in history to find the roots of this conflicted attitude.

The Invention of Childhood

Modern society's fascination with children's culture and with the psychical factors that shape children's maturation is possibly one of the most important inventions of the industrial era. As Edward Norbeck noted, 'It is still surprising for most of us to learn that various languages lack a generic term for play, and lack a concept of work and play in binary opposition.'[3] Our contemporary notions seem to be bound up in attitudes which link play and childhood. In early medieval life, however, children appear to have been more fully integrated into the daily flux of making and consuming, of getting along. They had no autonomy, separate status, privileges, special rights or forms of social comportment that were entirely their own.[4] Commenting on the parallel if somewhat miniaturized existence of the preindustrial child, historian J.H. Plumb notes:

> There was no separate world of childhood. Children shared the same games with adults, the same toys, the same fairy stories. They lived their lives together, never apart. The coarse village festivals depicted by Breughel, showing men and women besotted with drink, groping for each other with unbridled lust, have children eating and drinking with the adults. Even, in the soberer pictures of wedding feasts and dances the children are enjoying themselves alongside their elders, doing the same things.[5]

In the medieval imagery of an organic and integrated social milieu there is no evidence of the existence of either special prerogatives for childhood or of children's culture. Children were expected to participate in the household economy almost as soon as they could walk. They worked more or less as servants. They toiled in the fields with their parents, helped to tend livestock, or picked and sorted wool. Children in the 'lower reaches of society', perhaps as young as five years old, were apprenticed off to learn a trade for terms of seven to nine years. In feudal society, children were defined through the property rights of their progenitors, and their activities were defined by the role of their families in society. The objects that children handled were no different to the cultural objects that adults had, and children's lives were essentially no different from those of adults. The whole community shared work and leisure as well as games, songs and tales.

The feudal worldview contrasts sharply with our own centuries-deep concern with children's rights, leisure and pleasure – a change in attitude most clearly expressed in the profusion of toys and specially designed objects that fill a typical child's own room.[6] But more importantly the change is rooted in a framework of legal and social structures that have crystallized children's rights and prerogatives, expanding upon legal definitions first articulated in England in the cruelty acts of 1889, which for the first time extended to children the same protection from abuse granted to animals under the earlier cruelty-to-animals legislation. It is only during the twentieth century that children's legislation began to extend and elaborate on children's property rights and apply new principles that cushioned children from the common law, including the controversial exemption from the adult criminal justice system on the grounds that due to developmental inadequacies children were 'incapable of a guilty mind'.[7]

The significance of this major revision to the conception of childhood has gone almost unnoticed by a historical gaze narrowly directed towards the cataclysmic social transformation that followed the mechanization of production. Children's lives began to be featured in fictional and social historical accounts of the early industrial period, notably in the novels and stories of Charles Dickens, often either as warnings about the brutality of industrialism or as indications of social progress achieved by the factory acts of the opening decades of the nineteenth century and the 'free' schooling acts of the later third. Indeed, these changing attitudes had first taken hold earlier, prodded by an active social movement that had its protective aspirations focused on removing children from the industrial environments that were oppressing adult working women and men.

During the early decades of the nineteenth century children as young as five worked alongside their parents in factories and mines, maintaining patterns of work continued from the feudal order. In England the factory acts of 1802, 1816, and especially 1833, began to challenge the assumption that children were simply the property of their progenitors and to restrict the abusive practices of industrial managers to use this cheap source of labour as they wished. Under the banner of protection, children were gradually excluded from the industrial world, helping to destroy the system of apprenticeship that had made the family an important locus for the transmission of skills and craft knowledge.

Until a small coterie of social historians, starting with Philippe Aries, recently began to explore the issue, the sweeping changes in the conception of childhood and childrearing practice that occurred within the new framework of protection for children had rarely been carefully examined.[8] The related issues of family life and children's culture were largely ignored by the historians of the industrial era, who saw in the science, technology and the political economy more significant forces shaping social life. During the nineteenth century a powerful idea came to prevail as the dominant view of child development: that children are innocent beings in need of formation and learning, to be protected from the harsher realities of industrial society.

Historically, this was a radical idea, for within it we find the origins of a new, more self-conscious conception of children's culture. Throughout the nineteenth century the cultural matrix of socialization was changing dramatically. Children were being excluded more and more from the crucial arenas of life and the inherent conflicts and struggles that had shaped so much of the rest of history. They were similarly being denied the value and power such participation might bestow. In compensation they were granted rights of protection and a separate institutional space – the schools – which established the new agenda for their training. In that agenda, literacy and knowledge became the privileged objectives of socialization. This transition is critical, for it marks a period when the state was not only prescribing protective buffers for childhood but beginning to assert its own 'interest' in social communication with children.

As historian Lloyd DeMause has pointed out, the concern with children and the attendant conception of childhood were revised dramatically over the nineteenth century. The very idea of the family and schools as 'socializing' agencies – that is, as agents of conscious attempts to shape and mould children into civilized beings by orchestrating their learning and social experiences – gains its full force precisely during this intense period of upheaval. Interest in and concern with children's thought and experience permeate the second half of the nineteenth century. In the literature and popular writing of the period childhood became both a way of understanding the changes of industrialization and a fitting metaphor for growth and development.

DeMause's characterization of the Victorian approach to child-rearing as becoming less concerned with dominating the child's will than with protecting children and guiding them in the proper paths, teaching them to conform through more conscious and civilized means, seems an apt description of this revised attitude.[9] The expression of such progressive ideas can be traced back to social thinkers such as John Locke and Jean-Jacques Rousseau, and even to earlier community traditions that highly prized and valued children in their own right. But it was the industrializing Victorians who took this new attitude seriously, who worked at undoing the feudal matrix of socialization with its strict definition of children based on the family's property rights.[10] In feudal society the family was not only the means of organizing working life; it was central to the transmission of property and power. The undoing of this concept of lineage was a precursor to the acceptance of children's rights. In this sense the child-labour laws and factory acts were aimed as much at limiting the rights of families who were pressuring children into work as at rejecting the cruel and abusive practices of the industrial work-place.[11]

The factory acts in Britain, however, do confirm that throughout the early industrial era childhood was increasingly seen as a stage of growth that in the long-term interests of civilized society had to be isolated and guarded from an abusive world. This implied a radical realignment not only in the rights and interests of those major agencies of socialization – the family, church and state – but also in the means and instruments of acculturation. Implicit in the new attitude towards childhood was a gradual drifting away from the notion of control towards an approach that sought to instil models of self-control in children. This attitude conceived of civilization as expanding its hold around a core of transmitted moral (Christian) precepts. Protection brought with it an equally important conception of the child as a separate social stratum, as an innocent in need of protection, and as an underdeveloped mind in need of nurturing, guidance and instruction.

During the eighteenth and nineteenth centuries, the church followed these principles, becoming increasingly engaged in organizing an alternative to home and factory, hoping minimally to expand the religious, moral and ideological training within children's learning experience. Arguing that education 'civilized' the naturally enthusiastic but underdeveloped child and infused everyday experience with moral rectitude, the churches became outspoken advocates and supporters of educationism and built church schools as the preferred venue for children's guidance. Schooling was also seen as a liberating and progressive element by early socialists, such as Robert Owen, who set up schooling for his millworkers' children. Schools were meant to inspire and create the basis of a more humane

49

industrial order, an inspiration that similarly underwrote Friedrich Froebel's kindergarten, and later Rudolph Steiner's Waldorf schools and Maria Montessori's new system of education.

Through the activities of the schooling movement the issue of socialization became of increasing interest to the state. By 1871 the problem of educating children had become such an important social issue that the Free Schools Act made it compulsory for young children under the age of twelve to attend an institution of learning. The new mission for childhood was to become literate, numerate and well behaved. In accepting this mission, the school system was being built upon a less harsh vision of childhood: schools were to be a special world within which children could learn at a more leisurely pace, free from the demands and pressures of both parents and industrialists.

The Victorian state school and curriculum did not provide a children's paradise. Brutality was accepted and justified on the grounds that it was necessary to discipline the recalcitrant learner. Learning itself was defined and viewed as a very unliberating process of knowledge assimilation and repetition. Nor was the school completely without an industrial social purpose. The knowledge, skills and training offered children were praised widely as the training ground for the necessary attitudes, skills, knowledge and good work habits needed in both professional working and domestic life. Children were meant, as they progressed through the education system, to experience more fully the relations of production based on an industrial model: in the schools children encountered the 'educational' values of achievement, competition, authority, principled behaviour, obedience and reward and punishment in a significant way. The school curriculum featured these dimensions of social behaviour and moral growth as important dimensions of learning. For example, the London board schools included housewifery lessons that taught the science and practice of hygiene, home economics, and cookery as progressive innovations in girls' education.

The urgency of providing a truly engaging formative experience, including the social skills to participate in adult life, underscored much of the state's interest in schooling. It was at school, after all, that children would derive their first sense of their position in the broader social matrix of jobs, civic duty, social responsibility and moral choices. These liberating and democratizing possibilities for education were particularly taken up by twentieth-century educational theorists such as John Dewey in the United States and Susan

Isaacs and Teddy O'Neil in England. The same underlying social perceptions were leading to a dramatic expansion of children's organizations, many of them focused on cultural activities, including games and other play activities. Sunday schools, scouting movements, camps, playgrounds, organized sporting groups, youth groups, and even pleasure parks, were mostly directed at the poor and working classes, whose idle hands and leisure were somewhat mistrusted. In play, games and sports activities a model providing a wholesome focus to the patterns of children's development was discovered. Play, it was argued, was not simple idleness but the 'work of childhood' – the moral equivalent of labour. Street children were ushered into the playground to have a taste of organized collective activity. Structured game play and organized sport were also highly recommended as ways of preparing children for a competitive society and of creating a location for class mingling and negotiation. Games for the young in which children pretended to be animals were recommended as providing models of appropriate childlike behaviour to the very unchildlike street children of the working class. It was upon these formative foundations of the nineteenth century that toys, sporting and play equipment, uniforms, and other accoutrements have been added as a now common part of so many children's lives.

This idea of free play was most particularly celebrated in Friedrich Froebel's notion of the kindergarten, which gained acceptance in the twentieth century as the most appropriate and widely accepted modality of early childhood socialization. Froebel's kindergarten – or children's garden – was not only a place of natural innocence but also a site that granted children *Spielraum* – room to play and mature according to their own dictates and schedules.[12] Helping children to enjoy learning became the concern of most educationists, social thinkers and psychologists, who in detailing children's underdevelopment and special needs implicitly backed the idea of a unique role for children's culture – a cultural environment that would support children's own developmental agendas.

The Rousseauean theme of innocence develops through the educational writings of the period and continues throughout the twentieth century. The favoured comparison is between childhood experience and the garden. Sometimes the metaphor is there to ascribe to children a state of prelapsarian grace and the originary state of Eden. At other times the allusion is to the neat, well-tutored, and ordered rows of a more familiar landscape benefiting from well-managed nurturance. The ambivalence of the metaphor did not undermine the common emphasis on the need for new forms of social control and conformity, which within the emerging developmentalist approach could be achieved by recognizing and empathizing with children's needs, especially their needs for culture. The garden metaphor was particularly favoured by the writers and artists who furnished children's primary cultural artefact – the book.

Toys, pianos and sports equipment – and not the teacher's rod – were to become the privileged instruments of childhood enlightenment, delight and entertainment. Music, art, sports and dance lessons were expected activities for the properly civilized middle-class child. More broadly, an interest in the full spectrum of cultural development was being impressed on public institutions such as museums, art galleries, playgrounds and parks, places that became the mark of civic pride and achievement. From the narrow confines of literacy the garden of children's culture came to full flower.

The Commercialization of Childhood

During the closing decades of the nineteenth century, rapid industrialization was dramatically increasing the capacity of manufacturers to meet people's needs by supplying more goods. Much of the commentary on industrialization has focused on the changing relationship between capital, technology and labour within this process of social transformation, overlooking marketing's specific historical task in expanding the sale and distribution of these goods – that is, the insertion of manufactured goods into an ever wider sphere of human activity. Yet it was with a verve and energy equal to that of the engineers and designers that marketers sought new means of increasing the public's interest in buying the goods that the factories were producing. The motif of children's culture, which through the next century became ever more visible, emerged within the broad spectrum of the market's communication activity.

The neo-medieval art of the period gave vivid expression to the new sensibility of innocence and unassailable purity that grounded the Victorian perspective on childhood, and also lent itself to products. The cherub and fairy motifs long established in painting became part of the decorative frame and backdrop for goods. Indeed, this same imagery of childhood was featured in the poster art of the period and among the classics of turn-of-the-century advertising. The babe of the new century ventured optimistically on the sea of life, riding a wave of material goods or, fairy-like, bestowing the cornucopia of life. At the turn of the century this simple metaphor captured not so much the reality of industrial society as a sentiment of hope in an emergent order. In most turn-of-the-century advertising the child seems to symbolize not only the end to the rigidities of the past but also the promise of a gentler purer future. Within the world portrayed in advertising, personal growth, health and fulfilment were not incompatible with industrial progress and economic expansion.

The Victorian awakening to the preciousness of childhood helped ensure that children's goods would expand along with other markets. Childhood was being increasingly characterized by specific behavioural traits and products. The increasingly vivid image of a separate domain of childhood became standard in both the late Victorian arts and product appeals. Pears soap, for instance, focused on the images of childhood in its promotional efforts, equating cleanliness and spiritual purity. Pears commissioned the famous Pre-Raphaelite painter Millais to design one of its display ads, with memorable effect. Other advertisers followed suit, making the Victorian cult of cleanliness part of the essence of good parenting. But implicit in the soap manufacturer's invocations was a new sense of childhood: the young were no longer viewed as simply miniaturized replicas of adults.

Many families across the social spectrum – not just the wealthy – were benefiting from the rapid mechanization of production and the increasing availability of manufactured goods. The shift of focus towards youth helped ensure that children shared the industrial largesse. Along with soap, other products – shoes, clothes, foods, medicines for children – were being produced in greater abundance than ever before and distributed in rural as well as urban communities. Families now had additional resources available to purchase products in the market rather than having to make them within the household or buy them from local artisans. The ability to provide more adequately for the family became recognized as a touchstone of progress itself. One prominent example was the gentle expression of anxiety about the ill child, which in the context of advertising became a powerful reason for buying manufactured medicines.

The child's health was a bearer of another message locating childhood in a grander organic unit. As T. Jackson Lears was to point out, in response to the rationality and mechanization implicit in progressivism, a contrapuntal theme was being voiced in the nineteenth-century organs of popular culture. Ads were stressing a 'therapeutic' ethos with an emphasis on well-being, self-help and betterment:

> A characteristic therapeutic strategy linked domestic responsibilities with nostalgia for a pristine, natural state. 'Mothers do you not know that children crave natural food until you pervert their taste by the use of unnatural food?' a Shredded Wheat advertisement asked in 1903. Unnatural food develops unnatural and therefore wrong propensities and desires in children.[13]

Food and health always play an important role in family life, and specialized breakfast foods and medication were among the first brand goods to become associated with the theme of children's natural innocence and their unique nutritional and health needs.

The rounded and pliant images of the child convey these organic qualities. Pictures of both contented and suffering children began to decorate the packages and displays for an ever-increasing circle of products. Advertising repeatedly articulated the need for parents to become aware of the unique needs, vulnerabilities and sensitivities of their child. Most particularly, this idea was expressed through a madonna-and-child motif: the concerned mother and the frail and innocent child were coupled in the image of a bond rooted in a deep emotional concern for the child's well-being. Indeed, the theme of anxiety about children accompanied one of promise and innocence in the imagery of turn-of-the-century advertising. Advertisers found in the nurturing instincts of mothers a useful thematic warp into which they could weave their products complete with the evolving protectionist sentiments.

The increasing awareness of the domain of children's goods was also witnessed in the new and often elaborate department stores, which began to feature children's sections. Children's goods infiltrated the catalogues and display advertising of these early pioneers of merchandising. The department store established its place as purveyor to the whole family by bringing forth in one place a greater range of goods required for family life. This pattern of marketing continues today, with 65 per cent of the volume of children's wear still purchased in department stores. Stocked with a variety of general-purpose provisions for the family, the department stores thrived by responding to parents' perceived sense that family well-being was a matter judged across the whole spectrum of consumption and care.

Meanwhile, the educational interest in child development and welfare encouraged manufacturers and producers to consider a distinctive children's array of goods. Some of the new products of the period were even designed differently to strengthen their association with the new attitudes and activities that had arisen in children's culture. For example, during the nineteenth century clothes were being more extensively designed and styled for children's use: pinafores, knickerbockers and smocks, sailor suits and short trousers. In paintings and illustrations, too, clothing helped to signal the child's new station in life. Similarly, new items of furniture – for example, high chairs and chairs, school desks, and chairs that made children sit more erectly at the table – were among the design innovations at the end of the period.

A historian of design, Adrian Forty, writes:

> Only at the very end of the century were there entire ranges of nursery furniture that were different from those for adults, not only in scale but also in form and appearance. Some of these new articles, such as the purpose-designed toy cupboards, specially filled children's needs, some offered the advantage of being hygienic and easy to clean, while others were decorated with pictures of animals or with colours that were particularly appropriate for children.[14]

Forty quotes the 1914 Heal's nursery furniture catalogue, which gives the reasoning behind the changes in design:

> Formerly the children, even in the families of the well-to-do, were relegated to an attic or some room not thought sufficiently good for any other purpose.... Now the nursery is carefully chosen, well lighted and well planned ... suitable to the needs of the occupants, and in every way a fit training ground, both physical and moral for the young. Children are admittedly very susceptible to their environment, therefore, how important it is to surround them with things at once beautiful and useful.[15]

The special designs made children stand out from the social continuum. In his painting *Bubbles* which appeared in a famous Pears poster, Sir John Everett Millais had presented a boy caught in a reverie, dressed in clothing befitting not only his station in life but also his youthful position in the social spectrum. The uniforms of school, the neckerchiefs of scouts and the caps favoured by youth-activity groups helped to create a cultural stylization that levelled children but clearly demarked childhood. Children are much easier to recognize in the art and photography of the twentieth century for this very reason: a separate clothing style and, implicitly, a unique place in society were created for them. Together, the new designs, catalogues, advertising and consumer-magazine stories and advisories of the turn of the century jointly contributed to a new sense that children were at the hub of the domestic scene.

The stylization and voice in early consumer-magazine advertising were directed to parents. The advertising duplicated the content of much of the popular writing in women's magazines and books, which devoted increasing attention to advisories on childrearing practice and discussions of children's well-being. In the advertising of the period this 'advisory voice' was woven into many product appeals. It was, after all, the mother's attention that was being targeted by advertisers. It was the mother's concerns that were being discussed: health, ease of preparation, building strong bodies, gentle on the system. These were appeals designed to connect with the maternal anxieties and values being more broadly discussed. There is no doubt that the parent was supposed to buy the product. There are only a few examples in the advertising of the period of goods marketed to children directly: an occasional bicycle or train set. The merchandisers had little interest in motivating or addressing children themselves.

Symbols of Domesticity

Among the ads for general domestic goods after the turn of the century was a new motif which pictured the modern family as a unit. This was not the stern and forbidding autocratic patriarchy that psychiatry described as the roots of repression, but a more engaging image of family life – a vision of the household as a cultural sanctuary from industrial life. The image was increasingly repeated in the advertisements of the 1920s and 1930s for food, cars, houses, furniture, appliances and a variety of other products. As advertising historian Roland Marchand comments:

> If the view from the office window defined the dominant fantasy of man's domain in the world of work, another visual cliche – the family circle – expressed the special qualities of the domain that he shared with his wife and children at home. During the nineteenth century ... the notions of work and home had become dichotomized. The home came to represent a sheltered haven to which men escaped to find surcease from the harsh world of competition, ambition, and cold calculation. More than ever, the concept of the family circle, with its nuances of closure and intimate

bonding, suggested a protective clustering – like the circling of the settlers' wagons – in defense of qualities utterly distinct from those that prevailed outside.[16]

Stuart Ewen sees another parable in advertising's fascination with the family and home life. He argues that the emerging image of a modern nuclear family was not simply a reflection of broader social changes taking place in industrial society (for example, urbanization, mobility, population growth) but was more precisely connected to the conscious attempts by industrialists to solve the problems emerging with the maturation of industrial society. Industrialists during the 1920s, Ewen points out, were beginning to recognize that the family's home life, and with it the child's earliest experience, were growing beyond the family's grasp:

> On the one side stood the corrupting and masculine world of business; on the other, a home ruled by the father and kept moral and virtuous by the mother. Where the home and community had once attempted to comprise a totality of social existence, and patriarchy had been its 'legal code,' Victorianism elevated the patriarchal home into a spiritual sanctuary against the realities of the productive sphere.[17]

Ewen's reflections on the history of commercial culture see in industries a renewed interest in the social dynamics of the household and a rethinking of the problems of industrial overproduction. During the 1920s and 1930s, industrialists began to think seriously about the function of the family, and in particular of women, as a consuming unit. The family made its contribution in the form of the demand for goods rather than in terms of labour and its potential for labour. Youth became an element in visualizing the promise of consumption as a wholesome preoccupation of life:

> In the opening decades of the twentieth century, the symbolic role of youth was central to business thought. The fact that childhood was increasingly a period of consuming goods and services made youth a powerful tool in the ideological framework of business. Beyond the transformation of the period of childhood and adolescence into a period of consumption, youth was also a broad cultural symbol of renewal, of honesty, and of criticism against injustice – the young have always provided a recurrent rejection of the ancient virtues of the 'establishment'.[18]

Advertising therefore began to configure its discussion of the benefits and uses of manufactured goods within a continuum of domestic consumption that featured the child as central in the dynamics of the household.

Ewen's comments help show why women's work, portrayed in advertising as the labour of consumption, was continuously denied significance and validity until merchandisers began to reveal to industrialists the real dynamics of the marketplace. Given the belief in men's industrial work as the only valid form of labour, the non-waged work of the household, including childrearing, was granted only marginal notice among social historians – at least until feminist theory refocused attention on the social significance of the house-hold as a place of labour. Ewen's study suggests the importance of the merchandisers' increasing attention to the domestic scene. The marketplace is a meeting ground between producers and consumers: the expansion of production depends upon the expansion of consumption: yet the social dynamics of consumption are defined in and by the family unit – not the factory.

It is odd, therefore, that in the social commentary and advice that emerges around the topic of childrearing, so little attention has been given to children's place in the framework of consumption. In twentieth-century advertising the imagery of childhood became vital in the tapestry of the consuming family – as a motivation for adequate provisioning, as an indicator of family pride and virtue, and as an easily understood symbol of the long-term benefits of continued economic prosperity. In an age of anxieties about social progress, advertising's images of family solidarity provided some comfort. As Roland Marchand points out:

> This visual cliche was no social mirror; rather, it was a reassuring pictorial convention.... When father, mother, and child in an advertising tableau stood gazing off into the distance with their backs turned directly or obliquely toward the reader, it could mean only one thing. In the language of visual cliches they were looking into the future.[19]

The future, though lacking in detail, was filled with hope and promise – for which children were often the visual clue.

Although the present became more troubled during the war years of the 1940s, advertising did not lose sight of this promised future. Even in the depth of those years, the images of war's end indicated that in her airplane factory Rosie the Riveter still dreamed of the infinitely clean and modern domestic vistas of consumption. The kitchen, the hub of domestic labour and familial warmth, was to be transformed by the very technology and enterprise that was helping to win the war.

Indirectly, the advertisements for a remodelled domesticity in the first half of the twentieth century also provide a glimpse of the impact of the emerging philosophy of developmentalism on the conception of childrearing. In advertising's version of modern domesticity, appropriate clothing and the central positioning of the child on the floor clearly demarcate a status that stresses the legitimacy of childish aspirations and pastimes. Some of the ads convey directly the need to recognize children's own playful and imaginary approaches to goods. In others, the presence of books, toys, wagons, special furniture, games and learning equipment, along with school bags, playground equipment, sports equipment and other pastimes all imply the expanding sphere of children's cultural products.[20] These product lines were starting to consolidate in the marketplace a conception of children's goods which compounded the perception of the autonomy of childhood.

The carefully constructed commercial scenes of these advertisements reflect the importance that parents attached to finding the right vehicles and objects to encourage their children's development. Few of the ads depict adults unreservedly impressing their ideas and will upon the child. Most of them, rather, convey the sense that the common tools of childhood – the ball, the doll, the bicycle – are essential to good parenting. The moral force of the presentation of these objects is that parents who cannot provide them are in some ways inadequate.

The toy has a special significance among the symbols of children's cultural requirements. The ball or wooden train serves as a useful reference point in the scheme of domesticated consumption, because it connotes a different aspect of utility. Roland Barthes notes that the toy is a cultural signifier conveying not only the common preoccupations of children with play but also their changing experience of things.[21] The toy is a symbol of a world distinct from the processes and social relations of work. It is the possibility of a youngster's isolation and buffering from a harsh industrial reality that lies at the centre of these representations of childhood preoccupations. The child with toys is a symbol of the pleasures of consumerism, of the new objects primarily designed for leisure and fantasy. Play is a childhood labour whose essence is a mental transformation – the distancing from daily experience and the re-creation of self in an imaginary world. The toy is therefore an effective symbol of a simpler form of gratification steeped in pleasure alone and not in the rational adjudication of a product's attributes, benefits and construction.

In addition, toys are fitting symbols of economic progress because they direct consumers to the rewards of leisure and relaxation. The re-created atmosphere of domestic consumption takes its emotional cues and mood from the absence of labour implied by a playful child. The advertising of the 1920s ascribes to the family unit a new self-confidence and softer structure of feeling. For example, Roland Marchand notes how:

> 'Soft focus' defined the family circle tableau almost as readily as its specific content. Nostalgic in mood ... the soft focus atmosphere suggested harmony and tenderness.... the artist recognizing the moral ambience of the scene he was invading, washed an affectionate, rosy mist over the scene. It was the family circle, rather than the home itself, that laid claim to the soft focus treatment.... The addition of a child, connoting family, increased the likelihood of a soft focus treatment. The addition of the father completed the circle, more or less assuring that the scene would fall into one of the sentimentalized categories of leave-taking, homecoming, sharing of a meal, or evening leisure in the living room.[22]

During the 1930s the hues of family sentimentality were intensified, and the imagery of youthful play became increasingly crystallized as a symbol of the benefits of modernization.

Industrialists, notes Stuart Ewen, reconceptualized the family within the framework of their business interests by favouring a depiction of the household economy as an exemplar of the progressive democratic consumerism:

> To businessmen, the reconstituted family would be one which maintained its reproductive function, but which had abandoned the dogma of parental authority, except in-so-far as that authority could be controlled and provide a conduit to the process of goods consumption.[23]

Yet the imagery of domestic consumption was not an entirely placid affair. The image of the happily playing child had to assert itself against the traditional backdrop of industry and patriarchy. The tensions in the family often presented in allegory the contradictions experienced in the progressive period. In this respect much of the consumer advertising directed to women takes on an educational tone, instructing mothers on the values and practices implicit in new approaches to childrearing and contrasting these with the pre-modern values of unthinking autocratic paternalism. Sometimes a woman (generously armed with information provided by advertisers) is arrayed in argument with the old-fashioned forces of patriarchy. Sparing the rod can be justified, however, when another solution found in the market solves the problem. A rather typical ad shows a scene of family disputation centred on the failure of the father to understand the modern means of childrearing. Children were often caught at the middle of a tug of war, and an interest in children's needs turned out to be a metaphor for the struggles to establish a market democracy.

A corresponding tone of anxiety pervades much of the advertising of the 1930s, which overtly recognized the significance of a child's changing stature within the family. Much of the anxiety concerned parents' ways of relating to children, of controlling and directing their abundant energies, imagination and creativity. Sometimes mothers fretted over their lack of control of their children's well-being; sometimes experts intruded into the scene to help resolve this sense of insecurity; and sometimes parents disputed the appropriate ways to deal with the troubled moments of childrearing. These scenes seem to speak of a more fundamental unsettledness that went beyond the disputes over childrearing practice.

Children of Affluence

In the depression of the 1930s the whole project of industrial progress and the business leaders' ability to manage economic prosperity were called into question. Against these uncertainties, advertising offered a new vista of domestic stability emanating from the new technologies offered in the home. The family gazed proudly at the new car dad had brought home, or they gathered in rapture around the radio. As Marchand argues:

> The visual cliche of the family circle served to reconcile the past and the present, authority and democracy. It defined domain as security rather than as opportunity. Above all, it connoted stability. The products of modern technology, including radios and phonographs, were comfortably accommodated within the hallowed circle. Whatever pressures and complexities modernity might bring, these images implied, the family at home would preserve an undaunted harmony and security.[24]

61

No domestic technology was more comfortably accommodated into the family circle than television. By the 1950s the image of the family turned uniformly to the television set for its leisure, its knowledge of the world, and its self-identity spoke clearly of the well-laid plans of business and government leaders to make commercial television into a centripetal cultural force within a period of unprecedented industrial expansion. The image echoes and transforms the eighteenth-century idea of children gathered around the maternal storybook. During the 1950s the new technology became an emblem of the compatibility between cultural stability and domestic prosperity – but only, Americans believed, if the medium followed the model of commercial radio and left programming decisions to be based on marketing needs.

Imbued with a new purpose for industrial productivity, the domestic environment, including attitudes towards family life and child-rearing, underwent dramatic change. The postwar period saw returning soldiers and a new hope for peace and security result in the largest procreative bulge yet recorded – the baby boom. Starting in 1945 the birth rate rose 60 per cent; at the height of the boom in 1957, 4·3 million babies were born to 36 million women of child-bearing age. The social issues of raising a family and caring for children's needs were brought to the front ranks in the 1960s and 1970s, as working families struggled to discover what the new age of prosperity meant for them.

This moment in North America's history enunciates itself as a celebration of unprecedented affluence. War productivity was diverted to meeting new consumer needs and a building boom was under way to house the growing population. Although poverty lingered on in many 'hidden pockets', greater wealth did flow to ordinary working-class and middle-class families, bringing hopes for a new way of life that would transcend the depression and war years. This way of life was crystallized in the vision of a quest for easier and more leisurely lifestyles: houses would be filled with the new labour-saving devices that would free women from the drudgery of domestic duties and allow them freedom and self-expression in their role as house-wives. Television advertising gave vivid and repeated expression to the new aspirations of the suburban two-car families freed from want and toil by labour-saving devices. Public consciousness was diverted from the underlying problems of racial tensions and cold war with the promise of technologically enhanced ease. Social scientists proclaimed everywhere the emergence of a new era as personal happiness and freedom levitated to the summit of espoused goals.

Affluence presented a particular dilemma for the family and a new challenge for traditional patterns of socialization. The transformation of traditional family patterns and attitudes was founded on a hope that the experience of working-class and immigrant children might be different and better than that of their parents. Television provided a field of images of family life that enabled this 'anticipatory socialization' – the learning of new social roles and relations necessary in a mobile and fluid social order.[25] The age of affluence envisioned a new approach to childrearing, new responses to children, and new patterns of interaction in the family. In particular, affluence meant a less restrictive emotional atmosphere. Families would no longer have to contain their aspirations and save carefully for the future. The practice of delayed gratification seemed harder and more troublesome to the family than simply satisfying children's immediate needs with consumer goods.[26] The accumulation of material wealth became more important in defining social relations and social standing. The material effort to 'keep up with the Joneses' replaced hard work and good citizenship as a North American motive, and the way of life meant that children, too, had to display the necessary symbols of wealth.

David Reisman's 1950 study of the emerging patterns of American values argued that the new morality had its origin in the practices of socialization.[27] Freedom and control through reward was different from the rigid internalized moral principles and punishment that had guided the previous generation. For 'inner-directed' parents, the qualities of principle, duty, obligation and a strict sense of right and wrong had underwritten behaviour and informed the styles of childrearing. The new approach to the family did not develop these inner codes and instead exposed children increasingly to peer influence, making conformity and acquiescence to perceived norms more important than moral codes. 'Outer-directed' children, left to their own devices, would use the standards and values of those around them as the criterion for comportment and action.

The media were beginning to feed into this revised definition of freedom and peer control. The attitudes and behaviour of the reference group became a prime anchor for the behaviour of both parents and children. The new urgencies of socialization demanded that children learn to synchronize themselves with their peers, with the social world around them. According to Reisman, the underlying role of the mass media was to create cautionary tales suited to the new patterns of socialization. Contrasting the *Little Golden Book* with the story of Little Red Riding Hood, Reisman points out that:

> The story of Tootle would seem to be an appropriate one for bringing up children in an other-directed mode of conformity. They learn it is bad to go off the tracks and play with flowers and that, in the long run, there is not only success and approval but even freedom to be found in following the green lights.[28]

The theme of loosening the severe restraints of rigid disciple became a major item in parental advisories. Dr Benjamin Spock's *Baby and Child Care* was the invariable guide for families trying to modify their parenting to match the temper of the times. Parents forsook physical punishment in favour of new bonds of love and caring:

> We have learned a great deal bit by bit: that children need the love of good parents more than anything else; that they work hard, all by themselves, to be more grown-up and responsible; that many of the ones who get into the most trouble are suffering from lack of affection rather than from lack of punishment; that children are eager to learn if they are given school projects that are right for their age and are taught by understanding teachers; that some jealous feelings towards parents are natural and that a child does not need to feel deeply ashamed of them and that a childish interest in the facts of life and in some aspects of sex is quite normal; that too harsh a repression of aggressive feelings and sexual interest may lead to neurosis; that unconscious thoughts are as influential as conscious ones; that each child is an individual and should be allowed to be so.[29]

Parents were thus urged to establish a new quality of self-determination in the relationships with their children, giving them the appropriate objects and opportunities to help them 'discover themselves'.

Lloyd DeMause writes optimistically of this emerging postwar US childrearing practice, which he terms 'helping'. Helping reflects a family situation in which the parent believes the 'child knows better than the parent what it needs at each stage of its life' and parents struggle to 'empathize with and fulfill its particular needs'. The aims of such practices are the liberation of the child and to produce a generation that is 'gentle, sincere, never depressed, never imitative or group-oriented, strong-willed, and unintimidated by authority'.[30] Not surprisingly, in this mood of uncertainty concerning the fate of the family, new forms of fiction – the family drama and situation comedy – became television's main prime-time offering, with the open and understanding family as the narrative focus. *Father Knows Best, Adventures of Ozzie and Harriet, I Love Lucy* and *The Honeymooners* mirrored for the postwar generation their own difficulties in coming to grips with new family expectations. Conflict often revolved around the differing perspectives of husband and wife and always on the generational divide between parent and child.

The perspective of developmentalism, articulated in Erik Erikson's book *Childhood and Society,* was repeated assuredly in the popular media.[31] Advertising and a host of shows supported parental forbearance when it came to self-discovery. 'It's only a stage he's going through', was the rallying cry for parents who had become alarmed when they found themselves increasingly besieged by an assertive child. Maturation in the new era demanded psychological space – an arena free from guilt and parental interference. Children needed to experience leisure, to have autonomy and to engage in their fantasies – to have a 'rich inner life' so they could express themselves in meaningful ways in the future. Parents who did not allow youth to work towards maturation by resisting authority might inadvertently undermine the self-restraint required of mature citizens. Sociologists spoke of a widening generation gap as children reared under the new regime of freedom no longer responded to the discipline and self-restraint that had been urged upon their parents.

This generational conflict in families was itself interpreted as a microcosm of a broader social transformation. Sociologists popularized the idea that the baby-boom generation was a transition period on the road to a new way of life. They debated whether the rising divorce rates, the separation from the extended family and community ties, the generational differences, the family tensions and breakdown were a sign of stress or of inevitable progress. For the older generation to achieve their goals it was still important to maintain a sense of responsibility, self-restraint and hard work – in short, an adherence to unchanging moral principles. The youth generation did not seem to share these values. Rather, youth peer groups seemed driven by the need for rebellion, personal freedom, self-expression and autonomy – the values promoted by a new vision of consumerist democracy. If families failed to evolve a modified form of authority or adjust to the new freedoms, they were doomed.

Indeed, the forces converging on family life grew only in proportion as the baby-boom generation grew to maturity. Although the family did not 'disappear' as a social institution, it had undergone serious reorganization by the late 1980s, and divorce and remarriage continued to mark children's lives. Some 30 per cent of families were single-parent households. Likewise, many family units consisted of combined families from previous relationships. Unlike their mothers, the new generation of women went out to work to establish their equality, and they earned more money. Half the childrearing mothers were now in full-time work and many more in part-time and occasional work. As a result the amount of time available for childrearing interaction declined. Over 40 per cent of children were spending time in nursery and childcare before school age, increasing dramatically the role of the peer group. Children, it was argued, would learn social skills and develop their own identity best within the peer group.

The mobile, fluid and materialist industrial order, it seemed, required a new kind of bonding if the family were to survive. And if families could no longer share values, they could at least share things – the fridge, the family car and the television promised continued family solidarity. In the sitcoms of the postwar period much of the humour centres on this issue – Lucy's shopping sprees and Bud's car in *Father Knows Best* were symbols of generational conjuncture around domestic technologies and consumerism. And the image of the family gathered around the television set was a reassuring counter-stroke to the pall of doom and divisiveness that hung over social-ization.

The Imaginary Technology

Commercial television brought this domestic vista to the very foreground of popular discourse. The baby-boom years seemed to be built around the reinvention of modern family life accompanied by a more self-conscious approach to childrearing. In television's formative period, experimentation with and adaptation of program-ming form were necessary to constitute the familial audience for the new technology. Television quickly became the favoured means of articulating the new order of childrearing, not only through advertis-ing but also through the teary hard-luck stories of programmes like *Queen for a Day* or the bemused friendliness of Art Linkletter's *Kids Say the Darndest Things*. But the greatest innovation was a light and entertaining dramatic form that explored the internal texture and

66

feelings of family life: the sitcom. The rise of the family situation comedy may indeed signify a truly innovative but underrated direction in popular entertainment; it is easy to overlook how this narrative form brought into the public eye those important transformations taking place within the postwar household.

The conflict at the heart of the family drama is generational. Unlike *The Honeymooners* or *Burns and Allen,* which maintained the fictional battlelines drawn along the ground of gender and class stereotypes, much of the strife, humour and characterization in the family narratives pivoted on an emergent generational power struggle and the problems of childrearing. The narrative thread that links *Father Knows Best* or *My Three Sons* with the later *Family Ties, Cosby Show,* and *The Simpsons* is the predominating sense of the family as the site of chronic confusion and misunderstanding. The family is disrupted by the clash of culture. In comic terms, parents are often depicted as having grown out of touch with their children, in constant battle with them over mores and behaviour, or fussing about the diminution of their parental authority. Children, by way of contrast, emerge as wiser and more wily characters than the cherubs of early days. Their primary agenda may be maturation, but they are not docile, witless or complacent in the face of modern society.

Prime-time advertising also focused its attention on the celebration of the family's daily preoccupations. Advertisers treated these domestic practices and rituals as the vehicle for revealing the moral foundation of the familial order: the 1950s' family became preoccupied with possession and consumption and the satisfaction that goods can bring. The tensions of family life remain of course, but in the background: in the foreground is the product's ability to resolve those tensions inherent in changing generational relations: soup and motherly wisdom assuage the competitive instincts of the young hockey player, fast-food hamburgers provide the only food the whole family enjoys eating together, a laundry detergent saves an overly proud teenager from social embarrassment, the right dog food is the only way to keep the family pet contented and docile. In all of these domestic situations, products appear as the ultimate locus of in-depth emotions and the natural resolution of domestic misunderstanding.

In the face of increasingly demanding children who can only be satisfied with the 'right stuff', material caring and nurturance came to define both the purpose and responsibility of good parenting. The world of television product advertising resounds not only with a sense of generational conflict over consumption patterns but also increasingly with the vision of warm sentiments and endearing scenes from family life in which the consumerist solution to childrearing has been tried. Multiple generations of the family can be unified and understood in terms of common brand loyalties. By the early 1960s television advertising was producing a singular and harmonious social vision of the family pacified on the plane of consumption.

Television advertising helped the postwar era refocus its attention on domestic affairs and experience. Television was enormously useful in helping merchandizers to return to and finish the public projection of a picture of domesticated consumerism promised in the 1930s. It did so not only in the highly domesticated 'slices of life' portrayed in its advertising but also by developing this medium as a venue for family-orientated programming. Television could achieve the merchandizers' dream of a family gathered together to listen to its selling pitches.[32] In this sense, the advent of family drama and advertising should be seen not as an attempt to destroy family intercourse as much as a means of focusing attention on consumption. David Reisman and Roseborough speculated in the 1950s that 'previous theory and research indicate that young people may acquire from the mass media the expressive aspects of consumption and that family and other socialization agents such as school may be inadequate in teaching relevant consumer skills, knowledge and attitudes leaving room for the mass media to serve as substitutes in the socialization process'.[33] In the process of transforming television into the ultimate weapon of consumer socialization, a new interest in the imaginary family and new undercurrents in the depicted problems of childrearing appeared disguised in an entertaining and dramatic form.

Television and its Discontents

Since its inception television has been a much contested and much criticized medium in public policy debates about contemporary socialization. Although television is now clearly a significant channel of communication with children, many parents remain confused about why television matters. Do children watch too much of it? Do the simplicity and banality of the programming cause children harm? Does the television itself disrupt, interfere with and weaken family interaction? Are we producing generations of children who don't know the names of their political leaders or the simple structure of the atom?

Television is often pictured as the instrument of aggressiveness, degeneracy, mass ignorance and growing illiteracy for a whole culture. It is easy and convenient to attribute to television all the unsavoury trajectories of contemporary culture because it now dominates so much of home life, and through it popular culture. Little wonder that the introduction and growth of this medium have been accompanied by a chorus of uncertainty and doubt. These issues are repeatedly raised in discussions of the impact of television on the family, revealing both an uncrystallized discomfort with the medium and a growing sense of malaise in childrearing in the face of the pressure of television.[34]

The longstanding criticisms of television became readily apparent in a random telephone survey of 300 families in the Toronto Region.[35] Over 60 per cent of the sample expressed concerns about children's TV (including violence, excessive fantasy and low quality) but only 21 per cent offered any indication that their concerns were strong enough to motivate active restrictions on their children's TV viewing. Parents were most vocal about the amount of violence in children's programming (19 per cent) and many were worried about an excess of advertising.

However, most parents (63 per cent) reported that they felt the amount of their children's TV viewing was about right. Most parents also felt satisfied that they knew what their children were watching in spite of the fact that the majority only occasionally watched TV with their kids. Most importantly, less than half of this Canadian sample felt that government regulation was the best way to control children's commercial television; they preferred less direct measures. There was little sense of a groundswell of critical opinion around children's television and little to indicate that parents were deeply troubled by, or even noticed, the intensifying efforts of marketers to sell products to their children.

Although most parents reported minimal efforts to influence their children's viewing, few denied the positive side of television for the family: that it preoccupies and interests children, thus freeing up time for the adults. This tension lay at the heart of ambiguous parental attitudes towards television's intrusion into the family's responsibilities for socialization: accepting their children's fascination with television and their own inability to dislodge it from its place of prominence in their lives, parents seem to accept the mainstream criticisms of television and to feel a sense of guilt; but they do not know what should be done about it, and they are not likely to struggle to resist its influence. Any resistance amounts to urging children to watch educational programming and to occasionally viewing and talking about television with their children. These appear to be the only prophylactics against what many parents sense as an intrusion into the complex and difficult task of shaping children's culture. Few parents question, however, whether it is wise to hand over to others the task of early socialization.

Marie Winn's book *The Plug-in Drug* provides an indicative summary of popular concerns around children and television.[36] She argues that television is crucial to the erosion of family life not because it is boring and banal but because it has been too effective in gathering children to its bosom. Television is such a good babysitter and holds such strong attractions and fascinations for the child that it has become a hypnotic force for the destruction of the real family interactions that surround it. Winn draws particular attention to the *act* of watching television. 'It is easy to overlook a deceptively simple fact,' she states. 'One is always watching television ... rather than having any other experience.' For Winn the consequences of TV displacing other activities from children's lives demand that parents do more than know what their kids are watching: parents must try to guide, restrict and replace television-viewing whenever they can. Winn provides encouraging accounts of families who have undertaken this struggle.

Few parents in the Toronto survey reported attempting to do so. Very few of them said they were able to counteract the displacement effect of television, and fewer still could imagine how they might make this effort. The net feeling among parents is a mixture of uncertainty and powerlessness. Mostly, they seem to experience and express the inability to combat children's television-viewing as a pressure on parental time and energy. The harried modern parent finds it hard to imagine what children did before television came along to absorb 4·2 hours of their child's day. The activities that have been displaced from children's lives by television viewing become invisible to a parent who is merely content that the child is occupied placidly elsewhere. Moreover, forty years of taking the simulated interactions of television families as a model of normality appears to have erased from collective memory the array of daily preoccupations (conversing, playing and working together, music) that sustained families before the advent of TV.

Ultimately, the common-sense view leads parents to interpret their doubts and concerns as emanating from television itself. Without a historical sense of cultural change, baby-boomer parents have no bench-mark against which to compare childhood today except against their own experience of television. Only those who have experienced less commercialized media systems elsewhere can see the institutional connection between the struggles in the family over television and the commercial context of children's broadcasting.

Winn's arguments also reveal this common-sense assumption. She sees passive watching as inherent in the nature of the medium rather than residing in the choices made about its location in the matrix of socialization. The same peril of ignoring the commercial element in broadcasting is apparent in Neil Postman's much celebrated book, *The Disappearance of Childhood,* in which he prophesies the decline of the culture of innocence on the basis of television's effects on children.[37] Postman's account provides a novel twist to the common view that sees television displacing reading and other traditionally valued activities from children's culture. In his view, television has a direct effect on the traditions of familial socialization because it erodes the very differences that were sustained between the domains of adult and child:

> Television makes hash of this whole process because it reveals to everyone in the culture simultaneously all of the cultural secrets. . . . TV, because of its instantaneity, because of its simultaneity, because of its inability to segregate audiences, therefore eliminates the idea of having a special category of people, children, who are in need of protection and nurturing and who are in particular to be protected against knowing too early some of the things that adults know. Because this process is well under way, it seems to me that the idea of childhood is being rapidly eroded.[38]

Postman's prognosis rests on his argument that television drama presents images of children as 'adultified' and precocious while the adult characters are infantilized and immature. He bases this conclusion on an overview of popular prime-time programmes. Children, he summarizes, are being asked to share the more mature and troubled view of life that the mass media frames for the whole family.

Like most critics of television, Postman portrays this medium (and its treatment of childhood and family dynamics) as if the patterns of its use and meaning, as established in North American culture, were

71

inherent to the technology itself – as if the genres, audience orientation and patterns of programming adopted for television were the inevitable expressions of the inner workings of the medium. It is precisely this deterministic way of thinking about television that Raymond Williams has criticized for completely misperceiving the dynamics of cultural production.

The casual observer may be led to see in television's obsessions with family life a mere reflection and mirroring of broader demographic trends and shifting attitudes of the television generation. No doubt social realignment is part of the story. Yet television is a pivotal technology for reorganizing many dimensions of the household, including the social interactions that can take place in and around television. Because watching television is rarely totally atomistic and passive, one incidental effect of television is the construction of interpretive communities, groups of individuals that interact around and through the sharing of content.[39] But a historical inquiry into the motivation behind the patterns of television's cultural form and programming indicates that television did not passively receive family programming as a social fact or even an inherited tradition from other media. As Williams also notes, the motivation arises from the institutional context: at the critical moment when the foundations of commercial television were being formed, the guiding concept of a household medium of entertainment prevailed. All television programming had to serve the purpose of opening and maintaining the communicational passageways between the marketplace and the consumer that programme sponsorship entailed. The familial imagery from 1950s television serves to remind us how seriously broadcasters took their mission of 'constituting the family' as an audience for the medium. The popularity of recent family programming such as *Cosby* and *The Simpsons* is a token of the continuing success of this project. But this was not television's only audience.

Postman's assumed homogeneity of television as a 'mass' medium leads him to ignore historical audience segmentation patterns and the development of new audiences. His review of children's television somehow completely overlooks the presence of Saturday morning cartoons, the kind of children's programming that young children spend much of their spare time viewing. Before he drew his conclusions about what was happening to children's culture, Postman might have tuned his set to the *Smurfs, Flintstones* or *Super Friends* and reflected on what these children's animations meant within children's experience. To overlook the development of this programming ghetto, which specifically addresses the children's audience, is to fail to perceive a crucial change in television's role in socialization.

Focusing critical attention on the most popular familial imagery of prime-time only serves to distract us from the children's-time TV ghetto and the commercial voice nestled therein. There amid the images of happy children munching sweetened cereals and the incessant clatter of toy advertising is a different picture of family life – one where kids are kids and where adults are compliant. Children's television is the world of children's peer culture, peer interests and sentiments all projected into a narrative realm by its producers. But it is not a garden-like realm of innocence that is envisioned for kids in children's-time programming – not even on *Sesame Street.* Moreover it is a world almost devoid of play.[40] The only exposure that children get to the notions of peer interaction and play, and the freedom and self-expression they can experience in that interaction, may be in the abundant toy and food commercials.[41] It is a reassuring palliative that in the struggle for children's television in the United States, critics are increasingly focusing on the issues of quality and the commercial content of television.[42]

It is easy to forget that before the advent of children's television very little effort was expended in guiding the consumption practices of children. This meant an impoverished and undernourished children's programming. Networks had very little motivation to produce a children's culture. Postman's otherwise thoughtful examination of the history of childhood suffers badly from overlooking this historical fact. His failure to locate a 'children's culture' on television entirely misses the point that from the early 1950s television producers became engaged in developing a new kind of television product with a very different sensibility and imagery at its core. These creations were shown first after school, later on Saturday mornings, and later still in the preschool hours, whenever children could be drawn to the set without the parent in the room. Through their success, television has become an increasingly effective instrument through which marketers have been able to address the child as audience directly. Young children, some of whom watch up to seven hours a day, clearly get exposed to many ideas about social life from this specifically child-orientated programming and advertising. Currently, the majority of the average under-eight child's viewing is dedicated to children's-time television viewing. But is this really a childhood vision we can celebrate?

I don't think so, for the market brings with it its own set of problems. Critics of children's media can no longer ignore or wish away the marketing dynamic that frames contemporary television programming. Television does provide a distinctive cultural product for young children. But these children have been furnished with a cultural product of their own neither out of the magnanimity of broadcasters nor a sense of moral purpose. Commercial television is a business lodged in a competitive marketplace. This means that any analysis of it might well begin with the programmers' primary business considerations – audiences and what they purchase – which circumscribe their interest in children and shape all commercial television content.

Marketers of children's goods such as sweets, cereals and toys became dissatisfied with the opportunities offered by family viewing. The family gathered around television was only the precursor to a new project: marketers began to use television to talk more directly to children and through it to assert the market's right of place within the matrix of socialization. There was little discussion of whether commercial interests should have such licence, or whether their influence on socialization fits in with the border prospects for social justice and psychological well-being.

Marketing directed at children arose coincidentally with the television medium and its new position of command over children's culture. The television-viewing of children increased to what must be considered its natural limit; television has become the undisputed leader in the production of children's culture. Television constituted children as an audience so they could be integrated into the market. Although only a narrow band of children's goods were ever advertised on television there emerged sufficient advertising interest to assign the creative resources to this task.[43] In the thirty years from the first children's television advertising in the early 1950s to the explosion in commercial media, television has changed family life dramatically. Indeed, it is only the recent nature of this historical phenomenon that has made it easy to see how marketing became such a major force within the contemporary 'funnel' of childhood.

Notes

1. Lloyd DeMause, 'The Evolution of Childhood', in Lloyd DeMause, ed., *The History of Childhood*, New York, Harper & Row, 1974, p. 3.
2. Van der Kooij, Rimmert and Wilma Slaats-van den Hurk, 'Relations between

Parental Opinions and Attitudes about Child Rearing and Play', *Play and Culture*, 4, 1991, p. 120.

3. Norbeck, Edward, 'The Study of Play – Johan Huizinga and Modern Anthropology', in David Lancy and B. Allan Tindall, *The Study of Play: Problems and Prospects*, New York, Leisure Press, 1977, p. 17.

4. Ariès, Philippe, *Centuries of Childhood: A Social History of Family Life*, New York, Alfred Knopf, 1962.

5. Quoted in Tucker, M.J., 'The Child as Beginning and End: Fifteenth and Sixteenth Century English Childhood', in DeMause, *The History of Childhood*, p. 251.

6. Rheingold, H. and K.V. Cook, 'The Content of Boys' and Girls' Rooms as an Index of Parents' Behavior', *Child Development*, 46, 1975, pp. 459–63.

7. Adams, Paul, Leila Berg, Nan Berger, Michael Duane, A.S. Neil and Robert Ollendorff, *Children's Rights: Towards the Liberation of the Child*, Wellingborough, Elek Books, 1971.

8. See Ariès, *Centuries of Childhood*; DeMause, ed., *The History of Childhood*; Pollock, Linda A., *Forgotten Children: Parent–child relations from 1500 to 1900*. New York, Cambridge University Press, 1983; Jordan, Thomas, *Victorian Childhood: Themes and Variations*, Albany, State University of New York Press, 1987.

9. DeMause, 'The Evolution of Childhood', p. 52.

10. Marc Bloch, *Feudal Society*, Chicago: University of Chicago Press, 1961, pp. 134–42.

11. Adams, Paul, 'The Infant, the Family and Society', in Adams et al., eds, pp. 51–90.

12. Rubin, K., 'Introduction' and 'Early Play Theories Revisited: Contributions to Contemporary Research and Theory', in Pepler, D. and K. Rubin, eds, *The Play of Children: Current Theory and Research*, Basel and New York, Krager, 1982.

13. Jackson Lears, T., 'From Salvation to Self-Realization: Advertising and the Therapeutic Roots of the Consumer Culture 1880–1930', in Richard Fox and T.J. Lears, eds, *The Culture of Consumption*, New York, Pantheon, 1983, p. 23.

14. Adrian Forty, *Objects of Desire*, London, Pantheon Books, 1986, pp. 68–70.

15. Ibid., p. 72.

16. Marchand, Roland, *Advertising the American Dream: Making Way for Modernity, 1920–1940*, Berkeley, University of California Press, 1985, p. 248.

17. Ewen, Stuart, *Captains of Consciousness*, New York, McGraw-Hill, 1976, p. 126.

18. Ibid., p. 139.

19. Marchand, *Advertising*, pp. 254–5.

20. Snyder, Richard, 'Trends in the Sporting Goods Market', in M. Marie Hart, ed., *Sport in the Socio-cultural Process*, Dubuque, Wm. C. Brown, 1972, pp. 423–44.

21. Barthes, Roland, *Mythologies*, London, Paladin, 1973.

22. Marchand, *Advertising*, 248–9.

23. Ewen *Captains*, p. 139.

24. Marchand, *Advertising*, p. 254.

25. Mendlesohn, Harold, *Mass Entertainment*, New Haven, College and University Press, 1966.

26. Maital, S. 1982, 'From Pleasure to Reality: Learning to Wait Begins in Childhood', in *Minds, Markets and Money*, New York, Basic Books.

27. David Reisman, with Nathan Glazer and Reuel Denney, *The Lonely Crowd: A Study of the Changing American Character*, New Haven, Yale University Press, abridged edn, 1965.

28. Ibid., p. 106.

29. Spock, Benjamin, *Baby and Child Care*, New York, Pocket Books, 1979, pp. 364–5.

30. DeMause, *The History of Childhood*, pp. 52, 54.

31. Erikson, Erik H., *Childhood and Society*, New York, W.W. Norton, 1963.

32. Moore, Roy and George Moschis, 'Role of Mass Media and the Family in Development of Consumption Norms', *Journalism Quarterly*, 60, pp. 67–73.

33. Reisman, David and H. Roseborough, 'Careers in Consumer Behavior', in Lincoln Clark, ed., *Consumer Behavior II: The Life Cycle and Consumer Behavior*, New York, New York University Press, 1955, p. 68.

34. See the attitudes reported in Steiner, G., *The People Look at Television*, New York, Knopf, 1963.

35. Our survey interviewed 300 randomly selected parents by telephone for about forty minutes. The survey used the phone book for the Metropolitan Toronto region and included only parents who currently had children under twelve years of age. Analysis of this data is in the Appendix.

36. Winn, Marie, *The Plug-in Drug*, New York, Penguin, 1977.

37. Postman, Neil, *The Disappearance of Childhood*, New York, Dell Publishing, 1982.

38. Postman, interviewed by David Cayley, CBC Manuscript, *Ideas*, 1986.

39. Lindlof, Thomas, Milton Shatzer and Daniel Wilkinson, 'Accommodation of Video and Television in the American Family', pp. 158–92; and Morley, David, 'Domestic Relations: The Framework of Family Viewing in Great Britain', in James Lull, ed., *World Families Watch Television*, Newbury Park, CA, Sage, 1988, pp. 22–48.

40. Duncan, Margaret Carlisle, 'Television Portrayals of Children's Play and Sport', *Play and Culture*, 2 (1989), pp. 235–52.

41. Kline, Stephen and Debra Pentecost, 'The Characterization of Play: Marketing Children's Toys', *Play and Culture*, 3(3) (1990), pp. 235–54.

42. Palmer, Edward, *Television and America's Children: A Crisis of Neglect*, New York, Oxford University Press, 1988.

43. Doolittle, John and Robert Pepper, 'Children's TV AD Content: 1974', *Journal of Broadcasting*, 19(2), (1975) pp. 131–42; Atkin, Charles and Gary Heald, 'The Content of Children's Toy and Food Commercials', *Journal of Communication*, 27, (1977), pp. 107–14.

3

From Literacy to Comics:
The Origins of Children's
Fiction

To open a child's book nowadays is to discover some part of that unknown world which touches experience at so many points. The city beyond the clouds, the underground country, all the enchantments of woods and islands are open to the little traveller. From *The Water Babies* to *Peter Pan* there has been little else in nursery tales but the stuff of dreams.[1]

All cultures have myths and tales, stories and folklore – narratives that accumulate vital cultural knowledge and percepts and pass those bits of wisdom on to succeeding generations. Through their enactment in ritual, through story-telling or their dramatization in ceremony, arts and religion, narrative gives expression to mythic explanations of the world and provides the templates of a culture. Narrative is a means of negotiating the broad patterns of a culture's thought and feeling; through early exposure to the stories children gain their first intellectual framework within which they can integrate experience and perception. Such stories appear to be the primary means by which fundamental psychological and cultural values and needs are crystallized in every society. For this reason anthropologists have long held that mythic narratives are a useful point of access to the symbolic framework of a culture.[2]

As many folklorists have noted, the printed word has assimilated oral culture through the book; and many of the traditions, references, themes and motifs of earlier times have been preserved and passed on through the children's book. As the work of Iona and Peter Opie has shown, many nursery rhymes that we take to be our classic inheritance are formal versions of centuries-old oral traditions – of songs, verbal games, riddles, jokes and finger games that connect our culture with its earliest roots.[3] Likewise, children's fairy tales echo with the well-known biblical themes and even pre-biblical motifs of sibling rivalry, tricksterism, magical transformation, oedipal struggles to gain consciousness, enduring quests and animal–human relations – all the forms of unconscious thought and feeling that give shape to our myths.[4] The children's book became a key repository of preliterate thought and the means by which patterns of thought were reintroduced from one generation to another.

The preservation of these mythic narrative forms within children's culture is not without reason. For children, as Bruno Bettleheim notes, modern fairy tales serve a psychical function similar to the role of ancient tales, taking on particular importance in psychologically orientating children in the framework of their cultures:

> This is exactly the message that fairy tales get across to the child in manifold form: that a struggle against severe difficulties in life is unavoidable, is an intrinsic part of human existence – but that if one does not shy away, but steadfastly meets unexpected and often unjust hardships, one masters all obstacles and at the end emerges victorious.

In defining both the contradictory tendencies that buffet the child's life, and urging a culturally defined path to their resolution, mythic and folkloric narrative becomes a vital means by which the child assimilates and makes sense of both internal and social experience. As Bettleheim states: 'The form and structure of fairy tales suggest images to the child by which he can structure his daydreams and with them give better direction to his life.' For this reason the perpetuation of story-telling remains vital to the child's social and emotional development.[5]

Not surprisingly, when most of us think about our own early experiences the first thing that comes to mind is the stories we were told in childhood, especially the much-loved and long-remembered nursery rhymes, fairy tales, poems and exotic tales that were read or told to us in our very youngest years. The classics of children's literature, as collected and written over the past two centuries, have become definitional to our understanding of children's experience and culture in the modern era. The emergence of a lighter touch in children's writing during the Victorian period, with the enthusiastic support this more imaginative folklore received from children, is often viewed as one of the major cultural achievements of the era. The image of a group of young children gathered around a matron reading a story gives concrete form to the nineteenth-century idea of preserving the traditions of story-telling through children's literature. The communion of the children's book, and the image of the literate family it cultivated, became emblematic of the emerging refuge of innocence and delight constructed from the 'stuff of dreams' that took hold in the era of industrialization.

As Canadian theorist Harold Innis observed, however hard the prevailing oligopolies try, most innovations in communication eventually destabilize the established lines of cultural authority and give unforeseen power to new institutions and customs.[6] Children's books did not emerge from a vacuum. Like all early publishing endeavours, books for children at first fulfilled a limited set of purposes defined at the time of the Renaissance and firmly controlled by church and state. But as early manufactured goods they also became subject to the new dynamics of the marketplace and the changing interests that controlled their production and distribution. The book, as the first repeatable 'mass-produced' commodity, foreshadowed both the mechanization of socialization and the distribution of cultural knowledge through the market. The early publishing industry was at first constrained by a social order based on class distinctions in learning, the high cost of rags, low literacy rates and very limited opportunities for book merchandising. Yet, as literacy became a requirement for continued socialization, improvements were made in printing technology and paper production, and the state's tight grip on publishers faltered. The limited prospects of acceptable publishing permitted by church and state were usurped by the commercial press. Books, pamphlets, posters and newspapers became avenues for challenging and circumventing the most established institutions. Publishing in the eighteenth and nineteenth centuries became a vital route for distributing radical ideas.[7] In more modest terms, the children's book contributed to the might of the pen. The printing press ultimately helped to secularize knowledge by ensuring the ever-wider distribution of books and the ideas therein. And just as the book eventually usurped the monopoly that the church held over the printing presses, the children's book also helped to open society at large to new vistas and new ideas about childhood.[8]

Possibly the most radical idea was that books should serve children's needs. Whereas children's books were originally commissioned and bought as instruments of Christian moral instruction and aids to enlightenment for the offspring of the wealthy, by the nineteenth century children's literature had taken wing, soaring on updrafts of fantasy and adventure in a boundless quest to stimulate everychild's imagination. But service to the child's delight was an idea that could emerge only after the traditional channels of familial and church socialization and their implicit moral agenda had been diminished. The rise of fantasy and pleasure as the purpose of children's fiction is therefore a prime indication of the changing conceptions of childhood over the past four centuries.

As Marshall McLuhan noted, it is unwise to underestimate the enormous role that the book and literacy play in the social upheavals induced by the invention of the printing press.[9] This is not only because culture is transmitted through the communications media but also because a change in the medium of knowledge transmission can have profound social consequences. Perceptual modalities underscore the forms of consciousness and the means of organizing the storage and transmission of information. The improvements in printing enabled the ever-wider dissemination of written ideas to carry and ultimately replace oral forms of communication that relied on memory, simultaneity and collective participation. Reading subverted memory, isolated the reader from the collectivity, emphasized mental linearity and regularity, and placed a psychological focus on personal identity. Books promoted the necessity of literacy, McLuhan argued, not just as a skill for acquiring knowledge and power but as the dominant cultural frame of mind.

Pursuing McLuhan's argument, Neil Postman observes that 'there was no such thing as a children's literature' before the sixteenth century.[10] The emerging aura of innocence and naivety that surrounded the Victorian idea of the child, Postman argues, was closely linked to the demands for literacy inherent in the growing print media, which erected a cultural barrier between illiterate children and adults:

> A new communication environment began to take form in the sixteenth century as a result of printing and social literacy. The printing press created a new definition of adulthood based on reading competence, and, correspondingly, a new conception of childhood based on reading incompetence.... In a literate world to be an adult implies having access to cultural secrets codified in unnatural symbols. In a literate world children must become adults. But in the nonliterate world there is no need to distinguish sharply between the child and the adult, for there are few secrets, and the culture does not need to provide training in how to understand itself.[11]

For this reason, Postman regards the invention of the printing press as crucial to the invention of modern childhood. Literacy not only represents a radically different sensibility but also a departure in organizing the acculturation of the child and, implicitly, of organizing consciousness itself. Literacy became the dominating pedagogical agenda of the schools, and of parents' aspirations for their children, reinforcing the perceived innocence and naivety of those not inducted into the mysteries of reading. Yet a pedagogy based on literacy – and literacy's obsession with knowledge acquisition – also replaced some of the other social, moral and cultural aspects of a youth's maturational experience, except as mediated by books. What youth might once have learned on 'the playing fields of Eton' was now to be garnered from the pages of a book.

The book is not just a medium for communication, though; it is also a product that allows the market mechanism to play a significant role in socialization. Originally the role of the market was small, for other considerations and institutions dominated the writing, printing and distribution of books. Publishing was fully preoccupied with the task of 'educating and enlightening' children, and printers had to produce and sell children's books that served the accepted perspective on their role. Children were not in the market for children's books, and the books that came into their possession were given as gifts for instruction and moral inspiration. Yet during the nineteenth century those purposes began to broaden as a sense of the child's autonomy and freedom and its love of stories for their own sake became celebrated in children's literature. More than just instruments of pedagogy, the stories took on the ability to enthral and delight the child, an ability that emerged as the prime attraction of reading.

This change in content coincided with both an expanding market for children's books and an expanding role of fiction in their culture. Publishers began to reconceive of the children's book as a good – to be used by children for their own purposes. This simple appreciation of the marketing concept led them to encourage writers to loosen the bounds of their fiction; writers joyfully undertook experiments that charted new courses for the literate imagination. The increasing acceptance and sales of new children's works helped consolidate the idea that children experienced the world in a very different way from adults, and it revealed too the possibility of designing and distributing products that addressed children's special needs. Children's books were in fact the first 'products' of any kind to be designed with children's special status and needs in mind. The book, as redefined by the nineteenth-century publisher, challenged parental and church authority and subtly subverted the lines of force within the established order, making enjoyment the preferred structure of feeling associated with literacy.

Handmaidens to Literacy

Books for children were rare indeed before the close of the eighteenth century. Most education for young people consisted of being tutored or learning at the sides of their parents and relatives. Books were expensive to produce and only the wealthier members of society could read or teach their children to do so. The original forms and uses of published material for children were dominated, therefore, by the notion of the privileges of education. From the beginning there is evidence of the seriousness that wealthier segments of society ascribed to reading. The first book produced explicitly for children's use that we know of was published around 1578 by Sigmund Feyerabend, a German publisher who had become interested in the idea that books could be used by parents in their nurseries. His book's title, which translates as 'Book of Art and Instruction for Young People Filled with Legend and Fables and Folk Tales with Illustration' is overtly educational but, in a sense, more appropriate to an oral culture. Yet it helped to define the characteristics of a child's 'first reader' for generations to come. Its pedagogical method consciously relied on the motifs of folklore to guide the instruction of the child. In the plain and moralistic tales of folk society, parents were encouraged to continue using simple narratives to help teach their children to read. There is evidence, therefore, that early books published for children – that is, to be read to them and sometimes by them – were already being simplified to satisfy more limited capacities and interests. The picture alphabets and rhyming picture books so common in today's stores represent the revision to pedagogical technique undertaken during the earliest period of children's books.

Like many modern children's products, early books were often well-illustrated with vivid pictures, a practice that served to establish visualization as a pedagogical principle in the acquisition of literacy. The illumination of manuscripts was common to the adult works of the era before the printing press, but in the minds of educators such as John Locke illustration informed a new approach to instruction because pictures could rivet the attention and picture–word combinations could aid learning. Locke advocated illustrated picture books like *Aesop's Fables* for the young (male) reader because it will 'entertain him much the better and encourage him to read, when it carries the increase of knowledge with it; for such visible objects children hear talked of in vain whilst they have no idea of them.'[12] The book, unlike stories told in song, drama or tale, established links between linguistic and iconic symbolic fields that no other method of instruction afforded.

The whole aura of early children's publishing was tied to a strong belief in 'suitable works' approved by parents for encouraging the guidance and enlightenment of the child: many of the works that became popular family reading were originally written for adults who then referred them to their families for their mutual benefit. For example, the first part of John Bunyan's *The Pilgrim's Progress* was published in 1678 as a religious tract. Its moral purpose was clear. Yet for centuries the book was recommended to the young because its simplicity of language made it accessible both in thought and style. Bunyan later wrote *A Book for Boys and Girls or Country Rhymes for Children*, which was imbued with the fear of God and smell of brimstone; but this overstated work ended up being much less read by children.

Biblical stories and myths written for younger minds account for another path followed by early publishers. Isaac Watts's book published in 1715, *Divine Songs Attempted in Easy Language for the Use of Children*, provides clear confirmation that the retelling of biblical tales to children was a prime motive in the circulation of children's books. As Northrop Frye noted in *The Great Code*, where biblical tales were not being told directly to the child in books they were often the implicit symbolic foundation of all narratives. The mere title of James Janeway's *A Token for Children: Being an Exact Account of the Conversion, Holy and Exemplary Lives, and Joyful Deaths of Several Young Children* is sufficient to convey the intensity with which children's books strove to lay down the religious basis of reading. Through example, Janeway's tales urged children to live lives of religious ecstasy and forbade them toys of all shapes and forms because such goods were tainted with leisure. Commenting just as much on the whole spectrum of eighteenth-century publishing, British book collector Eric Quayle states:

Early children's literature was also constrained by the sense of moral urgency which hung over a child's education. Books were written at children rather than for them, and sought to terrify into docile obedience with threats of everlasting hell-fire all those youngsters who obstinately persisted in enjoying their leisure hours.[13]

Children's writing was being shaped by the rather limited sense of purpose to which books were put throughout the eighteenth and into the nineteenth centuries. Literacy itself was grounded in a moral mission, promoted by the Evangelical church. Robert Raikes's Sunday school movement became particularly influential in the United States during the eighteenth century and produced and distributed many of the books for children in that century.[14] Accompanying works also sought to improve the parents' relationship with their children, including instructions on how to use books in their childrearing. The quality of writing in these books indicates that the stories were written primarily to be read to children – as extensions of the parent–child relationship – or studied at Sunday school. Children could not be trusted to extract the right lessons if left to read on their own. This is why Maria Edgeworth offered advice in her book *The Parent's Assistant: or, Stories for Children* on how the reading of her stories was to be an integral part of religious upbringing. Parental advisories, including instructions to parents on the employment of literature and appropriate fables, commonly discussed the practice of reading to young children in the nursery and in family groups as a means for enhancing religious and cultural bonds within the family. Such works argued that religious stories and percepts were to be actively shared between adult and child and not simply parables for moral indoctrination. Consequently, even for those books that children were instructed to read on their own, the narrative and writing style often mimic the parental companion, using a moralizing voice.

Yet in pursuit of moral instruction through books, a number of compendiums of traditional folklore were published explicitly for children. *Aesop's Fables* was first published in England by John Ogilby in 1651 in Latin, not for children but for scholars. Yet because folk tales and fables were allegories with a clear moral question or dilemma at their core they seemed perfectly suited for both encouraging reading and instilling correct values. *Aesop* was quickly translated, illustrated and endlessly republished as a children's book, ensuring that these ancient tales of wayward animals would persevere as modern morality tales. In case the implicit moral lesson escaped the child, the moral lesson was usually and clearly enunciated at the end of each story: living happily ever after was the reward of hard work, persistence, or keeping faith with established principles; terrible punishments befell the wicked doer or evil thinker. Yet these tales represented an enormous broadening of children's stories because they employed natural allegory rather than religious example to frame moral issues.

Illustrated versions of folk tales, often rendered in verse, were common in the chapbooks and song-sheets that circulated among the literate middle strata of society. Chapbooks and flysheets loosely bound on low quality paper were the seventeenth century's equivalent of popular magazines. Sometimes religious tracts, sometimes political in nature, they also included short fictional works.[15] Some containing well-known rhymes and fables were obviously intended to be read to or by children and often related stories about children's encounters with heroes, monsters and ogres. It is in these flysheets and chapbooks that the first stumbling literary steps to a popular fiction for children appear to have been taken.

It is not clear whether these simplified and fantastical works were intended primarily for children, for general reading, or for parents reading to the children. Indeed, some historians have questioned whether the tall tales, miraculous stories, ballads of adventure, and even nursery rhymes so common in chapbooks of the period were intended for children at all. Certainly some of the rhymes and songs that we think of as classic children's fare were really political satires or allegorical references to historic events. 'London bridge is falling down' may refer to an eighth-century Viking attack on the city. Little Jack Horner's plums were the lands confiscated from the monasteries by Henry VIII. Yet as Iona and Peter Opie's encyclopaedic study also argued, many of the rhymes are based on nursery finger and counting games or play activities.[16] However uncertain scholars may be of the origins and uses of nursery rhymes and tales, it is clear that their popularity gave impetus for the French raconteur Charles Perrault to gather a number of these folk tales together and publish them in a single volume. This collection was translated into English in 1729 and called *Mother Goose Tales*, which quickly became a popular favourite. The profusion of collected fairy stories and folk tales published from this period on provides an indication of the gradual admission of new and more imaginative influences into the protected realm of the nursery.

Under the banner of moral guidance, children's books were also gradually opening the door to secularization. For example, books intended to aid in the acquisition of socially appropriate behaviour supplemented the biblical stories, allegories and doctrinaire diatribes. Francis Hawkin's *Youth's Behaviour or Decency in Conversation amongst Men* (1636) and *A Cap of Gray Hairs for a Green Head: or the Father's Counsel to his Son, an Apprentice in London* (1671) helped establish the role of the book as a key to 'civilized' behaviour. Armed with knowledge of social ritual, comportment, mannerly speech and social graces, youth were equipped to make their way more effectively in society at large. It is interesting to note that many of these works couched their advice in a simulated dialogue between father and son; the book was inserting itself within the channels of interpersonal communication by adopting that relationship as narrative form.

Travel, exploration, conquest and colonization undertaken during the seventeenth and eighteenth centuries also prodded the English-speaking world towards a more expansive and secular sense of what the child needed to understand. It became increasingly common in certain circles to introduce this expanding vista through stories from different civilizations. Travelogues and tales of adventurers' encounters with other civilizations became an important source of material for both fictional tales and scientific texts that were part of family reading.

Some early texts for young scholars also began to include translations and rewriting of important historical works. As the knowledge of different cultures grew through exploration and colonization, so too did the awareness of alternative patterns of thought and mythology become a significant input into the literary matrix. This growing intrigue with the expanding universe of the Enlightenment can be witnessed in publications such as *The Prehistory Representing the Fabulous Histories of the Heathen Gods*, translated in 1713 by Tookes, a Charterhouse don. Charles Lamb's rewriting of Shakespeare stories and a flood of books on myths and ancient history for children were published in the ensuing centuries following this more liberal notion of education.

These travelogues, bestiaries and accounts of exploration became an increasingly important source of direct instruction for eighteenth-century schoolchildren. Daniel Defoe's *The Life, and Strange and Surprising Adventures of Robinson Crusoe; of York, Mariner*, although published for an adult audience in 1719, laid the groundwork for adventure and travel themes that would hold great appeal for youthful readers. Equally popular was *The Swiss Family Robinson*, a romantic story of a resourceful family shipwrecked on a desert island, published in translation in England in 1814. Both these tales and their many imitators quickly found their way into the hands of school-age readers, and the adventurous spirit they inspired became associated with the aspirations of youth.

Likewise, Swift's satirical *Gulliver's Travels* (1726) and its many adaptations were quickly absorbed into the children's field of knowledge as acceptable literature. The *Lilliputian Magazine*, started in the 1750s, was probably the first periodical published for children, indicating how adaptations of these adventure stories were being increasingly incorporated into children's reading, bringing with them styles of expression and ideas that children would otherwise not encounter. The stories and tales included in this magazine were based on a more secular vision of their education.

The expanding reliance on books as a means of education meant that children's reading had to use more interesting literary devices, including more vivid and natural language, stronger character-ization, more exotic themes and excitement. When they were based on reworking tales found in other cultures they often brought with them a refreshing sensitivity to language and theme. For example, Edward William Lane's translation of Arabic stories, *The Thousand and One Nights*, was an enormous success as family reading from its first publication in 1838–40. This beautifully sequenced series of tales, which Scheherazade and her sister must tell to sustain the interest of the king who is about to kill them, has sold hundreds of thousands of copies in endless printings. Indeed, *The Thousand and One Nights* was particularly poignant, because it recalled for readers a social order in which story-telling was still the lifeblood of culture. This same infatuation with oral tales was gradually being squeezed out by the privileged segments of English society, which valued instructive books for children over the love of a good story.

Another important step in the development of children's books was an innovative type of nursery-verse book that took inspiration from traditional sources. First published in English in 1744 as *Tommy Thumb's Pretty Song Book*, these collections included many familiar rhymes, including 'This Little Pig Went to Market' and 'Little Boy Blue'. The morality of these works seems incidental. Their strength is the obvious delight in parable and the seemingly nonsensical references that afforded children their first delighted glimpse of a less didactic use of language.

87

These tentative steps taken by publishers to open the vistas of children's books were not without opposition. Although the seventeenth and eighteenth centuries were a period of robust and rapid expansion and exploration, there was also a powerful underlay of missionary zeal. The colonization of backward nations paralleled the task of civilizing the little savages at home too. Although some children were being introduced to a broader, more worldly set of ideas through books, the majority of works published for children offered little relief from the onslaught of controlling and moralizing social themes. Indeed, often in strident opposition to the trends in secular publishing, the moralizing voice seemed only to get more intense. Frivolity, adventure and dalliance were not thought fitting themes for the young to hone their minds upon. Those works that valued leisure and proffered nonsense were considered unsuitable for children. Indeed, the arguments of this period are the precursors of a debate that has engulfed all media, including the comic books in the 1950s and television today: books could serve the beguiling work of the devil as well as aid the maturation of moral judgement and righteous enlightenment.[17]

Anna Barbauld's response to the secularization of children's books was a work published in 1778 called *Lessons for Children from Two to Three Years Old*, which consisted of moral lessons consciously written as a missionary expedition into the very earliest ages of childhood. Her ambition was to ensure that stories instilled modesty, obedience and humility in children. She was just one of a group that Eric Quayle refers to as a

> heavy brigade of formidable matrons [who] seemed determined to root out any tendency on the part of the young to read solely for their own entertainment and amusement, especially such frivolous fiction as fairy tales and other pernicious rubbish. The superiority of virtue over vice was their reiterated theme; and vice was usually designated by these belligerent moralists as the type of conduct we should today class as merely youthful naughtiness or boisterous high spirits.[18]

Although advocates of children's literacy, these writers offered stories only in so far as they provided a strict moral lesson. Other prominent English commentators such as Sarah Trimmer – known as 'Good Mrs Trimmer' – were highly critical of the moral lassitude that secular children's literature encouraged in young women. She argued that *The History of Susan Gray, as Related by a Clergyman for the Benefit of Young Women Going to Service* – a book attacking vanity, pride and self-indulgence as well as ungodliness in no uncertain terms – was the only kind of literature a young girl should be allowed to read. The book derided a young girl's interest in pretty clothes and the desire for admiration, which qualified it in Trimmer's eyes to be 'put into the hands of mothers with the view of checking in them that thoughtless vanity which frequently contributes to the ruin of their daughters'. Other books written to be read by children themselves wove into their stories a finger-wagging parental voice that concluded in no uncertain terms by restating the moral lesson of the story. Even though a child would work through these books in the privacy afforded by the solitary experience of reading, the moral voice ensured that the parables and actions of protagonists would be correctly read, not simply as stories, but as lessons guiding the child's own behaviour. A story out of context held dire dangers for the unprepared child.

The Stuff of Dreams

The alternative to the didactic role of fiction was clearly articulated by those who saw pedagogical advantage in the child's simple delight with books. As Lady Ellenor Fenn wrote in her introduction to *The Rational Dame; or Hints Towards Supplying Prattle for Children*, published in 1783:

> In making amusement the vehicle of instruction, consists the grand secret of early education ... early impressions are perhaps, never totally erased – who forgets the nonsense of the nursery.... Children listen with avidity to tales – let us give them none but rational information – amuse them with real wonders – entertain them with agreeable surprises but no deceit; tell them plain, simple truth – there is no need of invention; the world is full of wonders. It is my ambition to have my little volume be the pocket companion of young mothers when they walk abroad with their children, it is my wish to assist them in the delightful task of forming in those children an habit of amusing themselves in a rational manner during their hours of leisure.[19]

Rationality and literacy were also promoted through reading, so it was important to encourage the childish love of good stories. Rather like the producers of *Sesame Street*, Lady Fenn saw in the child's fascination with the narratives a powerful technique for enlightenment. These more secular voices were also gathering in and around the schools and publishing industry, which lent support to Lady Fenn's call for a more intriguing fiction that would engage children directly.

The seventeenth and eighteenth centuries saw complex and often countervailing undercurrents struggle over the conception of childhood.[20] As literacy and self-discipline gradually replaced obedience and brutality as a means of controlling children, so too the celebration of literature for its own sake began to compete with the moralizing purport of the missionaries. The victory of the liberal conception of the purpose of the children's book has become so complete in our own century that one of the foremost twentieth-century historians simply excludes those works dragged down by didactic and pedagogical purpose as simply not being children's books:

> By 'children's books' I mean printed works produced ostensibly to give children spontaneous pleasure, and not primarily to teach them, nor solely to make them good, nor to keep them *profitably* quiet.[21]

In using this definition, Darton overlooks the many books that actually reached children – school books, texts, travelogues, pamphlets, spellers, nursery picture books and the high-minded didactic treatises – and avoids the important debates about the role of books in children's lives – debates that involved a rethinking of the cultural needs of children. Yet through this debate new conceptions of childrearing were being articulated, which in turn supported an expanding market for children's stories. Aware of this discussion, some independent publishers began to encourage their writers to devise books that reflected this new dimension in the demand for children's books.

Many of what we consider children's books were, in fact, first published for adults and passed down to children by parents or teachers. Adults were clearly the gatekeepers to the domain of children's literature, and independent publishers published with the parent in mind. There was, therefore, little impetus to publish stories that children themselves wanted to read. Whether authors were intimidated by the moralizers or simply failed to recognize the market for such fiction, the writing of children's stories remained a very minor part of the publishing trade until a select group of printers and publishers finally started to commission new kinds of books for children.

Yet by the eighteenth century folklore, fantasy and adventure elements had already been absorbed into the traditions of children's publishing through song-sheets and chapbooks. John Newbery was perhaps the first commercial publisher in England to realize that these elements were an excellent basis for producing a new kind of livelier and more entertaining children's book. He conceived of books that could be displayed in a format that made them attractive and desirable possessions in the eyes of young people and started to publish a series of lighter volumes that could be given to a child with a different purpose. He introduced this rationale in the introduction to his first collection of nursery rhymes with the following admonition: ''tis hoped the whole will seem rather an Amusement than a Task'. His 'Juvenile Library' consisted of a collection of original works that he commissioned from writers. The result was a new string of fictitious characters who have persisted in children's culture for three centuries, including Goody Two-Shoes (often accredited to the hand of Oliver Goldsmith, who worked for Newbery). Newbery's books had a light, humorous tone, as can be sensed in this advertisement which appeared in *Penny Morning Post* in 1744:

> A Little Pretty Pocket-Book, intended for the instruction of Little Master Tommy and Pretty Miss Polly, with an agreeable Letter to read from Jack the Giant Killer; as also a Ball and Pincushion, the use of which will infallibly make Tommy a Good Boy and Polly a Good Girl.

Newbery had proved the potential of the children's book trade and he devoted himself to developing a comprehensive list for every niche of the children's market: one source lists 250 books published by the Newbery publishing house over a twenty-five-year period, including magazines, nursery songs and books of an instructional character.[22] To break into the schools Newbery commissioned *A History of England* as a series of letters from a nobleman to his son, as well as Goldsmith's *Roman History Abridged by Himself for the Use of Schools*. Newbery's enormous success set the early pace of children's English-language publishing, but he was quickly copied by six other British publishing houses, which by 1800 were producing books almost exclusively for the young. Other publishers in Germany and the United States quickly followed suit.

This breath of artistic freedom, which eventually swept through all children's literature, appeared first in poems. Poetry collections for children were already a nursery tradition in the form of song books, rhyming alphabets and religious psalms. But *The Butterfly's Ball and the*

Grasshopper's Feast broke new ground in children's poetry when it was first published in 1807 in *Gentleman's Magazine*. Some forty thousand copies sold before the end of the next year, which suggests how willing many parents were to open up the literary exposure of their children. But few children's poetry collections proved as successful in the market or in defining the genre of children's poetry as the work of Kate Greenaway. Greenaway wrote and illustrated hundreds of children's poetry collections and stories in the course of her career, making her gentle, romanticized observations of a pastoral child-hood a widely emulated idiom. In her *Marigold Garden* (1885), within a versified conversation she clearly identifies the choice that lies at the root of secular children's verse:

> In September, when the apples were red,
> To Belinda I said,
> 'Would you like to go away
> To Heaven, or stay
> Here in this orchard full of trees
> All your life?' and she said, 'If you please
> I'll stay here – where I know,
> And the flowers grow'.[23]

The beguiling temptation of this poetry of natural innocence similarly inspired poets from William Wordsworth to Robert Louis Stevenson. The poetry of childhood began to reflect writers' interest in children's love of nature and their perceptions of themselves.

Stevenson's *A Child's Garden of Verses* (1885) was an overnight success not only with parents and teachers but also with children. The simplicity of style and exciting language were becoming a real way of encouraging the young to enjoy reading poetry to themselves. Parents and educators could rest easy with the consolation that rhymes and dramatic verse encouraged the child's literacy, improved diction, taught pronunciation, and gave focus to memory. Recitation and dramatic readings were likewise recommended both as fireside entertainment and school assignments as the notion of a liberal education promoted through literacy took hold in the nineteenth century. Possibly more than any other literary form, poetry articu-lated a reverence for the perceived gentle and natural innocence of the child, which was the underscoring of this new attitude.

In a similar way, folklore and fairy tales were a major inspiration for other kinds of children's publishing. After 1823, when the Grimm brothers' collection of folk tales was published in English, this scholarly work of folk history was quickly made available in versions suited to the parent and teacher too. Now included among the classics of early childhood education, these tales are most notable for their simplicity of language and plot, their unexpected twists of fate, and the evocative quality of their flights into the imagination. As oral stories they retain a strong sense of a moral universe where magic and revenge do the work of divine retribution and reward.

One of the first widely popular examples of fiction influenced by this folkloric sensitivity was Charles Kingsley's carefully crafted tale of sprites, *The Water-Babies; a Fairy Tale for a Land Baby* (1863), which demonstrated that a subtle blending of a softer moral undertone and traditional subject matter could co-exist with a lighter and more buoyant writing style. Kingsley did not merely set out to adapt old folk tales; he used their basic ingredients to create a new kind of fictional work that appealed to children. This same quality of a fantastical moral allegory was present in Hans Christian Andersen's *Wonderful Stories for Children*, published in England in 1846. Both works provided source material for hundreds of adaptations, installing folkloric overtones at the core of children's narrative.

Many of these tales included fantastical elements – animals that talked, fairies, sprites or magical interactions with the natural world – and a simpler and non-scientific vision of the natural world. Some of the characters, such as those in the Uncle Remus tales, traced their lineage to oral animal stories, rewritten for the Southern US audience but clearly based on story-teller versions. Later books, like J.M. Barrie's *Peter Pan*, expanded this genre to explore a more purely imaginary fictional style based on an interpretation of an 'enchanted world' that lies just beyond the characters' dreams. Like Peter Pan, children were generally thought to be more fascinated with that world beyond than with the humdrum nature of everyday life that scolds and intrudes so heavily on their own inner schemes. A.A. Milne's *Winnie-the-Pooh* similarly brought vividly to life a world of animal toy-beings who thought, acted and experienced the world in childlike terms. Pooh's bumbling escapades gain their humour from irony and subtle language, but the charm of Milne's writing lies in his creation of the childlike character of Pooh himself, a 'bear of very little brain'. Yet implicit in these literary explorations is an idea that moved the articulation of children's culture into an imaginary world beyond the delights of the natural garden. The late twentieth-century animators would rely extensively on these folkloric qualities of characterization and narrative for the development of their art.

The exploration of writing for children was also encouraged by the emergence of children's magazines and annuals, which became increasingly popular from the 1830s on. Adam Keys, for example, edited *The Excitement*, an annual collection of tales for boys with the stated sole objective of interesting and entertaining them. These periodical collections, rather like the comics in the 1930s, were for slightly older children and they defined a genre stressing exciting plots, a youthful adventurousness and a stronger sense of the need to involve readers in the story. Keys's introduction to the first collection stated that his annuals would contain only stories with 'narratives of such striking incidents as are fitted to rouse the most slothful mind – incidents in which the reader cannot fail to imagine himself identified, as it were, with the parties concerned, and to enter with the deepest interests into all their various feelings'.[24]

Trends in adult fiction also reflected the nineteenth century's changing attitudes towards childhood. As a literary form the novel seemed to give new impetus to a type of narrative melding biography and psychology. In Charles Dickens's novels *David Copperfield*, *Great Expectations* and *Oliver Twist*, like so much of the literature of this period, there is evidence of a growing interest in the experience of the child. Like many other books written expressly for adults, these biographical novels became children's classics, prescribed on children's school curriculum because of the lucidity and sensitivity with which Dickens treated problems of youth. His writing seemed to dredge from the collective depths of youthful memory a way of characterizing early experience that contained a new sympathy for the child's struggle to achieve understanding and control unruly feelings. In Dickens's time this was a radical point of view. His and other Victorian novels provided a fresh inspiration for children's publishers and writers, and children's publishing expanded rapidly in the period, which became something of a turning point. Eric Quayle specifies the year 1855 as the 'dividing line' between old and new literature for young people: the difference between 'soul saving didacticism and the modern children's book'. Although he admits there was considerable overlap, he says that after 1855:

> The majority of children's books contained characters who resembled real children in their attitudes to the family and the world. They were no longer paragons of virtue with the saintlike attributes; neither were they black-hearted little sinners plunging rapidly to hell.

The changes that took place in children's stories mirrored a more general change on the part of adults who saw that the young wanted books 'that would amuse and entertain them, without at the same time seeking to impose a nagging load of moral responsibility on their unwilling young shoulders'. Alert book publishers responded to this 'liberal-minded shift' so that 'Moralise less and sell more became the unspoken watchword of the leading London publishers'.[25]

By far the most successful new genre of children's book was a looser, more action-packed fiction that proved endlessly enter-taining, enjoyable and interesting to kids. The enormous appeal of this genre transcended the bounds of the real world. Imagination did not simply attract children's attention, it was their reality. The growing sales of children's books were built on this insight. Most of the innovative literary elements of children's fiction – the heroic characters, the exotic and far-flung situations, the fantastic beasts and cute animals, the sense of adventure and excitement in the world – can be attributed to writers' reconceptualization of the inner world of the child.

This growing cultural motif was strengthened by the free schooling movement, which had a huge impact on children's books. The publishing industry responded to the new mandate of literacy with an avalanche of books of all types: penny readers and accounts of history for the school system; moral tales and biblical stories for the Sunday schools; new illustrated books for the nursery; and books for children's private reading. All of these became an expected feature in the family libraries of the Victorian period. The school experience and children's struggles with it likewise became an acknowledged theme in the literature. *Tom Brown's Schooldays* (1857) was one of the first books to give a more realistic picture of school life and a child's jaded experience of it.

Hesba Tretton's *Fern's Hollow* (1865) is revealing, too, of the way the shift to a child's literary perspective was changing the orientation of the narrative. This work was among the first to make a girl's life seem exciting and adventurous. It sold over one and a half million copies in the author's lifetime, indicating how ready the audience was for this new kind of narrative. From this time, many fictions written for children began to be told from the child's point of view, focusing on a child protagonist and addressing problems in the child's experience of daily life. From *Anne of Green Gables* (1908) to *Swallows and Amazons*, books began to reflect back to children the experience of their own lives and the dynamics of their own peer groups.

Although most of these stories look at ordinary children and their experiences of growing up, they are often located in more exotic settings, with the characters engaged in highly charged struggles. Stories such as Richard Hughes's *A High Wind in Jamaica* (1929) presented experience aggrandized by adventure and mystery and gave a greater 'in-depth' sense of the characters' personal encounter with danger, challenge, disappointment and longing; there is simply a richer emotional texture.

The nineteenth century was indeed a turning point for children, in part because publishers risked staking out the ground for children's culture. Victorian book publishing exploded not only with a new energy but also with unfettered imagination. No book encapsulates this new freedom of imagination as well as Charles Dodgson's self-publication, under the pseudonym of Lewis Carroll, of *Alice's Adventures in Wonderland* in 1865. Dodgson's intense interest in pleasing the nine-year-old Alice Liddell unleashed from the period's prevailing plot devices the qualities of imagination, playfulness and innocence that make the Alice stories such an original work. Dodgson paid for the first publication of *Alice* from his own pocket, but the book sold over forty-five thousand copies within ten years. The strange characters, ironic language, adventurous wanderings and amusing reverse logic of a universe unrestrained by either physics or metaphysics brought together all the threads of children's literature.

During the next hundred years the market for children's books and the creativity of the writers did not diminish. By the 1980s over four thousand children's books were being published each year in the United States, and about nine hundred in Canada. The children's book trade had become the hottest expansion area in publishing.[26] But it is a niche market, based on a narrow segment of the population buying a lot of books: mainly the wealthy and educated book-orientated segment of the market, people who still see books as vital tools of socialization.[27] A survey of Toronto parents indicated that about 40 per cent of parents bought books as gifts for their children, although less than half that number did so regularly. Demographic and attitudinal patterns restrict the use of books in family socialization. With the average child watching so much television, books have become a much diminished source of cultural knowledge and entertainment, in part because they compete with cheaper and more readily available sources of entertainment offered in the cultural marketplace: toys, films, tapes, video games and television programmes.

96

Yet if the contemporary marketing of children's culture had a nursemaid, it was in the form of a book. The means used to nurture children as a willing audience for cultural products were the templates for all subsequent attempts to promote children's cultural products. Books demonstrated that children could be addressed as a market in themselves. Publishers may simply have been too successful in defining a literature of childhood that would capture children's hearts and minds. By showing the way to the childish imagination the publishers laid the groundwork for other forms of cultural enterprise that would grow to challenge them in the very market they had created. What the succession of competing media ensured was that the initial dribble of contact between children and the marketplace established by the first 'repeatable cultural commodity' would grow into a flood.

The growth of children's cultural products expanded most dramatically in the beginning of the twentieth century. Since then there have been ever-intensifying efforts to communicate with children through all available media – comics, films, radio and television. The literary traditions and attitudes towards the child cultivated by the book trade of the nineteenth century did not die: they were merely adopted and modified by and for these other media. Animators and toy designers especially relied on these same ideas, characters and themes: in the movies and television programmes of today, such as *Roger Rabbit*, *Strawberry Shortcake* or *The Care Bears*, we get a glimpse backwards along this cultural lineage to the children's book. Yet these new creations are rarely celebrated with the enthusiasm reserved for the book. Critics have argued, instead, that these narratives have robbed children's stories of their meaning, their exuberance and their innocence. The modern children's television narrative, they say, is more like an empty spectacle, a feast for the eyes lacking depth of meaning or reference – a literature that mirrors the underlying sensibilities of the industries that now produce the majority of children's fiction. With each of the new media, it seems, a transformation has taken place in the presentation of children's stories.

From the Comic Strips to Comic Books: The Children's Market

Developed at the turn of the century for adult audiences by the newly commercialized press, the comic strip was an extension of the illustrated satires common in the periodical press of the late eighteenth century. These illustrated satires were intended for the new mass audiences, which had lower levels of education and literacy and less interest in the corporate and political affairs that dominated the more literate and partisan press of the time.[28] The commercial press, with its lighter, more accessible journalism, relied on large circulation and hence relied for its economic survival on its ability to attract advertising. Headlines, illustrations and comic strips were among the key innovations associated with the rise of the newspaper's popularity.

The original impetus for the comic strip's visual form of sequential narrative derived from the market dynamics of turn-of-the-century journalism. R.F. Outcault's *Yellow Kid* comic was first run in 1895. The main character got his name from the attempt to print his shirt in yellow, and in turn the comic strip gave its name to posterity as the pseudonym for the down-market upbeat journalism of the mass-produced dailies of William Randolph Hearst and Joseph Pulitzer. As the commercial press struggled to increase its appeal to wider readerships, it experimented with layout, reduced the complexity of language, and offered more sensational human interest stories and less in-depth political analysis. The comic strip was simply an illustrated idea and as such was accessible to the supposedly less learned sensibility of the immigrant and working-class readers that were providing the expanded market of the commercial press. In targeting lower levels of literacy, the newspaper adapted styles derived from children's books: bold and large-print faces, plentiful illustrations and the description of 'deeds' rather than events – the established hallmarks of children's publishing. A bidding war that raged between Hearst and Pulitzer for the first *Yellow Kid* strip conveyed the enthusiasm of publishers to find the means to expand circulation.

The innovations in newspaper design were not primarily intended to include children as readers. Journalism has never established daily reading within the youth market, let alone with children; usually the only part of the newspaper that interests a youthful reader is the comics.[29] The highly visualized form of sequential story-telling that evolved as a comic strip and later the comic book arose, however, because of important features inherent in the early newspaper strips. Ironically, the characters in the early newspaper comics were almost exclusively represented as children. Many of the longest-lived and most beloved popular comic strips feature children (Buster Brown,

Little Orphan Annie, Peanuts, Dennis the Menace), reflecting a growing attention towards raising children in the twentieth century. Many strips actually adopted the perspective of children, playing on a naive satirical humour in connection to society and family life. But many of the characters also possessed strangely unchildlike characteristics. In Outcault's *Hogan's Alley*, for example, the characters were abandoned victims of a brutal world – children who wore bowler hats and smoked cigars mingled with bald little toughs who beat up dog-catchers. The *Yellow Kid* is important, Asa Berger argues, because it inaugurated a new kind of satirical perspective on US society, which included the 'everyman' represented as a child.[30] This perspective proved enormously appealing.

The Katzenjammer Kids, which made its appearance in 1897, was another prototypical strip. It extended the visual form to include a series of panels, giving an episodic focus to the story and exploring the implications of social 'events'. Following the Katzes, most newspaper comic strips became serialized, that is, the characters and situations became the defining aspect of the strip and were repeated from day to day. Serialization refocused the satire on a trait-specific humour, in which a well-known character responds to an equally well-known situation with a familiar quirkiness. Whether it is Jigg's riposte to Maggie, or Charlie Brown's annual kick at the football, there is a code of expectations linking each strip. Comic-strip humour differed from the more sophisticated political satire of *Punch* or *The Atlantic*: it assumed no inside information about the world of public affairs, referring only to the working knowledge of everyday experience that all readers possessed.

The subject matter of the Katzenjammer strip and its many imitators also seemed less concerned with the experience of the child than with vivifying the tension created between generations. The Katzenjammer Kids were inveterate practical jokers who were constantly getting thrashed for their misdeeds, just as Dennis the Menace has a provocative way of resisting his parents, or Bart Simpson of thumbing his nose at authority. As Berger notes, there was a double recognition inherent in this portrayal of generational conflict – of childhood as an autonomous realm, yet one increasingly out of the control of adults:

> The conflict between the Kids and the Captain, and other adults in the strip, can be attributed to the generation gap. In the perspective of the comics it is an old theme, and its existence at the turn of the century

suggests that generational conflict is a basic and long-time constituent of the American social personality. But there is an implicit democratic and anti-authoritarian bent to the humour and narrative that emerges in the comic strip that is particularly American in tone and stance.[31]

These simple narrative devices and the profoundly light commentary on everyday life permeated the newspapers' early comic-strip genre. By 1915 most of the sixty-odd strips in existence were being syndicated and distributed nationwide to newspapers.

Reinhold Reitberger and Wolfgang Fuchs see in these early strips the attributes that made the newspaper comic into an artistic laboratory that led to the working out of the eventual form of the strip. They call this phase the 'funnies' and see it characterized by an anarchical slapstick gag-orientated humour.[32] Gilbert Seldes, talking about the *Krazy Kat* strip, similarly notes the innocence and the anarchic and fantastical qualities that pervade the humorous adventures of the 'everyman' characters created by George Herrimann. Seldes concludes that these qualities result from 'a naive sensibility rather like a douanier Rousseau'.[33] These same attributes continue in newspaper strips like *Donald Duck* and *Peanuts*, but the real impact of this new comic foil left a stronger legacy in films and animation.

Yet historians of the comic strip note that the comic motifs of the funnies gained new scope and depth with the experimentation of the adventure strips in the 1930s, and the mystery, melodrama, romance and superhero strips of the 1940s. From the late 1920s comic-strip writers would test the limits of the visual episodic story, borrowing freely from other cultural forms. They incorporated elements of film, radio and book fiction. Adventure, social satire, science fantasy, romance, medicine and crime were the most notable new motifs witnessed in *Popeye, Blondie, Buck Rogers, Dick Tracy, Rex Morgan M.D., Flash Gordon, Li'l Abner, Superman, Batman, Pogo, Kathy* and *Doonesbury.* The simplest of forms demonstrated that it could accommodate complex story ideas.

Through this gradual diversification in content the comic strip gave rise to a new publishing effort aimed at children. Although collections of newspaper strips were published as books from the late 1920s, it was not until 1937 that DC (Detective Comics) launched its first proper comic book series. DC realized that children were interested in the stories but did not have enough money to buy books on their own. Comics could be produced on cheap newsprint. At ten cents a comic, these new books were marketed so that children themselves could become the purchasers, using their allowance, savings or disposable earnings.

The comic 'book', too, differentiated itself from early collections of newspaper strips in its generous use of colour and the sustained storylines made possible by multiple pages. The length allowed comic-book writers to work with more complex characterizations, motivations and plot structures. Still broadly episodic, the comic book was more literary. *Superman*'s life history, for example, is often re-enacted or alluded to in flashbacks. The story creates dramatic tension from the social interplay of the main character's hidden identity and the normalized world of Metropolis. The creators of comics dug deeply into the popular cultural repertoire, looking for contemporary characters and themes, borrowing from and inspiring similar experiments in radio, cinema, and magazines. 'Classic Comics', for example, were launched to retell famous literary stories and historical events in comic-book form. Some popular movie series such as 'Tarzan', plus westerns and detective and war films, likewise inspired imitations in comic books.

The comic book's episodic visual narrative was particularly adept at epic stories, adventurous characters and grand deeds. Launched by Action Comics in 1938, Superman was probably the most important and influential new character in this mould. The authors Jerry Siegel and Joe Shuster merged two popular motifs in one. They borrowed from detective stories like *Dick Tracy* the idea of an unending and dogged fight against crime and chaos. From the science fiction action adventures like *Buck Rogers* and *Flash Gordon* they worked in an imaginary universe where they could explore mysterious forces beyond the worldly powers. Superman was a more absolute kind of hero – his singular purity of motive, his unrelenting power, his other-worldly origins were far removed from the daily experience of children and the human models offered by the fall-guy stooges of the funnies. Superman was instantly popular, seemingly expressing important psychic underpinnings of childhood that were rarely expressed in other literary forms; on the one hand, Superman, in his secret identity as Clark Kent, was meek and mild mannered, an impotent denizen of the throng. Yet on another, fantasy, plane he was an invincible hero capable of overcoming all opposition. By 1952 *Superman* comic books had a monthly circulation of over 1,400,000.

The work of illustration in comics like *Superman* lent itself to action – exploits and exotic situations could easily be worked into plot. The humour was less verbal, the adventure more dramatic, and the fantasy ever more visibly exotic. The comic book nudged children's stories in the direction of heroic imagination. Batman, Green Lantern, Captain Marvel, and a myriad of similar heroic personalities emerged from the synergy of forms and ideas that poured through the channels opened by this first children's cultural market. Kids didn't have rigid literary preferences. They might buy a retold classic *A Tale of Two Cities, The Three Musketeers,* a lavishly illustrated monster tale, a homely teenage *Archie* comedy, or an exciting action adventure or western. Even if these works were rarely regarded as literature, they were fiction. By 1950 there were three hundred different series available. In the immediate postwar period and the early baby booming 1950s, comic books established themselves as the most important medium of direct communication with children; the production of comics had grown into a healthy children's industry capitalizing on kids' love of stories. At the same time, however, comic-book publishing had become associated with an unhealthy aspect of children's lives. In 1954, chastened by Dr Frederic Wertham's well-known book *Seduction of the Innocents,* and in the wake of a public outcry about the comics' influence on children, a code was drawn up to restrain the industry. As it turned out, the code was probably unnecessary because the publishing industry was being confronted by a major new competitor in the children's market for fiction – television.

Comics and the Preference of the Market

The initial growth in children's reading patterns had a stimulating effect on book publishers and a liberating influence on the books they sent into the market for children. The emergence of children's fiction from under the heavy rock of the pedagogy of literacy and moral teaching had been allied with the experiments undertaken by select publishers intent on redefining the child's place in the book trade. The magic of fiction was the key to this change. The freshness of the garden world replete with flower fairies and animal friends, and the credence publishers gave to children's fascination with the adventures of peers, had provided the framework within which children's fiction could flourish.

The comic book marks an important transition in this growing market for children's fiction because it not only broadened the base of children's reading but also changed the face of children's fiction. The comic-book industry clearly demonstrated the viability of a children's market by turning out a product that children could buy with their own hard-to-come-by pennies. Comic books also inspired a new set of literary formulas that could sustain a mass audience. They continued the comedy traditions of the newspaper funnies but also introduced new literary themes and motifs to solidify the enormous popularity that action adventure stories enjoyed among children. The comic book publishers were able to modify the stories to stay in touch with the new circumstances of distribution – mass readership and purchase by children themselves.

The social critics of the 1950s saw in the homogenizing, levelling and simplifying necessities of the mass market a force that could undermine the literary quality established by the book trade.[34] For them the vision of millions of children reading the same stories, venerating the same imaginary heroes and wanting the same Dick Tracy watches began to take on ominous tones. The standardization in children's culture seemed to be following the industrial model: culture reduced to the lowest common denominator that the market would bear.[35] And of course to some degree they were right, because in the search for a cheap, quickly produced and easily repeatable literary form that would ensure the comic was widely bought by children of diverse backgrounds, the logic of the mass market was beginning to assert itself within children's cultural industries. The publishers of the comics were most interested in the broad appeal of their product. They conceived of their product as popular entertainment rather than as literature or a form of socialization, and they worked at promoting children's fascination with the story.

As always, social theorists were divided in their response and evaluation of this trend. Some referred to comics simply as 'popular' culture, seeing in the comics' literary continuities and enormous popularity a levelling and democratizing possibility.[36] Others derided comics as 'mass' culture, bemoaning the subsumption of traditional literary values and artistic aspirations in the profit motive. Comics, they said, were 'valueless' artefacts produced by an industrial model of production and distribution.[37] They often overlooked the simple fact that comics were among the very few goods offered in the mass market that children could purchase by and for themselves. This fact added an enormous complication to the debates, because to deride children's comics the critics adopted a stance that denied children's rights to express their wants and preferences within the market.

Whereas books were fiction for children – to be read to, chosen for, and offered as gifts to children – the comic was the first cultural product cheap enough to be bought by them. To criticize the comic meant denying children's sense of choice, denying their wants and their literary tastes. Comics therefore symbolized the intrusion of the consumer-sovereignty dilemma into the realm of children's culture. Distribution in the mass market thus ultimately transformed the differences in taste, purpose, and values between adult's and children's fiction into a breach in socialization – the first sign of a cultural generation gap that liberal-thinking parents found ideologically problematic.

In this respect the comic book played an important role in defining the boundaries of a mass market for children's culture and the framework for debates about it. The continuity of literary genres, themes and characters carried over from books can obscure the important changes in storyline, emotional tone, characterization and plot wrought by comics – and by the other children's media as they competed with books and comics to establish their own specialized voices and niches. These subtle lines of force exerted by mass marketing on children's fiction were equally present in the development of animated cartoons.

Notes

1. Barry, Florence V., *A Century of Children's Books*, London, Methuen, 1922, p. 9.

2. Most notably the works of Frazer, James George, *The Golden Bough: A Study of Magic and Religion*, New York, St. Martin's Press, 1966; and Campbell, Joseph, *The Masks of God*, New York, Viking, 1959. Both have helped me recognize the oft-repeated mythic patterns that exist in children's stories.

3. Opie, Iona and Peter, eds, *The Oxford Dictionary of Nursery Rhymes*, Oxford, Oxford University Press, 1951.

4. Campbell, Joseph, *The Masks of God: Occidental Mythology*; Frye, Northrup, *The Great Code*.

5. Bettelheim, Bruno, *The Uses of Enchantment: The Meaning and Importance of Fairytales*, New York, Vintage Books, 1977.

6. Innis, Harold Adam, *The Bias of Communication*, Toronto, University of Toronto Press.

7. Williams, Raymond, *The Long Revolution*, New York, Columbia University Press, 1961.

8. I have relied on the accounts in the following books for my overview of children's publishing: Avery, Gillian Ellis, *Childhood's Pattern: A Study of Heroes and Heroines of Children's Fiction 1770–1950*, London, Hodder & Stoughton, 1975; Barry, Florence V., *A Century of Children's Books*; Darton, F.J. Harvey, *Children's Books in England, Five Centuries of Social Life*, New York, Cambridge University Press, 1970;

Hildick, Wallace, *Children and Fiction: A Critical Study in Depth of the Artistic and Psychological Factors Involved in Writing Fiction for and about Children*, London, Evans, 1970; Jones, Philip, *Children's Books of Yesterday*, London, The Studio, 1976; Moses, Montrose J., *Children's Books and Reading*, Detroit, Gale Research, 1975; Quayle, Eric, *The Collector's Book of Children's Books*, London, Studio Vista, 1971; and Thrwaite, M.F., *From Primer to Pleasure, An introduction to the History of Children's Books in England from the Invention of the Printing Press*.

9. McLuhan, Marshall, *The Gutenberg Galaxy*, Toronto, University of Toronto Press, 1962.

10. Postman, Neil, *The Disappearance of Childhood*, New York, Dell, 1982, p. 18.

11. Ibid., pp. 13, 18.

12. Locke, John, *Some Thoughts Concerning Education*, 14th edn, 1772, p. 229.

13. Quayle, Eric, *The Collector's Book*, p. 17.

14. Schneider, George A., 'Millions of Moral Little Books: Sunday School Books in their Popular Context', in *New Dimensions in Popular Culture*, ed. Russel Nye, Bowling Green, Bowling Green Popular Press, 1972, pp. 1–15.

15. Williams, *The Long Revolution*.

16. Opie, Iona and Peter, *The Oxford Dictionary of Nursery Rhymes*.

17. Barker, Martin, *A Haunt of Fears: The strange history of the British Horror Comics Campaign*, London, Pluto Press, 1984.

18. Quayle, *The Collector's Book*, p. 18.

19. Lady Fenn, quoted in Quayle, p. 49.

20. Illick, Joseph E., 'Child-Rearing in Seventeenth Century England and America', in L. DeMause, ed., *The History of Childhood*, New York, Harper Torchbooks, pp. 303–50.

21. Darton, *Children's Books*, p. 1.

22. Newbery, S. Roscoe and Carnan Power, *A Provisional Check List of Books for the Entertainment Instruction and Education of Children and Young People Issued under the Imprints of John Newberry and his Family in 1774–1802*, London, Library Association.

23. Greenaway, Kate, *Marigold Garden*, London, Frederick Warne, p. 23.

24. In Quayle, *The Collector's Book*, p. 12.

25. Quayle, *The Collector's Book*, p. 87.

26. Taylor, Jennifer, 'U.K. Children Publishing: Growing Up', *Publishers' Weekly*, 12 September 1986, pp. 50–3; 'Drive in U.K. to Push Children's Books', *Publishers' Weekly*, 20 March 1987, p. 38; Wishinsky, Frieda, 'A New Era in Canadian Children's Books', *Publishers' Weekly*, 20 March 1987, p. 36.

27. 'No Affront to the Children – Why is Britain's Children's Book Business the Best in the World?', *The Economist*, 13 December 1986, pp. 99–100; 'Printing, Publishing and Allied Industries', 1986.

28. Smith, Anthony, *The Newspaper: An International History*, London, Thames & Hudson, 1979.

29. Bogart, Leo, 'Comic Strips and their Adult Readers', in Bernard Rosenberg and David Manning White, eds, *Mass Culture: The Popular Arts in America*, New York, The Free Press, 1957.

30. Basic references on comics include: White, David Manning and Walter Abel eds, *The Funnies, an American Idiom*, Glencoe, Free Press, 1963; Lupoff, Dick and Don Thompson, *All in Colour for a Dime*, New York, Ace Books, 1970; Perry, George and Alan Aldridge, *The Penguin Book of Comics*, London, Penguin, 1971; Reitberger, Reinhold and Wolfgang Fuchs, *Comics: An Anatomy of a Mass Medium*, London, Studio Vista, 1972.

31. Berger, Arthur Asa, *The Comic Stripped American*, Baltimore, Penguin, 1973, p. 37.

32. Reinhold Reitberger and Wolfgang Fuchs, *Comics*.

33. Seldes, Gilbert, 'The People and the Arts', in Rosenberg and White, eds, *Mass Culture*, pp. 74–96.

34. Rosenberg and White, eds, *Mass Culture*; see especially Robert Warshow, 'Paul, and Horror Comics, and Dr Wertham'; Lyle W. Shannon, 'The Opinions of Little Orphan Annie and her Friends'; and Arthur J. Broadbeck and David M. White, 'How to Read Li'l Abner Intelligently'.

35. Roseberg, Bernard, 'Mass Culture in America', in Rosenberg and White, eds, *Mass Culture*.

36. White and Abel, eds, *The Funnies*.

37. Roseberg, 'Mass Culture in America', in Rosenberg and White, eds, *Mass Culture*.

4

Thralls of the Screen:

The Rise of Mass Media for

Children

> Television changes and modifies traditional formulas ... it
> begins to create a sense of the television formula with its own
> cultural significance ... it is also possible to define a set of artistic
> techniques, aesthetic devices that contribute to some unique
> capabilities on the part of television. The things television does
> best are related to the most formulaic and popular works.[1]

The concerns about the effects of a mass children's culture and the
debates about children's prerogatives in choosing their own cultural
products were, somewhat surprisingly, not transferred from comic
books to the movies, even though the trajectory of both media was
similar. Both of them relied on the same templates of literary taste
laid down in the nineteenth century and brought forth the traditions
in the form of lively visual entertainment. Comics were criticized not
for the retelling of ancient tales but for how they transformed those
narratives in the act of retelling. Early movie and television producers
also reworked the tried and true formulas of children's fiction
according to the technical, social and economic exigencies of their
media. The popularity of today's programming is testimony to the
success of those producers in refashioning narrative into a form that
children wanted to watch. Comic books illustrated the possibility of
a mass children's culture; the experimentation with children's films
and television programmes made that culture an actuality.

The pressures of the large-scale markets for stable audiences and
the need always to reduce production costs were the urgencies that
most dictated a formulaic approach to the development of entertainment products. These pressures led in turn to an ever narrower
conception of children's interest in fiction. The mass market

dynamic did create some enthusiasm for experimentation with children's fiction, but in the long run it also ensured that the most successful literary inroads would be repeated until they became a kind of superhighway to the child audience. The economics of mass marketing ensured that the successes were endlessly imitated and the failures closed the door to further experimentation.

Despite the more obvious commercial pressures, the debates about children's role in the world of movie-watching were less extreme and overheated than the debates over comics. The film media seemed to bestow its aura of art upon its early producers, and many of them strived to achieve goals beyond simple entertainment. The fact that film induced ever wider segments of childhood into the embrace of fiction was also celebrated as the prime indication of its inherently democratic nature. Preliterate children could now be introduced to good literature through the creativity of Hollywood. For some, of course, the growth in children's film simply certified the substitution of quality with quantity. Were Disney's cinematic tales the creation of an American folklore or the debasement of literary culture? The critics scoffed at the movies' pretensions to art – pretensions which, they thought, presumed cultured taste and critical intelligence applied by the viewer. Kids had too little sophistication and experience to discriminate. They watched whatever was offered. Unlike the controversy over comics, the early debates about the movies and television focused less on content than on quality and taste. Ironically, it was not until the 1970s, in the wake of twenty years of television broadcasting and intense research effort, that the issue of the content of mass culture reared its head again.[2]

The culture industries did not remain silent in these debates. Walt Disney happily offered his own belief that the mass market provided the vast majority of children with exactly 'what they wanted'. But the debates intensified only when it became clear that commercial television was having a profound impact on children. The consequences of television as culture were directly felt in the home, in part because the changes in children's patterns of daily activity had become so large. It was not a matter of a weekly trip to the movie theatre, or a comic book read under bed covers. Children obviously voted with their valuable leisure hours; they put even their comics aside to watch TV. This enthusiasm itself disturbed many critics: was this choice that children were making to watch TV good for them, they asked, or did it displace and contradict the values and activities of a healthier literate culture?

The early debates about television, therefore, also raised broader concerns about mass media and what they displaced from children's lives. In this view the inherent undermining of the literacy and education agenda seemed to pose a significant threat. As one critic, Harry Skornia, suggested:

> The slogans, catchwords, values, mottoes, and other lessons tattooed on young minds even before young people learn to read are not educational but commercial. They displace, contradict, and cancel, in many cases in advance, those lessons and values which education seeks and will seek at public expense to teach and inculcate.[3]

Is there, critics wondered, something inherently wrong in the commercial dynamic of the culture industries that has produced this sorry state of affairs? Early observers of television knew that the industry only developed 'properties' based on an elaborate and biased system of polling that made audience size the only relevant criterion for developing a new show. Where were quality, higher values, noble inspiration and broader vision going to come from? Certainly not from TV. Of course these early critics were right.

The Growth of Children's Film

By the 1920s, silent films had already assimilated most popular narrative traditions. Historical epics, slapstick comedy, westerns, mystery, science fiction, adventure and romance all demonstrated that the magic of the new medium rested in its ability to dramatize a story. The audience for cinematic culture had become so firmly entrenched that even in the Depression of the 1930s the film audience kept growing. Movie theatres were located in every community and improvements in cinematic technology (sound, technicolour, wide screens) helped to make film the most important source of popular drama and entertainment; the Hollywood dream factory became emblematic of the new massifying tendencies in American culture, criticized by a few but celebrated by most as the 'lively art'. Yet for all the historical commentary on the development of film art, surprisingly little attention has been assigned to the parallel development of children's movies.

A uniquely children's film genre emerged very early. Some of the first experiments in animation techniques involved adapting well-known comic-strip characters (The Katzenjammer Kids, Buster

Brown, Little Nemo) in attempts to capitalize on their established appeal, although these films were not conceived of as entertainments for children.[4] Some of the early animators were simply inspired by the possibility of bringing the comic strip to life, and they mimicked those strips by introducing characters like Felix the Cat and Coco the Clown. Yet the animated cartoons proved immediately popular as shorts when offered by movie theatres as an added enticement preceding an exciting epic adventure or western. Like the silent films, the cartoons tended to be bold in action and long on stunts and gags. In their short-circuiting language they were equally accessible to very young children, the functionally illiterate and foreign-language speakers. Visual humour and action-orientated plots were the proved guarantors of everyone's interest.

The original novelty of seeing drawings moving on the screen soon waned, but cartoons helped the theatre managers see children as a component of their clientele. If the development of animated cartoons derived to some degree from the comic strip, as an entertainment the new medium tended to supplant reading as an activity. If the funnies and later the comic book afforded a private moment of fantasy, the cartoon proved a highly dynamic and visually exciting way of experiencing a story. Because of this more immediate appeal to children, running cartoon shorts proved a clever way of encouraging an image of the movie house as a suitable site for family entertainment. Children's space within the theatre became defined through the cartoon. The institution of family Saturday matinée features with 'cartoon clubs' ensured that children became integrated into the audience rituals that grew up around the film. Giving a child permission to go to see a film became a prized reward for good behaviour. It also became a sign that, amidst the new ideas about children's socialization, entertaining them had a growing legitimacy.

If Hollywood became America's dream factory, the Disney studios became its nursery school. Walt Disney was not the first person to develop animation as a technique or to make a children's film, but he may have been the first film maker to specialize enthusiastically in the production of cultural products for children. There is no doubt that Disney had a fascination with and unique sensitivity to the special qualities of children's narrative. Although his first experience with film-making was a job with the Kansas City Film Ads Company, where he made animated cardboard-cutout commercials to be shown in theatres between movies, he quickly saw something very special about animation that connected him with children. Setting up on his own, he began to produce a series of animated fairy tales that he hoped would appeal to this little-heralded segment of the movie audience. Somewhat stilted versions of Cinderella, Puss 'n Boots, Goldilocks and the Three Bears, and Little Red Riding Hood were among the first efforts of the fledgling Disney studio.[5]

Disney was quick to recognize that children's love of imaginative fiction provided the real basis for their fascination with the magical technique of animation, and he sought to rework the inspiration provided by folk tales and traditional children's fairy stories. In doing so he discovered the appeal that unusual characters could have when rendered on the screen. Although Disney loved to portray himself as an animator and artist, his true contribution seems to lie in the unique flair he brought to narrative and in his sensitivity to characterization – qualities sustained by the Disney studio through most of its productions.

To keep his studio alive in the mid 1920s Disney and his collaborator, artist Ub Iwerks, embarked upon the production of a series called *Alice in Cartoonland,* a combined animation–live-action film featuring a young girl superimposed on an animated setting. The wide acclaim that the *Alice* series received helped to establish this Midwest upstart in Hollywood. But the live-action scenes proved harder to produce and in the end less compelling than the host of interesting animated creatures that Disney and Iwerks had invented to populate his Cartoonland. Disney would eschew these mixed live and animated productions in favour of the greater narrative licence afforded by cel animation.

The film industry was a high-turnover business, and Disney knew that to maintain his place as a leader in the market for lively shorts would demand innovation and bold experiments. In 1929 he launched a series of cartoon shorts called the *Silly Symphony* that proved very successful. The orchestra contained boundless opportunities for visual comedy given the various sight gags that could take place in and around the instruments. The trombone sliders were turned into amusing weapons and the sight of a conductor who cannot control his orchestra held a special fascination suited to the anarchistic streak in kids. When put to music, the characters seemed to dance to the rhythms in a perfect blending of action and sound. Indeed, throughout their history Disney studios maintained a strong sense of the role that music could play in adding emotional colour and punctuation to animation – a lesson that reached its finest expression in Disney's feature-length animation *Fantasia* (1940), often regarded as his most creative work.

The 1930s were lean years, and to hold its audience the cinema had to expand its offerings. MGM led a number of studios in seeing the family audience as the industry's salvation. Many Hollywood film producers looked for projects that would expand the movies' hold on the family market, and saw the answer in classic literature. The historical settings, high drama and swashbuckling action in *Treasure Island, Robinson Crusoe* or *The Three Musketeers* lent themselves well to the film medium, just as these same features ensured their serialization on TV. The less classic story of Tarzan also proved a great family success when restaged as a film. Zorro, the masked avenger of injustice, and Robin Hood with his socialist gang of merry men were two particular mythohistorical characters from literature who have sustained repeated fame in all media. Yet these efforts were little more than faint adaptations of the original fictions. Generally speaking, the action-adventure genres popularized by the penny dreadfuls (mystery, westerns, war and romance) provided the source material that was to be the mainstay of the studios. The action-adventure genre became associated with the broad appeal of the mass market because it established a type of narrative that would attract the whole family. Likewise, borrowing from vaudeville and the theatre, children's musicals featuring child prodigies such as Shirley Temple were another innovation that helped to cultivate new forms of family entertainment as well as establishing child stars in the constellation of the cinema. Yet it was the cartoon that would continue to be most associated with children's place in movie-going. Animation's zany comedy became the emblem of the cinema's most valued gift to children.

Engineers of the Imagination

Disney himself appreciated that animation's finest quality was the narrative freedom it offered to the animator; the obligation to find new ways to delight and entertain kids was not the only moral constraint Disney imposed on his animators, but it did provide the primary directive for their creativity. Imaginative freedom was the battle cry of the Disney animators, who revelled in the loosening of those constraints that camera technology and reality forced upon film. Animals could talk, walls could fall, the body could contort, and any imaginable situation could be created with ease through cel animation. Animators could emphasize images and visual situations that even the finest artists of silent comedy could never dare to portray. Animation also gave enormous freedom to characterization expressed through the drawing of faces, the use of voices and the depiction of movement and gestures.

The quick familiarity of the characters who emerged from the animation studios disguised a subtle ambiguity in this narrative form. Unlike the heroes and villains of adventure movies, these anthro-pomorphic cartoon characters bridged the divide between the everyday and the impossible. Toonland existed neither in the 'here-and-now' world of strife nor in the fairyland 'never-never' of pure imagination but, rather symbolically, somewhere between the two. Much in the cartoon is easily recognizable – the clothes, cars, houses – and references are to the normal world. Yet rather than convey the specific mannerisms and noble actions of historical characters, the heroes were amalgams – a pastiche of abstracted traits projected into an uncertain world. The childlike stylization of characters made their history and status in the social order hard to pin down. Mickey, the mouse that dressed and behaved like a human, wore shorts and had a high squeaky voice. Mickey was a changeling caught between reality and the imaginary universe of folklore – representing both the everyman and the innocent child. So too, Donald Duck, who from his quacking human speech to the waddling tail protruding beyond his sailor suit, symbolized the mixed-up status of the world alluded to in cartoon humour.

Disney referred to his enterprise as 'imagineering' – the engineer-ing of imagination. His terminology reveals both his appreciation of the role of technique in the work of the animator and his own deep belief in the power of the characters he created to capture children's imagination. Because they were drawn rather than enacted, ani-mated storylines permitted a greater scope for zany situational humour than the comic arts of the silver screen had ever enjoyed. The exaggeration of body movements (long arms reaching around a corner, eyeballs extending out from their sockets) and an emphasis on impossible events or actions (characters pancaked by steamrollers or crashing through walls and leaving outlines of their shape) became the conventional and repeated elements of the humour. In a cartoon, any board can become a catapult, spring or lever; objects can alternately be rubbery and rigid; a flight of angry bees can take the form of a squadron of dive bombers; a rushing 'head' of water can take on the characteristics of an angry face. The symbolic space that animation created on the screen was both visually immediate and highly abstract. Although the cartoon's plot-line followed well-known trajectories, the humour depended on normal events that would go awry and everyday objects that would violate the conventional behaviour of the world of things. In the mouse Mickey, that everyman butt of the world's never-ending pranks, Disney not only crystallized his trademark character but also perfected a genre of children's story-telling.

The belief in technique implicit in Disney's term 'imagineering' is therefore not ironic. His animators exhibited a particular fascination with technological themes. The slapstick comedy of Buster Keaton and Charlie Chaplin in silent films had established a humour revolving around technology: Keaton's gags were often based on the clever use of modified everyday objects – windows, doors, boards, ladders, glasses, roller skates – used as props. The classics are now simply part of the American sense of humour – a man carrying a long board with no one at the end, a banana skin carelessly abandoned on the road, or a long hall full of doors ready for a chase are all immediately recognizable. They were much-repeated devices in cartoons. The humour of slapstick, like stage magic, rested in defying the expectations of everyday physics. Animators exploited this idea by exploring our expectations of everyday objects. Chaplin's marvellous parody of working life in *Modern Times* (1936) bequeathed some indelible images of the perpetual battle with machines: machines are running the world; they have a logic and a will of their own. Chaplin's humour played on a new type of comic character, one who was very childlike in demeanour, an innocent in a world of mechanical complexity. The character was often repeated in cartoons, possibly most memorably in *Fantasia*, where Donald Duck as the sorcerer's apprentice experiences humankind's domination at the hands of our own implements.

The cartoons revelled in the comic possibilities of cogs and levers, machines and household equipment. Donald, Mickey, Goofy, creatures in Toontown – were all transformed by everyday technology into everyman fools. As clowns they were reminiscent of the classic buffoon and the ingenue of slapstick, but they suffered less from their own gullibility and innocence than from the inherent instability of both the natural and artificial worlds around them. As the endless butt of nature's pranks, life for a cartoon character was filled with vexation – one long picnic filled with broken cars, sinking boats, ants, wasps and bulls.

In the opening sequence of *Who Framed Roger Rabbit* (1988), Roger is hurled around the kitchen by a chain of events dictated by the actions of household technology, which only ends when a refrigerator pins him to the floor. This sequence is a tribute in parody to the original wild joy of the cartoon and its anarchic sense of visual humour. Cartoon machines, like nature, could be personified, given will and intent. Whether it was the face in a cloud that reveals the malevolence in the north wind, or the machine arm that works like a body part, animation turned the presumption of objectified nature on its head. Nature and technology were both infused with subjective qualities. Machinery was mostly pictured as mindlessly malevolent: Donald's quiet day cutting the grass turns into a chase with the lawnmower wheeling itself around to attack its victim in an unexplained but clear act of vengeance. A tug on an outboard motor, the cranking start of a car, the making of a piece of toast in a pop-up toaster, or a day's work on a combine harvester could each turn into a life and death struggle with technology that has a mind of its own.

The humour of the cartoon rested precariously on our assumptions about the everyday world. Life was certainly no fairy-tale garden although Donald and Mickey did often quest after an illusive peace with nature. Every action-packed episode guaranteed that the 'ordinary' would behave otherwise. The plot-lines often amounted to nothing more than a series of episodic catastrophes. For instance Donald is having a much needed holiday in the country. He decides to go fishing, yet his leisurely trip to the lake turns into one of the many variations of disaster: maybe he will hook an enormous fish that whips off with him and his boat; maybe he will catch an old boot while the kids get up to mischief in the cabin. When he and Goofy go shopping, the moment he enters the shop we know that the tottering piles of goods will ensure an endless series of calamities. In every nook and cranny of normal life the animators found potential for exploring a fragile physical order in the universe, only to have that world restored to normality in the closing frames.

This errant unpredictability was introduced into cartoons solely in the name of humour. Cartoons were not offered up as critiques of technoculture or bourgeois society but merely played with the humorous possibilities in the denial of everyday physics. These excursions into chaos were grounded solely in an epistemology of entertainment and therefore avoided questioning the social basis of the conflict. The rules broken were visual, not societal. That was the main difference between the 'stick' in the filmic and animation versions of slapstick. In film the stick wouldn't bend or spring; in the cartoon it always did. When Donald was rammed down a gun barrel we got to see the bulge. Though cartoon humour celebrated a cock-eyed physics arising in an unstable and unpredictable world where anything could happen and everything that could go wrong always did, it never linked that world to social conditions in the way that Chaplin had done. Disney never came near being banned from the United States for his promotion of anarchism in children's culture.

The Disney studio's successes demonstrated that the creativity of animation could be the royal road to children's audiences in the movies. The art and magic of figures brought to life in a darkened room demanded action, and other studios also got into the act, producing numerous short cartoon features and lots more action. This was particularly true of the episodic short as exemplified by MGM's *Tom and Jerry* cartoons, which remodelled the Disney formula by bringing conflict to the centre of the story. The creators of Tom and Jerry, William Hanna and Joseph Barbera, used the traditional cat–mouse enmity to motivate endless chase and torture sequences.

Tom and Jerry presented an innocent imaginary violence that was at least visually humorous. When Tom crashed into the ground at high speed he made a hole rather than hurt himself. Friction, resilience, the mechanics of the lever and the spring, and the flexibility of the body were the endlessly repeated visual ideas in the *Tom and Jerry* series, so it didn't matter that there was no pain and no lasting hurt. The endless battles never produced an injury or a death but simply ritualized violent acts as the pretext of humour. The kids knew it was 'only good fun'; Tom and Jerry were just light on a screen.

In these cartoons, dramatic conflict is treated primarily through the interactions between characters mediated by nature and everyday technology. There is no character development and no learning, and the scripts favour a highly stylized and violent sense of humour. Cartoons put the 'schtick' in slapstick: the accidents, crashes, bangs and bonks were narratively elongated and visually emphasized in a somewhat puerile celebration of physical conflict. Familiar gimmicks and conventions were lifted directly from silent films: the pulldown bed that flattened the unfortunate would-be sleeper, the spinning door that dizzied the chaser, the long board that acted as a catapult, the balls, barrels and skates that tripped and twirled the body, or the falling wall that buried an ill-prepared character. These oft-repeated oldies always got a chuckle. Given the endless opportunities at visual pyrotechnics, animators never bothered to push the bounds of verbal humour, satire or situational irony in their stories.

Kids didn't seem to notice that the plot-lines and visual humour were getting repetitious, confirming the edict that anything that could make kids laugh twice should become a cliché. Indeed, Tom and Jerry's immortal confrontations were so popular that its formula was imitated by Warner Brothers and other studios. The cartoon shorts for the movie houses made the memorable wars waged between Bugs Bunny and Elmer Fudd or Tweetie Pie and Sylvester appear to be Hollywood's gift to children's fiction. These same characters and motifs are still displayed on Saturday morning television.

An American Tale

Yet Disney believed animation could tell grander tales. Inspired by classic themes and relying on more literary conceptions of narrative, Disney asked his animators if they could sustain a less episodic full-length feature by working more closely on characterization and plot. In the highly experimental and costly *Snow White and the Seven Dwarfs*, Disney animators provided the answer. Released in 1938, this reinterpretation of a dark and moody fairy story proved that animation was more than a passing gimmick to lure kids into the movie theatre. The Dwarfs were transformed from the misbegotten denizens of the underworld into lovable little bumblers from the backwood. Snow White herself became the embodiment of American innocence and natural justice.

Disney's folk stories were entertainments and not moral lessons. Disney wanted to retell the classic folk tales for an American audience – without the same moral or religious imperatives that first inspired their telling and retelling. The feeling was bemused rather than fearsome and preachy – comic rather than tragic. Disney's production of *Snow White* relied on the stylized visual humour of cartoons, but with his lusher drawings, more detailed settings, and the subtler care in character expression, Disney established the feature-length animation as a new idiom for story-telling.

And this is probably the most important contribution of the early Disney studio, for in these richly animated folk tales the movies were seen to provide a more traditional kind of fiction that parents could regard as wholesome entertainment for children. Disney could count on kids' love of simple plots, lovable characters and magical pictures to bring adults to a recognition of the children's niche in the cultural marketplace.

Disney established animated folk tales as a fixture in the mass cultural market. The Disney studio earned its enduring reputation for its artistically successful and memorable experiments in feature-length cinematic animation, following *Snow White* with *Pinocchio, Fantasia, Dumbo, Bambi, Lady and the Tramp* and many others. These works exemplified the animators' sensitivity to beautifully illustrated and simply told tales. Yet in the dancing hippos, the gentle friendships of the Dwarfs or the class snobbery of the 'Darlings', other subtle threads of popular culture are being woven into the fabric of folk tales. The techniques adapted from other genres of light entertainment transformed the layered and complex tone of the folk tale into a lively dance of music and image upon a screen. Angst and uncertainty were banished from the scripts. Gracious movement co-ordinated with music to accent cute and coy star turns by the characters, rendering the stories in a lighter, more predictable mould. The Disney studio transformed darkly toned and psychologically ambiguous trials of folk heroes into simplistic parables about the triumph of bourgeois sentiments. Even the ambiguous dog Tramp had a good-hearted and misunderstood panache about him, which eventually won his acceptance within civil society.

Yet the feature-length *Snow White* did not only prove successful among the critics and at the box office. It also showed the great merchandising potential of animated characters. Mickey and Donald had already been reproduced in plastic, metal and cloth, but the immediate impact of *Snow White* on Disney Licensing was remarkable. Children loved Disney characters so much that they wanted them as toys or in comic books, or emblazoned on their curtains and plates, and this convinced Disney that the prelicensing of the characters would be a significant additional source of revenue for the studio. *Snow White* was the first indication of what eventually became a multibillion dollar revenue for the Disney empire constructed around the copywriting of images. Although the crowds of kids at the theatre door built Disney's fame and fortune, the innovative link that was forged between the producers, writers and designers and the licensed goods market was no less important.

Cartoons and the Narrowing of Television

In the 1950s, television became the pre-eminent medium, gradually eroding the movie audience and reducing children's reading time. Within ten years of its introduction, television had found its way into over 80 per cent of US households and absorbed almost two hours of people's leisure everyday. But although the public was ready for television, television may not have been ready for its public. As Raymond Williams noted, commercial television was introduced without a sense of mission or content. In the attempts to establish the new medium and build its audience, programmers borrowed heavily from all idioms of entertainment, including those established in radio, film and literature, to fill the void. Although chronically underfunded, the children's television of the 1950s was therefore diverse in programme offerings and experimental in approach. In this exploratory stage, children's broadcasters willingly tested the waters with circus programmes (*The Big Top, Super Circus*), variety shows (*Smilin' Ed's Gang, The Pinky Lee Show*), dramatized animal stories (*My Friend Flika, Lassie*), science programmes (*Mr Wizard*), puppet shows (*Howdy Doody*), nursery school programmes (*Captain Kangaroo, The Ding Dong Show*) and talent shows (*The Children's Hour*). They also included lots of science fiction, action-adventure dramas and cowboy programmes – genres that had proved so successful in the movie theatres.

The action-adventure drama and cowboy formulas sustained the main continuity in children's narrative through to television. The heroic postures and noble deeds of these simplified tales under-wrote many television series, ensconcing the cowboy-lawman (*The Lone Ranger, Hopalong Cassidy*), the frontiersman (*Davy Crockett, Hawkeye and the Mohicans*) and the superhero (*Superman*) in the pantheon of modern mythology. The specific inspiration of the comic books was also clearly evident in early television, for even the dramatis personae they made famous reappeared in dramatic form: the older order of literary heroes like Robin Hood and Swiss Family Robinson were thus supplemented with essentially comic-book creations like Superman and Lois Lane, Flash Gordon and Dick Tracy, so that the comics' structural and moral simplicity would span successive generations of youthful minds. It was also this mindless simplicity that inspired Newton Minow, the chairman of the Federal Communications Commission (FCC) to call television a 'vast

119

wasteland', raising the spectre of quality once again.

Yet as we confront the question of quality in children's television we must remember that most programmes in the early years were live-action dramas. Because television was rewarded as an essentially film-like venue (and most programmes were shot as films), live-action drama appeared to be the logical form for stories – even stories for children – to take. Cartoon shorts appeared in the 1950s' television schedules but these offerings did not rival drama. In sharp contrast, there is now no filmed human drama among the children's programming on commercial television. If kids want to see *Black Beauty* or *Doctor Who*, they must watch public-pay or educational television. Commercial television's Saturday morning offerings are uniformly animated, and so the question of quality must be framed within the transition from movies to television, in which animation stopped being the enticement and began to become the sole venue for children's story-telling.

In the 1950s, the prognosis for children's television did not include the disappearance of drama. Amidst the eager experimentation with all forms and genres of fiction, the introduction of those predictable and formulaic cartoon shorts to television was considered a minor concession with very little long-term consequence.[6] Few would have believed that the animal stories, the circus talent shows, musical comedies, variety shows and family-centred dramas would so completely disappear or that commercial television would become defined by such a narrowness of programming. Few then would have understood that the critical debates of the future about children's television would concentrate on the violence and consumerism that the cartoon programming helped to establish in children's lives.

The Return of the Diminished

In retrospect, we can see that the diversity once valued as an intrinsic part of children's culture was sacrificed by the television industry's monopoly on entertainment. The changes that took place in audience programming, then, had a direct relationship to the different economic base established for children's cultural production in commercial TV and to the subsequent quality of the TV fiction offered.

There is no single economic mechanism in the cultural market-place, no unified way that cultural goods are bought and sold.

Children's books and comics, as goods sold in stores, closely follow the framework of classic commodities. Although their price bears some relationship to the input of materials and labour and the demand for them, it is also to some degree a reflection of their value to those that buy them. Comics were a mass media, but they were never a commercialized one; the advertising base was very limited. Profits flowed from finding stories that kids liked.

The movies were slightly different. There was a separate system of distribution (the theatres) which meant that there were more intervening considerations in the marketing of films. Studios were interested in their access to theatres, and theatres were concerned about renting more seats and increasing their flow through those seats. Children's films were profitable largely because of the size of the audience, a film's ability to attract children to the theatre. As in the classic notion of the market, the survival of the producer was based on direct sales of the product itself.

But in the commercial media the economic dynamics are different. This was immediately apparent in the very limited interest that early radio expressed in children and in the poverty of the television sequels. Indeed, *Children's Story Time* and *Listening with Mom* were the rather paltry early preschooler offerings of children's radio, and the television networks followed radio by locating their very limited offerings (*Howdy Doody, Captain Kangaroo*) in the big holes of the morning and afternoon schedule when Mom was preoccupied. But the fact that, unlike reading comic books or seeing movies, watching television fiction costs children nothing was extremely significant, for they no longer had to earn money, save up their allowance or beg from their parents. The advertising subsidy not only circumvented kids' lack of resources and power in family choice; it also subverted the assumed market relations of supply and demand. Any preferences expressed by kids for television programmes were only indirectly related to what was offered by programmers, because to watch TV kids had only to have time on their hands and access to the tube. Television seemed to provide children with free entertainment.

But in fact, without advertisers who sold expressly to the children's market, there was little money to produce programmes for an exclusively children's audience. The limiting factor was the inherent dynamic of commercial media, which is based on the sale of audiences to advertisers. If advertisers are not interested in sponsoring a certain type of programming or in buying a particular audience's viewing time, there is little motivation in the networks or the production houses to produce that kind of programming. In commercial media, demand is mediated by marketing considerations such as market reach, positioning and competition. The under-funding of children's television production reflected advertisers' general lack of interest: children did not spend enough money and programming could not be devised that would grab a large enough audience to make peer strategies work. To maintain a communica-tion link with the market the networks were content to finance a dutiful level of children's entertainment, but that was all.

Although within fifteen years of television's introduction over 90 per cent of US homes had television, children's programming was still very restricted – as was the willingness of advertisers to invest in it. Therein lies the irony of early children's TV. Although children met the requirements of an avid audience, they did not appear to be in the market as consumers of the goods TV was selling so advertisers had little interest in sponsoring their programmes. The networks in turn had little incentive to produce any programming for children, let alone high-minded quality programming. Commercial broad-casters could only afford to be interested in programming for audiences that spent money on goods. Kids had little money, and they spent what little they had on an occasional comic book and a few sweets. In the marketers' minds television simply provided a direct link between themselves and the family home. For advertisers of products aimed at least partly at children it made commercial sense to sponsor 'family programmes' (which would include both children of all ages and parents in the audience) over programmes more narrowly aimed at young kids alone. The networks argued that their obligations to children would be best accommodated by what television provided best – mass family entertainment. Throughout the baby-boom years, therefore, the production of children's special television programmes received the lowest priority. The minimal-cost children's productions of the early years of television were diverse in form but grossly underfunded as the marketers failed to have the concept of a kids' market.

Within a family-viewing context, Disney's move from cinema to television, therefore, did not involve major changes in the company's production philosophy. Still an advocate of the importance of children's fiction, in 1953 Disney inaugurated the *Disneyland* pro-gramme, a Sunday evening pot-pourri including animal fictions, animation and action drama. In the opening minutes Disney intro-duced his philosophy by stating that he thought his mission was to produce for kids of all ages. Disney wanted to be viewed by children and parents together. Watching TV should be like reading together, an act of family solidarity. The programming itself was designed primarily for children, for their proved love of simplified and reduced stories – though it lured the child in all of us to the television set.

Disneyland's appealing formula made it a regular feature of many families' viewing time. In the course of this popularity, Disney began to realize that the potential of television for merchandising was even greater than that of the movies. In 1954 Disney's *Davy Crockett* frontier adventure ('King of the wild frontier') experienced such breath-taking and immediate popularity that several million coonskin caps were sold in the first three months. Through television Disney imagery and Disney mythology found its way into many million more homes than it ever did via the movies.

This success inspired Disney to try another innovative project. He set about creating a commercially viable television programme *exclusively* for children – the kind of brave departure that made Disney the industry leader. At the time kids' shows on TV tended to run in the late afternoon 'dead spot' when Mom, finished with her daily ordeal with the soap operas, was busy preparing dinner and Dad wasn't yet back from work. Researchers had proved that audiences 'ebbed' around this time, and that networks could minimize lost revenue by handing it to local affiliates showing low-cost children's programmes. These programmes might not make money but they gave a responsible gloss to the television networks.

This attitude was challenged in 1955, when Disney's Mickey Mouse Club brought in a new formula attractive enough to appeal to advertisers. Disney's own cartoon shorts were interspersed with slice-of-life children's dramas, nature tales and musicals, all forming a kind of children's variety show. The programme was hosted by a gang of talented and well-scrubbed kids who spanned the targeted ages of four to sixteen. The mouseclubbers themselves, singing the Mouse Club song with their special mouse ears on, provided a sense of tribal organization and belonging, with Mickey as its totem animal, which Disney hoped would inspire children to rush home from school to watch TV.

The Mouse Club's commercial success issued a siren call to children's marketers. Before the Mouse Club, advertising expenditures for children's television only amounted to a million dollars a year in 1954 and this was mostly aimed at getting children to

123

influence the family's breakfast and snack choices. Cereal marketers such as Ralston and General Mills had gravitated to sponsorship of family programmes in the expensive after-dinner slots. Now they would consider ads on kids' programmes. Meanwhile, toy manufacturers were on record as saying they could thrive without mass-market advertising on television. Since television advertising on kids' shows (especially before the development of the videotape machine) was restricted to sponsor announcements and product demonstrations, it hardly seemed worth the trouble. Yet the quick growth of mouse guitar and ear sales indicated the potential of featuring toys within a peer context and made the toy companies prick up their own ears.

Disney had given children's television production an important boost. As a medium, TV did not totally supplant comics and films within children's culture, but no one could deny that it was engaging children for a considerable part of their waking day (about 1.5 hours in the United States in 1957). Marketers who were interested in communicating with and selling to children could no longer deny that the opportunity was there.

By the early 1960s, the Saturday morning and after-school children's ghettos were firmly established TV institutions. Given the low adult ratings at these times, the interest among children's marketers grew steadily (further encouraged by lower than prime-time rates). Saturday morning came to mean up to three hours of children's programming that included cartoon shorts regrouped into thirty-minute collages along with children's adventure programmes (*Sky King, The Lone Ranger, The Cisco Kid, Captain Midnight, Hawkeye and the Mohicans*), animal dramas (*Lassie, Fury, My Friend Flicka, Rin Tin Tin*), and other family entertainment reruns that drifted into the children's ghetto when they could no longer muster the prime-time ratings (*Our Miss Brooks, The Bob Cummings Show, I Love Lucy*). Although no one got excited about the quality of children's television, at least there was some variety in the types of programmes being offered – they included live drama, sitcoms, cartoons, animal stories and nature programmes.[7]

The Plot Thickens: The Formative Years

By the mid 1950s, the children's movies were experiencing declining audiences due to the popularity of television programming.

Television seemed to provide a movie theatre in the home. Some film producers, including Warner Bros, saw this as a new opportunity, but MGM decided in 1957 that its cinematic animation department should be disbanded. Hanna-Barbera, thus released, set up their own studio with the sole intent of continuing their production of cartoons directly for television. Their first offering was *The Ruff and Reddy Show*, a seven-minute animation modelled on their ever popular *Tom and Jerry* formula. Packed with accidents and mishaps, the cartoons proved popular in the new children's viewing slots. Struggling to survive in hard times, Hanna and Barbera probably had no sense that the innovations in technique and the plots simplified around combat they were to forge in children's animation would eventually swamp children's culture with over one thousand new characters.

The move to television presented the animators with a difficult problem. At MGM they would have had a budget of $50,000 to produce seven minutes of animation. Their contract with NBC was for only $2500 a programme. As their own corporate history puts it:

> What Hanna and Barbera had created was a wholly original animated product. If necessity is the mother of invention, then the budget limitations the fledgling company initially faced proved to be extremely fertile forces. The network's budget restrictions unleashed Hanna and Barbera's full creative powers. They found ways to get the same amount of laughs for a lot less money.[8]

Television animation proved more demanding than movies from the production point of view. As the audience did not have to spend money or decide to see a programme, lavish production on the scale of the Disney features was unnecessary. More often than not the audience was inherited from the previous programme. The task was to motivate them not to switch or leave, and the quality of drawing and illustration mattered far less. Children would more or less watch anything that moved sufficiently. Production for television therefore imposed extensive economic disciplines on animators, especially given the lower rates for advertising in the children's ghetto.

To produce for television Hanna-Barbera learned how to economize on the expensive cel animation production techniques by simplifying drawing and storyline while making movement more stylized and less expressive. Since drawing the cels was the most labour-intensive and time-consuming aspect of animation, the new methods involved substituting action and effects for the old elegantly illustrated expressions and visual humour. Hanna-Barbera relied on conflict between very clearly defined characters as the pretext of plot, with highly ritualized and repetitious stories. Borrowing from advertising, each character had a characteristic voice and a saying that provided easy recognition: 'I hate these meeses to pieces' or 'smarter than the average bear' became part of a verbal iconography that could substitute for clever visual humour.

The cartoons were not only extraordinarily popular with all children, it almost seemed as if children never got tired of them. Unlike a story with a strong plot-line, there was no unfolding of events and no sense of 'I've seen this before'. As early commentators were to complain, television fiction proves popular when it regularizes narrative:

> The quality of continuity, even repetition, is important to [television] viewers (fans). They are people who readily become involved with a TV series to the point where a sense of familiarity develops and sustains their interest and involvement. Knowing the recurring people, their relationships, and what is likely to happen – the set patterns of events and relations that so often typify a television series – is of value to them. Variation on a theme is desired, but too much change in themes is likely to disrupt their ability to identify with the program or series.[9]

Cartoons could be repeated ad nauseum, and many of the early ones continue to run even now. Plots never took unusual directions and dialogue actually became more important; in *Tom and Jerry* there had been nothing but sound effects, but now dialogue was used to fill out time and save on drawing. The opportunity for verbal humour was sacrificed on the altar of highly predictable interactions and uncomplicated characters. The abbreviation of social interaction allowed for economic scripts.

The success of *Ruff and Reddy* led to the widely syndicated *Huckleberry Hound* series, which won the first Emmy for animated television and quickly built the studio's reputation. *Huckleberry Hound* was a cartoon omnibus, but the leading character with his 'cowboy' drawl and western ways was implicitly taking the animators in a new direction. Many of the scenes and situations seemed to be drawn from or to be parodies of other cinematic genres, the favourite being westerns. The characters thus gained their easy familiarity by resonating with known qualities. More importantly, the references were socially specific. Bugs Bunny or Mickey Mouse were clearly American personalities but they had also retained a universal quality as

126

'everymen'; Huck was unmistakably a strictly American persona derived from American TV.

The Hanna-Barbera studios parlayed their initial success by gradually adapting the form and focus of the cartoon and spinning off new characters from previous series. Huckleberry Hound's omnibus was the entrée for one of the studio's most durable characters, Yogi Bear. Yogi was a bit of an American nerd; living in the Jellystone National Park, he spent his days cadging picnic baskets from unwary tourists and eluding the rules-conscious Ranger Smith. The personality traits of this lazy trickster overshadowed the limited drawings, jerky movement and repetitive tales. Yogi was not so much an animal as a character from a sitcom placed in an animal suit and let loose in the park. Yogi got his own show in 1961 and still appears on TV today.

Yogi showed the way to *The Flintstones,* which was not only the first programme-length TV cartoon series but also the first attempt to animate the family sitcom. Fred and Wilma were the Honeymooners removed to one million years BC. Attempting to attract adult viewers to cartoons, *The Flintstones* was first shown in prime-time, an innovation that was hard to sell to the industry, according to the Hanna-Barbera historian:

> That the Flintstones scared off many sponsors was not really surprising, because it was the first animated sitcom, the first animated show to go beyond the six or seven minute format to half hour, and the first animated show to feature human characters.[10]

As primitive humans whose lives parallel those of the typical American family, much of the humour (as indicated by the canned-laugh track) was thought to pivot on the archaic technologies; whether in their stone-wheeled car, the bowling alley, or the multi-applianced kitchen, the Flintstones reassured North Americans about the normality of their suburban reality.

The ease and economy of production, it was soon discovered, were not the only economic advantage of animation. *The Flintstones* only lasted a year in prime-time; but like its spin-off, *The Jetsons,* the series survived hundreds more showings on Saturday morning, proving, it seemed, that the cartoon was essentially a children's idiom unable to compete effectively in the prime adult market. A similar fate may await the more recent *Simpsons* series. The hidden economic benefits of an animated series rested in its durability in the children's schedule. Hanna-Barbera went on to dominate children's television with hundreds of cartoons produced over the subsequent thirty years, because on the basis of cost live-action drama, children's variety, and even reruns of old westerns found it hard to compete. As recycled programmes, cartoons were cheap properties. More importantly, the repeated exposures achieved 'saturation', making the characters household names. The familiarity meant that the Flintstones were excellent licensing material. Over one hundred licences were spun off from the series, including a Pebbles doll (over three million pieces sold) a cereal, and a brand of vitamins, all of them adding considerable income for the studios, which, like Disney, became fully aware of the merchandising possibilities in children's cultural production. When Hanna-Barbera was taken over in 1967 by the Taft organization, it was with the corporate intent of gaining full advantage of the spin-offs that derived from popular kids TV programmes.

In their continued exploration of the comic possibilities of technology, ordinary-life and everyday-people cartoons proved capable of adapting many of the elements of prime-time television for children. The Flintstone premiss that 'people don't change, only their situations do' provided a new formula that extended both forward and backward in time, and spanned the enchanted circle of television. Hanna-Barbera used the American fascination with space in its follow-up series *The Jetsons*, which was based on Fred and Wilma projected forward in time. Futuristic technology might offer as many comic possibilities as anachronistic ones, and you never had to worry about the star demanding a rise for the next season's run. Hanna-Barbera studios expanded their production and in so doing made their contribution to television: the cartoon at a very competitive price.

Indeed, throughout the 1960s and 1970s, as the volume of children's advertising continued to rise, animated programming grabbed an increasing share of the children's production dollar. Most of these efforts were scheduled for Saturday morning but some also migrated to the after-school spot, competing with family western series (*Bonanza, The Rifleman*) and reruns of prime-time comedy and sitcom series (*Mary Tyler Moore, Lucy, Dobie Gillis*) with their proven appeal.

This period was a difficult one for programmers because of growing parental activism around the issue of the quality of children's programming. In mixed broadcasting systems, such as in Canada, Japan and Britain, public broadcasters recognized that the commercial logic was not suited to children's audiences. They therefore interpreted their public service mandate (inform, educate and entertain) broadly as sufficient reason to produce children's shows. Variety shows, classical puppet theatre (*Sooty, Muffin the Mule*), educational contests (*Spelling, General Knowledge*) and musical comedy (*Maggy Muggins*) were the preferred fare, both because they were accepted forms in children's culture and simple and cheap to produce. Japan and Britain eventually developed special offshoot channels for educational programming and both countries still have a better blend and diversity of programming – although increasingly their national public networks accept this mantle reluctantly. In Canada it fell to the provincial governments to establish educational TV, as the CBC gradually abandoned this unprofitable sector of the cultural market with few apologies to parents or children.

In the United States, stung by FCC Commissioner Newton Minow's 'vast wasteland' accusation of the early 1960s, the networks offered a few educational ventures, such as *Reading Room, Exploring* and *One, Two, Three = Go*. As advertising executive Cy Schneider noted, this response was destined to fail because the programmes had to compete on commercial terms:

> Despite the fact they didn't get much of an audience, the shows were sponsored by more enlightened advertisers – at first. The advertisers eventually lost heart and were not willing to pay high rates for poorly rated shows. They preferred to concentrate their money on the cartoon shows where the audience was.[11]

Indeed, this resistance to quality was so deeply rooted in television's financial arrangements that it took another seven years of lobbying effort to launch the Public Broadcasting System, with its educational and quality mission. The concern about quality did help to launch the American Public Broadcasting Network and to fund the Children Television Workshop's preschooler flagship *Sesame Street* in 1969. Two decades later the impact of this effort would be disputed and children's quality production would still be underfunded.[12]

Yet for all the complaints about the commercial network's abysmal children's production budgets, one fact could not be denied: whatever the content – or perhaps because of it – children wanted to watch TV. The average child was viewing over three hours a day and a good portion of this time was accounted for by the Saturday morning cartoon barrage. Television had fulfilled its commercial mission: it had cultivated an eager and loyal audience composed of young people. The network executives simply followed the commercial edicts of light entertainment programming. The critics, it seemed to them, were conflating the very elements that made television attractive and entertaining to kids (action, pace, anarchistic humour) with the effects of the medium when they worried about the increasing aggressiveness of US culture.

For the mass-society critics, the predictions had simply proved right: television was structurally incapable of providing a well-rounded diet of information, education and fiction to children. As an instrument for enlightenment and for strengthening culture it was hopeless. The violent fantasies provided only mesmerizing entertainment – entertainment devoid of criteria other than audience size. As critic Harold Mendlesohn argued at the time, television had no set of guidelines concerning 'quality' of entertainment, and there was insufficient discussion among critics as to what 'standards of value' ought to be applied.[13] The critics' assessment implied that after years of television addiction, children were left with no basis to judge what they wanted to watch, and no basis to understand the world they lived in or the forces that shaped it. How could they, when the programming was so thematically narrow? As Dr F. Earle Barcus pointed out in a study of programming commissioned by Action for Children's Television (ACT), commercial television produced only light and frivolous entertainment:

> Dominant subject matter of the programs included domestic (home/family) topics, interpersonal rivalry between characters, crime and the supernatural. Little or no emphasis was given to topics such as history, religion, race/nationality, education, business, government, war, literature and the fine arts, crafts and hobbies or language.[14]

The Barcus study was only one of the many to document what had happened to children's television in the 1960s and 70s.

This study of children's television by Barcus certified that the earlier dream of quality and diversified commercial television was dead.[15] The networks' afternoon television programming (three to six p.m.) included about 43 per cent of programmes orientated towards children, about half of them cartoons. About 60 per cent of children's afternoon programming on independent stations included mindless violent animations. In general there was nothing educational (with the exception of programmes on Public Broadcasting stations), very little historical drama, a few family-type

comedies, and a steady stream of highly ritualized cartoon aggressiveness. The study reported: 'Programming on the ten independent
stations studied was almost entirely entertainment (99.9) dominated
by cartoon comedy, situation comedy, children's variety and crime/
mystery drama.' What could you expect given the audience dynamics
of commercial television?

By the mid 1970s, three important tendencies were dominating
commercial programming. First, children between the ages of three
and twelve had become an increasingly attractive audience with its
own tastes and preferences. Second, like the Saturday morning slot,
programming in the children's afternoon ghetto (especially on the
independents) was consistently using cartoons and reruns as the two
most economically viable options for maintaining the children's
audience. Third, there was a clear preference for comedy, either in
rerun or cartoon form. The networks clearly believed that the 'light
entertainment' format was most appropriate for children's television
– it kept kids watching, which is what counted most. All together this
meant that the networks would assimilate whatever increased revenues arose from the growing advertiser interest in children into a very
narrow production mandate.

At the top of the heap was the cartoon, riding a wave of continuous
popularity with kids. Yet, significantly, animation also survived and
prospered as a programming idiom because it tended to take in most
of the elements it ultimately displaced from other light entertainment traditions: *Quick Draw McGraw* was a parody of the western;
the 'Top Cat' character was a cartoon wheeler-dealer in the mould of
the 1950s sitcom character Sergeant Bilko; *Rocky and his Friends* was
structured as a cartoon version of a kids' television variety show
complete with its own 'fractured fairy tales' and an absurdist humour
borrowed from *Mad Magazine*; even highly popular family sitcoms
(which were self-referential if not satirical) were rendered in a
cartoon format (*Dennis the Menace, Peanuts* and, more recently, *The
Simpsons*), which added a social dimension and a satirical edge to
animation.

Because of their assimilation of other television genres, animated
cartoons turned out to be in one respect an excellent primer in
media literacy; cartoons taught the basic forms of television in an
enjoyable way because cartoons assumed children's understanding of
the highly structured nature of those formulas, providing parodies of
the rules in *Rocky and Bulwinkle* or *Sesame Street*.[16] Much of the
incidental learning that children derive through watching television

131

cartoons over the years concerns the literary conventions of characterization and plot used in the programmes.[17] This fact complicated the debates about the causation of violent behaviour because, although cartoons contained a surplus of violent acts, it could be argued that the clearly understood conventions ensured that children would not confuse the formulas with real everyday social behaviour. A better explanation of observed correlations than imitation or modelling from cartoons could perhaps be derived from studying the amount of television-viewing, the attitudes of family, and the general activation levels stimulated by cartoons.[18]

Critics still called children's TV a cultural wasteland, a violent distraction, obsessed with fantasy and escapism. Only the establishment of the educational broadcasting networks had served to blunt the criticisms of quality and diversity. Some parents were concerned that their children were learning little of value from cartoons and sitcoms, and even educational television had its detractors. Ironically *Sesame Street*'s most effective segments were its animated educational commercials for concepts and letters. The creators chose animation not only because it was an art form that had proved appealing to kids, but also because it was relatively cheap and easy to produce. But these criticisms had a minimal impact on television programmers, who knew that if they amused kids and kept them occupied in front of the TV sets, they were doing their jobs. Maybe it was the parents who were failing to understand children and how they saw the world. If the cartoon action was exaggerated and the situations fantastic, this surely reflected the fact that children's sense of humour was itself uniquely zany rather than subtle. The TV characters were so unreal, after all, that it made no sense to say that one of them bashing another was 'violent'. Children loved action in their cartoons, no one was hurt, and it was all in an atmosphere of fun. Even in the supposedly educational *Sesame Street*, the letter B-ee will get up and sting a B-ehind.

Adventure Capital

While audience management remained the undeniable dynamic of commercial media, the 1980s would witness several important changes in the children's culture industries, including the introduction of video games and VCRs, the increased spread of cable television, and the deregulation of commercial TV. None of these changes reduced television's continued hold on child viewers. Children watched about an hour more television each day than they had done in the 1970s, in addition to watching videotapes and playing with Nintendo sets. The audience studies also reveal that much of this growth was due to intensified viewing during the weekday afternoon, preschool mornings and Sunday morning time slots, which continued to be opened up as children's time by the independents,[19] and exploited by the children's, educational, cable and pay TV networks as well. Yet for all this expansion, the programming schedules of the networks continued to reveal a paucity of live-action drama programming suitable for kids. Stories that featured child characters and focused on children's lives from their point of view disappeared with the reruns of family drama (*My Three Sons, Little House on the Prairie, Leave it to Beaver, Happy Days*), and animal stories (*Lassie, Flipper, National Velvet*).

In the 1980s the most popular shows on children's television, the audience studies showed, were defined by two characteristics: they were animated and they followed the fantasy-adventure formula in their narrative. For this reason it is worth tracing the rise of the action-adventure cartoon in some detail.

The action-adventure formula of the nineteenth-century children's novel defined an important narrative tradition, popularized in the comic books and films of the 1930s. Children crowded around their family radios to listen to these new legends – Zorro, Green Lantern, The Lone Ranger – and later convened around their TV in the same family spot: The Lone Ranger, Zorro, The Cisco Kid, Dick Tracy, Superman, Batman, and scores of other well-known heroes made a successful transition to television, bringing with them the action-adventure genre.

Filled with high action, the stories focused on the heroic exploits of a superior being – a man on a quest, a survivor, an individual of power, someone who knew right from wrong. These were the ingredients of mythology; they were basic tales of cosmic scope whose characters confronted the enduring struggles of life – human progress, enlightenment, personal triumph and moral rightness. Some of the heroes brought to early television drama were based on historical figures, legends or events (Robin Hood, The Three Musketeers), and some like Zorro had survived exposition in each and every medium from penny dreadful to movies. Others, like Superman, Batman, and The Fantastic Four, seemed to emerge only from the more visual and mythic comic. Whatever their origins, these tales had a constant narrative structure which prevailed whatever role or situation defined the character.[20] Whether the character was detective, cowboy, sailor, policeman, frontiersman, soldier or alien, the unifying heroic theme implied a narrative structure emphasizing confrontation, rescues, captures, escapes, combats and enduring trials; these social motifs were the pretext that allowed for the hero's triumph, for the victory of good over evil, humanity and civilization over greed, base nature and disorder. This mythic content became the prime focus of cinema criticism.[21] Enjoying these predictable action-packed narratives has brought pleasure to most North American children since the western first introduced American myth into children's culture.

Hanna-Barbera were the first producers to try animating the heroic adventure formula. Significantly, in choosing their hero for the 1960s they turned not to the west but to space. In 1964 they released *The Adventures of Jonny Quest*, the first animated adventure for prime-time family viewing. Jonny Quest's protagonist was an eleven-year-old towhead who travelled the universe with his scientist father in search of adventure and intrigue. The programme used a realistic style for drawing the human figures (about as realistic as comics, anyway) and the plots were motivated by the adventure motifs of action, danger and escape. Although the series was gone from prime-time within a year, like *The Flintstones* it was featured in Saturday morning reruns for years to come. *Jonny Quest* blazoned a cultural trail across the terrain of children's television, introducing the science fiction themes that had become increasingly popular in family viewing (*Science Fiction Theatre, The Twilight Zone, Superman*).

During the 1960s, children's science fiction television was given another enormous boost by *Star Trek*, whose epic sagas proved one of the most durable formulas of television. The very young child, it seemed, might miss the subtle philosophical dimensions that made the stories cult material with teens and critics but still enjoy the intergalactic scale, strange objects and ugly monsters that gave tone to the series. Space technology defined an important symbolic texture in children's narrative, for through the adventures on board the Star Ship Enterprise children's culture began to project forward into a fantasy future where 'no man has gone before'. So when the Taft company took over Hanna-Barbera, it stopped the prime-time animation experiments but continued the production of science fiction adventure animation for children. *Jonny Quest* was followed by *Space Ghost and Dino Boy, The Herculoids, Birdman and the Galaxy Trio,*

The Fantastic Four, and *Super Friends.* Other animation houses joined in with similar animated adventures such as *Wonder Woman, The Bionic Man* and *The A-Team.*

The science fiction motifs that had become such a strong part of children's popular culture partly reflected the growing uncertainty surrounding the vision of a rapidly technologized future. They also provided a wider scope for adventure. Science fiction moves the characters out of an 'ordinary' world and resituates the heroic act in a technologically modernized social context, an imaginary world freed from the normal constraints of everyday reality. As Celia Anderson was to note:

> In this genre, resolution after resolution of plot encourages the notion that some suprahuman power will save modern civilization in its last extremity. There is a difference between this and the magical happy ending in fairy tales. In fairy tales both problem and solution exist in never never land of archetypes; in cartoons, the problem is often from current reality – the energy crisis, the destructive potential of machines and bombs – while the solution is mere fantasy.[22]

Science fiction therefore gives great scope to animators not only for envisioning new inventions but also for creating new bizarre, monstrous or even surreal characters. The characters and actions are no longer constrained by the limits of ordinary human experience.

Animation, although not as directly representational as live-action drama, can still be developed around stories in which events, situations and characters resonate with familiarity and normality and partake in everyday human experience. *The Flintstones* and *The Jetsons,* wherever they lived, still exemplified the normal. The *Dennis the Menace* and *Peanuts* cartoons are two instances of highly popular creations that map the typified experiences of ordinary life. But the science fiction writers stopped worrying about everyday experience; they borrowed freely from the storehouse of legend (mostly as preserved in the comic book) and projected those legends into a technologically contoured imaginary universe. In this sense reference to normal social situations, interpersonal relations, family life, and the experiences of growing up were implicitly abandoned in favour of a more cosmic and fantastical scope and tone. Heroic animation brought to children's television an implicit bracketing of those literary points of contact with reality and with the social dilemmas associated with the child's experience.

135

The Corporate Pinwheel

The licensed spin-off was a well-trodden path in children's media. The Disney studio had sold product licences for some of its earliest characters, including Mickey's predecessor Oswald the Lucky Rabbit. But these licensing arrangements remained minor financial considerations for the studio. During the 1930s, however, Herman Kamen, an advertising executive, showed Disney that his animated creatures could be the foundation of a much more extensive marketing effort. Disney designed his products to appeal to the imagination, and Kamen pointed out that for children the process of imagining happened not only while they were playing but also while they were eating and dressing and even going to bed. So Disney became a major purveyor of character imagery that could appear in other venues besides film. By 1933 Disney was selling over $10 million of its merchandise including models of all Disney's famous characters.

By 1988 the licensing of cartoon and fantasy-world characters was helping to make $3·44 billion worldwide for Disney enterprises. Disneyland itself was further proof of the way characters could transcend a particular medium and enter the mainstream of culture. Lovable characters, not films or television programmes, had become Disney's major product – a product attractive to a wide range of merchandisers because the Disney studio had itself become so effective in implanting the characters within children's hearts.

In the 1950s, Disney's move to television brought with it mouse ears and mouse guitars, in an attempt to strengthen the bond between the world of kids' media and associated marketing. In turn, the Flintstone characters were associated with over a hundred products introduced throughout the 1960s and 1970s. The saleability of these popular anthropomorphic characters left a deep impression on children's marketers, who began to use animated characters as brand-image devices in children's advertising: the breakfast tables of North America became populated by Sugar Bears, Honey Bees, Tony the Tiger and a myriad of snap-crackling creatures that advertising executives interspersed in their product appeals to children. Similarly, the establishment at the centre of children's culture of television, with its huge audiences and its star system, made the medium especially suited to toy spin-offs because the characters would get extensive exposure: successful characterizations came to saturate children's media. Children's responsiveness to these lovable characters is probably the best-tested maxim of marketing, and television became the major source of new characters for the children's toy industry. The convergence of cartoons and merchandising makes perfect sense, Mark Crispin Miller points out, 'because the ad and the cartoon each present a fantasy of perfect wish fulfillment that seems both immediate and absolute'.[23]

The biggest boost to spin-off licensing in the toy industry was the *Star Wars* trilogy, which along with other Lucas Films sequels had spawned over $2 billion in product licences by 1989. The merchandising revenues accrued by Lucas Films revealed the importance of merchandising considerations in raising the funds for media productions. By 1988 licensing had become a $54·3 billion-dollar-a-year business, with a 15·5 per cent share of the toy market. In 1988 Mattel itself sold $55 million dollars' worth of licensed identities to the other children's merchandisers. Spin-offs were transforming the economics and infrastructure of the culture industries. Specialist licensing agencies and symbolic designers became familiar faces around the corporate tables. The stars themselves began to look for added income from contracts with children's merchandisers: professional wrestlers, Farrah Fawcett, Michael Jackson, Mr T, and Madonna all parlayed their exposure on television into a marketable commodity. But more significantly, the producers of successful adventure dramas found that they could cheaply animate a story concept for children's TV time-slots with some assurance that previous exposure through family viewing had tested the market and the added economic incentive of spin-off licensing deals. Examples are *Wonder Woman, Super Friends, The A-Team, Droids.* Children's producers understood that there was a lot of money to be made in licensing the characters and accessories made popular by a TV programme – most of the money being in the children's market for action toys and vehicles.

The manufacturers and merchandisers of children's toys and vehicles were particularly pleased with the free advertising they received on these programmes. Licensing arrangements also reduced the expense of market research and the creative risk involved in bringing new action toys into the market.[24] Licensed goods sales had already ascended from insignificance to a healthy 20 per cent share of the toy market in 1977, the year of *Star Wars'* release. The excellent kids' ratings for animated adventure programmes in turn helped to increase the toy advertisers' interest in television advertising, and their proportion of total advertising expenditure in children's TV grew from 15 per cent in the early 1970s to over 50 per cent in the 1980s (over 60 per cent in the pre-Christmas quarter). As the authors of a book on the toy industry note, it was 'promotional toys' that changed everything: 'Promotional toys are the toys heavily promoted on television, and most of the large companies sell them. Promotional toys create the booms and the busts; it is the promotional toys that make the industry a fashion and entertainment business.'[25]

Character licensing then has had a wide impact on both children's television and on the toy industry.[26] It has meant that personas crafted for television have become the predominant social identities that children play with in the form of fashion dolls, plush toys and action figures.[27] It was around this matter of television spin-offs, licensing and marketing of toys that the logistics of the toy trade became a fact of life amidst the business plans and programme decision-making in children's television. Licensed character toys grossed $8·2 billion in 1986, proving to the toy makers that television exposure was the key ingredient in the children's toy market.

Through the promotional toy strategy, toy-marketing and children's culture industries were invisibly drawn together. As Sydney Stern and Ted Schoenhaus note, the marketing of toys depends on an understanding of children's culture, because

> The secret of success lies inside the head of an eight year old child. That is the eternal paradox of the toy industry. Adults running multimillion-dollar toy companies are always trying to climb back inside that eight year old head. Creative people in the industry love to boast that they have not grown up, that they have retained enough youthful enthusiasm to know what children will consider fun.[28]

Toy makers now shared this paradox with the TV networks.

Unfettered Fiction

In the late 1950s, sponsored television had been replaced by 'spot' advertising after several scandals had revealed problems in advertiser control over the development of programmes. Direct sponsorship was now prevented by broadcast policy, and the new arms-length approach at the networks seemed to promise some protection against advertiser abuse of the airwaves. As a result, as early as 1969, when Mattel had tried to launch a programme featuring its Hot Wheels toys the FTC frowned on this approach and prevented stations from showing it. Such promotional tactics violated the established principle that advertisements and programmes should be separate.

But something dramatic happened to children's television in the 1980s. In the business climate of the Reaganite 1980s, the FTC and FCC did not seem to object when licensed character tie-in programmes began to be produced to promote new toy lines. Tom Englehardt has termed this strategy the 'Strawberry Shortcake' strategy in recognition of the product that crystallized the first really successful use of this new marketing concept.[29]

Brought out in the early 1980s, Strawberry Shortcake wasn't just another doll promoted by mass-market advertising. She was a sellable image conceived of by a company called Those Characters from Cleveland, the licensing branch of American Greetings Cards Ltd, to provide instant strong public identification for a new series of children's products. The image was worth several hundred million dollars in sales of a wide variety of licensed goods ranging from the Kenner doll and accessories to stickers, cut-out books, clothing, cups, jewellery, shoes and food. Moreover, Strawberry Shortcake was not just a decorative motif but an identifiable character, carefully crafted and conveyed through advertising and two of her very own TV specials – thirty-minute animated commercials provided as cheap programming to syndicated private TV stations.

He-Man, GI Joe, Thundercats, The Transformers, She-Ra, My Little Pony, and The Care Bears quickly followed this lead as all the major toy makers tried to get into the act. The television special was extended into a sixty-five-episode animated serial, providing even higher definition to the character toys and their licensed iconography imprinted on clothing and shoes. The iconography of children's television became a fantastic bestiary: *Insectoids, Jem, Centaurians, Bravestarr, Inhumanoids, Voltron, Droids, Ghostbusters,* and *C.O.P.S.* are but a few of the science fantasy adventures produced for children's television. In fact, by the late 1980s close to sixty different product-tied animation programmes had been showcased on kids-time TV. By the early 1990s there was no television show brought to television without at least one licence associated with it. These programmes represented about 65 per cent of children's programming and 90 per cent of the new production effort. They filled children's television with the narrative projections of 'character toys' on the most watched shows for the under-twelves. In interviews, children have indicated that these programmes are the ones they are most interested in. Children were watching adventure-fantasy

139

television programmes with rapacity and loyalty, which is why such programmes were featured prominently in the Saturday and Sunday morning and weekday afternoon schedules.

Children also watch TV in prime-time and, as Neil Postman notes, in doing so they become voyeurs gazing into a somewhat incomprehensible world of quizzes, sport, soap operas, crime dramas and crime re-enactments. Many stay up late and watch the late news. But it remains clear that during the 1980s a major transformation took place in children's scheduling thanks to the interest of toy merchandisers in promoting their products through animated television. By way of consequence, contemporary youngsters have been catapulted into a fantastic and chaotic time–space continuum of action toys. There is in fact nowhere to be found a purer example of how the 'postmodern revolt' has become one with the official children's culture of Western society. As Fredric Jameson explains:

> What has happened is that aesthetic production today has become integrated into commodity production generally: the frantic economic urgency of producing fresh waves of ever more novel-seeming goods (from clothing to airplanes), at ever greater rates of turnover, now assigns an increasingly essential structural function and position to aesthetic innovation and experimentation.[30]

No clearer articulation of the postmodern aesthetic is offered than in the globally popular Ninja Turtles, one of the most recent marketing formulas to try and cash in on children's love of play and lust for fiction. This sewer gang of avenging mutoids, led by their karate sensei in their fight against a demonic brain that lives inside an androidal body, reflects the recombinant formula that television animators began to rely on to establish their place on the luminescent screen. Mutant turtles seem unlikely heroes of classic socialization drama, and they would seem even harder to sell as toys. Yet as promoted through the well-developed marketing plans of clever character merchants their conquest over children's hearts and minds seems inevitable.

Most parents are familiar with the characters that marketing has made famous, yet few understand the changes in the television industry that spawned them. Parents are slow to make the connection between this revolution in childhood mythology and the drain on their pocketbooks. Yet the US toy market enjoyed enormous growth, from just over $2 billion in the mid 1970s to well over $12 billion by 1986, thanks to some important changes in the children's cultural market. These changes include the new television services and technologies associated with VCRs and cable, the deregulation of children's television and competitive factors within the electronics and toy industries. Although there has been constant criticism of the tediously violent stories that television feeds to children, one factor has tended to be overlooked: that the rise in character marketing has all but eliminated images of real children playing in the normal course of their lives – in dramas or narratives about and for the young.

Notes

1. Newcomb, Horace, *TV The Most Popular Art*, New York, Anchor, 1973, p. 23.

2. Huston-Stein, Aletha, and J. Wright, 'Effects of the Medium, its Content and Form', *J. of Research and Development in Education*, 1979; and Wartella, Ellen and Byron Reeves, 'Historical Trends in Research on Children and the Media: 1900–1960', *Journal of Communication*, Spring, 1985, pp. 6–21.

3. Skornia, Harry J., *Television and Society: An Inquest and Agenda for Improvement*, New York, McGraw-Hill, 1965, p. 158.

4. Crafton, D., *Before Mickey, The Animated Film 1889–1928*, Cambridge, MIT Press, 1982.

5. Finch, Christopher, *The Art of Walt Disney: From Mickey Mouse to the Magic Kingdoms*, Walt Disney Productions, 1975.

6. The history of programming is well documented in several historical references: Schneider, C., *Children's Television: The Art, the Business, and How It Works*, Lincolnwood, Ill, NTC Business Books, 1987; Bogart, Leo, *The Age of Television*, New York: Frederick Unger Publishing, 1955; Fischer, Stuart, *Kids' TV: The First 25 Years*, Facton File Publications, 1983; Grossman, Gary, *Saturday Morning TV*, New York, Dell, 1981; William A. Henry III, 'The Big Turnoff, The Rise and Fall of Network Television', *Lears* (Nov 1989), pp. 97–108, 164.

7. The programmes mentioned are there because they are the shows that impressed themselves upon my viewing, and stayed with me through my life.

8. Hanna Barbera Productions, *News: History of Hanna-Barbera Productions*, Hollywood, California, p. 3.

9. Glick, I.O., and S.J. Levy, *Living with Television*, Chicago: Aldine, 1962. Cited in H. Mendelsohn, *Mass Entertainment*, New Haven: College and University Press, 1966, p. 88.

10. Hanna Barbera Productions, *News: History of Hanna Barbera Productions*, Hollywood, California, p. 6.

11. Schneider, *Children's Television*, p. 169.

12. See, for instance, Edward Palmer, 1988, *Television and America's Children: A Crisis of Neglect*, New York: Oxford University Press.

13. Mendelsohn, *Mass Entertainment*, pp. 155–8.

14. Barcus, F. Earle, *Television in the Afternoon Hours*, Newtonville, MA, Action for Children's Television, 1975, p. 8.

15. Barcus, F. Earle, *Children's Television: An Analysis of Programming and Advertising*, New York, Praeger, 1977.

16. Salomon, Saloman, 'Shape, Not Only Content: How Media Symbols Partake in the Development of Abilities', in Ellen Wartella, ed., *Children Communicating: Media and Development of Thought, Speech, Understanding*, Beverly Hills, Sage, 1979, pp. 52–82.

17. Hodge, Robert and David Tripp, *Children and Television: A Semiotic Approach*, New York, Polity Press, 1988.

18. Potts, Richard, Aletha Huston-Stein and John Wright, 'The Effects of Television Form and Violent Content on Boys' Attention and Social Behavior', *Journal of Experimental Child Psychology*, 41, 1986, pp. 1–17; Huston-Stein, Aletha, and John Wright, 'Effects of the Medium, its Content and Form', *Journal of Research and Development in Education*, 13(1), 1979, pp. 3–29.

19. BBM Bureau of Measurement, *Television Statistics for Toronto*, Toronto, Bureau of Broadcast Measurement, 1984, 1986 and 1987.

20. Marchetti, Gina, 'Action-Adventure as Ideology', in Ian Angus and Sut Jhally, *Cultural Politics in Contemporary America*, New York, Routledge, 1988, pp. 182–97.

21. Wollen, Peter, *Signs and Meaning in the Cinema*, London, Martin, Secker & Warburg, 1969.

22. Anderson, C., 'The Saturday Morning Survival Kit', *Journal of Popular Culture*, (Spring 1974), pp. 155–64.

23. Miller, Mark Crispin, 'Hollywood: The Ad.', *Atlantic Monthly*, April 1990, p. 54.

24. Ladensohn Stern, Sydney, and Ted Schoenhaus, *Toyland: The High-Stakes Game of the Toy Industry*, Chicago, Contemporary Books, 1990.

25. Ladensohn Stern and Schoenhaus, *Toyland*, p. 28.

26. Englehardt, Tom, 'The Strawberry Shortcake Strategy', in Todd Gitlin ed., *Watching Television*, New York, Pantheon Books, 1986, pp. 68–110.

27. See Stephen Kline, 'Limits to the Imagination: Marketing and Children's Culture', in Ian Angus and Sut Jhally, ed., *Cultural Politics in America*, New York, Routledge, 1989.

28. Ladensohn Stern and Schoenhaus, *Toyland*, p. 23.

29. Englehardt, 'The Strawberry Shortcake Strategy'.

30. Jameson, Fredric, 'Postmodernism, or, the Cultural Logic of Late Capitalism', *New Left Review*, 146, 1984, pp. 53–92.

5

Marketing Toys to Children

and Youth

Culture arises in the form of play. It is through this playing that society expresses its interpretation of life and the world. By this we do not mean that play turns into culture, rather that in its earliest phases culture has the play-character, that it proceeds in the shape and the mood of play. In the twin union of play and culture, play is primary.

J. HUIZINGA[1]

Play, the historian Huizinga argued forcefully, is the central creative principle of culture: 'In this sphere of sacred play the child and the poet are at home with the savage' because underlying the cultural forms of play is the instinctive basis for a type of human action 'accomplishing itself outside and above the necessities and serious-ness of everyday life.'[2] Yet as a social activity that expresses a society's particular interpretation of life and the world, play takes different forms – in sports, drama, literature and ritual. The forms of play give a sense of the social fabric: its definitions of freedom, of what is sacred, and its sensibility of order. And these abstract elements are represented in all things associated with play, with the costumes, rituals, rules and objects that are bound up in this sociocultural process.

Noting that some of the basic forms of children's playthings (rattles, dolls, pull toys) occur in all cultures, historian Antonia Fraser agrees that the play instinct seems to be universal. Yet because their use is essentially cultural, toys are objects that acquire unique symbolic content and meaning in a particular social context. 'Nothing is more natural than that a toy should reflect the life of its period,' Fraser states. Designed as miniatures of ideas, people, animals and things, or working indirectly through the structures they impose upon the play activity, toys and games are signs of the social world and the way it is organized. Fraser finds, especially in the way toys are designed and used by the older child, 'something more elaborate, and more connected with the world around him. It is these more advanced toys which are likely to show the natural fluctuations of the social and economic changes.'[3] It is not surprising, therefore, that the gradual industrialization of toy-making over the last hundred years has enscripted industrial forms and functions and the meanings and uses of marketing into the realm of playthings. As in all societies, our own modern definition of play and preferred play forms are integrated into the conceptions of childhood and the regimes of childrearing and collective socialization.[4]

The Industrialization of Play

The transformation of play by mass marketing is difficult to characterize until we contrast the contemporary images of play in television advertising with those depicted in the imaginary garden of Victorian childhood. Though in both scenes the child will be involved in a game of 'let's pretend', the Victorian child's pretending is a simple sociodrama with a personal dynamic. The television child, in contrast, is always pretending that the toys change them in some way or transport them into a more exciting world. Until relatively recently pretending did not sell toys, for play was seen as an expression of the natural spirit of childhood and not of a bonding with objects. The picture books depicted children who communed with one another, and with the things they found in the garden (animals, butterflies, sticks, rivers) through pretending. They did not rely upon toys as a tool for projecting the imagination or on television narratives to script their imaginary adventures. Rather, they searched out some deeper repository of cultural memory.

In short, the Victorian world of child's play was not a world of manufactured things: sometimes it included found and discarded objects (wheel hoops, sticks, rags) and very occasionally folk toys of archetypical form (dolls, balls, carved animals, wheels) – things that parents, relatives and children themselves might carve, sew or otherwise craft. So too the sports, street games, language and singing games, dramas and rituals, and board, string, and card games that defined the diversions of friends, family and community were essentially social play-forms requiring little material commitment. Victorians did not assume that the child needed a profusion of toys to mature, and most traditions of play (rules, songs, references, phrases, rituals) were transmitted socially.

In fact most Victorian children had few or no toys.[5] Until the beginning of the twentieth century, toys, like books, had been a specialist product mainly enjoyed by the wealthy. Mechanical soldiers, ceramic dolls and toy theatres – however beautiful they were – were not for the ordinary child and not necessarily associated with childhood at all. Indeed, many of the seventeenth- and eighteenth-century miniatures that we retrospectively see as toys – dolls, carved objects, houses and soldiers – were objects intended for adults. Like books, these objects sometimes found their way into children's possession. Toys were only one of the means of satisfying the play instinct and, for many children, not a very important one. Before they were factory manufactured, toys belonged in the sphere of folk culture. They were objects produced in one of three ways: by the kids themselves, by parents for their kids, or by local specialized craft producers as gifts or for ceremonies and special occasions. In this context toys had a very special and personal meaning for the child. They were rarely regarded as just another thing to use to while away idle moments.

The expanding market for factory-made goods changed the situation dramatically. The fine array of handcrafted folk toys, cleverly devised mechanical delights and homely dolls that grace toy and folk museums gave way to the contemporary profusion of plastic, nylon, and metallic artefacts that currently circumscribe child's play. This transformation took place in two phases. The first wave of manufactured toys began to hit America in the beginning of the twentieth century. At the turn of the century, 50 per cent of the toys sold in the United States were actually imported, predominantly from German craft producers; yet by 1920, 90 per cent of the toys sold were being locally produced, and many of these toys and games bore the stamp of the factory. In the first half of the twentieth century, factory production meant lower costs and wider distribution, allowing the basic lines of toys and games to be more broadly and readily integrated into the schools, clubs and family leisure activities. It became customary at this time to give the infant rattles and the toddler pull and manipulation toys or the occasional stuffed animal as presents; the older children were provisioned with toys that replicated the roles of adults (baby dolls, animals, hammer and peg, construction sets, cooking sets, vehicles).

Commenting on the impact of this industrialization of toy-making, the French semiotician Roland Barthes proffered a more critical view. In the emergence of the mass-produced toy he lamented the loss of folk traditions and sentiments associated with earlier toys:

> The bourgeois status of toys can be recognized not only in their forms . . . but also in their substances. Current toys are made of a graceless material, the product of chemistry, not of nature. Many are now moulded from complicated mixtures; the plastic material of which they are made has an appearance at once gross and hygienic, it destroys all the pleasure, the sweetness, the humanity of touch. A sign which fills one with consternation is the gradual disappearance of wood, in spite of its being an ideal material because of its firmness and its softness, and the natural warmth of its touch. . . . Wood makes essential objects, objects for all time.[6]

In his rhapsody to wood toys, Barthes makes clear (if not explicit) his own cultural bias and preferences, harkening back, no doubt, to the world of his own childhood and his own toys, which he takes to be timeless. He is right to note that toy forms have been changing due to the mass production of toys. The expansion of toy-manufacturing has replaced the organic imagery of handcrafted toys with the 'industrial' sensibility of look-alike objects which are merely miniaturized versions of the technologies or goods of industrial society (cars, planes, kitchen- and tea-sets, tool benches, weapons, construction sets). Partly too, industrial values are seen in the new materials and the resultant uniformity of toy products. To Barthes, the repetitious plastic forms represent the triumph of an 'inhuman' industrial feel over the innocent, more organic playthings of children's traditional culture.

The second reverberation felt in the sphere of play began in the 1950s, as mass-marketing strategies and television advertising were adapted to merchandising toys. Until the 1950s the top toy makers such as Marx, Ideal and Knickerbocker had thrived through efficiencies gained in production methods. In 1955 Marx's, with $50 million in sales, spent $312 on advertising. This is why, as Stern and Schoenhaus note 'Mattel's decision to advertise toys to children on national television fifty-two weeks a year so revolutionized the industry that it is not an exaggeration to divide the history of the American toy business into two eras, before and after television.'[7] Guided by tried and true marketing methods, toy-making emerged as a big business with toy sales increasing tenfold between 1955 and

1985. In the 1970s the average American child had not just a single doll, bear or truck, but well over ninety playthings scattered around the bedroom.[8] By the late 1980s, 70 per cent of gross toy sales consisted of 'promotional toys' – those plastic replicas of television characters with which children simulate the contours of the universe 'as seen on television'. The sweeping invisible hand of mass-merchandising strategies likewise transformed toy stores into citadels for playthings, making Christmas seem like a festival of toys. Toys have become the supreme emblems of the young child's dearest pleasures, a parent's way of saying how special and precious the child is. Meanwhile our conception of play has narrowed its scope: the very word 'play' now conjures first and foremost the activities that revolve around the relationship between child and toy. The twin dynamics of mass production and mass marketing has penetrated deeply into all aspects of children's culture: few people can look at children's play and not see there a 'timeless' source of energy and creativity that can never be subdued by toys. And many of the standard toys are still available in the contemporary market. Yet the changes in play can be witnessed in the new materials and processes of toy production, in the toys' shape, design and social reference, and in the child's experience of play. Yet, remarkably, few critics have questioned the consequences of the mass marketing of play or carefully examined the pressures upon children's experience this change has brought about. For the most part the contemporary commentary on play and culture assumes that the marketing of toys has little impact on children's play.[9]

Toys of the Early Industrial Period

The new stamping, turning, and forming technologies and factory production methods have regularized the appearance of toys. Factory-made dolls all had the same faces and clothes; the wooden animals the same features; the doll's houses the same furniture. Industrial production brought standardization to toy design and through it demanded greater uniformity in children's play. It was their mass-produced 'individuality' that made Cabbage Patch dolls sell $1 billion of merchandise in the mid 1980s. More than the standardization, though, the national distribution of playthings has enormous consequences for a product's design, packaging and distribution in the mass market. This fact became abundantly clear with the emergence of toy 'fads', a phenomenon in which a single toy or game captures the popular imagination throughout the country and often the globe for just a short time. These toy crazes would be picked up by celebrities, by the news and by journalists as signs of the times. Jacks, originally a Roman pastime, enjoyed enormous and widespread popularity after the First World War. The yo-yo (depicted in Egyptian temple drawings) was reinvented and marketed in the United States in 1929 by Donald S. Duncan and quickly became a worldwide fad. In the late 1950s the 'craze' that flashed through the United States with the Davy Crocket hat and, a little bit later, the hula hoop indicated that television could now accentuate the fashion dynamic in the toy market and help a product achieve instant recognition. Thus 'cultural penetration' became integral to modern toy-marketing as a way of capitalizing on the national scale of consumption.

Play became the visible unifying mode in children's mass culture – bringing together in common possession and use the areas of daily life and custom previously marked by more local traditions, history and ethnic composition. Across North America, children began to want to own and play with the same toys, to play the same sports or games with the same rules and the same equipment. Mass-produced playthings, like compulsory schooling, reflected the universalizing expectations increasingly shaping children's socialization and pene-trating North American culture. The mass marketing of toys was just one of the ways of forging a unifying bond across the diversity of North American childhood.

A Bear Market

The refinements in manufacturing processes ensured that factory-made dolls, doll's houses, vehicles, rattles, blocks, puzzles, balls and marbles were quickly competing in the market with craft objects of a similar nature. But factories and mass-production methods also enabled toys to be produced in ever greater abundance and distributed more broadly in the market, at modest cost. The scope of the mass market in turn encouraged some local manufacturers to reconsider the possibilities of national distribution and to conceive of new designs and uses for children's toys to match the changing dynamics of the age.

The gathering of industrial forces around children's play at the turn of the century was clearly witnessed in one of the toys that now stands as an emblem both of children's innocence and their simple emotional attachments to their playthings – the teddy bear, introduced to the United States early in the turn of the century. No other toy so successfully symbolized the growing mood of universality engulfing childhood, or left such a lasting impression in children's culture. The teddy bear was first marketed in 1906 by the Ideal Toy Company under a licensing agreement with Theodore Roosevelt. Teddy's appearance and his soft, furry, cuddly nature appealed to children in a way that adults could understand: it represented the child's innocence and emotional attachment to animals. Meanwhile teddy's popularity immediately revealed to toy manufacturers how new conceptions of childhood were beginning to influence the design of products.

More significantly, the teddy bear's success proved an important point about the link between toys and children's culture. Teddy's identity as a bear was originally associated with Roosevelt's 'conservation' stand on forestry and resource issues. Product endorsements were a part of political campaigning at the time but few had focused on children's toys. Bears, however, seemed a thematically appropriate hook on which to hang Roosevelt's political campaign. An encounter with a bear that Roosevelt refused to shoot because it was across a state boundary stimulated a newspaper cartoon depicting the hunting scene. The cartoon was in turn the stimulus for Ideal's president to seek a licensing arrangement for the teddy bear. The bear provided a popular focus for Roosevelt's stand on conservation as well as a clearly identifiable – amiable but strong – personification of the president.

It is not clear whether the teddy bear was originally intended for children at all. Licensed dolls had been used in promotions before that time. P.T. Barnum, the great innovator in promotional gimmicks, had sold over fifty thousand Jenny Lind dolls in support of the Swedish soprano's legendary tour of the United States in 1855. Similarly, R.F. Outcault's comic-strip character Buster Brown inspired a host of products, including shoes, sweets, clothes and toys – enough to rent a museum of his own. Character promotions for children's goods were already clearly in evidence in turn-of-the-century America. Over his career Roosevelt had himself endorsed other products, so that the teddy bear took pride of place alongside Rough Rider Tea and a variety of other products associated with Roosevelt's rise to fame. However much this venture into image politics helped the election, the teddy bear's association with either Roosevelt or conservation was outlived by its strong impact on the toy market. In providing a valuable lesson about the role of publicity in the mass marketing of toys, teddy turned out to be the godfather of the nationally loved character toy.

Bears, of course, were deeply ensconced in children's folk culture and in this sense teddy fitted neatly into a familiar cultural universe that stretches from Goldilocks to Yogi Bear and beyond. Yet once embodied as a toy, teddy quickly lost his direct connection with Roosevelt and established himself as a generic children's plaything– the fluffy, soft, lovable animal companion. A toy was something children could cuddle and caress – a powerful symbol of childhood affection embodied in toy form. Children responded to a teddy's cuddliness with a depth of attachment they gave to few other objects. This helped toy makers to realize that children's relations to goods are grounded in emotion and not in rational choice.

The vision of universal childhood attachment to a lovable toy was quickly popularized in many illustrations of family life, in ads and stories about childhood, and indeed was enhanced by innumerable children's books that, like *Winnie the Pooh*, made personable bears into fixtures in children's fiction as well as the constant companions of children. Indeed, plush toys have today become the standard companions of early childhood, given at birth as tokens of the emotional latitude that should be allowed children. The marketing of the teddy bear, therefore, was to provide the first index of a reformulation of public thinking about socialization and children's play that extends unbroken into our own era: Teddy Ruxpin and the Care Bears are merely the inheritors of this legacy, which made toy animal companions the iconography of emotional innocence. Plush toys remain a major force in children's lives, accounting to almost 20 per cent of the contemporary toy market: bears still make up 53 per cent of all plush toys sold, giving a sense of the stability established around this unifying play value.

The Maturation of Play

If the teddy bear opened a gateway to childhood by establishing a new archetype of the plaything in popular consciousness, toy makers were quick to realize that national marketing was opening up the possibility of redefining attitudes towards play. Toys would sell only when parents willingly accepted the purpose of providing toys to children. The expansion of toy-manufacturing throughout this century depended on emerging attitudes towards children's play and the creation of new social forums in which toys were used as the tools of socialization. Manufacturers realized that demand was contingent upon changing social attitudes and practices.

Recognizing the need to consolidate the educational use of toys, by 1903 the American Toy Manufacturers' Association began to issue pamphlets advising on the maturational benefits of toys. The idea had been circulating in educational circles for a long time, but now the toy manufacturers consciously endeavoured to promote the perception of toys as instruments of education and vital to a child's development. Although many of the turn-of-the-century toys were simply variations on traditional forms – dolls, carved pull toys, noise-makers, puzzles and manipulation games – their place in social-ization was beginning to be dramatically reinterpreted. Toys not only became a regular feature of the kindergarten and nursery environ-ment but were also bolstered by new educational theories of development. Toys were being seen by parents as appropriate gifts for their young – as symbols of the bonds of love and affection at Christmas and on birthdays.

The lowering of per unit costs ensured that toys were available in greater profusion. This also implied that the dynamics of demand and price were to play as great a part in shaping the uses of toys as manufacturing methods and materials. Indeed, a much more com-plex social process was also shaping the toy market, rooted as it was in the interplay between industrial production and national market distribution. Popularity and parental acceptance turned out to be a significant requirement of the continued expansion of production, and the emphasis shifted to the manufacturing of 'demand'. The twentieth century's broad rethinking of 'childhood' was crucial to the toy makers, and in its changing social relations of familial consumption the fate of the modern toy took shape.

Market demand has always been rooted in broader social attitudes and practices. Long before there were toy factories, the industrial values of hard work and seriousness had already significantly under-mined the legitimacy of many traditional forms of play, games and sport as community rituals. Gradually during the nineteenth century play became an activity more narrowly associated with the protected realm of childhood and therefore with the innocence, freedom and psychological immaturity associated with children. By the end of the nineteenth century play was being thought of as the 'stuff of childhood', the special means by which the young prepared for and adjusted to the world. Writers and educators of the time began to extol play as having three advantages in socializing the young: play was a way of harmlessly releasing excess energy, of rehearsing the skills necessary for adulthood through enjoyable practice, and of working and mastering maturational problems through recapitulation in fantasy.[10] These virtues brought play as an issue into the arguments of the playground and youth movements, the sporting movement and the attempts to encourage the use of play within schools. Play became the legitimate means of socialization in the industrial era and an excellent means of social control without force. A popular new conception of play as the 'work of childhood' emerged in the twentieth century, and toys appeared to be the natural tools of this work. This attitude circumscribed and fuelled the demand for toys.

Many new toy designs originated with the need to supply the playgrounds, youth groups and schools with a means of structuring children's play activities with objects and equipment.[11] Turn-of-the-century teachers or play leaders thought of play equipment (at first mainly playground and sports equipment) as useful in promoting appropriate patterns of development (co-ordination, will, concentration, hard work, team co-operation, obedience). They had the added hope that the new play venues would distract children and draw them away from the less esteemed but often popular activities of street play and petty crime.

For these reasons, sports, play and arts activities were increasingly integrated into school curriculums and organized community activities (scouts, Sunday schools) for children promoted. Influenced by nineteenth-century pedagogical theories, toys were already being used in some kindergartens: sand boxes and puzzles, tops, balls and skipping ropes were accepted as useful preoccupations for young learners, ways to facilitate the transition from home to school. Specially built playthings were also being invented and tested by the more innovative turn-of-the-century educationalists. Maria Montessori, for example, devised a number of toy-like learning devices for helping the formation of mathematical concepts. Playskool, an important US toy manufacturer, got its start in 1923 producing hammer-and-peg games for children. During the 1930s in London, Susan Isaacs began her well-known work with children by organizing the kindergarten classroom around sociodramatic and role-play activities that included dress-up, domestic equipment, and the 'wendy house'. Miniature sets of household, workshop and medical equipment were similarly prescribed for preparing the young at home, to supplement the board and card games, construction sets, puzzles and crayons.

The manufacturing plans of toy makers were to benefit from a new breed of educational toy inspired by this idea that play was the primary teaching technique of early education. As the conception of the uses of toys broadened to encompass the social, emotional and conceptual development of the child, new toys were introduced into both home and school. The rationale for this new commitment to play was the belief that it laid down in sensation and experience the basis for all learning:

> Because he cannot learn in the 'real' world by doing 'real' things which would be too large, too dangerous, too difficult, too complicated he has to play in a protected situation where the world is presented in a manageable form – toy cars, toy dolls, building material and raw materials in safe, controlled quantities, pretend situations and relationships.[12]

New teaching methods were used in nursery schools and kinder-gartens because play was 'the starting point for cognitive development'. In the British Department of Education (where this philosophy was taken to heart in the 1960s), a document stated the pedagogical benefits: 'In play, children gradually develop concepts of causal relationships, the power to discriminate, to make judgements to analyze and synthesize, to imagine and to formulate.'

Play was accepted and valued as an excellent instrument of social learning by teachers and psychologists mainly because of a child's apparent intensity, autonomy and involvement in it. This aspect of volunteerism and self-production seems to imply a depth of experience and creativity that distinguished play from the traditional patterns of rote memory and rehearsal learning. The Swiss developmental psychologist Jean Piaget buttressed these educators' arguments with his observations about the role of symbolic play in developing the rudimentary cognitive schemas of children.[13] In play children appear to be less resistant to being taught because they are more intensely engaged in the learning: the depth of engagement with toys seems to speak of a quality of involvement that serves important functions of psychological adjustment. Throughout the twentieth century parents have been urged by popular advisors to make sure their young children are given adequate opportunities to play.[14]

Eric Erikson urged parents to recognize the psychological as well as educational benefits of fantasy play in which a child 'condenses into scenes of unitary place and time, marked by a set and populated by a cast, the tragic and comic dilemma of representative individuals caught in the role conflicts of their time'.[15] Seeing play as a form of social and emotional learning, Erikson was to 'propose the theory that the child's play is the infantile form of the human ability to deal with experience by creating model situations and to master reality by experiment and planning'. The value of play is that in 'utilizing his mastery over objects, the child can arrange them in such a way that they permit him to imagine that he is master of his life predicament as well'. Erikson felt this point was particularly important in reconciling children to their social as well as their physical limitations.

Children, therefore, should be encouraged to play out their inner feelings and thoughts in order to gain mastery over them and give harmless expression to unconscious ideas. As Bruno Bettelheim was to advocate:

> When there is no immediate danger it is best to approve of the child's play without interfering, just because he is so engrossed in it. Efforts to assist him in his struggles, while well intentioned, may divert him from seeking and eventually finding the solution that will serve him best.[16]

Play should not be censored, and to some degree parents should let children play by themselves and with their peers.

This principle of engagement in the play process was also central to the perceived educational benefits it afforded. In play children experiment and plan and in so doing apply pre-established concepts and test them out. They are building basic intellectual structures that serve their cognitive growth. Jean Piaget, the greatest exponent of the educational value of symbolic play, argued:

> Symbolic play is the apogee of children's play ... it corresponds to the essential function that play fulfils in the life of the child. Obliged to adapt himself constantly to a social world of elders whose interests and rules remain external to him, and to a physical world which he understands only slightly, the child does not succeed as we adults do in satisfying the affective and even intellectual needs of his personality through these adaptations. It is indispensible to his affective and intellectual equilibrium, therefore that he have available to him an area of activity whose

154

motivation is not adaptation to reality, but on the contrary, assimilation of reality to the self.... Such an area is play, which transforms reality by assimilation to the needs of the self, whereas imitation is accommodation to the external models.[17]

Such arguments underwrote an acceptance of the notion that all forms of play were important for growing children, and that the kinds of objects used in play mattered less than the degree of being engrossed in play. Other contributors to this argument have advocated training exercises in imagining as a way of enhancing the role of this kind of play in schools.[18] This cumulative emphasis on the benefits of imaginative play created a situation in which toys were rarely criticized and rarely denied to children.

There was early evidence of the reconceptualizing of toys as developmental tools in some of the games developed for children over the last one hundred years. Parker Bros, Playskool and Milton Bradley are three of the toy companies whose origins lay in the conceiving of 'educational' games for the expanding market. Well before the turn of the century, card games, checkers and simple board games were well established as rainy-day activities that children enjoyed and parents accepted because they preoccupied their children. 'I spy' and 'twenty questions' were among the social pastimes handed down in families. Similarly, puzzle-solving, strategy games such as chess and guessing games were thought to invoke basic problem-solving and analysis skills and promote better memory in children. These traditional pastimes could be made up into sets and sold as educational aids. But the game makers' marketing plans also quickly included the development of new games for the home, which like Scrabble or Clue supplemented a child's formal education. The traditional board and card games of snakes and ladders and checkers were quickly joined in the contemporary games market by a broader spectrum of acceptable preoccupations for children: card games (Old Maid), knowledge and guessing games (Trivial Pursuit, Memory and Junior Scrabble), societal games (Monopoly and Stock Ticker), manipulation and co-ordination games (Tiddly Winks and Hungry Hippos, and strategy games (Risk and Dungeons and Dragons).

Games are broadly educational. All games at least teach children to play together and to follow rules. Competitiveness ensures that games are interesting to play. Parents have perceived that the sociality of game play and the implicit structure game play provides for social interaction are important benefits – especially if the games also help children while away a rainy afternoon. This same rationale of 'useful preoccupation' has been picked up and promoted throughout the history of mass marketed toys. Computer and electronic games were promoted, however, around the same educational benefits that earlier board and card games promised, minus the social interaction. And if improved eye–hand co-ordination and hours of wide-eyed rapture are not sufficient to convince the reluctant parent, computer games marketers argue that at least children using the games acquire the familiar skills that a computer generation needs.[19] A major boom–bust cycle resulted as the toy companies competed with computer companies (Atari, Commodore) in the computer games market with electronic and educational products during the late 1970s. Riding on the 'educational' aura of computers, electronic toys generated a lot of excitement in the early 1980s and most of the major players, such as Mattel and Coleco, invested heavily in what they saw as the 'future' of their sector. Sales amounted to almost a billion dollars by 1981, but the bust was even bigger as the novelty wore off and it became recognized that the poorly written software did not deliver continual play value. Coleco's consumer electronics division lost $258 million in 1983. Meanwhile, with the educational pretence abandoned, the new dedicated 'entertainment' systems introduced in the mid 1980s grossed $4 billion in US sales by 1990.

But pitching toys as maturational aids remains a central tenet of mass toy-marketing. The nature of this parental demand was clearly understood and accommodated by the toy makers as the basis for much of their communication about the benefits of play. The contemporary popularity of preschool educational toys reminds us how a deep concern with children's mental development that took root in American attitudes also provided the foundation of the preschool market. In the rapidly changing conditions of the postwar period it proved possible to introduce new toys into the market to the degree that the products matched prevailing parental attitudes and social practices. Toy companies had to learn how to cultivate trends and parlay those trends into growth markets. Fisher-Price's continuity as a force in the toy market is testimony to its appreciation of the basis of consumer preferences for developmental toys. The company always understood that parents – and especially mothers – would buy certain toys, even if they were mass produced, if those toys seemed likely to provide suitable experiences for their youngsters 'by engaging and stimulating' them. Fisher-Price remained true to this concept and focused its marketing on the delivery of toys that parents wanted their young children to have. The company cultivated a market for educational toys, transforming it into an ever larger array of 'tools' for meeting the intellectual needs of the preschooler. The company fortunes depended in large part on trends in parental concern.[20] These optimistic ideas about the benefits of play are now so deeply engrained in popular attitudes that they constitute a dogma for early socialization.[21] Few indeed are the critics who have challenged or opposed the growing importance of toys in education and contemporary childrearing or analysed why particular toys get to market. The violence and aggression associated with war toys seems to be the only reservation that teachers have extended to the growing role of free play in the modern classroom, although there is some professional debate over what kinds of toys are best.[22] Parents interviewed showed a similar concern with war toys. A few also expressed a vague sense that their children had too many toys and that somehow they weren't getting as much out of them as they might have got out of a single, much cherished toy.

The Industrialization of Demand

As toy production gradually shifted into post-industrial gear, toy makers had to develop new attitudes towards management – towards technology, planning and the design and distribution of their products – if they were to survive in a competitive market. They faced essentially the same management dilemma as all businesses relying on the increasingly national markets to offset capital investment and achieve lower per unit production costs.[23] The trick was to have very popular toys. To achieve the new larger-scale factory production, toy-making became increasingly capital-intensive rather than labour-intensive; in consequence toy makers replaced the security of traditional demand with a reliance on marketing as an important criterion in production planning and product design. They had to balance the potential of far greater losses against the introduction of a new product line with its increased retooling and advertising costs. Herein lay a complex and dangerous dynamic of growth, for manufacturing innovations and the introduction of new products depended upon the consolidation of demand through marketing. Knowing how to negotiate through the complex undercurrents of merchandising became the vital craft knowledge of the surviving toy maker.

The logic of industrial merchandising is witnessed in the corporate history of Lego. This toy company, founded in Denmark and later bought out by a US corporation, was selling over $1 billion of toys worldwide annually. The case of Lego is particularly interesting because it reveals how new materials and industrial processes involved with the development of plastic were essential to the toy designs that increasingly emerged after the Second World War. Plastic was an expensive material but whose production technology vastly reduced the costs of labour and materials. It could also be moulded with great precision and variety, giving it considerable flexibility as a construction toy. The advantages of plastic guaranteed the lightness and mobility of the hula-hoop, the physiognomic detail of the Barbie doll, the verisimilitude of model airplanes, the motility of transformers, and the durability of the Rubik's Cube joints.

Lego originated with Kirk Christiansen, a Danish woodworker who in 1932 had diversified into making wooden toys including dolls' furniture, yo-yos and construction sets. Like other toy makers after the war, Christiansen turned to construction and modelling sets which, following Lincoln Logs and Meccano, were gaining popularity with the baby boom's parents. Such toys were an advance on the more traditional building blocks yet presented much the same demands – for concentration, eye–hand co-ordination, and patience – thus providing benefits that parents appreciated. Christiansen's experimentation with the idea of a quality learning 'construction' toy led in 1955 to the development of the 'Lego System', plastic bricks that easily snapped together and could be combined to build different objects, from cars to houses to monsters.

A Lego executive later attributed the longevity of the plastic bricks to Christiansen's discovery of a 'type of play that transcends [a product] label'.[24] But it is probably more accurate to say that the success of Lego was assured by the company's shrewd modification of its products based on a marketing analysis of the demand for toys. While concentrating on the proved construction toy niche, Lego chose to stratify and diversify its product line. Lego historian notes, 'Children pass through an incredible process of development during their first five years, and their toys must live up to their needs ... it is important to clarify the demands that can be made on each age group in order that every set can hold a challenge which the child can undertake with pleasure.' Rather than toys for all time, successful marketing demanded that toy makers understand that kids need to experience challenges appropriate to their age and maturation level.

Lego devised an age-related strategy for its product line: by bringing out Duplo, essentially the same toy in a larger, more easily manipulated version, for younger children, the company made construction play accessible to the very young. Moreover, children could work their way up the Lego ladder of products, thus achieving a strong brand identity from a very early age.

In 1966, to keep up with a changing market, Lego designers took another step forward by introducing model sets that included building instructions. These predesigned models seemed to extend the time children were willing to spend at play and they added the element of learning to follow plans. The introduction of thematic sets no longer accorded with Christiansen's original philosophy of using bricks to build anything at all, but it helped reposition Lego in the market, and even though it was less open to children's innovation, it ensured their enjoyment and loyalty to the product line.

Similarly, the longest surviving toy manufacturer in the United States grew out of simple innovations necessitated by industrial production and national marketing techniques. Fisher-Price, a small company founded in the early 1930s, adapted mass-production techniques to produce, as a first line of toys, sixteen wooden pull toys – ducks and horses – that looked like traditional craft toys but were produced in much greater quantities than was previously possible. The company was founded on the belief that mass-produced toys could combine 'intrinsic play value, ingenuity, strong construction and good value for money and action'. In its recognition of parents' desire to aid learning through toys, Fisher-Price found the basis for promoting a new line of worthwhile and quality gifts for the young.[25]

The production of toys accelerated dramatically as postwar affluence and the baby boom intensified demand. Over the next forty years, innovation in design and the introduction of popular new toys became the standard tactic for corporate survival. By the late 1980s, for example, Fisher-Price was introducing about fifty new toys into the market each year, on the assumption that only a few would become popular enough to last. The continuing innovation in design, however, had to be supplemented with an accumulation of expertise in production methods and materials. A company had to understand the basis of demand, although overspecialization in a particular line or sector could also be a hazard. Toy makers in general were beset by the standard problems of corporate growth and product innovation; many were reorganized or bought out by larger firms with deeper experience in mass-distribution methods. The toy industry has known its share of turmoil. Increasing corporate concentration and specialized marketing seems to characterize the survivors of the toy market.

Of the major toy companies who were merchandising over 60 per cent of the toys in the United States by the mid 1980s (including Coleco, Kenner, Mattel, Hasbro, Tonka) only Fisher-Price had started corporate life as a traditional toy maker as far back as the 1930s. Mattel got its start in the marketing-intensive merchandising environment after the war, and others, including Coleco and Hasbro, moved into toy production after starting by trading in other areas such as leather goods, hat liners, and pencil boxes.[26] Fisher-Price itself became part of the Quaker Oats empire, and Lego was taken over by Samsonite. By the 1970s toy production had become part of vertically and horizontally integrated corporate strategies. What the shift in ownership indicates is both the appreciation of the economic potential of toy merchandising and the way non-toy strategies were increasingly shaping the toy industry. Toy-making emerged as just another sector of the highly concentrated industrial economy.

A willingness to test new product concepts in the market distinguished the US toy makers and led to a number of innovations in toy design and marketing methods. Research became the hallmark of this approach to marketing. Many of the new toys introduced in the 1960s emerged only after extensive testing; others were inspired by the insights garnered in research. For example, through its simple observations of children, Fisher-Price began to realize the fascination that ordinary household technology held for children. Introducing the Chatterphone in 1962, the company proved how simple and easily manipulated objects offered a vast potential market. Throughout the 1960s it continued to extend its traditional lines with brightly coloured, safe and durable plastic toys: lever-pulling crib sets, noise-making manipulation and pull toys, brightly coloured counting and shape toys, and record-player music boxes. Through its attention to developmental benefits and careful research, Fisher-Price established a reputation for producing excellent maturational toys and came to dominate the preschool market, with gross world sales of over \$2 billion by 1989. The company became a keen believer in research and the careful observation of children's use of the new toy designs. It used its nursery school laboratory to refine toys for specific cognitive operations. Object manipulations, which researchers such as Jean Piaget had been able to encourage with simple everyday objects (keys, matchboxes), were reworked as toys that promoted particular conceptual or technical operations. Focusing jointly on learning and the preschool market, the company became adept at coming up with toy designs for the anxious coterie of 'concerned' parents who wanted to accelerate their child's intellectual growth. Toys were designed around a 'unique' learning task at a particular maturation level, implying that the children would quickly outgrow the toys and move on to others.

Fisher-Price's position of dominance in the preschool market reveals how important the tactic of concentrating corporate resources can be for adjusting to the changing circumstances of competitive merchandising. Corporate planning had to consolidate both manufacturing and marketing expertise while giving clear definition to corporate or brand identity. Fisher-Price developed its reputation for early developmental toys by specializing in durable toys that demanded simple manipulation and taught basic skills to young children. It sometimes proved wiser not to produce a whole range of toys but rather to focus expertise on a given product sector or a particular market demand – managing diversity within narrower limits. The consequence of specialization, however, is a fragmentation of play – a fantastic diversity of toys with little difference in function or play value. Hasbro has excelled in marketing action and fantasy toys; R. Dakin and Co has likewise emerged as the leading maker of plush toys.[27]

Knowing Consumers

In the emerging age of affluence, toys and games focused the social vision that increasingly ascribed freedom to childhood. These values were appreciated readily by toy manufacturers when they multiplied them by the demographic pressures that promised increased demand for toys. Between 1950 and 1987, spending by parents on their children rose faster than disposable income, for childrearing had become an expensive venture. The average first baby was demanding an initial $2500 expenditure in the United States, a sum that increased steadily as the child progressed through to college.

Toy makers had to become careful observers of the social trends influencing parental consumers. A research industry grew up to feed demographic, attitudinal and lifestyle information to the market planners as a vast array of social data proved necessary for understanding the changes in demand that would determine the fate of a new toy. Hasbro's Playskool division, for example, competing with Fisher-Price in the preschool market notes:

> that with over 50% of mothers of preschool children in the workforce, young parents increasingly are interested in products that occupy their children's time and attention. Playskool's focus on innovation reflects the emphasis that young couples place on products that have developmental and learning attributes as well as play and entertainment value.[28]

Harried parents wanted toys that preoccupied as well as educated. Such sociological interpretation clearly had become a valued means by which the toy makers adjusted to the new family conditions of postwar affluence and developed their merchandising strategy.

Retailers and marketers realized too that the willingness to spend more money on children – and especially on individual gifts or acquisitions for them – presented a market opportunity for any manufacturer that could take advantage of changing attitudes and childrearing practices. These changes were abundantly discussed in the literature of the time, but more significantly toy makers were beginning to encounter them in their in-house marketing research and their studies of children's play. The need to adjust to the baby boom forced toy makers to rethink the place of toys in the context of contemporary family life and to rethink the idea of children's marketing.

Consumerism gave all objects, but particularly toys, new meaning within the practices of socialization. With their emphasis on self-expression, exploration and fun, toys represented a bond of love that fuelled their popularity as Christmas gifts. In the 1950s toys achieved 80 per cent of their annual sales at Christmas time, when establishing a child's happiness peaked on the family agenda. Toys embodied the idea that successful families consisted of children who were thoroughly contented in their idle or leisure moments. As Brian Sutton-Smith notes, the toy idealized the familial bonds of love being forged through the toy as gift: 'The modern idea is that we are giving children or others a gift to show our love or friendship . . . but the gift helps to maintain the social bond between the parties, parents and children.'[29]

The relations of the modern family were built on ideas about emotion and freedom.[30] A perceived intensity of needing, an impulsiveness in the marketplace and a decreasing willingness to delay, defer or channel gratification were the basis of an expanding consumer credit. The same patterns of feeling that permeated family

162

life were unwittingly conveyed to children through discussion, identification and modelling, so that the behaviour of parents, siblings and friends helped to build a mood of excitement that infused consumption generally and toys specifically.

A father's return home from the workplace might be greeted by an eager toddler expecting a small treat. Such gifts reveal how the new ideas and childrearing practices that used reward rather than punishment as a means of social control could influence patterns of demand. As fear and respect became proportionally less important dimensions of family interaction, parents expected children to bring their immediate desires and behaviour under conscious control for the sake of promised future rewards. The subtle skills of negotiation and guilt, of love and its withdrawal, lay at the roots of bourgeois family practice, which was embodied in the 'treat'. With the decline of authority, the contemporary parent was forced to substitute force with new psychological instruments for rewarding appropriate conduct: snacks, sweets, toys and television-viewing privileges became the tangible negotiated rewards – the reasons for channelling immediate desires into parentally accepted conduct.

Increasingly, toy designers had to take into account children's response to those ambiguous symbols of love. Although children rarely purchased their toys directly, their enjoyment of their toys had a great influence on their parents' decision-making. One of the first researchers to investigate children's marketing labelled this new factor 'passive dictation', a matter of 'mothers observing what their children consume willingly and what they resist, and govern their purchases accordingly'.[31] Parents wanting to provide their young with useful experiences increasingly chose toys that made their children appear happiest as well as publicly docile and contented.

Towards Marketing to Children

Prewar toy advertising only occasionally expressed an interest in selling directly to children and rarely did the ads themselves refer to children's participation in household decision-making. The absence of these references reflects the limits of marketing's interest in the child. For half a century the child depicted in advertising was merely a symbol of consumer aspirations – a way of interesting a parent in a product, or of referring to children's growing expanding consumer needs.

James McNeal, a noted researcher into children's marketing, has defined marketing's orientation to children as consisting of three analytically separable parts: because children purchase goods; because they are an influence on their families' purchases (mainly by moms); and because they are prospective customers who will at some later date decide to buy goods or services. In the early 1950s there were few far-sighted industrialists who were interested enough in long-term markets to get seriously involved in the broader social effort of consumer socialization. There was little awareness of children's consumption practices or influences on the family. It was not until the late 1950s that marketers began to recognize the conditions that would transform children into a real market.

Classic marketing theory postulated that a market exists only under specific circumstances, in which the following conditions are met:

1. the product is needed by a group;
2. individuals have authority to buy the product;
3. they have the money to make the purchase; and
4. they must be willing to use that money for that purchase.

Before 1955, marketers generally believed that children did not meet these conditions and therefore there was little interest in them. Marketing is interested in consumer power, and children lacked that power. In the 1950s, innovations in marketing by toy merchandisers began to challenge this assumption.

During that decade the marketers' attention increasingly focused on attempts to bring the more affluent and accessible teenage baby boomers into the market. The youth emphasis of the late 1950s and early 1960s, along with the saturation of certain consumer markets, helped to awaken marketers to the ascendance of this segment. Indeed, they expended much effort and gained practical experience in marketing to teens, learning about the growing consumer power and peer influence of adolescents.

Marketing's interest in the teenage market went beyond that of socializing future consumers. The boomers, it was discovered, were growing up and beginning to be serious spenders. More importantly, they were not buying the same products as their parents and they were using their media differently. Advertisers were the first to take note of the 'trend of the 12–24 market becoming more independent. This is a very important market segment since this is when buying habits are being set. But due to their on the go lifestyle, it's a difficult market to reach and motivate.'[32] Even more of a problem for the advertisers, the television-viewing of baby boomers was not increasing as quickly as the viewing of other audiences. As a result, new distribution systems had to be nurtured for youth products. Advertisers learned to address youth in new ways (music), through a specific medium (radio) and use advertising styles and appeals geared to their interests. The importance of cultural style, resistance and the supposed inner reality of teen lives, helped marketers discover ways of adjusting their sales pitch by emphasizing the peer situation and youth-cult sensibility. In short, it was marketing that discovered the youth subculture. Marketers appreciated that this subculture was a separate way of life built around a cohesiveness, mutual interest and belonging, as well as its own set of shared symbols, language, idols and rituals. Business with a stake in the youth market became sensitized to the need to invoke these distinct cultural stylistics as a crucial part of the marketing process.

Two crucial psychological lessons were learned and applied during this period, lessons that crystallized marketing's full recognition of youth culture. The first was the need to create 'special symbols' or situations for the youth market niche, and the second was the use of peer group processes as a means of social involvement and persuasion. Together these approaches combined to create the 'youth ethos' that helped to manage youth as a separate part of the marketplace.

Communicating with children was harder. There were few successful magazines aimed at youngsters, children read little that contained advertising – newspapers, for example – and on the radio they listened mainly to family programming until they were in their teens. Kids' films were not an advertising medium. The points of contact between the marketplace and children were few and unsuited to advertising. So it fell to television to open up new lines of communication with children making marketing to young children possible.

A few merchandisers had been directing their messages to families in the hopes that children might influence their parents. Kellogg, for example, financed a pioneering research effort on children's attitudes towards various product brands, confirming that older children held strong preferences for particular food products.[33] Some national advertisers therefore tried television to test the possibility of an influential children's market based on these preferences. Several breakfast food companies that had sponsored radio programmes decided to transfer their accounts to family-orientated prime-time television. At first these ventures were clearly limited to a narrow band of product ranges in which influential marketing was already a tradition: cereal, snack food and toothpaste.

This is why Disney's *Mickey Mouse Club* television programme was such an innovation in children's marketing: it focused on the notion of peer culture. The club was intended to parlay Mickey's established popularity with youth by including a visible and attractive peer group whose adventures and exploits provided the narrative link to the pot-pourri of other animated and dramatic offerings. Daily 'meetings' of the club hosted by a range of kids of all ages provided the pretext, but the mouse-clubbers also featured in live-action drama and intro-duced the Disney cartoons. Mickey Mouse was simply the integrating personality of the mouse-club clan, a gang who wore mouse-club ears and espoused Disney values.

Prior to the *Mickey Mouse Club*, children's television advertising totalled only about $1 million and the product array was narrow. Mr Potato Head might have been the first toy advertised on television in 1952, but generally toy manufacturers were on record as believing that they would thrive without mass market advertising. Television advertising formats, especially before the development of videotape technology, consisted solely of sponsorship announcements and product demonstrations. TV was only beginning to gain a hold over the children's audience. Children often preferred playing on the street to watching funny men with puppets in the electronic toy box. Only someone of Disney's reputation could induce NBC to envision the *Mickey Mouse Club* programme as a route to a mass audience composed of children. The programme was put together by finding twenty advertisers willing to buy at least $500,000 of time for the first series. Mattel was the only toy company to partake of this outrageous gamble, and was rewarded by pride of place among the cereal, toothpaste and sweet ads.

The *Mickey Mouse Club* was a fantastic success. Kids, it turned out, flocked to the screens to see a more engaging programme tailored to their very own cultural inclinations. If they didn't have their own set, they went over to the neighbours to watch – and they watched regularly. For the first time television had offered a programming format for children that could provide up to 90 per cent exposure ratings and a loyal audience. The scene was thus set for marketing more directly to children.

The *Mickey Mouse Club* also provided a first glimpse at an exclusively children's subculture formed by television. Advertisers could now direct their communication specifically at children – to explore new ways to shape children's wants and win their influence within the family circle. Television advertising to children rose quickly, from about $25 million a year by 1956 to about $750 million by 1987. In opening up a vision of children's culture, television brought the children's segment from the fringes of influential marketing into the inner regions of targeted marketing. The growth of children's advertising thus highlights a fifth condition for the existence of modern marketing: there must be a means by which the marketplace can communicate with consumers. It is in this respect that television contributed to children's marketing proper – that is, marketing communication directed specifically at the child.

Mass Marketing and the Age of Television

Through the *Mickey Mouse Club* a number of businesses began to explore the new possibilities of mass advertising. Mattel, one of the most innovative of the toy companies, had become fascinated with the potential of television. Mattel had been producing a limited range of musical products and now found that its Mouse Guitar – actually a wind-up music box in a ukulele with mouse ears – benefited enormously from the association with the club, which included a good deal of group singing and guitar strumming by the Mouse-keteers. Mattel attempted to expand its television advertising and during the 1960s sought to duplicate its success with mousemania by introducing product promotions based on a principle enunciated by children's marketing guru Cy Schneider as: 'A brand that is popular with children takes on a meaning far beyond personal preference.' A toy 'character takes on special meaning in the same way. There is peer pressure within the child's world to use the right one – a pressure that doesn't exist to the same degree with adults.'[34]

These early campaigns had demonstrated to Mattel that mass advertising could result in purchase and overcome parental resistance to particular kinds of toys. Mattel's Burp Gun was one of the first toy products to be introduced through intensive television advertising. Within one month of the first ads Mattel noted that the demand for Burp Gun was going to outstrip all the campaign's expectations. The Mattel brand name and the slogan 'You can tell it's Mattel, it's swell', which featured significantly in all its advertisements, seemed to register with kids. Using a TV commercial featuring a young boy as a pint-sized sheriff stalking around the living-room with big-game pictures projected on to walls, Mattel was to become the pacesetter for a generation of new toy manufacturers.

In the years following these early efforts, television advertising would have a major impact on the toy industry. As Sidney Stern and Ted Schoenhaus state:

> The most important effect of national television advertising in Toyland was not the growth of the industry or the increase in off-season sales or even the change to a demand- instead of a supply-driven market. It was more subtle than any of these, but at the same time more profound: the growing importance of television advertising changed the nature of toys themselves.[35]

The toy product emerged from a very different kind of development and research process. Stern and Schoenhaus quote Russ Alben, Mattel account manager:

> We were shaping products to the needs of the television eye and ear ... what a successful plaything must be able to do to perform in the commercial to sell itself at its best.... We strove to identify the single-minded preemptive qualities which would distinguish our toys from those of our competitors.

Mattel was likewise the innovator in using market research in the development of its toys. It didn't just monitor sales on a weekly basis, it used focus groups and other qualitative studies. Children obviously couldn't afford to buy the Burp Guns themselves, the toys were too expensive. They had to convince their parents to buy them and to sympathize with the urgencies of faddish children's products. The Burp Gun was hard to justify on the grounds of enhancing education and skills. Children had effectively to lessen their parents' concern to have only educational toys and convey how important the special nature of this object was to them. The success of this television promotion was enough to convince some toy marketers that it was possible to change the family dynamics around consumption by TV campaigns directed at children.[36]

As academic research subsequently confirmed, Mattel was right. Children's personal preferences could be targeted and altered by television advertising.[37] More importantly, advertising could aid children's influence in the family, arming them with strong preferences for their negotiations with parents.[38] Television advertising proved a successful weapon for changing family dialogue. The evidence was that kids who watched a lot of television, and who zeroed in on commercials, began to make more requests for specific goods in the supermarket. Heavy advertising therefore increased children's influence and consumer 'power'. As one marketing analyst baldly states: 'The trend is for children to get more decision making authority and exercise that authority at a younger and younger age.'[39]

Children, by way of consequence, were gaining experience and expertise in responding to marketing communications. They learned how to identify and respond appropriately to advertising and promotions aimed at them. Research has shown that by five years of age about 50 per cent of children understand the persuasive purposes of advertising.[40] By eight, almost all know that advertising is intended to make them buy things. Moreover, they do have the ability to formulate product choice: they think about more than one attribute of a product, and in certain product areas they base their decisions on product information.[41]

As their research investigated children's responses to promotional material, marketers became more aware of the development of kids' preferences. It was clear that marketing to children, as elsewhere, necessitated prying open new areas of experience – the miniature universe of the children's orientation to life was distinct from the aims and rationale defined for them by the adult world. This meant examining the peer group and its influence on children's responses to advertising.[42] Toy marketers often view their research as entitling them to champion children's desires, on occasion publishing tracts attempting to resolve their apparent conflict with parental opinions.[43] But their interest in children's opinions and dreams was practical. For example, when Hasbro researchers asked little girls what they imagined in bed before they went to sleep, the answer was turned into a billion dollar series of clothed horses called My Little Ponies.

Similar qualitative research was also crucial in the development of one of the most successful toy-marketing efforts of the 1960s. Barbie – the best selling doll of all time – provided an object lesson in the role of television in marketing personality. As Cy Schneider, the former advertising agency executive who worked on the Barbie campaigns, stated: 'The people at Mattel and the agency ... began thinking of toys in an entirely new way. We began to see toys as concepts that could be depicted or demonstrated in television commercials.' Schneider provides an honest account of the detailed thought that went into Barbie's introduction into the market in 1959. Barbie was carefully and consciously designed not as just another plaything, but as a personality: 'We didn't depict Barbie as a doll. We treated her as a real-life teenage fashion model.' And so Barbie was provided with a 'back-story' – a narrative that established her personality profile within an imaginary but familiar universe.

In the campaigns to market toys on television, the role of fantasy quickly emerged as an important dimension: 'In showing our earliest television commercials to children, we also realized something more important that persists to this day. The play situation in which you place a toy becomes a fantasy for the child. The fantasy presented becomes as important as the product.'[44] Toy marketers realized that they were not so much promoting a toy's use-value as marketing a particular imaginative relationship with the toy. Barbie was not a baby doll but a fashion model; her identity was tied in with the imagery of the glamour world of teenage fashion and romance.

This 'back-story' brought the symbolic context of play into a narrative form. Barbie's attraction as a doll was that children identified with her character rather than with her 'role' as a toy. Hence the way they played with her changed. Cy Schneider points out: 'Somehow Barbie filled a very special need for little girls' imaginations. She was the fulfilment of every little girl's dream of glamour, fame, wealth and stardom.' Young girls identified with Barbie and became deeply involved with her. They didn't rehearse motherhood as they did with other dolls but spent a lot of time just staring at and admiring her in her various outfits. Some 90 per cent of their playtime was preoccupied with dressing and undressing Barbie; given this ritualistic and repetitious form of play activity, Mattel concluded that Barbie's appeal lay in her ability to evoke fantasy in the child – what went on in their heads during play. The television back-story worked and Barbie sold in the millions in the first few years after her introduction.

Through extensive product-testing Mattel also detected how important passive dictation was in the demand for playthings. Watching girls playing with Barbie, the premarketing researchers were impressed by the intensity of the identification and the vividness of fantasy that engaged the children. The activities were repetitious but the fascination with Barbie's teenage imaginary horizon was clearly more compelling than the parental roles that traditional baby dolls offered. Ironically, when the tested children's mothers were asked after watching their own girls playing with Barbie whether their daughters would want to have such a toy or whether they would buy one for their daughters, most mothers replied with an unequivocal no.[45] These moms seemed to have little understanding of the imaginative basis of their children's play or of their own susceptibility to persuasion in the stores. Mattel chose to ignore the parental point of view. What mattered was the company's research, which had convinced them of the attractiveness of the new product and of television's ability to sell it to children. Similar research helped reduce the risk of innovation throughout the toy industry; marketing decision-making increasingly demanded that children's own reactions be brought into the plan. Less obvious was the fact that through research, children themselves increasingly added their voices and their fantasies to the product development cycle.

In the course of marketing toys through television, Mattel also discovered that the peer dimension of toys was the key to 'children's marketing'. Kids liked to watch other kids on TV or in the ads for toys – to gauge their own reactions against those of other children. They were incredibly fussy about the particular kinds of kids they identified with. Adult presenters (unless well-known kids' personalities) didn't work well on kids' TV. After all, play was a form of social interaction. Children expected to see toys presented and used with others around. Promotion on television demanded that the specific toy be valued and clearly integrated into the social milieu of childhood. The ads that best shaped the formation of preference tended to set up a meaningful relationship between the toy and the children playing with it.[46]

Just as television had awakened marketers to teen subculture, 'kids peer groups' became equally a part of the dynamics of marketing toys. Children's marketing would be viewed as a cultural process – a problem of choosing a certain style and design, of demanding sensitivity to new values which matched the felt realities of the young consumer. Marketing to children required its own unique methods of product design and testing. Langbourne Rust, a noted researcher in children's marketing, summed the point up:

> Children constitute a unique market. A lot of American business is run on the assumption that everyone ... sees things in pretty much the same way. Manufacturers make products they like, advertisers make ads they find persuasive. And when the market consists of adults, especially adults that share culture and values with the producers, the system can work pretty well. With children it works less well.[47]

The reason for the difference is that kids do not share the same cultural values as the adult producers of products, and the task of research became to help marketers understand children's sense of value. Television advertising forced the toy makers to start listening to the child consumers, empowering them as consumers.

Notes

1. J. Huizinga, *Homo Ludens: A Study of the Play-Element in Culture*, Boston, Beacon Press, 1955, p. 46.

2. Ibid., p. 26.

3. Antonia Fraser, *A History of Toys*, London, Weidenfeld & Nicolson, 1966, p. 18.

4. Helen B. Schwartzman, *Transformations: The Anthropology of Children's Play*, New York, Plenum Press, 1979.

5. Jordan Thomas, *Victorian Childhood: Themes and Variations*, Albany, State University of New York Press, 1987.

6. Roland Barthes, *Mythologies* (trans. Annette Lavers), London, Paladin, 1973, p. 53.

7. Sydney Ladensohn Stern and Ted Schoenhaus, *Toyland: The High-Stakes Game of the Toy Industry*, Chicago, Contemporary Books, 1990, p. 55.

8. H. Rheingold and K.V. Cook, 'The Content of Boys' and Girls' Rooms as an Index of Parents' Behavior', *Child Development*, 46, 1975, pp. 459–63.

9. Brian Sutton-Smith, *Toys as Culture*, New York, Gardner Press, 1986.

10. K. Rubin, 'Early Play Theories Revisited: Contributions to Contemporary Research and Theory', in D. Pepler and K. Rubin, eds, *The Play of Children: Current Theory and Research*, Basel, S. Krager, 1982.

11. Richard Snyder, 'Trends in the Sporting Goods Market', in M. Marie Hart, ed., *Sport in the Socio-cultural Process*, Dubuque, Wm. C. Brown, 1972, pp. 423–44.

12. Kathleen Manning and Ann Sharp, *Structuring Play at the Early Years at School*, London, Ward Lock, 1977, p. 12.

13. Jean Piaget, *Play, Dreams and Imitation in Childhood*, New York, Routledge & Kegan Paul, 1951, ch. v.

14. Benjamin Spock, *Baby and Childcare*, New York, Pocket Books, 1977.

15. Eric Erikson, *Childhood and Society*, 2nd edn, New York, W.W. Norton, 1963, pp. 217, 222.

16. Bruno Bettleheim, 'The Importance of Play', *Atlantic Monthly*, March 1987, p. 36.

17. Piaget, *Play, Dreams and Imitation in Childhood*, 1951, p. 170.

18. Jerome Singer, 'Imagination and Make-Believe Play in Early Childhood: Some Educational Implications', *Journal of Mental Imagery*, 1(1), 1977, pp. 127–44.

19. Joshua Meyrowitz, *No Sense of Place: The Impact of Electronic Media on Social Behaviour*, New York, Oxford University Press, 1985.

20. 'G.I. Joe, the American Retailing Hero', *Chain Store Age*, Oct. 1986, p. 81.

21. B. Sutton-Smith, *Toys as Culture*, New York, Gardner Press, 1986.

22. Nancy Carlson-Paige and Diane Levin, *The War Play Dilemma: Children's Needs and Society's Future*, Columbia University, NY, Teachers College Press, 1987; Kathy Silva, Carolyn Roy and Marjorie Cants, *Childwatching at Play Group and Nursery School*, London, Grant Macintyre, 1984.

23. Daniel Pope, *The Making of Modern Advertising*, New York, Basic Books, 1983.

24. 'Construction Toys Are Solidly Building', *Chain Store Age*, Jan. 1985, p. 106.

25. Fisher-Price Canada, *Fisher-Price Corporate History*, Mississauga, Ont., Fisher-Price, 1987.

26. In addition to toy manufacturer histories and annual reports I have relied upon the following sources: Sydney Ladensohn Stern and Ted Schoenhaus, *Toyland: The High-Stakes Game of the Toy Industry*, Chicago, Contemporary Books, 1990; Andrew Weiner, 'Suffer the Little Consumers', *Quest*, Dec. 1982, pp. 66–72; William Crawford Woods, 'The Littlest Arms Race', *Harpers*, April 1983, p. 6; David Owen, 'Where Toys Come From', *The Atlantic Monthly*, Oct. 1986, pp. 65–78.

27. 'Rise of Licensed Plush: Where are Profits?', *Chain Store Age*, Feb. 1986, p. 89.

28. Hasbro Corporate Report, 1987.

29. Sutton-Smith, *Toys as Culture*.

30. Maital, *From Pleasure to Reality: Learning to Wait Begins in Childhood*, pp. 54–81.

31. William Wells, 'Children's Marketing', *Journal of Advertising Research*, March 1965, p. 9.

32. Scott Dorman, *The Hollywood Reporter*, 2 June 1987.

33. Lester P. Guest, 'Brand Loyalty Revised: A Twenty Year Report', *Journal of Applied Psychology*, 48, 1964, pp. 93–7.

34. Cy Schneider, *Children's Television: The Art, The Business, and How It Works*, Chicago, NTC Business Books, 1987, p. 90.

35. Ladensohn Stern and Schoenhaus, *Toyland*, 1990, p. 56.

36. James McNeal, *Children as Consumers*, Austin, Tex., University of Texas, Bureau of Business Research, 1964.

37. TV effects studies, i.e. E. Wartella et al., 'The Young Child as Consumer', in E. Wartella, ed., *Children Communicating*, Beverly Hills, Sage, 1979, ch. 9.

38. Charles Atkin, 'Observation of Parent–Child Interaction in Supermarket Decision-Making', *Journal of Marketing*, 42, 1975, pp. 41–5; Joann P. Galst and M.A. White, 'The Unhealthy Persuader: The Reinforcing Value of Children's Purchase-Influencing Attempts at the Super-Market', *Child Development*, 47, 1976, pp. 1089–96; Thomas E. Barry, 'Children's Television Advertising', *American Marketing Association, Monograph Series 8*, 1977.

39. Peter Fancese, *American Demographic Trends and Opportunities in the Children's Market*, Ithaca, New York, 1985.

40. Stephen R. Levin, T.V. Petros and F.W. Petrella, 'Preschoolers' Awareness of Television Advertising', *Child Development*, 53, 1982, pp. 933–7; Kenneth D. Bahn, 'How and When Do Brand Perceptions and Preferences First Form? A Cognitive Developmental Investigation', *Journal of Consumer Research*, 13, 1986, pp. 382–7; G. Sydney Burton, James M. Calonico and Dennis McSeveny, 'Effects of Preschool Television Watching on First Grade Children', *Journal of Communication*, Summer 1979, pp. 164–70.

41. D.B. Wackman et. al., 'How TV Sells Children: Learning to be Consumers', *Journal of Communication*, Winter 1977, pp. 138–57; Charles Atkin, 'Television Advertising and Socialization to Consumer Roles', in D. Pearl et al., eds. *Television and Behaviour: 10 Years of Scientific Progress and Implications for the Eighties*, vol. 2, *Technical Reviews*, National Institute of Mental Health, Washington, US Government Printing Office, 1982.

42. Del Hawkins and K.A. Coney, 'Peer Group Influences on Children's Product Preferences', *Journal of Academy of Marketing Science*, 2 Spring 1974, pp. 322–31.

43. See, for example, the American Toy Manufacturers' publications.

44. Schneider, *Children's Television*, 1987, p. 23.

45. Ibid.

46. M. Goldberg and J. Gorn, 'Television's Impact on Preferences for Non-White Playmates: Canadian "Sesame Street" Inserts', *Journal of Broadcasting*, 23(1), 1979, pp. 27–32.

47. L. Rust, 'Children's Advertising: How It Works, How to Do It, How to Know If It Works', in *Everything You Should Know About Children's Research* (Proceedings of ARF Key Issues Workshop), New York, April, 1986, pp. 13–22.

6

Building Character

The children's market has come of age. Offspring of the 25–39 year old baby boomers have captured the attention of the advertising world because of their numbers and influence on the purchasing power of the family.[1]

In the 1980s there was considerable excitement among children's marketers as the promotional methods formulated during the baby-boom years were updated for the baby-boomers' children. As marketing experts note, 'The large number of children being born during the '80s and projected to continue during the '90s is causing astute manufacturers and retailers of children's products and services to reexamine their marketing strategies.'[2] There were opportunities in the contemporary marketplace that had to be exploited, and the 1980s witnessed a strong growth in children's marketing departments and a threefold increase in promotional expenditure among toy makers. But the most significant of the changes was the wholesale adoption of character marketing as the dominant means of strengthening the sales of children's goods.

Looking beyond the puffery of the marketing press, we can see now that the 'discovery' of children's marketing in the 1980s did not represent a sudden cataclysmic event but was instead a gradual reorientation of marketing and media practices within the new sociopolitical environment of the decade. When Reagan made new appointments to the Federal Communications Commission (FCC), which led to *de facto* deregulation of children's television, the marketers were already positioned to produce the glut of animated programmes that would flood TV screens with commercial fiction. These 'thirty-minute commercials' attracted attention and criticism, yet largely unnoticed in their shadow was a new toy-marketing enterprise that had firmly fixed children's consumption in its sights. The enterprise was spearheaded by well-tested marketing techniques that guided product design by relying jointly on research and on keeping in touch with children's culture. But while promotion had become the pivot of marketing plans, new product design was a matter of discovering the right cultural symbols and projecting them into the market through television fiction. The very notion of 'play value' – the central notion of a toy's use – had to be reworked for the new realities of the marketplace created by deregulation.

The Importance of Research

The marketing concept and its implicit interest in the consumer helped to steer children's marketers to children themselves – to their responses to goods and the media through which these goods were sold. This simple insight inspired not only the dramatic increases in the quantity, scope, and quality of children's research during the 1960s and 1970s but also the development of a research industry upon which children's marketers depended. This research, ironically, embodied and applied the same 'helping' philosophy that modern psychology had urged for contemporary parenting: find out what children say they need and then help them get it. Marketers simply took this idea more seriously and did the research more conscientiously. The consumer in this case becomes a complex mass market for the product. Testing a new design involved more than the toy maker taking it home to see what the kids said. As James McNeal, marketing teacher and researcher, pointed out in his overview of children's marketing, research fulfilled the obvious requirement of 'recognizing the needs' of the various consumers in the market. Unlike contemporary parents who appear anxious and confused about their children, 'marketing researchers nonetheless seem to have no trouble recognizing the desire among children for need expression through consumer behaviour and providing advertisers with appropriate information about children's needs.'[3]

The objective of understanding the various practices and contexts of children's consumption led early researchers to study kids in new ways and to isolate those special features of behaviour that were influencing their desire for goods.[4] Unlike educational and psychological research (which also took off at this time), marketing

175

researchers used as their starting position the ordinary circumstances of contemporary life unclouded by high-sounding goals. They offered a more practical perspective on childhood, and their evidence had immediate consequences in the formulation of marketing plans in various product ranges – most significantly in family restaurants, in snack, fun and breakfast foods, and in the array of children's entertainment (including films, music, fashion and toys).

The published investigations into children's responses to television programmes, to everyday activities, to their consumer habits and to their way of choosing and using products grew steadily in the 1970s;[5] but this marketing literature reflects only a fraction of the proprietary research undertaken by the food and toy industry – research that guided the development of new products, new tactics and new strategies for selling. The Gene Reilly Group's mammoth study conducted under the guidance of Scott Ward – it was called simply *The Child* – came into the public domain only thanks to a 1978 Federal Trade Commission (FTC) hearing on children's television advertising.[6] This four-volume report provided a wealth of detailed information on the attitudes and behaviours of the six-to-fourteen set in the early 1970s, material that was of enormous use for the manufacturers of children's goods. The study included a careful examination of children's television viewing and preferences, their knowledge of the brands and products in children's goods, their allowances and spending practices, and their consumer preferences, attitudes and behaviour in key markets including restaurants, snacks, toys and sports equipment.

Much of the information in *The Child* came as no surprise to those active in children's marketing. The study said children came home from school wanting to grab a snack and watch TV. They liked activities that were social and involved their peers. Children, even very young ones, knew what they wanted as presents and felt that they could influence their parents to buy their favourites. Consumerism was part of their lives and they reported that shopping was their 'favourite activity'. Indeed, shopping was one of the few activities that they liked doing with their parents, along with eating in restaurants.

According to the study, children were no *tabula rasa*. Their preferences had long ago been shown to be well formed and stable; many showed loyalty to their favourite products. Moreover, what they wanted was predictable. They all seemed to desire bicycles or dolls or sports equipment; the wealthier and older ones might aspire to a television or tape player. They expected these goods as presents.

Comparing the results of the study's child and adult samples with regard to preferred activities, the report noted four activities – having snacks, going to movies, watching television and going out to eat with friends – 'which reveal that children like the activity more than mothers' attitudes would suggest. The obverse case where parents' encouragement is high and children's liking low does not appear.' The report also stated:

> Even more interesting is the fact that each of the four categories mentioned here – snacks, movies, television, and restaurants – represent products which throughout the 1970s are heavily advertised to children. While this finding may be coincidental, it strongly suggests the power of advertising in determining children's activity preferences.

Parents and kids agreed that bicycles and sporting goods made suitable gifts for the older child, but the report also showed that about half of parents of the under-eights bought toys as birthday gifts. Surprisingly, then, children rated playing with cars or trucks and playing with dolls negatively among their preferred activities. Noting this anomaly, the report commented: 'The low ranking assigned to playing with toy cars/trucks and dolls/play people deserves some comment . . . and it may perhaps be explained, in large part, by the loss of interest in these activities reported by children beyond age 10.'[7] In fact, the under-tens showed significantly more interest in toy play, a fact obscured by the tendency to group children together. This finding also suggested that given the low levels of advertising expenditure by toy manufacturers at the time, toy sales might not have been achieving their full potential with the under-tens.

The Child revealed the importance of demographic break-points in merchandising efforts aimed at the children's market. As data from the study revealed, gender differences among older children and a juncture at around age ten mark significant divides in attitudes, activities and preferences. As children grow they change, and it was crucial for marketers to be aware of this maturational process. Certainly, advertising to the very young was not easy. *The Child* showed that children, especially the eight year olds and under, had trouble remembering brand names. Of the toy manufacturers only Mattel seemed to register with more than one in five kids, and this was mostly among the older children, who were already not particularly interested in toy play. Under-sevens had a perceived inability to form, retain and communicate brand attitudes.[8] Brand-image advertising did not seem a particularly useful way of promoting products and was particularly ill-advised in the toy market.

Other research from the 1970s showed that children's advertising was probably most effective in maintaining an already established brand profile.[9] Promotional tactics rested on repetition or media weight (gross expenditure) and advertisers relied on a limited set of appeals. Many breakfast and snack foods and restaurants were content to create easily recognized 'likeable' characters (Tony the Tiger, Ronald McDonald, Snap Crackle and Pop), which they had associated with their goods through long-running commercials. The familiarity of these characters seemed to be the only way they could circumvent the limited retention and attention. Personification of the product was a favoured tactic of children's advertising through-out the 1970s. The creation of an imaginary 'persona' was a simple extension of the use of testimonials in advertising; many ads had used stars or well-known personalities to make products more attractive and familiar. The psychological principle of evaluative transfer between the persona and the product was well documented in research tests, as William Walls points out:

> A somewhat more permanent solution to the individualization problem is to associate the brand with a personality children admire. Because children do ask for certain brands just because the brands are identified with someone they like very much, this tactic is apt to remain effective as long as the association is continually reinforced and the personality remains popular.[10]

Children didn't have to remember a corporate name or logo: all they had to do in the supermarket was find the box with Tony on it.

Children's advertising appeals have converged, then, on a narrow range of symbolic rather than rational strategies.[11] Food ads aimed at children seemed particularly to appeal to sentience (the sensory or pleasure-giving dimension of products) with taste and touch, feelings and excitement being the most important elements – especially in ads for snack food, where eating was pictured as a pleasurable and exciting experience. One research study itemized the use of appeals in children's ads:[12]

Sentience	64 per cent
Play	52 per cent
Affiliation	33 per cent
Nurturance	21 per cent
Achievement	14 per cent

The notion of the 'utilities' to be derived from children's consumption, such as nutrition and achievement, played a much less significant role in children's advertising than pleasure, play and peer sociability – the values that marketers preferred to invoke. Many other values (for instance hard work or social responsibility) were almost never mentioned in children's advertising. Interestingly, toy ads featured scenes where children played (about one-third of this sample), but images of children at play were also featured broadly as an abstract value associated with other goods – in snack food, cereal and even toothpaste advertising. Play as an exciting and pleasurable activity provides a useful symbolic linkage to the feelings of an enjoyable world that advertising more generally promotes. Children's marketers recognized that play was both at the centre of children's perceptions of themselves and a desired activity in its own right.

The Strategy of Affluence

Still, new toy lines advertised heavily on television had to overcome enormous barriers to get established in the market. Not the least of these barriers was the parent, who either bought the toy, supplied the money, or at least approved the child's purchase.[13] Marketing had to adopt social research techniques, including focus tests, mail-intercept tests, in-depth interviews and direct mail questionnaires, just to keep abreast of parents' feelings about children's toys. The information gained from communication with the consumers helped companies to decide what new toys they should introduce to the market.[14] Attitude research was an important addition to trend analyses in tracking the undercurrents of childrearing practice and parental concern.

Through expanding their market research, children's marketers gradually came to understand the importance to their planning of the psychological dynamic of family restructuring. One marketing document baldly identifies the problem as keeping up with social changes and the 'new demographics [and] new family structures that affect marketing to today's children'.[15] Even in the declining family sizes of the 1980s clever marketers could divine trends crucial to product design and pricing: 'Today's woman is having 1.8 children as opposed to 3.7 children in the Fifties and Sixties. People spend more on a first child. Not only is there the exuberance of the "big event", but more people are buying childhood products because there are no hand-me-downs.' The Television Bureau of Advertising document pointed out that because more than 50 per cent of mothers worked: 'They may have more money, but they have less time to spend with their children. To compensate, they may buy more things for their children.' The process of social research helped toymakers reconceptualize the role of the toy in maintaining the emotional ties of the family.

Examining the rising divorce rates in the 1980s, this same report also advised that 'many children have several sets of parents, and several sets of grandparents. Divorced parents see even less of their children than do working parents. Spending for children's products often helps ease the pain.' Because people in general lived longer, grandparents were having an increasing effect on the children's market: 'Because they often do not live close to their grandchildren, they may not know their grandchildren, they may not know their grandchildren's specific needs (clothing sizes) and, as a result, feel less bound to give what is practical.' Grandparents therefore became an important focus of toy marketing.

The demographic changes were also noted by distributors in terms of the parents' changing shopping habits and growing sense of how much they should spend on children. By the mid 1980s about 50 per cent of families were spending at least $50 on toys every year, with up to 25 per cent of families spending over $250. A retail survey of toy shoppers showed both a willingness to make trips to special stores to get what they wanted and to spend money on preferred gifts.[16] Department, convenience and variety stores had to compete harder with the speciality shops for their share of toy sales, as toy purchases became a more considered and extravagant element in the family budget. The distribution networks built by companies like Toys R Us and Lyons were based on these perceptions of the changing role of children's toys in socialization.

Toy supermarkets succeeded because they allowed for much greater diversity of product but concentrated toy-purchasing into clusters within a few outlets that parents could drive to. Because they were keeping prices low, the non-specialized retailers had to carry items with rapid turnover. To some degree these new outlets solved a problem for manufacturers who were competing intensely for shelf and floor space to display their broadening lines. Although for a long time toy purchases had been integrated with general shopping at department and discount stores, now modern parents were willing to make a separate trip for toys. This trend grew stronger, so that by 1983, 33 per cent of toys were being bought at discount stores, 19 per cent at toy speciality stores, and 9 and 7 per cent at variety and department stores respectively. By 1985 speciality stores had climbed to 47 per cent of toy purchases, taking business away from the discount stores. The speciality stores had also become a powerful force within the toy industry. Toys R Us controls about 20 per cent of the market and Lionel is not far behind.

Merchandisers also discovered from pricing surveys that families were not only making multiple toy purchases at the shop but were also willing to spend more on individual purchases, and the 1980s became a period of higher price-points. One analyst suggested that since grandparents and parents often know rather little about their children and what is appropriate for them, they are increasingly subject to the child's expressed opinions and are willing to spend more to overcome their anxiety. The rising costs of a speciality toy market was therefore not discouraging to all consumers.[17] In the area of gift-giving marketers know that consumers have a special price-point that they consider appropriate for spending on a particular occasion: a birthday party gift, a Christmas gift or a casual treat – each has its own range. Increasingly, toy buyers have shown a willingness to raise the level of spending on special toy gifts, which in part reflects the rise of first-child and only-child households. In addition, the industry has seen a trend of grandparents and older first-time parents spending more money on children's merchandise that they perceive as the 'best' of its kind for their children.[18]

Marketers began to introduce new ranges of toys at higher prices to meet this segment's needs: the success of Teddy Ruxpin, Cabbage Patch dolls, and other more expensive stuffed toys clearly illustrates that consumers have been willing to spend more than $19·99 for a toy. Some plush toys on the market can cost up to $100, making them the cost equivalent of a bicycle. But merchandisers still found a built-in price resistance. Higher-priced toys with special appeal do well, while other toys that offer good value at higher prices wither from neglect unless they offer something unique. So added value (including gimmicks such as electronic voices, computer-individuated faces, extensive publicity) became a requirement at the higher end of the toy market to attract parents' attention.

The Affluent Child

Market researchers also found that the children of baby-boomers had become more a part of the market than their predecessors because they were being given the power to practise and influence consumption. As James McNeal noted, children from the 1950s and 1960s gained their most formative experience of the economy through the marketplace. When they are four many children begin making solo trips to corner stores – sometimes on family shopping missions and sometimes for their own choice and amusement.[19] By the age of five most children are making these trips, so that by the age of eight the average US child is in a shop alone three times a week. Though they might have a very tentative understanding of the world of jobs, wages and corporations, children learn quickly to conduct themselves in shops, to exchange money for goods and to use storekeepers as helpers.[20] In the era of affluence, parental emphasis on consumer socialization far outweighed their concern about what happens before and after their children spend money. Baby-boomers encouraged their own children to learn about economics directly – from products themselves, from advertising and from experiences in stores.

The mood in the boomers' households changed as delayed gratification was no longer a predominate feature of the 'me' generation's values or childrearing agenda. The traditional middle-class skills of saving and accumulating wealth were balanced with a newly perceived need to teach children how to spend money and derive personal meaning and satisfaction through the use of goods. Children were taken and then sent to the store on family missions, in part to teach responsibility and in part to give them direct experience of the marketplace.[21]

The most important means of consumer socialization was the allowance. Whereas parents once gave out an allowance in return for work or regular achievement, or to help teach children to save and plan for the future, they now gave money to children as a reward for good behaviour, as a gift or as a way to teach children the skills of buying for themselves. Children were granted increasingly large sums of money and encouraged to spend it. When a parent gave seventy-five cents to the three year old and told her to pay the shopkeeper for the chocolate bar she wanted, everybody smiled, for this was introducing patterns that would come to serve the child for life. Allowances and occasional work were increasing the discretionary income of the under-seventeen set. Young children of five were being

Millais' *Bubbles* not only helped to crystallize a new perspective on childhood innocence, but provided a direct link between cleanliness and childhood that was sustained in turn-of-the-century soap advertising.

The innocent child of the new century even graces this corset advertising.

Mothers induct their daughters into the traditions of beauty and product use.

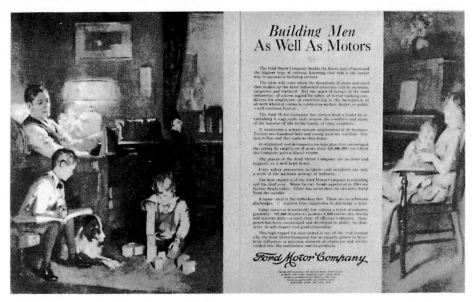

The home is the respite from work as symbolized by children at play on the floor.

In the 1930s, the new approaches to child-rearing permeate popular journals and advertising; fathers learn tolerance while mothers learn nutrition.

1950s television: a vision of the familial community.

Moms were told to instruct their daughters in the ways of consumerism by advertisements with an educational component.

A nineteenth-century illustration that whimsically envisions the automation of literacy in the year 2000.

IN AN APPLE TREE.

In September, when the apples were red,
To Belinda I said,
"Would you like to go away
To Heaven, or stay
Here in this orchard full of trees
All your life?" And she said, "If you please
I'll stay here—where I know,
And the flowers grow."

Kate Greenaway's children express their preference for the natural innocence of the garden.

Heroic hubris and symbolic powers permeate the comic book versions of Thundercat narrative.

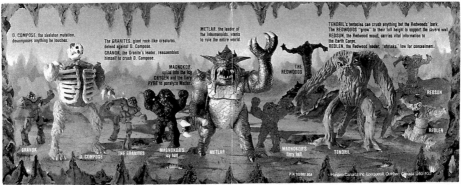

Action toys come in lines that together define a universe of play as depicted on television.

Only in the logic of total marketing does this symbolic relationship between a Barbie and breakfast cereal make sense.

A thoroughly modern Barbie reminds us that life is really just a play.

Princess of Power: She-ra's powers may only be skin deep.

Hasbro Makes it Happen: each new promotional line had to muster corporate support spanning the widest range of industries to ensure market saturation.

Jem, and the Misfits: fashion and music are configured as a
modern battleground.

Hasbro's idea of a children's room: full of toys.

How to advertise to the changing child

There are 4½ million children in Canada 12 years old and under. Today they enjoy greater independence, have more money to spend and take a more active role in family purchasing decisions than ever before. Children accompany their parent(s) to the supermarket 1 in 4 times, and choose where the family will eat out 40% of the time. They're very brand-conscious, particularly when it comes to names, labels and brand symbols on the clothing they wear.

It is vital for marketers to understand the complexity of the children's market, which is not one market but three, with children's preferences and values showing major differences according to their age: (1) Pre-schoolers (relying on parental decisions); (2) the 5-8 year olds (the magic years, but also the "age of why"); (3) The 9-12 year olds (with strong peer orientation). Key characteristics common to the 5-12 year olds are: Egocentricity; fun orientation; a need for continuity; the desire to be a little older and the desire to be like other boys or girls. And 7-8 years is the important breakpoint in children's reactions to advertising.

How best to reach this young, aware and growing consumer? Studies by communications experts and psychologists offer some directional guidelines.

1. **Consider the effects of the media themselves on children.** Print fosters reflection and imagination. Radio stimulates imagination. Television leads to an impulsive rather than reflective style of thought. Typically today's child eats, drinks, plays games, and does homework while the TV set is on and is thus exposed to over 4 hours a day.

2. **Children need a reward/reason to watch.** Children have a low threshold for frustration and boredom. They need an immediate reward either from entertainment provided by the commercial execution or from the product shown as giving pleasure through consumption or use. Show the product big and advertise **the brand** to children, not the category. Identify and individualize some characteristic of the brand or endow it with 'magic power' which may not be believed at the rational level but can create an aura about the brand. Brand names should receive special emphasis and repetition. Fun is the critical element in appealing to children.

3. **Children enjoy plot or story.** They identify with action and characters in a story, which should be simple, clear, concrete, moving quickly to completion or resolution. The pace, however, should not be too fast, particularly for the under 6's. Story line should not be dependent on audio. Create a personality for your product, it helps promote loyalty. Children respond well to a variety of strategic and tactical elements:

   A. **Fantasy/Role Playing:** Children enjoy a make-believe world they can enter into; and are also drawn to characters with extraordinary capabilities (super heros, folk heros, sports heros or entertainment stars and celebrities). Boys prefer invincible action figures (younger boys animatic or fantasy figures; older boys living male role models and athletes). Girls prefer cuddly creatures, fashion figures or incline to romanticism.

   B. **Conflict:** Children find the use of a conflict situation emotionally arousing and its resolution brings happy feelings.

   C. **Mystery:** The unknown intrigues children, generating curiosity and interest.

4. **Children respond strongly to emotional, non-verbal stimuli.** The following are extremely effective with children:
   Sound Effects/Music/Rhythm—Children are captured by catchy sounds, tunes and tricky combinations of words, which they frequently repeat. They are more attention-getting than dialogue.
   Humor/Comedy—Physical humor (slapstick, surprise and shock effect, etc.) communicates to children of all ages. Adults looking foolish (unsuitable for the very young). Verbal humor (puns, satire, jokes, riddles, dialects, mannerisms) is more effective with the over 8's.
   Action/Movement—Graphic motion is most important in attracting and holding children's attention—people doing things or the product in use.

5. **Children like things that are uniquely their own.** They enjoy non-adult situations and a non-restrictive environment.

6. **Children like to see themselves.** They enjoy watching children like themselves having fun with a product or mastering a problem. The children should be cast a little older than the target group since children desire to be older/stronger/masterful. If there is only one main character, make it a boy since boys will be accepted by both genders, but girls will be accepted only by girls.

For an agency that's not just "kidding around" but knows how to handle this volatile market, please call or write **Rupert Brendon, President and C.E.O., D'Arcy Masius Benton & Bowles Canada Inc., 2 Bloor St. West, Toronto, Ontario M4W 3R3, (416) 922-2211.**

DMB&B

The D'Arcy Masius Benton & Bowles and
Léveillé Group of Companies

This advertisement summarizes marketers' conventional wisdom about marketing to children.

given on average one to two dollars weekly, which rose to five dollars by the age of twelve. An allowance became a kind of tithe to children's independence and responsibility that parents gladly paid in the hope it would help their kids become more effective in making economic decisions.

Youth spending expanded enormously, accounting for up to $40 billion of purchasing power in the US economy by the mid 1980s.[22] Much of this spending is distributed across a constrained range of goods, including clothes and cultural goods. An analysis of under-twelve spending in 1986 found $1·4 billion was spent on snacks, $1·1 billion on toys, $0·765 billion on video games and $0·771 billion on movies. Most of the younger (under-ten) children's wealth is spent quickly and within an even narrower range of products, food treats and toys, so that marketers could encourage significant sales through direct marketing. Children had little tendency to accumulate savings, and toy and snack advertising could take aim at the impulsive quality of their consumerism.

The Influence of Children

From the early 1960s, children's marketers well knew that new family patterns also granted children greater say in family decision-making. In the age of affluence, shopping at the mall on weekends became a family ritual. Parents took their children shopping with them and included them in product decision-making.[23] Children responded eagerly to the opportunities by making requests for goods and expressing their preferences more forcefully. Researchers began to observe and study the family interactions in the stores, eventually describing a progression in a child's consumer socialization: it started with infants accompanying their mothers to the shops and culminated at age eight, by which time children had become highly skilled consumers.[24]

Because of this the family 'dialogue about preferences' became a crucial element in the marketing of toys. Advertisers had to get kids to want a 'particular' toy and to be able to communicate that want to a parent, friend or relative. This made parent–child interaction a strategic issue. Research confirmed that children shopped with parents and made frequent requests for specific products, such as cereal or candy, at strategic moments. The children would cause embarrassment if ignored. A marketing executive from Kenner estimated: 'Kids are the determining factor for toy purchases 90% of the time.'[25] Studies of parent–child interaction in the store also confirmed a growing ability on the part of the children to influence parental purchase. There was even evidence that children learned to communicate their interests more effectively as they grew older. Older children attempted fewer interventions and got what they wanted more often.[26]

Even those marketers who primarily targeted parents had to remember that parents wanted both to 'please and prepare' their kids. As researchers observed, parental influence was mediated by parental concern, and different parenting approaches resulted in different kinds and frequency of attempts to influence them.[27] Changing childrearing attitudes gave more room for children to influence the purchases of parents and relatives.[28] Direct requests in stores and at home along with the influence of peers were supplementing the 'passive dictation' of family life.

The concern about this increased pressure on parents was strong enough to influence the industry's self-regulatory advertising guidelines drawn up during the 1970s: advertisers were advised that 'commercials must not directly urge children to purchase, or urge them to ask their parents to make inquiries or purchases'.[29] These guidelines were superfluous, however, because marketers had already realized that children needed no instruction on the tactics of getting what they wanted. Indeed, as children's researchers learned, a useful way of evaluating the success of an advertisement at the test-market stage was simply to ask whether the child would make a request for that product to his or her parents.[30] Requests were understood to be a part of family dynamics.

The Values of Play

Competitive marketing also demanded a more precise understanding of how consumers make choices. In children's marketing the parents are the purchasers while the children are the users of goods – a problem that the marketing strategies of the 1980s resolved by recognizing the limitations of parental resistance. Toy makers realized that a toy has meaning only in the context of children and play, and a sense of 'play value' emerged as the primary motivation of purchase, even in the preschool market. This marked a vital step in the reorientation of character-toy marketing.

All the major toy makers began to research play carefully so as to refine their products for children. An executive at Milton Bradley stated: 'Our management philosophy maintains that contact with children through the product development cycle is the best way to ensure that we make toys that children will enjoy.... Research is that vital link between management and the most important people in our business: the children.'[31] Observing children choose and use their products in labs and talking to kids about play became essential steps in bringing a new design to market. Defining their conception of play value as 'the value a toy has for the child in their play', researchers set out to maximize a toy's appeal to children.[32] Play value was determined by 'the time the child spends with the toy', by the duration and intensity of play. As passive dictation and the children's own purchases became the basis of demand, play value served as an excellent predictor of marketability.

The toy's capacity to preoccupy the child became the means of selling even to preschoolers' parents. Fisher-Price, for instance, increased its investment in research, hoping to leave 'few stones unturned'. The company established its own nursery school. In that school 'play time is closely scrutinized', a Fisher-Price document states. 'Behind a wall of one way mirrors trained staff carefully observe the way children react to a large assortment of toys many experimental and some Fisher-Price's and some the competition's.' The document notes that the crucial element is research on children: 'Ours is a pragmatic research effort. We try to relate what we're doing to children, how they act, how they develop. Their likes and dislikes. We want to know what parents think of course but our real concern is for children. We're out to create toys that are fun for children.'[33]

The priority given to the sense of pleasure in a child's play clearly reflects a new focus on toys as the tools of children's delight. Toy marketers felt confident when their product produced obvious signs of enjoyment on the part of the player. A comment in the yearbook of the Canadian Toy Manufacturing Association notes this change in philosophy:

Toys have traditionally mirrored the adult world in size and in form which can quickly and easily be mastered by children. Scientific advances, technological changes, social attitudes and customs, personal values and moral convictions can all be found reflected in the playthings we offer to our children. But perhaps most important of all, the true purpose of a toy or game is to entertain.[34]

The erosion of the other qualities of play reveals the underlying reconception of the toy and its purpose within the toy industry.

Research with a Difference

Research enabled marketers to reconceptualize their idea of the appeal that toys held for children. To the marketer, play value is not a 'benefit' accrued through learning; rather, it is a seemingly mysterious quality of a particular toy that makes children want to have and play with it. In fact, most of the toys marketed were similar in their basic design. For instance, if they were dolls they were action figures, plush toys, or fashion dolls. In talking to children, researchers became increasingly convinced that the secret of the relationship to toys rested in the symbolic design of the product.

The research enterprise of the marketers became quite different from the perspective on childhood developed by academic psychologists and the educationists, who shared an interest in play but not in the pragmatic framework for investigating it. So too, the testing methods the researchers used for penetrating the inner world of the child's psyche diverged increasingly from standard tests of educational psychology. While the psychologists focused on cognitive growth and structure, the marketing researchers were interested in preferences, emotional attachments to toys and the feelings and fantasies experienced in play activities. Even while academic psychology argued over the operationalization of these concepts, marketing researchers took at face value the importance of imagination, the process of identification and involvement with characters, and the secret inner world of children's culture invoked by toys. By carefully observing what children were doing with their toys, marketers came to appreciate the potential of advertising to communicate the symbolic dimensions of toys.

The marketers' desire to study children in more pragmatic ways inspired pioneering efforts in research methods. Market researchers began to connect the social symbolism of children's toys to more sensitive and open-ended 'qualitative' methods, which they adapted from clinical practice, play therapy and school observation schedules rather than from experimental research. Marketing's pragmatism resulted in a less restrictive approach to research. It was immediately clear, for example, that communicating with children was different from communicating with adults. William Wells, an academic and researcher with Benton and Bowles, was a pioneer in the new efforts to build an understanding of the distinct children's market. In the mid 1960s he suggested: 'Perhaps the most pervasive difference between children and adult respondents is that children find abstract concepts very hard to understand and even harder to express.' Children proved not to be as articulate or self-reflective in their responses to research questions. They were less abstract and cogni- tively developed in their view of products, and the very young had a doubtful understanding of advertising's purpose. Very young chil- dren couldn't distinguish the ads from the programming, so uncover- ing their preferences for advertised products and their responses to the messages was a difficult research task. Wells said, 'Children are harder to interview than adults but they can provide useful informa- tion if they are approached in the right way.'[35]

As research methods Wells suggested those that 'rely on pictures rather than verbal brand identifications', and he emphasized the importance of establishing rapport and encouraging a sense of relaxation and fun. Children, he found, gave negative responses simply to avoid difficult questions and situations. Wells argued for new ways of talking to kids and urged the researcher to get 'inside' children's language. He also insisted on letting children set the agenda by encouraging unsupervised play with the product. He also invented the smiling-face scale, which is now widely used in chil- dren's opinion research.

Carole Hyatt recounted that her own early work at Children's Research Services entailed using drama and role-playing activities.[36] James McNeal and Scott Ward were likewise innovators in research- observation techniques with children. The research methods com- monly used with adults, such as focus groups, story-board tests, direct observation and interviews, had to be adapted for use with children. Indeed, children's researchers were forced to innovate in their methods because the standard linguistic procedures of market research failed to work well in the kids' market. Some of the new inquiry tactics have since become standard practice: hiding behind one-way glass to watch children choose toys and play in groups with toys; running focus groups and story-board tests, watching children watching television commercials in the home, noting the subtle interplay between friends, siblings and parents; asking children to write letters to Santa Claus as a means of eliciting wish lists with greater ecological validity. Researchers even engaged children in 'depth interviews' and free association sessions regarding particular snacks and they found that kids were quite willing to act out different candy bar names. They also closely observed the conversations children had with their moms in shops.[37] These methods were used to supplement the sociodemographic statistics that market planners used to track family trends and estimate children's spending power and influence on purchases.

Children's research became a booming business. As the workshop leaders of the Advertising Research Foundation (ARF) advised, a contemporary approach includes both more numerically elaborate multivariate analysis techniques and flexible and open qualitative approaches. An ARF seminar pointed out that marketers had to consider the unique dimensions of children's television-viewing patterns and the special qualities of children's responses to advertising – responses that are more emotional and visual and less dominated by language and cognitive order – as the critical aspects of children's consumer behaviour.[38]

Television's Children

In building up models of children's cultural experience, researchers inevitably turned to TV. It seemed safe to assume television's importance for children, given the hours of attention and devotion it inspired. Besides, from the point of view of communicating with children, television was the only available channel for serious marketing efforts. Through their efforts researchers gradually assembled a picture of how children responded to TV advertisements and, to some extent, the programming. The more academic wing of marketing research was particularly interested in the abilities of children to process information transmitted by television – their capacity to learn from TV. Television was known to be a very limited medium for conceptual learning and instruction.[39] Children processed abstract information slowly and with difficulty. They did gain ideas from television but the information had to be presented simply and repeated often.

Young children were especially fickle watchers. It seemed they did not watch TV very attentively and therefore were not bothered by endless repetition; rather, they often developed viewing strategies based on musical cues or references to the reactions of others present. They always had to be attracted to the screen either by seeing kids of similar age or by exciting music and images. Television, therefore, could be used to raise interest in a product, to give it peer appeal or excitement. Marketers were sure that television marketing had the potential to influence the preferences and purchase behaviour of children. One report concluded:

> Children aged two to eleven are probably the heaviest users of television in the country. . . . For the average child, television has pre-empted much of the traditional pattern of childhood development . . . rendering passé, or at least unremarkable, the normal experiences of growing up. Television also denies much of the normal conversational interchange between parents and children, a process essential to maximum development.[40]

Television did soon prove itself a useful tool for marketing toys. In 1973, J. Frideres reported that children were hearing first about new toys on television some 75 per cent of the time.[41] When children were asked about their sources of information about toys, they rated television and friends the highest.[42] Television seemed to be particularly effective in leading young children to products through 'perception without awareness' – a kind of learning based on a 'perceptual' orientation to the product.[43] Children, especially the youngest ones, primarily used perceptual cues to distinguish advertising from programming.[44] Although they had trouble remembering the multiple attributes of products, they responded to and remembered advertisements that were designed with 'child appeal' and repeated often enough. More importantly, researchers confirmed that children formed preferences for products based on simple brand-image attributes and they perceived social standing of products among peers. Television commercials for kids placed heavy emphasis on social and contextual information rather than on product attributes in isolation.[45]

Playing with Symbols

Marketers have long believed that all goods have social meaning – that they embody for consumers symbolic values beyond those of strict functionality or utility. Children's marketers, too, have realized for some time that at a very young age children begin to see goods as being instrumental in achieving social goals rather than filling a functional need.[46] Marketers have also realized that children are a special category of consumer because they have a limited intellectual foundation for understanding the dynamics of markets and the range of goods available and, indeed, a limited experience of the variety of 'functional' aspects of those goods. According to this stream of thought, children do not make 'rational' judgements about goods as the means of satisfying their experienced needs. Possibly because of the limitations of their other channels of communication, their preference for non-verbal communication, and their less elaborate system of self-identity, the issues of having the right toys, eating the right food and dressing for others become matters of great emotional intensity, even for very young children. A 'Topline' report on interviews with children from ages six to twelve noted: 'Kids today are very brand conscious, particularly so when it comes to names, labels and brand symbols on the clothing they wear. Clothing has become more important to kids at an earlier age, and stature is conferred when the right brand name is on display.'[47]

The marketing researchers therefore tested their products by watching kids in groups isolated from parents. They knew that parents muffled the strong emotional reaction that they were looking for. Researchers also noted that children reacted negatively to parents intruding into play, a realm they jealously regarded as their own. When they talk about weapons and war toys, for example, boys of six and seven clearly distinguish their own liking for these toys from the views of their parents and teachers. Many children even reported modifying their play activities in the presence of parents or teachers to disguise what really interested them. Researchers found strong sex-typed attitudes to toys and portrayals of children in advertisements so that even mixing boys and girls in focus groups had a disturbing effect; it made the reports of young boys and girls less representative of peer attitudes.[48] *The Child* report had correctly noted that peer groups were vital: playing together in a familial group was an activity pattern neither parents nor children preferred. Of all the activities afforded them, children most valued activities that brought them in contact with peers – playing, eating and socializing together.

Children's peer culture offered marketers the opportunity of designing products with this social influence process in mind. 'Children like things that are uniquely their own. They enjoy non-adult situations and a non-restrictive environment,' said the marketers. In the consumer society, as in all societies, people communicate to others through the things they own and use; for children this modality of communication through 'things' was especially vital because goods helped to integrate and identify them with their own peers. Advertisers had to become sensitive themselves to the changing flux of children's social symbols and to learn to convey those symbols effectively.

Peer Influence

The research on television was particularly helpful in establishing peer group desirability as a factor in marketing. Scott Ward had found that peer influence was one of the most important aspects of product requests, particularly in the toy market. Play, after all, was often a social activity in which the toy synchronized the behaviour of two or more children.[49] Children expected to share toys with others. Research had also confirmed that the social judgement of peers fulfilled a crucial role in orientating children's liking for a product. Mattel had based some of its earliest advertisements on this notion of peer acceptance and cultural positioning.[50] As an article in *Marketing News* pointed out, children are 'highly sensitive to rejection' and 'want to belong, to be accepted, to be part of the group'. The writers found that youngsters in a focus-group session they conducted reacted negatively to a commercial 'showing a boy who was treated as an outcast by his peers'.[51] Other research teams found that children preferred to play with kids whom they thought had the most attractive toys as demonstrated on television; it seemed that products rather than the likeability of other children was influencing social choice.[52] If a product was accepted into this exclusionary peer environment and registered as a symbol of it, children would want to buy it. Interviews conducted for McCollum Spielman found that modern kids suffered from a form of consumption anxiety over clothing:

> Children who are unsure of themselves will postpone clothing purchases until after they've seen how the class trend-setters are dressing. While they want to be individualistic, they'll stay within the boundaries of what is popular and acceptable. Kids are highly aware of what they look like.[53]

Watching themselves (in the form of their peers or idealized others) at play in TV commercials was appealing to children, which is why images of children at play have been featured in cereal, snack and toy ads. The world of children's advertisements is rarely populated by parents: it is overwhelmingly a kids' world.[54] The realization of peer power was at the very root of the saturation strategies in television advertising campaigns.[55] It is not simply a matter of reach and frequency: kids must have the sense of being surrounded by others who share their judgements about products. Some children's marketers felt that reach figures as high as 80 per cent of market and five repeated exposures are the minimum needed for product recognition in the children's market to establish peer pressure.[56] Creating a fad through television saturation was seen to be the best way of weaving a toy into children's social perceptions.

The marketers found that children saw themselves as part of an age stratum; but experience with message evaluation also demonstrated that it wasn't sufficient to use just any peer in ads. Kids were harshly judgemental of ad children who violated subtle peer expectations and evinced improper style. A youthful focus group might just as easily reject a model as being unrealistic as identify with him or her. Oddly, young girls preferred identifying with and liked models who were slightly older than themselves. Children in the same age group also had clear ideas about gender differences: boys reacted badly when girls appeared in ads for 'their' products, and girls reacted badly to the presence of boys to a somewhat lesser extent. If a toy company failed to recognize these implicit assumptions about the peer world it might jeopardize the potential success of its products.

Idol Moments

During the 1980s, children's marketing strategy concentrated its energy and innovation in the toy market: 'The toy companies are not only the leading spenders, but also the most ardent seekers of marketing options,'[57] declared one industry report. After deregulation, toy companies flocked to television animation tie-ins to promote action, plush and glamour dolls. It was a change in tactics that involved no original insights into children's psyches. Indeed, the irony is that marketers relied on fundamental, almost primitive elements of psychic structure, the sort of thing to which academics are so often blind. The sales charts and research reports of the industry provided convincing documentation of a twinned magic: television and the 'character doll'.

Throughout history dolls have played a unique cultural role. In various societies dolls have acted as fetishes, as medicine, as religious devices and as artistic models of forces beyond humanity's ordinary experience. There has been at times something strangely powerful tied to their symbolic force in people's lives – to their representations of the social world – a force not limited to childhood. The doll had this power because it was a miniaturized and abstracted representation, a condensation of the impulse towards drama, and a symbol that could be used in religious or mystical contexts. The doll was rarely a symbol of the ordinary and everyday in life; it referred to something more.

The earliest dolls or female figurines were simply that – representations of abstracted, more spiritual human attributes. This is why, as historian Antonia Fraser points out, some societies saw dolls as a way to ward off illness or evil spirits, to give protection and, in some cases, to provide direct access to the spiritual dimension of life.[58] This mystic aspect of dolls has been present in societies as different as Egypt and Melanesia. It is a particularly notable element in the children's festivals of Japan, in which the ritual display of a set of dolls in full period costume is regarded as an act of dedication for the children – a way of heightening their awareness of well-founded cultural percepts and the spiritual inheritance of the Japanese people.

Some time during the nineteenth century, the notion of dolls as adjuncts to role play and representations of everyday life emerged in children's culture. Dolls of that era were fashioned as baby dolls or little girls, primarily to help young girls develop the attachments and role behaviour of nurturing mothers. The baby dolls – and toy soldiers for boys – were abstract representations and usually did not embody specific personalities, identities or characters. Their featureless neutrality embodied the industrializing world's objectified sensibility and very limited conception of role play.

It was the more ancient form of doll, the one embodying a world of mystery and myth, that re-emerged with the rise of character-marketing tactics. The power of the doll as idol had been first demonstrated by Mattel's early Barbie campaigns: the popularity of Barbie helped doll makers realize the enormous cultural force embodied in a doll – especially the doll's capacity to represent an imaginary world beyond the ordinary world of everyday roles and rituals. Barbie had showed that girls become involved with a toy through a complex identification process rooted in the imagination – a process that could be prompted by television advertising. More importantly, the Barbie campaign revealed that toy makers could borrow heroes from established media and redesign them for their own purposes, retaining control over the 'identity profile' and positioning. Marketers fully understood the raw emotional appeal of kids' heroes and idols – sports and media stars, superheroes, especially accomplished children – and tied these to the doll.

Of all the lessons learned by toy makers probably none was as beneficial to sales as the idea that 'personality promotes loyalty' to a product line in the toy market. Personalities were easily remembered and therefore circumvented young children's inability to remember the functional attributes or characteristics of the products. More importantly, personality provided a way to involve children emotionally in the product. Finally, it enabled children to communicate easily to their parents which toys they preferred without having to know brand or corporate names. Kids could ask for Barbie, Jem, Liono, or He-Man without needing to know the names of the companies that made them. Giving toys distinctive names and memorable personas provided a better way of communicating to kids and, through them, to adults.

A McCollum Spielman study of children's marketing noted the impact of this approach on contemporary marketing:

> Underneath it all, however is the simple truth that children's personalities are very big business with virtually infinite marketing possibilities. This makes it critically important that youth marketers understand the vicissitudes of their juvenile targets for maximum appropriation of the youth dollar.[59]

Yet as attractive as the appeal of character toys appeared, promoting them meant that marketers had to plumb the depths of children's identification with heroes and role models. This was no simple task, and after the first blush of success many properties failed to establish themselves in children's culture to the extent that Transformers, He-Man, Jem, G.I. Joe, and the Ninja Turtles succeeded in doing. There was clearly a certain amount of artistry in constructing an attractive hero and in orchestrating the fantasy back-story that would lodge the character in children's culture. As the children's market became cluttered with more and more rival identities, personality marketing demanded more exacting research, as the McCollum Spielman study indicated:

> Research is recommended at early stages of character development and licensing to identify which new figures have or do not have potential and to identify which segments of the kid market are most likely to accept the

194

new character. This is the classic case of early application on small expenditure research, protecting very large investments in product, position name association and media.[60]

The McCollum Spielman report summarized an early investigation into children's heroes, confirming as expected that television characters had a special hold on all ages of children. 'To a much greater extent than adults, children are extremely interested in their own brand of glittering stars, anything from actual Hollywood celebrities to animated characters who appear in Saturday morning TV movies and holiday specials.' Children's strong preferences in television programming revealed an inclination towards particular kinds of characterization that engaged their imaginations. But in the highly competitive market it seemed there was no universally acceptable kids' character. The report notes, somewhat sadly, 'Digging deeper we discovered that it was extremely difficult to find kid idols that exhibited truly broad, universal appeal to both sexes and both major age groups studied.' The researchers also found that trademarked characters (like Tony the Tiger or Snap, Crackle and Pop) ranked at the bottom of the likability scales even if they were well known, 'because they have no lives outside of being emblems. They do not live on in achievements, serial battles between good and evil, or with retinues of relatives and associates in continuing sagas and epics. Kids are very conscious that these figures are advertisements' and not fictional characters with their own shows.

Rather than suggesting a single set of character guidelines for toy designers, the report urged marketers to recognize the 'remarkable segregation' in character preferences, most notably along age and gender lines. 'Indeed boys are inclined to prefer masculine, invulnerable, invincible, strong-arm dominant action figures – rough and tumble characters who are on the right side of cataclysmic struggles between good and evil and win.' But 'Girls are apt to revere whimsical cuddly, cute, sweet and gentle creatures ... anthropomorphic who require nurture, or fashion figures or they have begun to veer towards their romantic inclinations.' The study, done in 1983, predicted great gains for boys' action heroes, because 'boys were more inclined to prefer animated and fantasy figures, although they still observed the typical male kid preference for the invincible and the invulnerable'. Character-marketing should therefore adopt segmentation strategies in order to develop attractive properties for the toy market.

Age segmentation also proved crucial in devising strategies for promoting children's products. The researchers noted a 'distinct under six group' who continued to be most fascinated with the perennial TV cartoon characters like Bugs Bunny and Garfield – the 'immortals' of kids' TV culture. Television producers obviously had a good bead on this audience because these long-time characters had become especially recognizable in all age and gender groups, although they were weak on appeal among the over-fives. These 'immortal' characters were the current favourites of the very youngest preschool segment, but the report saw potential 'growth area ... in new characters that appeal to kids after they outgrow their early childhood friends'.

As investment in promotion increased, so too did the spending on research to secure this investment. Toys became the most researched product in the children's market, with testing taking place from the conception of a new toy to the advertising-design stages of marketing. Children are fussy about their toys.

The New Toy Box

Armed with their new research and theories on specific children's likes and dislikes, and guided by lure of television promotion, toy companies began to concentrate their attention on the profitable attractions of character-marketing.

Instead of simply finding a suitable and popular TV programme to sponsor, or waiting for a popular series to survive a season and then creating spin-off characters in the time-honoured fashion, toy makers and licensing agents got together early on to develop their own 'property' – their own TV characters and programme concept. The basic strategy of character-marketing was to create a children's television series that would provide the overarching means of promoting a whole range of licensed products. An integral part of the goal was media saturation.

The Mattel toy company, for example, came up with the idea of its *He-Man and the Masters of the Universe* programme in the early 1980s. The series cost over $14 million to produce, but this roadblock was overcome by financial arrangements between television producers, licensing agents and the toy maker. The up-front financial commitments along with guaranteed advertising contracts also proved a strong and necessary inducement to the toy distributors, who would see that the programme's products got priority space in stores.

The enormous risks of product development and introduction were thus spread across a number of co-ordinated interests in the children's marketing system. The animated television programmes resulted from protracted negotiations that had to satisfy each sector's expectations. The appeal of the programme and characters had to be well documented with research and the targeting clearly stated, and all parties were interested in the kind of exposure the character would get. Because the series also had to fuel toy sales, its hero had to have all the known qualities that inspire not just children's interest, but their devotion. Furthermore, a story concept had to include a host of characters complete with various accoutrements and technologies, all of which would become saleable products. The line of toys became the flagship for a flotilla of secondary imprinted products that would cash in on all the attention stirred up by the series and its cultural heroes. Given the expense of producing a television series, production costs had to be balanced against the better product positioning and display space in stores achieved as a result of the excitement generated among kids about the new series. The licensed goods that appear in the stores (stickers, books, films, T-shirts, pyjamas) are part of the saturation factor; they provide a visible manifestation of peer acceptance. As Cy Schneider so aptly points out, the proliferation of the licensed products in the marketplace becomes a form of advertising in itself, a promotional extension of television.[61] Timing is vital. A two-year planning process is usually necessary to develop programming and product agreements and to get the goods in the stores for the pre-Christmas season opening.

Nothing illustrates the impact of this new regime of character-marketing better than the Barbie doll's failing sales in 1985. Barbie, the first true personality doll, had been a top seller for Mattel for well over twenty years. Her miraculous longevity is testimony to the perspicacity of her creators. In part her success can be explained by the constant updating of her image achieved through advertising and accessory design. But Barbie represented the old promotional strategy for personality toys. She was not the product of a comprehensive TV marketing plan: she did not have a show of her own and hundreds of co-ordinated licensing arrangements. She was a stand-alone character toy promoted simply through a fashion-orientated imagery projected in advertising. Barbie had many challengers but few could replicate her appeal.

Barbie's first serious rival in the market – Jem – was launched by Hasbro in 1986 complete with a Japanese-produced animation series and a comprehensive marketing plan. Deregulation of television allowed Hasbro to portray Jem/Jerrica as a dynamic modern woman of the 1980s – a manager by day and rock star by night. The designers paid excruciating attention to all the symbolic dimensions that would appeal to girls in the four-to-nine market, and the media buyers made sure that Jem's saturation through syndicated television and extensive spot advertising was well targeted. They used an impromptu syndicated network of independent stations, mostly in the after-school and Saturday morning slots. The stores were filled with Jem sticker books, posters, T-shirts and tape recorders. Girls might receive the Jem doll at Christmas, but they would be buying her accessories all year round. A catalogue ad shows the range of goods associated with the Jem character and the careful attention to narrative detail implicit in the marketing strategy.

Barbie's sales were lagging while Jem was capturing an important share of the fashion doll market. As Hasbro executives explained:

> The glamour of today's music scene and the time tested appeal of doll hair play and beautiful fashion are among the ingredients of Jem's popularity. Talking to children is part of the ongoing marketing process at Hasbro. Although Jem launch was successful, our conversations with girls suggested the market would be responsive to new styling, fashion and accessories. As a result, we resculpted Jem's features to develop an even prettier doll for 1987. We have also introduced new members of Jem's band and other special friends, a new fashion collection and new play accessories priced at levels that consumers should find attractive year round.[62]

Jem's challenge to Barbie was a test of the power of comprehensive marketing to take a market share away from an industry leader. Jem had to be more than a fashion doll like Barbie: she was a co-ordinated, punkishly modern package of accoutrements, T-shirts and music tapes bundled together around a vividly portrayed animated television series with a lively storyline scripted for preteen girls – all pretested and monitored carefully to ensure success.

Barbie clearly had a problem. The solution, the new management at Mattel decided, was for the doll to fight back: to do so she needed her own TV show and rock band, and she got them both before the 1987 season was over. By her thirtieth birthday in 1989, Barbie was back in the limelight and Jem was just another flash in the pan.

In making these changes, Mattel had to violate the ideas of Barbie's original designers. Ruth and Elliot Handler of Mattel had believed that Barbie's personality should never be overly specified in her advertising or design because this might limit the imaginations of the girls who played with the dolls. Ruth Handler said, 'Each little girl has her own dreams about who Barbie is.... If you give her a specific personality, it could mean that little girls will lose their ability to project whatever personalities they want onto Barbie.'[63] In reworking the Barbie concept Mattel conceded that their own fiction and fantasies of marketing worked more effectively than leaving it up to little girls' imaginations. It seemed that the fantasies researched, designed and scripted by marketers were the best means of engaging children with a particular personality.

Mattel's triumph in the end was really that of a comprehensive marketing strategy. In fact the whole toy industry benefited from the escalating scope of marketing competition. The rivalry between He-Man, Transformers and G.I. Joe had fuelled the threefold increase in action-doll sales. Similarly, the interest generated by the fashion-doll wars was by no means limited to Barbie and Jem: Maxie, Jazzie, and Little Miss Makeup also appeared in the attempt to cash in on this play value. The excitement that the marketers brought to the toy business meant that the whole fashion-toy market grew in the process to yearly sales well over $1 billion. Indeed, between 1982 and 1986 US toy sales zoomed from $4·2 billion to $12·6 billion, an increase partly due to the general boom in licence merchandising.

Saturated Markets

No company has benefited as much due from the tie-in strategy as Hasbro, which has specialized in character-marketing and in the process has become the leading toy manufacturer in the United States. Its net revenue of $136 million in 1982 rose quickly to $1344 million in 1986 as the company took advantage of deregulated television to bring out a string of fabulously popular new lines – although its growth resulted primarily from a relatively small number of innovative character toys, including G.I. Joe, My Little Pony and Transformers. In 1982, Hasbro remodelled the G.I. Joe doll that it had initially introduced in the 1960s and gave the product an action-packed television series. Some 20 per cent of boys from ages five to twelve had two or more G.I. Joe toys within two months of the launch of the television series, and a hundred million G.I. Joes were shipped since 1982. Action-doll sales transformed Hasbro from a middle-size toy maker into a pre-eminent business. In 1982, the G.I. Joe sales of $49 million represented a full 36 per cent of Hasbro's revenues, but by 1986, with gross sales of $185 million, the toy accounted for only 14 per cent of the company's revenues. Hasbro learned quickly from its initial success in importing Transformers, which soon became another success story. Transformers outsold all other toy lines, with $214 million in sales by 1986, although this was down from its 1985 sales of $337 million. My Little Ponies had a similar success, establishing the Hasbro touch with character-marketing in the less developed girls' market. In 1986 Hasbro had thirty-four of the top one hundred sellers in the toy market largely because of its faith in character-marketing and its investment in advertising and promotion, which rose quickly from $81 million in 1984 to $170 million in 1985.

But Hasbro's failures as well as its successes indicate the new dynamics of the toy markets. The Inhumanoids, one of the most gruesomely violent attempts to merge the horror and science fiction elements of the toy market, flopped miserably with kids. The property had a range of faults, including weak characterization, but the toys also invoked parental resistance because they frightened children. Hasbro had to cut its losses and take Inhumanoids off television. Likewise, Hasbro's attempts to venture into film production with the Transformers and My Little Pony movies ended up losing the company $10 million.

In 1986 Hasbro found that intensive and expensive promotion did not guarantee success. Advertising and promotions were a necessary but not sufficient condition of children's marketing. Moreover, when certain heavily advertised lines failed to achieve their targeted sales, the effect was often to increase the advertising–sales ratio on those lines, leading to lower profit margins and distributor resistance. As a result, to maintain its steady 7.7 per cent profitability, Hasbro became more circumspect in the development of its new product lines. Similarly, character-marketing came under review in the board rooms of a number of toy manufacturers as the competitive market forced adjustments.

As the entrance costs and perceived risks of the toy market grew, research and development took on a greater importance. As Hasbro saw it, growth required figuring out which products would most benefit from the character strategy,[64] although the company remained convinced, as it said, that 'the development of new products is the driving force in our business'. Hasbro doubled its research and development staff in 1986 to a world total of 550 people to try to ensure that its products were on target and well tested. In the competitive environment of character-marketing, cultural research became necessary at all stages of product planning:

> At Hasbro, the development of new products involves a close linkage between R and D and marketing, as well as active participation of engineering, operations, sales and many other functions. New product ideas are rigorously evaluated from a number of different standpoints. These include design, safety, quality, lasting play value and market opportunity as well as advertising and promotional possibilities.[65]

This expansion of R and D reflected the Hasbro realization that the 'desire to create and maintain a broad spectrum of products and to extend the product life cycle requires a significant investment both in people and technology'. The company's general marketing plan called for more introductions and higher promotion costs that were more carefully researched to avoid future failures.

Research into children's feelings about their heroes was particularly fruitful and this included attempts to get at the roots of success in order to repeat it. As Hasbro executives explained, 'Such research for example helped to identify ways of continuing the popularity of the Joe team' so that 'by introducing new characters to the established team they were able to lengthen the product life cycle and amortize the expense of programme and product development'.[66] The popular wrestler Sargeant Slaughter was introduced into the Joe squad in 1986 and the Fridge (Refrigerator Perry) was added in 1987. Licensed sports-action figures became an increasingly important part of the market in 1988, when Kenner launched its Starting Lineup figurines, which grossed $50 million that year.

Coleco is another interesting, if less successful, case of corporate adjustment to the changes being wrought in the toy market. Coleco had built a successful toy company by answering the expanding demand for electronic computer and education games in the late 1970s. Diversifying in the early 1980s, the company enjoyed an initial success in the doll market with its Cabbage Patch line, brought out for Christmas 1983. Cabbage Patches were personality dolls of a different type, using certificates and slight changes in design to 'individuate' the product. The gimmick was successful for several years, but Coleco did not modify its promotional style to exploit the possibilities of television. When the computer games market declined in the mid 1980s and the Cabbage Patch dolls got stale, Coleco found itself in increasing financial trouble but lacked the infrastructure to bring new megatoys into the market. The fate of Coleco is a message writ large in the toy industry. It's a lesson learned too by the high-flying World of Wonders company, which brought out its Laser Tag to much acclaim and interest but suffered from competitive imitation, high promotional costs and the short life of such toys.

Other major toy makers struggled to adjust to the demonstrated new marketing realities created by character toys. Fisher-Price, which was experienced in licensing with its *Sesame Street* line, sought new licensing agreements with television production houses and also developed Construx, a thematic construction toy wrapped in the futuristic mood of the 1980s character universe. Lego too had to revise its longstanding practice of diverting only 15 per cent of its advertising budget to promotions directed to children. In addition to a $10 million expenditure in TV advertising, Lego also got involved in a co-operative advertising deal with the McDonald's chain, which gave Lego up to 400,000 exposures to its product line. Like Fisher-Price, Lego recognized that only by expanding the theme orientation of its classic construction product to accommodate the new emphasis on fantasy play could it keep the product in the market.

The Objects of Orientation

In the saturated toy markets of the 1980s, marketers found it essential to position their products ever more carefully. 'Positioning' is marketing jargon for a type of strategic thinking that attempts to situate a product within the everyday experience of children's lives and to specify the unique nature of the toy in relation to other products in the same niche. Toy manufacturers gradually learned that symbolic design for imaginary peer play was a subtle design problem fraught with enormous difficulties and risks. The broad methods of toy marketing were all well known and intensely employed: mass popularity, peer appeal, personality, media tie-ins. Toy merchandisers during the 1980s merely worked these methods up into a practical formula – a strategy stressing 'symbolic design' that made communications research a necessary part of the positioning, charting and assessment of how new characters were faring.

It was in this uncertain market that children's researchers were able to establish their credentials with toy merchants, because they provided practical ideas that could be used to sell toys. The validity of their work lies in the fact that the research helped to interpret children's experience. There is no coherent and well-developed body of theory among marketing researchers, but the trade journals are full of accounts of their services. Langbourne Rust, one of the better-established children's researchers, has synthesized some of the general research findings about children's response to the market-place into what he calls an 'orientation' model for children's consumer responses:

> Marketers tend to draw some inappropriate distinctions (mostly carry overs from models of adult consumer behaviour) which make it very difficult for them to see the holistic nature of children's thought. I have found it useful to downplay the term 'decision' and stress, instead, an orientation model.[67]

Rust once again confirmed the notion that children as consumers don't make rational choices about products. Rather, they

> move through life following one orientation after another. They seldom make decisions, in the classic sense of the term. Their involvement with the marketplace is characterized by very global, undifferentiated tendency to approach things.... For most kids most of the time liking and knowing are part of the same global response ... researchers should talk to children more about objects and less about attributes. And advertisers should keep the focus on the objects too.

The problem for marketing research, it seemed, was that of specifying how to orientate the child towards the product.

Rust suggested three means by which the toy business could change or form a child's orientation: definition, association and proposition. These principles would allow marketers to 'position' their own products in children's culture so that they could be differentiated from other competing products. Definition establishes the existence of a product in the child's mind; association links that product to other things – emotions, activities, products and people – in a child's awareness; and proposition asserts that the children will get something else they want just by having the product: possibly status, new energy, or happiness.

Definition, Rust argued, 'may be the most primitive level at which advertising works. With children it is often the most effective. If a product is strongly defined children will orient to it.' The methods he suggests for enhancing the definition of a product are show and tell, personification, and plot pivots. Next, through association, the product image is connected to 'desirable people and celebrities as well as familiarity associations'. These associations basically work because children orientate themselves to products on an emotional level. The last method, proposition, is the least effective, Rust suggested, because it is difficult to communicate to kids in simple terms about the consequences of product ownership, beyond the tactics of special promotions or offers. Explaining consequences or gratifications was an overly difficult communicative task when values such as belonging or status could be effectively communicated through association. But Rust's central message to marketers was: don't worry whether or not kids understand the advertising concept or even the story, but rather test for whether they latch on to a distinct identity for the product and make positive associations.

Rust's orientation theory illustrates what was learned by children's marketers through research and experience. His advice may seem obvious and commonsensical, but the very legitimation of common sense was an important contribution of children's research. After being rediscovered in research and tested in the marketplace, pragmatic simplification and the repetition of tried methods became the gospel of children's marketing. The lure of television promotion gradually transformed the toy industry and its marketing approaches. And when marketers concluded that television was the magical medium of communication with children because it promoted an 'impulsive style of thought', the face of children's advertising would change yet again.

Notes

1. *Marketing News*, 3 Jan. 1986. p. 3.
2. Ibid.
3. James McNeal, *Children as Consumers*, Lexington, Lexington Books, 1987, p. 7.
4. James McNeal, *Children as Consumers*, Austin, Tex., University of Texas, Bureau of Business Research, 1964.
5. The major overviews of children's consumerism are: Thomas Barry, *Children's Television Advertising*, Southern Methodist University, American Marketing Association, Monograph Series 8, 1977; James McNeal, *Children as Consumers*, Lexington,

Lexington Books, 1987; Scott Ward, 'Consumer Socialization', *Journal of Consumer Research*, 1 September 1974, pp. 1–14.

6. The Gene Reilly Group, *The Child*, Darien, CT, The Gene Reilly Group, vols 1–4, December 1975.

7. Ibid. p. 54.

8. Kenneth D. Bahn, 'How and When Do Brand Perceptions and Preferences First Form? A Cognitive Developmental Investigation', *Journal of Consumer Research*, 13, December 1986, pp. 382–7; Ellen Wartella, Daniel Wackman, Scott Ward, Jacob Shamir and Alison Alexander, 'The Young Child as Consumer', in Ellen Wartella, ed., *Children Communicating: Media and Development of Thought, Speech, Understanding*, Beverly Hills, Sage, 1979, pp. 251–80.

9. Lester P. Guest, 'The Genesis of Brand Awareness', *Journal of Applied Psychology*, 26 December 1942, pp. 800–8; Lester P. Guest, 'Brand Loyalty Revised: A Twenty Year Report', *Journal of Applied Psychology*, 48, 1964, pp. 93–7.

10. William Wells, 'Communicating with Children', *Journal of Advertising Research*, March 1965, p. 12.

11. Charles Atkin and Gary Heald, 'The Content of Children's Toy and Food Commercials', *Journal of Communication*, 27, 1977, pp. 107–14; and discussion, McNeal, p. 72.

12. John Doolittle and Robert Pepper, 'Children's TV AD Content: 1974', *Journal of Broadcasting*, 19(2), 1975, pp. 131–42.

13. Joann P. Galst and M.A. White, 'The Unhealthy Persuader: The Reinforcing Value of Children's Purchase-Influencing Attempts at the Super-Market', *Child Development*, 47, 1976, pp. 1089–96; James Frideres, 'Advertising, Buying Patterns and Children', *Journal of Advertising Research*, 13, 1973, pp. 34–6.

14. Sydney Ladensohn Stern and Ted Schoenhaus, *Toyland: The High-Stakes Game of the Toy Industry*, Chicago, Contemporary Books, 1990.

15. Television Bureau of Advertising, 'Target Selling the Children's Market', 1986.

16. 'Shoppers Rate Toy Speciality Store Tops', *Chain Store Age*, Feb. 1986, pp. 123–7.

17. 'Deck the Aisles with Lots of Basics', *Chain Store Age*, Sept. 1986, pp. 67–9.

18. TVB, 'The Children's Market', 1986; 'Can Retailers Afford To Grin and Bear It (Plush Add-On Sale Programs)', *Chain Store Age*, Nov. 1987, pp. 29—31; 'Deck the Aisles with Lots of Basics', *Chain Store Age*, Sept. 1986, pp. 67–9; 'High Prices Put Retailers in a Quandary', *Chain Store Age*, May 1987, p. 80; 'No Clear Winner Emerges in Toys', *Chain Store Age*, July 1987, p. 30; 'No Playing Around in Toyland', *Chain Store Age*, Sept. 1987, pp. 39, 40, 42; 'The Year of the Bear in Plush Toys', *Chain Store Age*, Feb. 1985, pp. 109–11.

19. McNeal, *Children as Consumers*, 1987, chs 2 and 3.

20. Hans G. Furth, *The World of Grown-ups: Children's Conceptions of Society*, New York, Elsevier, 1980.

21. Jo Marney, 'The Importance of the Children's Market', *Marketing (Advertising Research)*, 27 June 1983, (TVB); Jo Marney, 'Catch Them While They're Young', *Marketing (Advertising Research)*, 15 Nov. (TVB).

22. McNeal, *Children as Consumers*, 1987.

23. Daniel Wackman, Ellen Wartella and Scott Ward, 'Learning to Be Consumers: The Role of the Family', *Journal of Communication*, 1977, pp. 138–51.

24. Lewis Berey and R. Pollay, 'The Influencing Role of the Child in Family Decision Making', *Journal of Marketing Research*, 5, 1968, pp. 70–2; S. Ward and D. Wackman, 'Television Advertising and Intrafamily Influence: Children's Purchase Influence Attempts and Parental Yielding', in E.A. Rubenstein, G.A. Comstock and J.P. Murray, eds, *Television and Social Behavior*, vol. 4, *Television in Day-to-Day Life: Patterns of Use*, Washington DC, US Printing Office, 1972.

25. Laura Jereski, 'Advertisers Woo Kids with a Different Game', *Marketing and Media Decisions*, Sept. 1983, p. 73.

26. S. Ward and D. Wackman, 'Television Advertising and Intrafamily Influence'.

27. L. Berey and R. Pollay, 'The Influencing Role of the Child in Family Decisions', *Journal of Marketing Research*, 5, February 1968, pp. 70–2.

28. Charles Atkin, 'Television Advertising and Socialization to Consumer Roles', in D. Pearl et al., ed., *Television and Behaviour: 10 Years of Scientific Progress and Implications for the Eighties*, vol. 2, *Technical Reviews*, National Institute of Mental Health, Washington, US Government Printing Office, 1982, p. 191; Charles Atkin, 'Observation of Parent–Child Interaction in Supermarket Decision-Making', *Journal of Marketing*, 42, 1975, pp. 41–5.

29. Canadian Association of Broadcasters, *Broadcast Code for Advertising to Children*, Toronto, 1980 (revision).

30. Personal interview with Goody Teachman, children's researcher, Toronto, Ontario.

31. Brenda Daily (manager, product-testing, at Milton Bradley) in *Communicating to the Youth Market: A Child's Perspective*, Research report circulated by TVB, p. RC–7.

32. Information and Public Relations, LEGO System A/S, 1987, *Factors and Figures, Lego*, Denmark.

33. Fisher-Price Canada, *Fisher-Price Corporate History*, Mississauga, Ontario, Fisher-Price Canada, 1987.

34. The Canadian Toy Manufacturers Association, *Mixing Business and Pleasure: An Outline of the Canadian Toy and Decoration Industry*, 1979, p. 2.

35. William Wells, 'Communicatintg with Children', *Journal of Advertising Research*, 5, June 1965, pp. 2–14.

36. Carole Hyatt, 'Learning the Child Research Ropes', *Everything You Should Know About Child Research* (Proceedings of the ARF Key Issues Seminar), April 1986, New York, p. 101.

37. Jane Rae, 'If You're Going to Advertise to Kids on Television Do it Right', *Stimulus*, (May/June) p. 24–5.

38. ARF, *Everything You Should Know About Children's Resesearch*, Transcript Proceedings, New York Hilton, April 28 1986.

39. André W. Collins, 'Children's Comprehension of Television Content', in Ellen Wartella, ed., *Children Communicating: Media and Development of Thought, Speech, Understanding*, Beverly Hills, Sage, 1979, pp. 21–52.

40. Rae, 'If You're Going to Advertise'.

41. J. Frideres, 'Advertising, Buying Patterns and Children', *Journal of Advertising Research*, 13, February 1973, pp. 34–6.

42. A. Caron and S. Ward, 'Gift Decisions by Kids and Parents', *Journal of Advertising Research*, 15, August 1975, pp. 15–20.

43. Subhash C. Lonial and Stuart Van Auken, 'Children's Perceptions of Characters: Human versus Animate, Assessing Implications for Children's Advertising', *Journal of Advertising*, 14(2), 1985, pp. 13–22; Stuart Van Auken and S.C. Lonial, 'Children's Perceptions of Characters', 1985, p. 61.

44. Stephen R. Levin, T.V. Petros and F.W. Petrella, 'Preschoolers' Awareness of Television Advertising', *Child Development*, 53, 1982, pp. 933–7.

45. David Bloome and Danielle Ripich, 'Language in Children's Television Commercials: A Sociolinguistic Perspective', *Theory into Practice*, 18(4), 1979, pp. 220–5.

46. S. Ward, 'Consumer Socialization', *Journal of Consumer Research*, 1, Sept. 1974, pp. 1–13.

47. McCollum/Spielman Topline Report, New York, vol. 2(2), 1983.

48. Marsha B. Liss, 'Learning Gender-Related Skills through Play', in Marsha Liss,

ed., *Social and Cognitive Skills: Sex Roles and Children's Play*, New York, Academic Press, 1983; Terry Balaban, Joel Cooper and Diane Ruble, 'Gender Constancy and the Effects of Sex-Typed Televised Toy Commercials', *Child Development*, 52, 1981, pp. 667–73; Chris A. Downs, 'Letters to Santa Claus: Elementary School Age Children's Sex-Typed Toy Preferences in a Natural Setting', *Sex Roles*, 9(2), 1983, pp. 159–63; Lori Swartz and William T. Markham, 'Sex Stereotyping in Children's Toy Advertisements', *Sex Roles*, 12(2) 1985, pp. 157–70; Helen B. Schwartzman, *Transformations: The Anthropology of Children's Play*, New York, Plenum Press, 1979.

49. S. Ward, 'Consumer Socialization', *Journal of Consumer Research*, 1 Sept. 1974, pp. 1–14.

50. See, for instance, Cy Schneider, *Children's Television: The Art, The Business and How It Works*, Lincolnwood, Illinois, NTC Business Books, 1987, p. 90.

51. Elaine Morgenstein and Marvin Schoenwald, 'Success in the Children's Market Rests with Showing the Familiar', *Marketing News*, 12, 12 Sept. 1986, p. 48.

52. M. Goldberg and J. Gorn, 'Television's Impact on Preferences for Non-White Playmates: Canadian ('Sesame Street') Inserts', *Journal of Broadcasting*, 23(1), 1979, pp. 27–32; M. Goldberg and G. Gorn, 'Some Unintended Consequences of TV Advertising to Children', *Journal of Consumer Research*, June 5 1974, pp. 22–9.

53. McCollum-Spielman Topline Report.

54. Charles Atkin and Gary Heald, 'The Content of Children's Toy and Food Commercials', *Journal of Communication*, 27, 1977, pp. 107–14; Stephen Kline and Debra Pentecost, 'The Characterization of Play: Marketing Children's Toys', *Play and Culture*, 3(3) 1990, pp. 235–54.

55. Schneider, *Children's Television*, pp. 31–5.

56. *Marketing and Media Decisions*, March 1983, pp. 68–9, Interview with Felice Kincannon.

57. Laurie Jereski, *Marketing and Media Decisions*, Sept. 1983, p. 72.

58. Antonia Fraser, *A History of Toys*, London, Weidenfeld and Nicolson, 1966.

59. McCollum-Spielman Topline Report, 'Star Power 2: Understanding Kids and their Stars', *Topline*, 4(2), 1985.

60. Ibid.

61. Schneider, *Children's Television*.

62. Hasbro Corporate Report, 1987.

63. Schneider, *Children's Television*, p. 34.

64. Hasbro Corporate Report, 1987.

65. Ibid., p. 12.

66. Ibid., p. 8.

67. Langbourne Rust, 'Children's Advertising: How It Works, How to Do It, How to Know If It Works', in *Everything You Should Know About Children's Research*, Proceedings of ARF Key Issues Workshop, New York, April 1986, pp. 13–22, and summarized in Langbourne Rust, *Journal of Advertising Research*, August 1986, RC 13–15.

7

Limited Imaginings

Television has wrought no violent revolution. It has not destroyed conversation or revived the intimacy of Victorian family life; it has not converted Americans from an active people into a passive one; its psychological effect on the young has not always been for the best, but at the same time it has not produced a generation of delinquents. Americans continue to work, play, make love, and raise children. Our world, in the age of television, is still the same world. But we experience it in new and different ways.[1]

From the earliest broadcasts, the power of television has inspired widespread concern about its impact on children.[2] Television has been cited for a vast array of misdemeanours over its forty years of cultural ascendance, and the critical litany, often sung in academic circles, has placed seemingly little pressure on the medium itself. The cynical chorus is well known: commercial television produces a fiction of the lowest common denominator. It favours banal, mindless and trivial programming that strives not to enlighten but to entertain children with violence. It therefore encourages and legitimates violence in children. Its illiterate baubles also distract children from healthier activities, such as reading and sports, and have thus produced a generation of mean-spirited, aggressive and illiterate slobs.[3]

Television does appear to be a powerful instrument of socialization, with a wide scope to influence children's attitudes, behaviours, views of the world and cognitive abilities. For one thing it has been able to attract most children's attention for an average of 4.2 hours per day. Wouldn't all the received information influence the way children think, feel, act and interrelate?

The critics have long argued that television does have a significant impact on children. It has been credited with promoting passivity, lack of concentration, and an inappropriate understanding of the surrounding social universe.[4] Television has displaced other activities from children's lives – activities that happily preoccupied children before TV.[5] Given these enormous powers to influence children, the critics have asked if television shouldn't be guided by a cultural mission and a clear social responsibility to entertain, enlighten and educate children, to play a positive role in promoting community values and civic responsibility.

Throughout its brief history, then, television has been among the most contended arenas of cultural policy, particularly in the United States, where the commercial media system has been most firmly entrenched. Over the past two decades the battle has raged at the two regulatory bodies with authority over the production of children's culture – the FTC (Federal Trade Commission) and the FCC (Federal Communications Commission) – primarily over the issue of low investment and violent programming. For a long time the critics appeared to be winning. In the late 1960s, the US government did fund programme Head Start which launched *Sesame Street*, and it mandated the Public Broadcasting Service (PBS) to address educational concerns. Moreover, in 1974, after ACT (Action for Children's Television) had presented strongly expressed arguments about violence and the over-commercialization of children's television, the FCC imposed a set of guidelines restricting children's advertising in a number of ways and supervising the establishment of standards for advertiser self-regulation and the development of broadcaster codes for programming. The guidelines were supposed to impose limits on the merchandisers' influence on and through the medium by defining a framework for acceptable commercial speech to children.

The public battles over television also began to stimulate research into the effects of television, leading, for instance, to a massive series of studies on violence funded by the Surgeon General.[6] Yet for all the research effort devoted to proving television's effects on children[7] – especially on their aggressive behaviour and thoughts[8] and their cognitive functioning[9] – few researchers have been able to isolate empirically these 'effects' or to attribute changes in children's behaviour to television alone in isolation from other continuing cultural processes.[10] The theories concerning TV's effects had to take account of the consequences of the medium's general arousal as well as of the role of social learning through imitation, identification, attitude change and catharsis.[11] Most critics concluded that television does not have a hypodermic effect on children.[12] Studies of television now prefer to talk about what happens to some children under some conditions when exposed to particular kinds of ideas repeatedly; researchers argue that children may incorporate some of the information provided into their behaviour patterns and conceptual schema. Researchers are also well acquainted with the part played by siblings and parents in restricting and counteracting the input from television.[13] In the end it comes down to the influence of television being understood within the broader patterns of social cognition and social behaviour.

Ironically, the failure of research to document any monolithic social impact on children watching television has been used time and again by television's promoters to vindicate and justify the current commercial arrangements. If television cannot be proved to be harmful, why regulate its producers, when they are so evidently producing pleasurable entertainment for children? The very willingness of children to give so much of their time to television, and of families to permit this activity presents a dilemma for critics, who risk appearing élitist and moralistic, somehow distanced from the mainstream of American life. The critics would seem to underestimate the capacity and abilities of children to understand for themselves what's going on. The toy makers and TV producers have been quick to point out that children are more sophisticated than the simple-minded critics might believe.[14] They say that most children don't unthinkingly imitate television violence or model their behaviour directly on the roles of television superheroes, that children understand the difference between reality and fantasy, between advertising and programming. Television has, as Leo Bogart argued in 1958, wrought no revolutions in childhood, other than on the level of experience – a level that continues to elude the empirical researchers who have taken television out of context and have few tools for studying its true impact on children's culture.

A theory to account for the more complex children's 'experience' of television has only recently begun to be developed. First, it is now recognized that television is not monolithic in its content. So there is no singular form, set of role models or ideology which dominates children's TV – or if there is it has rarely been carefully studied. Yet children's television is formulaic – it follows definite patterns of representation which means that divergent themes, characters and ideas get squeezed into restricted narrative structures. Children's

210

narrative on television, for instance, uses humour and satire to make sure that the kids don't take the cartoons seriously. To understand children's television necessitates understanding these narrative structures.[15]

Second, the children's audience is far from homogeneous. The studies of children's viewing patterns have revealed the importance of different subgroups, segments and viewing environments, all of which regulate the amount and nature of the viewing process.[16] The audience has a certain structure, a factor that becomes especially important in marketing considerations: different demographic groups watch television differently. Moreover, because parents from different demographic strata follow different childrearing approaches, their control of their children's viewing and consumption is also a factor. Some parents restrict and regulate television-watching. Some children are heavy viewers but are guided by parents. Some children have to negotiate their viewing with peers and siblings, and others just watch what they want on their own. The patterns of heavy viewing, peer viewing, and parental influence are significant mediating factors in what or how children learn from television.[17]

Third, the theory holds that children are active processors of television content. They choose to watch particular programmes, and they make sense of them in their own ways. Children understand the differences in the forms and genres of television and use this knowledge to make sense of the content.[18] Children are therefore not easily gulled or taken in by television. They don't believe everything portrayed on commercials, identify with every hero, or imitate behaviour. They understand the difference between television and real life.[19] As Andrew Collins stated in a discussion of this issue, the child uses both abstract categories of social knowledge and the memory of specific social events to make sense of television:

> After viewing typical programs, attributions of causality and predictions about future behavior reflect not only the content of the stimulus, but also what viewers know about the types of characters and incidents portrayed, the conditions under which causality is appropriately imputed, and expectations about the temporal stability of behaviors or traits, as well as skills for processing the implicit and explicit contents, per se.[20]

Because of differences in how children interpret television, effects cannot be predicated on simple mimicry, but are mediated by the processes of social learning and identification.[21]

Howard Gardner has compared the situation of a child in front of the television set, to that of the anthropologist who, 'relying primarily on common sense and general knowledge of human nature', works at describing and almost single-handedly constructing models of society – 'its language, its kinship structure, its values, and its beliefs'. Anthropologists test and revise formulations as necessary, until they feel relatively secure in the 'characterizations'.[22] For children the complexity of this process of 'social decoding' demands that they quickly become skilled in making sense of fiction: 'The most formidable puzzle confronting the young television viewers is the status of, and relation among, the multiple levels of reality and fantasy within the variegated fare presented.'[23] This social decoding process is precisely what the character marketers saw as the appeal of character toys; the careful construction of fantasy-world back-stories and attractive imaginary characters was the basis of their craft. They themselves became ethnographers of children's daydreams in order to create mini-worlds that resonated with the social knowledge and preferences of their target markets – all so their product lines would stand out.

Robert Hodge and David Tripp summarize this new perspective:

> Television is refracted by children's minds, which develop different strategies for coping with the 'realities' on television and in the world they come to know; that the child's 'construction of reality' is a process of negotiation that unfolds in time under specific social circumstances; that both the content and the forms of thought that mediate it evolve in ways that will determine the ideological effects of television; and that the years from 0 to 12 are a crucial period for us to study if we are to understand why television has such a variable effect on the formation of ideas and world views.[24]

Hodge and Tripp provide a ten-point summary of a more sophisticated approach to children and television:

1. Active coding of programmes potentially rich in meaning implies that viewing can be of variable benefit and harm.
2. Developmental sequences underwrite decodings.
3. Television carries dominant ideologies but also oppositional meanings.
4. The perception of the relationship between reality and the world of television is developmentally determined.
5. Children need both fantasy and reality in their programming.
6. Conflict depiction is rooted in traditions of fiction but, as

212

fictionalized representation, it is different from real violence.

7. Children use the contents of television in other discursive practices.
8. Ideological forms have a determining effect on the decoding of television content.
9. The family is a site for determining and countering the child's decoding of television.
10. The schools should draw the interpretation of television into their curricular purview.

Unfortunately, the resources available for research have not been channelled into more comprehensive designs that could aid the study of this more illusive 'cultural effect'. In spite of the growing sophistication in media theory and research, the critics of television are losing ground in the policy arena.

After some forty years, the question of what it means to grow up in a generational culture predominantly framed by television-produced fantasies no longer seems to trouble the public. Those who question the quality of children's television seem strangely out of touch in that they fail to understand the realities of the commercial broadcasting system and the way the central belief in the market and consumer sovereignty has underwritten programming decisions. Cy Schneider believes that the critics completely misapprehend the business of television production:

> What these people fail to realize is that commercial television, even for children, is just another business. It is a business that makes its money by helping sell products, a valuable stimulator for gross national product which in turn helps to create jobs and greases the wheels of our economy. Is it fair to ask the television industry to be different from other businesses?[25]

Programming and production decisions have always been made within the commercial media for broadly economic reasons related to marketing and advertising criteria. Indeed, the networks – which had no delusions about their social obligations – did not choose ritualistically violent or mind-numbingly banal programming because they liked them; they did so because the market dynamics and advertiser demand made these the only economically viable options. As Schneider unequivocally states, quality programming (even the likes of *Sesame Street*) that fails to draw a sufficiently large audience simply cannot be justified on commercial television:

Before anyone judges television, he or she must first understand that decisions in the television industry are economic decisions. The television business works on three simple principles: keep the audience up, the costs down, and the regulators out. The reformers forget that television's first mission is not to inform, educate, or enlighten. It isn't even to entertain. Its first mission is to entice viewers to watch the commercials. If commercial television cannot move goods, it cannot be in business.[26]

The sole purpose of children's television, as Schneider points out, is to make money for the people who have a stake in the business.

Schneider's admonition is useful for critics of the 'cultural impact' of television. The first and foremost issue remains the purpose of this new technology of socialization: the impact of television on culture is to a great degree a function of how society chooses to use the medium. If we license this institution to entertain and preoccupy our children and pay no thought to questions of education, family life or the quality of fiction, we should not be surprised that this is what television accomplishes. But during the 1980s, US television was further mandated as a legitimate tool of merchandising. Deregulation allowed children's merchandisers to use the medium more fully in their business plans, and we should not be surprised by the enthusiasm that children's marketers showed for this expanded access to children's culture. Television performed this role well, effectively increasing the market for children's character toys, snack foods and cereals. One consequence was that more resources were funnelled into children's animations. Yet this revolution in television has often been overlooked. Schneider was right in reminding the cultural critics of television that they must first understand the new business dynamic – they must understand the changing dynamics of children's television production before they attempt to delineate and assess the impact of the changes on children's experience.

Deregulation of Children's Advertising

The rise of 'business culture' during the 1980s was not simply an ideological blip on the cultural scene. Reaganomic policies resulted in profound changes in the regulatory structure of the culture industries, enabling a cycle of enterprise that expanded the manufacture, marketing, licensing and retailing of children's goods. The reverberations that swept through children's lives were created by the

214

turnaround at the FCC. The fact that overturning a few provisions that had imposed some minor limitations on children's commercial programming could have made such a profound impact on children's toy preferences is an indication of the delicate web linking economic and cultural matters in post-industrial society. The fact that policy changes caused so little public protest is a further indication of a major shift in public opinion concerning the culture industries: it was not only élitist for critics to argue for quality in children's programming, but it was also anti-democratic to oppose the changes in the marketing of children's products unless there was proof of harmful effects.[27]

Yet in 1974 similar public arguments about the 'over-commercialization' of children's television had led the Federal Communications Commission to impose a set of guidelines restricting children's advertising. The agency had also supervised the establishment of standards for advertiser self-regulation and the development of broadcaster codes. At that time, under threat of an outright ban on children's advertising, the US television industry had agreed to guidelines for children's advertising that extended control over a number of merchandising practices for children's commercials, including product testimonials by television characters, exaggerated claims, deceptive pricing, the presentation of misleading product sizes and the abuse of children's credulity and imagination. In 1978 the FTC had become active in studying the children's advertising issue and added its opinion that children's advertising was inherently 'unfair and deceptive' because children were 'too young to understand the selling purpose of, or otherwise comprehend or evaluate, the advertising'.[28]

All this regulatory activity appeared to be backed by widely held public opinion (and a very articulate lobby group – Action for Children's Television – led by Peggy Charren), influenced by the apparent general failure of industry self-restraint in children's advertising. A report written in 1979 on behalf of the American Academy of Advertising conceded:

> Advertisers have done a poor job of self-regulation up to this point. The Broadcasting Code and other efforts at industry standards are recognized as being ineffective. These industry efforts have also lacked a sound empirical base. In this sense, children's advertising is centered on what works rather than a knowledgeable model of children as a special audience with particular needs and characteristics which must be addressed.[29]

After a decade of hearings and considerable research calling for special safeguards against abuses in children's marketing, it seemed probable that a tougher framework for children's television was in the offing. Yet in early 1980 the FCC suddenly reversed its position and began the *de facto* deregulation of children's television advertising. Under the sway of Reagan's administrative appointments, the FTC also removed the 1978 'unfairness' ruling. In 1984, the guidelines that had restricted television commercial time to nine and a half minutes an hour on Saturday and Sunday mornings were also lifted, leading to more children's commercials with almost no supervision of their content.

The arguments for restrictions on children's commercials have their base in a principle of jurisprudence rooted in conceptions of family life concerning the protection of vulnerable children – a view widely held during the twentieth century.[30] For reasons of developmental inadequacy, children are to be protected from having to make decisions that are beyond their capacity and experience. 'Children are viewed as a "special" audience, one that is particularly vulnerable to television's messages.... Young children, because they lack cognitive skills and the life experiences necessary to evaluate messages as adequately as might an adult, are likely to learn from and be influenced by TV content, even though it is essentially intended only to entertain them.'[31]

The implications of this argument for advertising policy is that children should have special status in the marketplace (with concomitant restrictions on the freedoms of commercial speech to them) because they cannot be assumed to have the knowledge, experience and emotional background to act as rational consumers in the market. This argument was taken seriously, for instance, by the Parti Québecois, which legislated a provincial ban on children's advertising in Quebec in 1978. In a recent case initiated by Irwin Toys against the Quebec governments, the Supreme Court of Canada upheld the ban, citing consumer protection as a legitimate legal doctrine:

> In sum, the objective of regulating commercial advertising directed at children accords with a general goal of consumer protection legislation, viz to protect a group that is most vulnerable to commercial manipulation. Indeed, that goal is reflected in general contractive doctrine.... Children are not as equipped as adults to evaluate the persuasive force of advertising and advertisements directed at children would take advantage of this. The legislature reasonably concluded that advertisers should be precluded from taking advantage of children both by inciting them to

make purchases and by inciting them to have their parents make purchases. Either way the advertiser would not be able to capitalize upon children's credulity ... materials demonstrate, on the balance of probabilities, that children grow up to the age of thirteen manipulated by commercial advertising and that the objective of protecting all children in this age group is predicated on a pressing and substantial concern.[32]

The Canadian court based its decision on the evidence of research that the judges felt underpinned the three primary reasons for protecting children: namely, that children (especially the under-eights) do not understand the purpose of commercials (persuasive intent), are too impulsive in their responses to persuasion, and have particular trouble distinguishing between fantasy and reality.

For a long time these same arguments were mustered at the FCC, yet with increasingly little effect. In his review of policy efforts directed at improving the way television serves the child audience, Dale Kunkel pessimistically concludes 'It seems unlikely to resolve the many children and television issues once and for all. As long as the system of American television broadcasting remains structured as it is, the issues of the past seem likely, in one way or another, to resemble the issues of the future – with no ultimate solution in sight.'[33]

The FCC's dramatic U-turn in policy caused considerable tribulation among children's advocates and produced continuing pressure on governments to re-establish restraint on children's advertising. To many people it seemed incomprehensible that the research had not established sufficient grounds (as found in the Canadian case) to place restrictions on advertising and commercial programming for children.[34] The US Court of Appeals recognized in the FCC's action a fundamental shift in ideology: 'The Commission has suddenly embraced what had theretofore been an unthinkable bureaucratic conclusion that the market did in fact operate to restrain the commercial content of children's television.'[35] Given widespread protest about the 'program-length commercials', which had been prevented by previous guidelines, the FCC was forced to reconsider its ruling in 1987, yet it again reserved judgement, demanding that critics prove such programmes 'caused more harm than good'. A new piece of legislation was rejected by Reagan's presidential veto in 1988. As a recent review of children's advertising policy points out, the situation in the United States is 'far from being settled':

All of the various parties recognize that children constitute a special

217

advertising audience, with distinct needs and vulnerabilities. All agree that care must be taken in designing and presenting television advertising to children. They disagree, however, on specific issues and solutions. If the past is an indicator, trying to resolve these children's advertising issues promises to be a complex, protracted, costly, and frustrating process.[36]

Watered-down restrictions on commercial programming worked their way through Congress emerging as the Children's Television Act of 1990 which limited the amount of commercials to ten and a half minutes on weekends and twelve minutes on weekday children's television and provided an impetus for 'pro-social' and educational programming on a local level. This limitation did not, however, restrict the 'thirty minute commercials' (unless the same product was advertised in the programme)[37] and left the matter of the special status of children in the market unresolved. Toy industry spokespersons in fact thought this legislation would have little impact as for most of the year children's advertising time was still unsold, and the legislation imposed no restrictions on their advertising and tie-in strategies.[38] The long battle over children's television is not over yet because until the hidden tension between the two ideological principles – one supporting the unfettered operation of the free market and the other stressing the need to protect children from marketing – the battle will continue. These are clearly incompatible principles, and as it stands the ideology of the marketplace continues to dominate US television policy.

Let's Make a Deal

As merchandising deals were increasingly underwriting more and more film and television productions, the business of children's television was changing.[39] Deregulation allowed the merchandising tie-in to operate as the preferred tactic of children's programming and consequently made the ability to move product the overriding consideration in the scripting of television. As Cy Schneider states: 'What was once the sole province of children's authors, comic strip artists, and film artists ... has now become a creative outlet for toy and greeting card manufacturers.'[40] The revised purpose and arrangements for the production of children's fiction are thus much harder to expiate with a shrug of the historical shoulder.

The character-toy strategy proved effective for merchandising interests because it enabled them to harness the two most important cultural forces in childhood: stories and play. The business objective was to achieve a kind of synergy between children's fascination with television programmes and their intense engagement in imaginative play. This would be achieved through a comprehensive market-planning that prompts the synergy by using a unified thematic framework (including imagery, narratives, characters and music) to establish a product concept linking toys and television. The product concept would be maintained consistently and firmly throughout the in-store displays, interpersonal communications, advertising and television-programming.

In character-toy-marketing, then, the carefully controlled campaign imagery, using toy designs laid out in briefing books, detail the actions, postures, colour, expression and accessories to be used for each character. Licences stipulate that merchants accept these limitations. As Cy Schneider states concisely:

> Easy and correct definition of the character is most important. The character must be – or become – an essential part of the American popular culture mainstream. While the character can relate to or be reminiscent of characters which have come before, he or she must be unique in some important way. Uniqueness is usually achieved by a difference in personality, design, graphic execution, story line, or identity. It is seldom achieved by what the character stands for or the values associated with the character. These characters are usually larger than life. They are super special and can often perform extraordinary feats.[41]

The attention to detail can be astounding. When, for example, Hunts licensed the Smurf characters for a new spaghetti product, Smurfa-getti, they were presented with strict limits on the use of voice, characterization and storyline.[42] Similarly, the Ghostbusters briefing book defines the precise colours, clothing and facial expressions (only three per character) – the unifying imagery – that can be used by advertisers, T-shirt printers, animators and toy designers. Licensing agents and children's marketing specialists had become the quarterbacks of the new marketing campaigns, sometimes acting as consultants and often as account managers.

The comprehensive marketing approach implied economic arrangements that differed markedly from the ones that flourished under national spot advertising on network TV.[43] Licensing agreements and distribution deals are the warp and woof of commercial

219

relations, and the deals that were cut had to package film, clothing, toy, publishing and accessories' rights.[44] The licensing of toys accounted for over 15 per cent of the $54 billion industry in 1987.[45] Developing a character property brought all the diverse sectors (toys, clothes, television, animation houses, publishers) together; they shared an interest not only in children's marketing but also the deregulated marketplace that allowed the energetic promotion of their character on commercial television.

The most important affiliations are between toy manufacturers, toy distributors and film production companies. The campaigns have led to co-production and subsidized production arrangements and to the expansion of vertically integrated investment between toy manu-facturers and communications conglomerates. For example, the $14 million development costs of the *He-Man and Masters of the Universe* animation, one of the first syndications, were split between Mattel (the toy company), Filmation (the producers) and a licensing agency. Likewise, Hasbro's offer of 10 per cent of local area sales of Thundercats toys to local television stations showed the programme was a clever alternative to the outright buying of advertising. Such deals became the mainstay of this intensely competitive and dynamic marketplace. Nailing down distribution exclusives in a chain, proving the ability to deliver volumes on time and introducing a massive advertising plan are vital steps in garnering the kind of joint commitment the plans require. Mattel, for example, hooked up with Disney to enter the preschool market with its Duck Tale character revivals. Sears negotiated an exclusive arrangement for distributing Steven Spielberg's American Tale products in its stores. Rainbow Brite was brought to market with similar distribution arrangements, and Toys R Us captured an exclusive distribution for Muppet Baby accessories. This kind of deal-making and collaborations continue as the underpinning of the children's culture industries.[46]

One important sign of change was witnessed in the plethora of animation houses that emerged in the 1980s. A constellation of new corporate names (DIC, Filmation, Lorimar, Nelvana, Harmony Gold, Marvel, Ruby Spiers, Saban, Amblin) has established its place beside Disney, Hanna-Barbera and Warner, amounting to a new production infrastructure. Outflanked by the upstarts, the established children's producers responded to the challenge by also contracting co-production deals with the toy majors, especially after the networks eased up on their own children's production. Much of the actual animation work is carried out by studios in Japan, South Korea,

Taiwan and Hong Kong, with the US arm taking responsibility for concept development, scripts, story-boards and account management. The expensive drawing and cel animation work is done in Asia in the interest of economy and efficiency, but also because of the technical prowess and skilled personnel there. Some of the US-licensed character animations (*Robotech, Voltron, Transformers*) were actually first produced in and for the Japanese market. Because many of the toys are produced offshore as well, the toy makers were already in the position of being marketers rather than manufacturers.

The new researchers, licensing agents and animators of the 1980s were all motivated to produce the big hit with a promotional toy. Everyone in the industry had watched Kenner's success with Star Wars products. They had seen Mattel's He-Man and Hasbro's G.I. Joe take off, and they thought they could do the same. The promise of a toy concept that would sell several hundred million dollars of merchandise was the silver lining that helped to create a very open business climate – one in which clever marketing schemes and intricate deals were more important than track records, experience and solid financing.

The Rise of Syndication: Licensed to Kill

Throughout the 1970s, network and affiliated advertising time had experienced slow growth. The Saturday morning cartoon ghetto drew an audience composed of 53 per cent children, but the most-watched network was commanding only a 20 per cent share of this audience, making for a relatively high cost per million viewers (CPMs). With these small shares, there was little incentive or capital available for experimentation or for changing children's programming. Until the 1980s, the advertising expenditure for children's programmes rose at a rate slightly lower than the expenditures for television programmes in general.

The network programmers of the 1970s were content to offer well-worn cartoons, which kept costs down and proved an effective way of retaining children's advertisers. The low promotion–product ratios embedded in this cosy arrangement ensured the stability of the children's marketing sector in spite of the complaints of parents and activists who wanted higher quality and more funding directed into

221

kids' TV. Given restrictions on commercial time, children's advertising time was relatively expensive. Half an hour of animation cost from $250,000 to $300,000 to produce, and a network advertising spot, at about $26,000 for a Saturday morning screening (up to $40,000 for the top-rated *Smurfs*) represented a significant expenditure for children's advertisers. In turn the networks repeatedly argued that if the advertising interest wasn't there, they were unlikely to spend much money taking risks developing new kids' programmes or experimenting with new schedules. Innovations in programming were left to public television and later to the cable and pay TV networks such as Nickelodeon, which were forced to innovate to draw audiences. But then, in the dynamic and fluid environment of the 1980s, such head-in-the-sand tactics proved fatal.

The deals that brought licensed animation to television began to disrupt this longstanding hiatus in television. The new thirty-minute animation programme turned out to be essentially a commercial with its development costs subsidized by a toy manufacturer's promotion budgets so that it could be sold more cheaply to networks or station syndicates. These production arrangements helped to distribute both the escalating risks and the profits of a character-promotion venture. The TV syndicates also began to deliver the children's audience at much cheaper national rates, enabling the marketers to divert more money to production of the ads and elaborate promotions at toy fairs. The World of Wonders company, for example, produced a series of ads for its Lazer Tag that cost over $1 million each to make.

The excitement and fervour inspired by character-marketing was manifested in the rise of the syndicates, which took the lion's share of the expanding promotional budgets. Syndicates are 'temporary' networks – groups of independent stations that arrange to show a particular cartoon or group of cartoons (often with the advertising presold directly to agencies), but with some arrangement for individual stations to sell local advertising time as well. The syndicates circumvented the networks' hold on children's production and became the primary outlets for character-marketing. They were able to offer much cheaper advertising spots with considerable shares of the children's audience.

The already limited children's production of the networks was thus further shaken in the 1980s as the advertising revenues from children's programme times began to flatten and drop.[47] The syndicates took up to 25 per cent of the advertising revenue in 1984, for example, and this share increased with the rapid expansion of character-marketing. The networks were particularly threatened by the loss of toy advertising, which can account for up to 65 per cent of total income from children's programming in the pre-Christmas 'last' quarter when new programmes are introduced. The syndicates were also able to draw away some of the cereal and snack food advertisers, who were attracted by the higher exposure ratings that syndicates were getting with popular shows such as *Transformers* or *G.I. Joe.*

The development of syndicated TV was more suited to the highly targeted marketing strategies of promotional toys because in these arrangements the advertising rates could be calculated against 'target exposures' rather than depending on total audience draw. For example, the *G.I. Joe* media buyer would be interested in buying time that maximizes the number of boys between the ages of three and eight as a percentage of the whole viewing audience. The buyer is not interested in paying higher rates for exposing these ads to girls, youths or adults. Syndicates could more closely control the demographic and regional exposure, and by commanding larger numbers of stations for a particular programme they could bring the potential exposure to above 70 per cent of a carefully designated audience. These efficiencies in targeting an audience segment could ultimately cut the cost of advertising expenditures in half when calculated as CPMs.[48] For this reason many advertisers preferred the more efficient vehicle of afternoon programming offered by the syndicates to the Saturday morning schedules of the networks. After-school schedules became syndication time. Toy ads soon became more noticeable in these after-school blocks than on a network's Saturday morning schedule. During the late 1980s up to 60 per cent of syndicated children's-time advertising was being bought by toy makers.

The trend towards character-marketing was reflected in a change in the purpose and design of the toy commercial. Because TV programmes now served the function of introducing products and creating excitement in the market, the commercials could concentrate on dramatizing the imaginative 'play value' of the toys. Many of the new advertising agencies were relatively unconcerned about self-regulation and the dangers of eroding the line between reality and fantasy. The networks generally continued to use the guidelines of the advertising codes (developed in the 1970s), which warned against the abuse of children's imaginations. But the syndicates didn't apply the networks' advertising guidelines, so character marketers preferred to advertise on the less fussy syndicated stations.

The network time-sales people recognized that the syndicators' 'relaxation of standards and practices governing advertising in children's shows', particularly with regard to issues of fantasy and reality, was contributing to the erosion of their volumes. They generally included 'bumpers', which separated the programmes, and discouraged direct endorsements and unrealistic presentations. Some of the toy companies chose to produce two versions of their toy spots – one for networks and one for syndication. But the majority preferred to take the easier and less costly route offered by syndicated shows.

The result was a lessening of the networks' impetus to produce children's television and a reduction of their children's schedules. NBC threatened to do away altogether with its Saturday morning cartoon shows. In 1988, Brandon Tartikoff, the president of NBC entertainment, said: 'It might be much more profitable for the network if Saturday-morning cartoons were replaced by other types of programs (talk programs, news and sports for example) that would give NBC a whole new audience in that time period.'[49] In the late 1980s the ratings for NBC's cartoon spots showed signs of decline and, as Tartikoff said, 'For the last three years we have not made the kinds of profits that we did five or six years ago.' The reason he identified was the new arrangement forged over the previous eight years for children's cultural production based on the rise of character-marketing. As he explains: 'The shrinking profits are due to the boom in recent years of children's shows sold in syndication to independent TV stations', making network interest in children's audiences wane. By 1991, NBC was out of the Saturday morning sweepstakes and Tartikoff was producing films for the family.

The Limits of Character-Marketing

All products have a limited lifetime, toys more than most. Kids lose interest in particular toys and quickly move on to new ones. After all, emotional and cognitive maturation implies that new psychological needs and states are being regularly expressed and worked out through a child's imaginative play. Kids are also extremely peer-orientated, subject to the collective whims of their immediate cultural environment, which is constantly changing shape and focus.

The toys – whether Strawberry Shortcake, He-Man, My Little Pony, or Cabbage Patch dolls – all come and go. This fact – of market burnout – is even more true of character toys.

In a sense, Mattel's dilemma with the Barbie became the problem of the children's culture industries as a whole. It is the dilemma of a media environment geared towards intensely competitive character-marketing and an audience grown jaded, cynical and wary by an overdose of similar products. Successful innovation was often followed by slavish repetition. Once the basic tactics of the character-marketing were clear, all the toy companies began working with the same givens, but in a much more cluttered market. In most cases marketers tried to repeat the formulas that had proved successful, with minor adjustments in imagery or in marketing sizzle. Barbie has successfully fought back with a stronger presence in the toy market than any other fashion doll, grossing close to $700 million in 1990.

It wasn't so easy to define a new symbolic niche for all promotional products. A typical case of the difficulties of repeat magic was the task demanded of the Strawberry Shortcake innovators, 'Those Characters from Cleveland' (TCFC).[50] Lady Lovely Locks was a TCFC and Mattel collaboration that tried to target

> the niche of play pattern that we were so successful in capturing with Strawberry Shortcake ... letting a girl be a little girl .... Lady Lovely Locks is her friend. Lady Lovely Locks is not her baby. She doesn't have to play mother and she doesn't have to act like she's 17 to enjoy Lady Lovely Locks.

As *Chain Store Age* noted, TCFC was 'betting on this license to be a winner' because the product relied on the tried and true playmaking attractions of hair – although it updated the image with current fashion trends. 'The soft coloring of Pixietails and the long hair of all the characters' were designed with the niche appeal in mind. The launching of Lady Lovely Locks was backed by a multi-million dollar ad campaign undertaken by Mattel and by a thirty-minute TV special shown in syndication. Yet for all the combined experience of TCFC and Mattel, Lady Lovely Locks made only small inroads into the more youthful end of the fashion-doll market: she had plenty of competitors in that tried and true hair-play niche.

The toy makers applied character-marketing to an ever wider range of toy categories (plush, games, weapons) and tested it with different segments (girls, preschoolers, youth). Commenting wryly from the retailers' point of view, one writer noted that the sunny forecast invites comparisons with the profitability of Masters of the Universe, G.I. Joe, Go-Bots and Voltron. The good news in those categories continues to be strong sales; the bad news is small profit margins. . . . Can retailers afford another category . . . of exciting toys that must be sold at slashed prices to generate traffic and preserve a store's value image? The answer seems to be 'not for long'.[51]

By 1990, this paradox of the promotional toy was being felt throughout the toy industry.[52] The changing position of plush and electronic toys between 1985 and 1986 clearly indicated the impact television tie-ins could have on gross sales. The toy makers targeted these sectors with toys like Captain Power and Teddy Ruxpin. Whereas action-figure sales were down by 30 per cent, plush toy sales rose by 82 per cent and electronic toy sales by 79 per cent. The role play, riding toys, infant, arts and crafts and sports toys were all up a more modest 2–13 per cent. Vehicle toys dropped by 9 per cent.

For a couple of years the market expanded. Clearly, the licensing and promotional strategy could be successfully translated to new niches. Plush, electronic and even board games tried their hand at this marketing gambit, and some very successful new lines were produced. But the same problems emerged as creative competition intensified among the new lines which all used the same approach to marketing communication. How many dancing-animal animations would children watch? Character-marketing began to encounter limits in the business realities that had proved to be both the hope and bane of the toy industry. As a writer in one trade journal said:

> Brightly colored, cuddly plush characters have been licensed to kill – profit margins, that is, say many retailers. Plush, until recently an oasis of profitability in a desert of loss leaders, is now a category poised to enter big-time licensing. Because of this, the category will become more important and gain higher recognition among consumers as more plush characters are firmly installed as 'TV toys'. But the toys will be higher priced and, as they become more popular, price competition will force retailers to lower profit margins to stay in step with competitors. Most retailers and manufacturers agree that the impact of licensing on plush over the last two years could prove damaging . . . as retail customers are forced to limit licensed assortments in the cause of selectivity. Retailers expect the effects of licensed plush to produce a backlash against new lines that will generate momentum for a back to basics movement.[53]

The major problem of the character marketers became how to devise ways of keeping their promotional products attractive long enough to survive a season or two in the shops. The limits to success in marketing promotional toys lay in cultural uncertainties. First their timing had to be right. Their success hinged on being able to create enough excitement among kids at the right time so that purchases could sustain the product for a couple of years on the store shelves. The excitement had to be so specific that the product couldn't be undercut by imitators and discounters. For this reason the product had to be designed correctly – perfectly tuned to the subtle inflections in children's cultural preferences of the moment. It was almost impossible to be consistently creative and timely in this business, yet that is what success demanded. The children's toy and marketing industries survive by managing creativity, but that creativity does not embody the same quality that goes into the best fiction or magical animations.

The Limits of the Marketplace

All marketing strategies are ultimately tested in shops where money is exchanged for goods. The rise of the toy speciality stores such as Lionel and Toys R Us and a number of discount retailers helped to concentrate toy-buying, but it also gave these distributors of toys greater power in marketing plans than had been the case of the disaggregated small retailers and variety store merchants of the past. These toy majors are particularly interested in rapid turnover and more effective use of shop space to cover their enormous overheads and large staffs.

The saturation of the market presents additional problems for retailers concerned about giving as little space as possible to slow-moving lines. Yet from the marketers' point of view, shelf space is a critical form of display advertising. Popular fast-moving toys get the best position in a shop. Successful action figures and highly promoted products will benefit from stronger visual presence in the stores. As one store manager explained, 'These changes will be made at the expense of space for wheel goods and board games.... wheeled goods have been sku'd down by 40% and games by 25%.'[54] Competitive positioning in the shops was becoming an ever more crucial part of character-marketing. The merchants' interests are served best by having a product available when demand is high and having no stock left on the shelves or on order when demand drops off.

All goods eventually have to be bought in shops. The elaborate shows and wheeling and dealing of the annual toy fairs is a critical time in a toy's life because it is when the new lines are exposed, the advertising demonstrated and the deals made. There is an atmosphere of uncertainty lurking behind the façade of glamour in toyland.[55] Much hinges on the presentations, and access to the displays of the toy majors is by invitation only. The buyers have to believe that the toy will sell, and guarantees of heavy advertising and an animation serial became the prerequisites for gaining the optimum stocking and display space. As one toy retailer stated: 'Cartoons really moves them.' Another retailer explained: 'I look for company presence and the amount of TV advertising. We know, for instance, that Hasbro gets behind a product. They give a lot of force.... Action figures are the most advertised and the most shopped toy category.'[56] That is why merchandisers devote space to them.

In 1986, it seemed that promotional toys were in danger of squeezing all other toys off the shelves. But the specific problems of character-marketing from the point of view of the distributor began to reveal themselves that year as the dramatic growth in action-doll sales slowed and lines failed. The unhappy truth began to reveal itself to most retailers, and it was noted that 'Toyland is not a universally happy place'. Some 6 per cent fewer units were shipped in 1985, which meant that a higher sales volume was being derived from price increases rather than faster product turnover:

> Emotion similarly seems to have gone out of the licensing game. It is becoming increasingly hard for a licence to last beyond a year or two, a victim of knockoffs and inadequate strategic marketing. Though license goods accounted for approximately 50% of all toy sales last year, their value as a retail favourite diminished. With their invasion of even the highly profitable plush area licensing reached a stage where too much produced too little.[57]

The sales of gross $12·5 billion in 1986 appeared to flatten when compared with $12 in 1985 and the rapid gains of previous years. By 1990 merchandise-licensing and animation production had both stabilized as Nintendo took a $2·6 billion annual bite out of the US toy market. Indeed, by 1991, the US toy industry grossed $13·4 billion, but it was video games at $4 billion that enjoyed all the growth.[58]

Merchandising economics defines the limits of character-marketing, as the commentaries in the retail industry testify. A survey of toy department managers indicated that they thought the promotional nature of the licensed goods would 'increase traffic' yet 60 per cent said they were apprehensive about increasing their own promotion of licensed goods. Toy buyers were most cautious because they felt that the 'additional promoting promises to shrink margins which are in some cases already relatively low'. Some 65 per cent of toy buyers said they were already getting less than 25 per cent margins on licensed merchandise.[59] This made the whole industry more cautious and conservative in its development of new promotional products.

The subsidization of expanding toy-promotion budgets to pay for television productions, expensive advertising and other promotions was being felt by retailers, whose success is contingent on the profit margins. If their profit margins are reduced because of large promotional expenditures or special distribution rights, then in spite of huge volume sales of one line, a retailer may gain little profit. For example, action figures are relatively low-cost items, and their accessories can take up a lot of space and produce little profitability. Retailers have to be 'savvy buyers' when it comes to promotional toys – more than with the basics which enjoy steady and predictable demand – because of the accelerated cycles of demand and satiation. The consequences of stimulated demand is that retailers either run out of hot items or must severely mark down slow movers after the fad has passed. Discounters themselves preferred more basic lines. Promotional toys therefore began to run up against price barriers and profit margins in a saturated market.[60]

The hidden danger of licensing, then, is the investment in promotion, which takes a bigger share of the product's cost without necessarily increasing profits:

> The business of selling character licensed products has become so competitive that some discount buyers who expect sales to continue growing nevertheless will not enlarge their strings of licensed merchandise. More than 72% of discount buyers responding to a recent survey say they believe character licensed product sales will surge ahead. Despite this vote of confidence, slightly more than 40% of the buyers do not plan to expand their commitment to the category.[61]

Increasingly in the late 1980s, toy makers had to divert promotional effort into convincing the big toy retailers that their syndicated shows would be popular. Retailers had to be kept excited about a product. They had to be absolutely convinced that a new product would really move so they would devote significant shelf space to it. The toy fairs and trade shows have become exotic and expensive venues for promoting the next hot new lines.

On the other hand, their margins go down as the promotional budgets push up the toy's price. Burdened with high promotion costs, the repetitive stylistics and limited themes, a number of expensively developed character-lines were failing both to draw children's audiences and to promote toy sales. An example was Captain Power, an attempt to reinvigorate the electronic toy market with a game that had children fighting battles with television characters. Captain Power was the most talked-about toy of the trade shows in 1986, but he was so pricey that some marketing people believed he had blasted right out of the price universe. In competition with Lazer Tag Academy and the cheaper Nintendo games, Captain Power had to include costly hi-tech production values in its retail price. Moreover, it was becoming hard to stand out and break through the clutter of the promotional toy market, as a flood of imitative products such as Wuzzles, Lady Lovely Locks and Rock Lords poured into every product niche. Teddy Ruxpin, a talking plush toy, did well, but not well enough because of parents' price barriers for plush. Many character toys failed to meet sales projections as the toy merchandisers found that a family's expenditure on toys was not unbounded. Their animated lives were never extended a second year. Moreover, a few of the product concepts – Rambo and the Inhumanoids, for example – had resulted in such violent or frightening TV shows that they disturbed parents and alarmed kids. There was growing parent resistance to buying more action-toy products, especially militaristic and war toys, and the rumblings of the critics of war toys were being heard once again.[62] For this reason, the promotional toys of the late 1980s and early 1990s have taken on a more responsible caste, including the reinvigoration of well-known and more cartoon-like characters (Muppet Babies, Tiny Toon Adventures, Duck Tales and Bucky O'Hare) or programmes for the young caste in more overtly 'pro-social' roles (Smoggies, Toxic Crusaders).

A Global Play: Unintended Consequences

The harvest of Reaganomics has to some degree rebounded on the toy industry, making it ever more expensive and difficult to bring out a new line of toys – to be truly innovative. With escalating promotion and research budgets, intense competition and growing retail and market resistance, the pace of new character-toy development slowed, leaving a weary, more circumspect and more concentrated toy industry. Yet in the wake of the biggest surge in children's television production, the three networks had begun to abandon their traditional role as the contracting arbiters for children's television fiction, even while the new licensing agencies stalled in their search for new product concepts. It was impossible to sustain the creativity and energy required by the new strategy. A report from the American Toy Manufacturers said: 'The US toy industry turned in a lacklustre performance in 1986.... These declines reflect the inability of the industry to develop substitutes for the excitement generating products of previous years.' The report added that not only had toy exports declined in 1986 but also 'imports will continue to supply the bulk of US demand for dolls and toys'.[63] By 1988, imports of toys into the USA accounted for 2.4 billion dollars of retail sales.[64] In other words, as toy-marketing paid more attention to symbolic design, the industry actually decreased its domestic toy manufacturing, preferring to sell the more cheaply produced imports. Many jobs were lost, even as the new entrance barriers for alternative and smaller toy makers were erected. The toy industry had participated willingly in its own restructuring.

One of the only ways the highly concentrated toy majors could continue to grow was to expand internationally – to market their symbolic designs on a global basis. Companies such as Hasbro had no option but to position themselves as international corporations, to take up a global strategy by gearing their product development increasingly for the world market. The television serials produced by character merchandisers are subsidized by US toy sales, so that when they are offered on the international market they prove to be attractively cheap programming for commercial networks and satellite broadcasters. Many of the television programmes have achieved global exposure, including frequent showings in Britain, France, Germany and Australia, helping to turn the character-toy market into a global affair. Where national policies for children's television take offence at the banality, violence and commercial biases of these animations in the highly protected children's broadcasting environment of Scandinavia, satellite, video and cable technologies have managed to undercut those policies.[65] Canada has most fully experienced the cultural forces unleashed by the deregulated US toy market: its cable networks were overrun by the syndicated programmes and the sales of imported toys grew steadily through the

1980s as a percentage of the total market as toy retailers gave space to these well-promoted lines.[66]

If character-marketing is such an effective tool for shaping toy preferences, could it also be responsible for other changes in the way children experience or understand their world? Every parent has reason to believe that children derive some of their knowledge and a fair bit of understanding of social roles and relations from television.[67] Yet the marketers' designs have reorientated television fiction and advertising for the general purpose of selling toys. Could these new ideological dimensions also be influencing children's attitudes? There is, then, cause for concern for those people who still believe that the quality and content of the stories told to young children and the way that they play are important for their socialization.

Notes

1. Leo Bogart, *The Age of Television: A Study of Viewing Habits and the Impact of Television on American Life*, New York, F. Ungar, 1958, p. 331.

2. In addition to Bogart and Schramm in the USA, there is also Himmelweit in England: Wilbur Lang Schramm, *Television in the Lives of our Children*, Stanford, Stanford University Press, 1961; Hilde T. Himmelweit, *Television and Children: An Empirical Study of the Effect of Television on the Young*, London, Oxford University Press, 1958.

3. The most significant critiques of commercial television are well laid out in: Harry Skornia, *Television and Society: An Inquest and Agenda for Improvement*, New York, McGraw-Hill, 1965; Jerry Mander, *Four Arguments for the Elimination of Television*, New York, William Morrow, 1978.

4. Neil Postman, *Amusing Ourselves to Death: Public Discourse in the Age of Show Business*, New York, Viking Penguin, 1985; Marie Winn, *The Plug-In Drug*, New York, Penguin, 1977.

5. Tannis MacBeth Williams, *Impact of Television: A Natural Experiment in Three Communities*, Orlando, Academic Press, 1986.

6. E.A. Rubenstein, G.A. Comstock and J.P. Murray, eds, *Television and Social Behaviour*, Washington DC, US Government Printing Office; D. Pearl, L. Bouthilet and J. Lazar, *Television and Behaviour: Ten Years of Scientific Progress and Implications for the Eighties*, vol. 2, Technical Reviews, National Institute of Mental Health, Washington, US Government Printing Office, 1982.

7. George Comstock, S. Chaffee, N. Katzman, M. McCombs and D. Roberts, *Television and Human Behaviour*, New York, Columbia University Press, 1978; Bradley Greenberg, 'Television and Role Socialization An Overview', in Pearl et al., *Television and Behaviour*; Robert Hawkins and Suzanne Pingree, 'Technical Reports from Violence and TV', in Pearl et al., *Television and Behaviour*, p. 224, and 'Television's Influence on Social Reality', in ibid.

8. Albert Bandura, 'Social Learning Theory of Aggression', *Journal of Communication*, 28(3), 1978, pp. 12–28; W. Andrew Collins, B.L. Sobol and S. Westby, 'Effects of Adult Commentary on Children Comprehension and Inferences about a Televised

232

Aggressive Portrayal', *Child Development*, 52, 1981, pp. 158–73;Guy Lommetti and Alan Wurtzel, 'Researching Television Violence', *Society*, 21(6), 1984, pp. 22–8; David Pearl, 'Violence and Aggression', *Society*, 21(6), 1984, pp. 17–22; Richard Potts, Aletha Juston and John Wright, 'The Effects of Television Form and Violent Content on Boys' Attention and Social Behavior', *Journal of Experimental Child Psychology*, 41, 1986, pp. 1–17; Nancy Signorelli, Larry Gross and Michael Morgan, 'Violence in Television Programs: Ten Years Later', in Pearl et al., *Television and Behaviour*, pp. 158–73.

9. Daniel Anderson and Patricia Collins, *The Impact on Children's Education: Television's Impact on Cognitive Development, Working Paper #2*, Washington, US Dept. of Education, 1988; W. André Collins, 'Children's Comprehension of Television Content', 1979, pp. 21–52, in Ellen Wartella, ed., *Children Communicating: Media and Development of Thought, Speech, Understanding*, Beverly Hills, Sage, 1979.

10. J. Bryant and D. Anderson, *Children's Understanding of Television, Research on Attention and Comprehension*, New York, Academic Press, 1983.

11. David Pearl, 'Violence and Aggression', *Science and Modern Society*, 21(6), Sept.–Oct. 1984, pp. 17–22.

12. Ellen Wartella and Byron Reeves, 'Historical Trends in Research on Children and the Media: 1900–1960', *Journal of Communication* 12, Spring 1985, pp. 6–21.

13. Elizabeth J. Roberts, 'Children's Sexual Learning: An Examination of the Influence of Parents, Television and Community Service Providers', *Dissertation Abstracts International*, 43(5-A), 1982, pp. 1400–1; Reid, Leonard, 'Viewing Rules as Mediating Factors of Children's Responses to Commercials', *Journal of Broadcasting*, 23(1), 1979, pp. 15–26; David Morley, 'Domestic Relations: The Framework of Family Viewing in Great Britain', in James Lull, ed., *World Families Watch Television*, Newbury Park, Sage 1988, pp. 22–48.

14. Bradley Greenberg and Byron Reeves, 'Children and the Perceived Reality of Television', *Journal of Social Issues*, 32(4), 1976, pp. 86–97; Albert Bandura, 'Social Learning Theory of Aggression', *Journal of Communication*, Summer 1978, pp. 14–29.

15. Robert Hodge and David Tripp, *Children and Television: A Semiotic Approach*, New York, Polity Press, 1988; Gavriel, Salomon, 'Shape, Not Only Content: How Media Symbols Partake in the Development of Abilities', in Wartella, ed., *Children Communicating*, pp. 53–82; Collins, W. André, 'Children's Comprehension of Television Content', in Ellen Wartella, *Children Communicating*, pp. 21–52.

16. James Lull, 'The Social Uses of Television', *Human Communication*, 6(3), 1980, pp. 197–209; Thomas Lindlof, Milton Shatzer and Daniel Wilkinson, 'Accommodation of Video and Television in the American Family', in Lull, ed., *World Families Watch Television*, Newbury Park, Sage, 1988, pp. 158–92.

17. Winn, *The Plug-In Drug*; Jerome L. Singer and Dorothy G. Singer, *Television, Imagination and Aggression: A Study of Preschoolers*, New Jersey, LEA Publishing, 1981; Sydney Burton, James Calonico and Dennes McSeveney, 'Effects of Preschool Television Watching on First-Grade Children', *Journal of Communication*, Summer 1979, pp. 164–70.

18. Richard Haynes, 'Children's Perceptions of "Comic" and "Authentic" Cartoon Violence', *Journal of Broadcasting*, 22(1), Winter 1978, pp. 63–70; Salomon Gavriel, 'Shape, Not Only Content: How Media Symbols Partake in the Development of Abilities', in Wartella, ed., *Children Communicating: Media and Development of Thought, Speech, Understanding*, Beverly Hills: pp. 53–82; Quanforth, Joanne M., 'Children's Understanding of the Nature of Television Characters', *Journal of Communication*, 29(1), 1979, pp. 210–18; Reeves, Byron, 'Children's Understanding of Television People', in Wartella, ed., *Children Communicating*, pp. 115–56.

19. Hodge and Tripp, *Children and Television*.

20. Andrew Collins, *Children's Understanding of Television*, New York, Academic Press, 1983, p. 125.

21. Albert Bandura, 'Social Learning Theory of Aggression', *Journal of Communication*, 28(3), 1978, pp. 12–28.

22. Howard Gardner, *Cracking the Codes of Television: The Child as Anthropologist*, Transmission, p. 93.

23. Ibid., p. 99.

24. Hodge and Tripp, *Children and Television*, p. 75.

25. C. Schneider, *Children's Television: The Art, the Business and How it Works*, Lincolnwood, Ill., NTC Business Books, 1987, p. 5.

26. Ibid.

27. Dale Kunkel, 'Young Minds and Marketplace Values: Issues in Children's Television Advertising', *Journal of Social Issues*, 47(1), 1991, pp. 57–72.

28. FTC Staff report 1978, cited in B. Armstrong and M. Brucks, 'Dealing with Children's Advertising: Public Policy Issues and Alternatives', *Journal of Public Policy and Management*, 7, 1989, pp. 98–113.

29. Roy Ashman, John Hasenjaeger and H. Keith Hunt, *Advertising and Government Regulation: A Report by the Advertising and Government Panel of the American Academy of Advertising*, April 1979, p. 47.

30. Dale Kunkel, 'Child and Family Television Regulatory Policy', in J. Bryant, ed., *Television and the American Family*, Hillsdale, NJ, Lawrence Erlbaum, 1990.

31. D. Roberts, 'Children and Commercials: Issues, Evidence, Interventions', in J. Sprafkin, C. Swift and R. Hess, eds, *Rx Television: Enhancing the Preventive Impact of TV*, New York, Haworth Press, 1983, p. 20.

32. Attorney General of Quebec v. Irwin Toy Limited, April 1989, Supreme Court ruling, Quebec City.

33. Dale Kunkel, 'Child and Family Television Regulatory Policy', in J. Bryant, ed., *Television and the American Family*, Hillsdale, NJ, Lawrence Erlbaum 1990, p. 366.

34. Dale Kunkel, 'From a Raised Eyebrow to a Turned Back: The FCC and Children's Product-Related Programming', *Journal of Communication*, 38(4), 1988, pp. 90–108.

35. B. Armstrong and M. Brucks, 'Dealing with Children's Advertising: Public Policy Issues and Alternatives', *Journal of Public Policy and Management*, 7, 1989, pp. 98–113.

36. Ibid., p.99.

37. *Globe and Mail*, 'Some Kids' TV Shows Deemed Commercials', 10 April 1991.

38. 'Viewpoints: How Will the New Regulations Governing Children's Television Affect Toy Advertising?', *Playthings*, Jan. 1991, p. 52.

39. Mark Crispin Miller, 'Hollywood: The Ad', *Atlantic Monthly*, April 1990, pp. 41, 68.

40. Schneider, *Children's Television*, p. 156.

41. Ibid., p. 124.

42. Susan Kastner, 'Lovable Little Smurfs Have a Hidden Darker Side When They're Crossed', *Starweek*, 18 July 1987.

43. T. Englehardt, 'The Strawberry Shortcake Strategy', in T. Gitlin, ed., *Watching Television*, New York, Pantheon Books, 1986, pp. 68–110. The setting up of these arrangements have been excellently described by Tom Englehardt in this ground-breaking essay.

44. 'TCFC Are at It Again', *Chain Store Age*, November 1986, pp. 57–8.

45. B. Lowry, 'Tie-ins: Raising the Bottom Line in Kidvid', *Hollywood Reporter*, 2 June 1987.

46. Michael Fleming, 'Will Hideous Green Things Bring Lotsa Green? Toy Companies Think so, Judging by their TV and Film Tie-ins on View at the Toy Fair', *Variety*, 18 Feb. 1991, p. 104.

47. 'Children and Media Conference Focuses on TV', *Broadcasting*, 13 May 1985, p. 98.

48. 'Daylight Spending Time', *Mediaweek*, 15 April 1991, pp. 30–1.

49. P. Boyer, 'NBC Considers Risk of Killing Saturday Morning Cartoons', *The Globe and Mail*, 20 Sept. 1988, p. A23.

50. 'TCFC Are at It Again', *Chain Store Age*, November 1986, p. 57.

51. 'Rise of Licensed Plush: Where Are Profits', *Chain Store Age*, Feb. 1986, pp. 87–8.

52. Donna Leccese, 'Toy Manufacturers, Retailers Battle Profit Squeeze', *Playthings*, June, p.75.

53. Ibid., p. 87.

54. 'New Toys May Boost Summer Programs', *Chain Store Age*, Jan. 1986, p. 75.

55. This uncertainty is well captured in Sydney Stern and Ted Schoenhaus, *Toyland: The High-Stakes Game of the Toy Industry*, Chicago, Contemporary Books, 1990.

56. Stephen Karp of Lionel Leisure Inc. quoted in 'G.I. Joe, the American Retailing Hero', *Chain Store Age*, Oct. 1986, p. 80.

57. 'March of the Toy Soldier Retreats', *Chain Store Age*, July 1986, p. 34.

58. Frank Reysen, 'Industry Reports Slight Gains in 1990 Toy Sales', *Playthings*, March 1991, p. 29.

59. 'Profits Still Tough on Characters', *Chain Store Age*, Feb. 1986, p. 93.

60. Michael Harnett, 'Rise of Licensed Plush: Where Are the Profits?', *Chain Store Age*, Feb. 1986, pp. 88–9; 'High Profits Put Retailers in a Quandary', *Chain Store Age*, May 1987, p. 80; 'Profits Still Tough on Characters', *Chain Store Age*, Feb. 1986, pp. 93–4.

61. 'Profits Still Tough on Characters', p. 93.

62. Jane Hall, 'TV's New Toys Send Critics Scrambling for their Guns', *People*, 27(12), 1987, pp. 34–5.

63. 'Toys and Games', *US Industrial Outlook*, 1987.

64. Eugene Gilligan, 'Imports Help Retailers Find their Niche', *Playthings*, November 1989, pp. 34, 35, 57; Rosemarie Del Vescovo, 'Foreign-Made Toys Broaden Retailer Mix', *Playthings*, November 1988, pp. 40–1.

65. Stephen Kline and Peter Smith, 'A Global Play? Comparing British, Canadian, American and Japanese Toy Advertisements', *Ethnographica*, Autumn 1992.

66. The Canadian Toy Manufacturers Association, *Mixing Business and Pleasure: An Outline of the Canadian Toy and Decoration Industry*, 1979.

67. Robert Hawkins and Suzanne Pingree, 'Television's Influence on Social Reality', in Pearl et al., *Television and Behaviour*, p. 224.

8

The Parables of Play:

Policy, Strategy and

Advertising Design

> While the marketplace has been there for some time, the coalescence of that marketplace in the form of toy barns and toy cities, with the incessant advertising of toys along with children's highly magnetic programs such as cartoons, has created an enormously powerful agency for the control of play. Many more children than ever before are spending more hours playing with television-sponsored toys which simulate the television characters or events in front of the television set.[1]

The marketers of children's toys do not set out to produce banal, repetitive, empty, violent programming and advertising that distorts children's values and sense of reality. Their intentions are simply those of business: to increase the profitability of their firms through the expansion of the market share for toys. But business goals must be translated into marketing strategies. The dynamism and booming sales in the promotional toy market were aided by the more upbeat high-pressure sales techniques developed after the deregulation of children's advertising in the United States. He-Man and Jem may no longer be seen on store shelves, but the lessons they taught advertisers continue to be evidenced in the new conventions for and standards of toy commercials.

Until the Federal Communications Commission (FCC) revised its stance to allow promotional programming and up to twelve minutes of advertising per hour, the designs of toy ads had remained pretty tame. US advertising regulation consisted traditionally of two provisions: first there were limits to the amount of advertising time that could be sold in each hour of the children's television schedule. Second, a code of self-regulation prevented a host of misleading and

236

unfair message designs, including injunctions against unrealistic or incomplete product demonstrations. Also included in the guidelines were prohibitions from using popular programming personalities in the ads and recommendations for 'bumpers' to ensure that children recognized the actual programme content as distinct from the advertising messages. The networks supported this regulatory protocol at least partly because it clothed them in a mantle of responsibility: throughout the 1970s, the regulations buffered the TV producers against the criticism of children's advocates while preserving their power and autonomy in programme decision-making.[2]

Advertising is a key element in the toy industry's marketing mix because it serves two important functions. First, it announces the availability of the product, differentiates it from other products in the market, and makes its ownership desirable. Second, it shows kids what they are to do with the product – how to play with it and what the benefits of having it are. All advertising strives to fulfil these functions in as direct a way as possible. All ads must first attract children's attention and then deliver the product concept. They must differentiate the toy's attributes and uses from competing goods and make children want to request or buy the product.

But research on advertising to children had taught marketers to be circumspect in their communications. It had been shown that children did not retain product information very well and that they tended to be impulsive in what they wanted. Especially among the younger segments of the audience, promoting the attributes of certain brands appeared to be a waste of money.[3] Most traditional TV commercials aimed at children, therefore, consisted of attractive shots of the product and scenes showing the fun, enjoyment and excitement of kids playing with the product. The ads usually portrayed one or two of the product's symbolic attributes known to interest and attract children and used whatever technical finesse they could to catch attention.

The removal of the long-established restrictions on advertising realism and tie-ins during the 1980s allowed marketers to explore new ways of communicating with children. Now they could attempt to circumvent the assumed limits of children's information-processing and retention of product information, and they no longer had to avoid unrealistic product portrayals.[4] Although the children's marketers all gravitated to personality-based selling, some of them began to experiment with new kinds of advertising that treated the personality of the product in a more imaginative mode. As one advertising commentator noted: 'The pre-schooler lives in a world of fantasy in which fantasy is reality. Hence, he is unable to tell truth from fiction. He does not see a story in terms of plot, but in terms of isolated sequences, and is unable to distinguish programming from advertising.'[5] Using television 'personalities' from children's programmes (for example G.I. Joe or Jem) within the ads meant that advertisers could now strengthen the connection between the toy, the kind of play it induced and the television series.

At the major networks, where a large portion of children's advertising revenue came from cereal and snack food advertisers, executives were at first not alarmed by deregulation. They no doubt secretly hoped that the freedom to include more commercials would increase advertising revenues, which might in turn help them fund better children's programmes. It was a while before they realized that their programmes had to compete with the syndicated toy company productions for a share of the children's audience. They then grew alarmed at the drift of advertising to the syndicates. The character marketers gravitated to the independents and syndicates not just because of the lower CPMs and schedules filled with attractive animations produced under licensing agreements. They also appreciated the syndicates' flexibility and less restrictive scrutiny of some of their more dramatic advertising executions.[6]

By 1987, toy makers were spending over $350 million on television advertising (enough to fund the production of up to twenty new television series) but less than half of that amount went to the networks. Each new licensed line to hit the market had to compete on television with forty other animated series and innumerable discounted knock-offs in the stores. Advertising placement and design – along with careful timing – proved to be a critical factor in promotional toy-marketing. Animated series could make a character famous, but the advertising made the child want the toy. The commercials primed the pump of mutual opportunities by introducing in a visual form the exciting play opportunities of the product, and for the licensing agents, animators, syndicates and manufacturers this often meant not only dynamic but also expensive advertising. Toy marketers that couldn't play the game right and make the product launch work had to be prepared to suffer the losses.[7] The ones that developed the skills and alliances necessary for high-stakes promotional marketing were able to enjoy the multi-million-dollar trajectories that were the dream of all businesspeople engaged in this volatile market. Advertising remained the key to such success.

The children's marketers had long believed that 'personalizing' their products helped to promote consumer loyalty. Yet not everyone involved in the children's market could successfully take advantage of the deregulation of children's advertising in the same way that the makers of promotional toys could. The Ninja Turtles' culinary habits no doubt helped to boost pizza sales, but not half as much as they helped to sell action figures. The boom in children's marketing had a built-in bias. Shoe and clothing manufacturers, for example, had to be content with licensing established characters to feature on their children's lines – they couldn't successfully develop a character on their own. It wasn't easy to write a TV series with a chocolate bar as a superhero or produce an animation special about a community of cuddly running shoes. The Gummi Bears did have a snack food tie-in, and McDonald's and Burger King got into the act through exclusive promotional deals with toy makers, but generally the cereal and snack food merchandisers either licensed characters (as in Smurfa-getti) or continued to use their own animated brand personalities (Tony the Tiger or the Sugar Bear).

By the early 1990s, there was hardly a children's product advertised on television that didn't have a 'personality' associated with it. Ads that reiterated known character traits ensured that even the youngest viewers would recognize what the ads were about. They also reinforced the associational link between those specific attributes and the product. Personality remained the best way to differentiate a product without depending on brand-name recognition or the retention of product attributes.

Yet only the toy makers could feature their products as the hero of a TV series. In the case of character toys, the personalities featured in the television series were the products – so their unique abilities, weapons, styles, voices and identities could be much more clearly defined and communicated than by advertising back-stories. A character toy appearing in a commercial easily renewed the child's established interest, just by using animated highlights from the series. Moreover, when they made requests for their favourite toys children didn't need to remember brand names ('J-E-L-L-O') or product attributes ('air cushioned heel'). All they had to learn to say was, 'I want Liono, leader of the Thundercats to play with.'

Advertising Unbound

The deregulation of advertising brought a new communications design for toy commercials. The modern toy commercial became the whole strategic enterprise of character-marketing condensed into one thirty-second, densely packed communications package. As the guidelines lapsed advertisers became less rigorously realistic in their depiction of the product and its uses, less concerned about merging the animated television sequences and the play scenes, less restrained in dramatizing the unique selling features of their product.

Marketers knew that kids could more easily describe toys in terms of what they did or how they were used. Kids paid little attention to what the toys were made from or how they functioned.[8] Many agencies scripted their ads as a sequence of dramatic events, based on evidence that children best understood and retained information from simple 'episodic' or 'dramatized' sequences. Children's advertisers never lectured their audiences on selling points or merely demonstrated the product. Instead they dramatized the product using a mini-plot, demonstrating the product's attributes in a specific fantasy location. Most toy companies connected to TV action series introduced action bases, equipment and play sets related to the series as part of their toy line and instructed the TV producers to feature these in the stories. Fantasy play required not only a troupe of characters but a proscenium – a site for the production of fantasy. Television provided the script.

Researchers have demonstrated that categorical and schematic cognitive systems are deployed selectively by children watching advertising and that younger kids pay particular attention to schematic information.[9] Categorical cognitive structures define relationships among objects in terms of class membership (swords are used by good guys) and similarity among class members (swords and ray-guns are both good-guy weapons). Schematic cognitive structures consist of expectations about objects (ray-guns beat swords) and representations of scenes or events based on what they look like (swords glow in use) or on the order in which they occur (the character throws away the empty ray-gun and uses his sword). The researchers showed that children could make sense of advertisements best when they could use their schematic knowledge or 'scripts' to process the product information. They also indicated that improved retention of commercials occurred among children who remembered them as sequences of events or behaviours memorized in order (schematic encoding) rather than by storing the attributes (category encoding).

The changes in advertising design that resulted from ignoring the edict of realism were not superficial, although many parents would hardly notice. Advertisers found that an easy way to dramatize the product was to make the products move on their own in the ads. For example, having action shots of the Rock Lords (warriors that were transformed from a rock shape) lumbering through an imaginary rocky landscape demonstrating their power and ruggedness to dramatic background music proved more impressive than showing them as they really are, life-size on a table being played with by kids. The two types of scenes could be intercut without children worrying about the differences in the setting. The fantasy was no longer a toy but a television character. In visualized play fantasies children could be seemingly projected inside doll's houses, they could drive their toy planes, dolls could converse with their friends or perform magic tricks in the bedroom. The advertisers didn't have to worry about the credulity of the young anymore. These kinds of commercials would never have gotten through the regulatory net before deregulation.

The advertisers also knew, though, that peer play was a highly valued activity. Kids liked to watch other kids having fun, and through the psychological process of evaluative transfer they would associate this pleasure with the product. This meant that toy companies had to target their TV audiences to make sure they had the right peer group for a particular toy. They had carefully to adjust the specific tone and appeal of a commercial to viewer audience profiles. Children would only take preference cues from commercials that depicted children whose play they found attractive or interesting. The boys tended to like driving music and action; the girls preferred pink glows and magical twinkles. Targeting by peer strata enabled toy advertisers to concentrate on communicating just the right play values and communication stylistic to the right age and gender segments, rather than trying to depict generalized values that would appeal to all children.

From their animated programmes the boys' action-toy lines brought an emotional intensity that also could be communicated in the ads. The advertisers used forceful, loud music and fast cutting to raise the ads above the clutter and make them noticeable in the programming. They accentuated or exaggerated the range of emotionality by dramatizing extremes of anger, cruelty, terror and triumph – far beyond those seen on network TV of the 1970s. But children's syndicated television was on in the afternoons, when few parents watched or noticed what was happening to the toy ads. On occasion, after complaints from parents a few of the worst offenders were pulled off the air by the toy companies; but, in general, action-toy commercials notched up the emotional heat in children's advertising without much public debate.

The decreased emphasis on realism didn't benefit all children's advertisers, or even all toy advertising – it didn't help games or pull toys, for example. Yet for the toys that involved pretending and imagination the depiction of make-believe and the visions of an alternative imaginary world to be found through play could now also be presented unrestrained by the need to be realistic in the depiction of product use, attributes, size or benefits. Animated sequences were taken from the series and intercut with kids playing with toys, emphasizing the visualization of the play fantasy.

A Study of Toy-Marketing

The communications style developed by the character marketers obviously had an influence throughout the children's advertising industry as snack, cereal and other toys all tried to use these new methods to update their advertising. Yet as Table 1 shows, character-toy commercials stand apart from other toy advertising on television because of their production values, their depiction of peer play, and their reference to imaginative engagement with toys.[10]

Significantly, the commercials for licensed toys that never showed children at play with their parents were more likely to include scenes of social play among similar sex groups, and more likely to indicate an imaginative transition to an alternative fantasy world through the use of the toy. There was no dominant formula, only several repeated patterns of representation used for different market segments, classified predominantly by gender and by age groupings. The designs for persuading each audience segment were tuned by stereotypic age and gender considerations.

The Production of Values

All advertising must attract children to the screen despite their fickle watching patterns and the counter-attraction of siblings, friends and

Table 1 Content of Toy Commercials (occurrence %)

	Character Toys	*Other Toys (verbal)*
References to play:		
imagine/pretend	34	20
power to build/control/master	6	29
Voice-over:		
describes play	14	29
product info	38	21
Parents in play:	0	9
Play activities involve:*		
laughing	0	10
talking	30	20
manipulating toy	24	8
competing	4	12
fighting	10	2
building	6	15
Play elements:		
care for toy	20	9
skills/operate/assembly	8	23
role play	0	6
objects imitate real objects	0	17
games	0	13
narrative	16	0
manipulate/hold product	14	15
Play sociality:		
alone	14	23
two same sex	46	33
familial	6	15
Play styles:*		
functional	12	33
skills/construction	4	21
sensory	18	9
role-taking	26	45
fantasy play	92	32
game play	0	15

Note: * indicates multiple coding.

toys. Believing that 'television leads to an impulsive rather than reflective style of thought' D'arcy, Masius, Benton and Bowles (DMB&B) recommend that advertisers become concerned about the affective dimension of their messages – the excitement and happy feelings generated. The advertising industry spends a lot of research money ensuring that the ads they produce are attractive to their prospective audience and convey the product idea effectively. As the DMB&B ad recommends, 'children are captured by catchy sounds, tunes and tricky combinations of words, which they frequently repeat. They are more attention-getting than dialogue.'

Children's commercials are dense in their production values because they must not only condense their message into thirty seconds but also communicate it on a stylistic register. As DMB&B state, 'Graphic motion is most important in attracting and holding children's attention – people doing things or the product in use.' Producers of commercials have therefore become adept at stylizing action sequences, coining memorable slogans and choosing music and graphics to establish mood, pace, and tone for particular target groups. In their use of non-verbal 'emotional' techniques (sound effects, music rhythm, humour, action, graphics) to establish the contours of the imaginary social universes promised in play, the

Table 2 Content Analysis of Formal Characteristics of Ads (occurrence %)

	Girls	Boys	Both
Mood of Music			
Powerful, dramatic, loud	0	57	9
Playful, cheerful	13	1.5	39
Cute, sweet	25.5	0	3
Romantic, soft	17	0	0
Discordant	0	9	0
Pop tune	28	4.5	12
Narrator/Voice-over			
Male	6	97	79
Female	83	1.5	15
Adult	85	97	91
Tone of Voice-over			
Happy, cheerful	45	4.5	42
Aggressive, loud, dominant	0	52	0
Sweet, tender	36	0	9
Authoritative	0	39	3
Confident	0	36	9
Excited	15	22	24
Sing-song	11	0	3
Number of cuts			
6–10	15	1.5	18
11–14	40	13	30
15–19	19	36	21
20–24	21	28	15
25–29	2	10	6
30–34	2	7.5	3
35 and more	0	3	6

marketers clearly make strong assumptions about each market segment and the different methods that should be used to communicate to those segments.

The linguistic themes of these character-toy ads perfectly match non-verbal communicators: action, power and conflict define the boys' action toys; friendship, affection and nurturance define the plush preschool toys; and glamour, admiration and friendship define the older girls' dolls. These production values augment and visualize the linguistic cues and peer portrayals, effectively conveying the emotional ideas and play styles associated with the character toy. Indeed, it appears that the stylization of emotion has become a major means of targeting in the children's market.

Fast cutting, loud music and excited drumming set the aggressive mood of the boys' commercials. Ads for action toys are visually dynamic, with many more scene changes (averaging from fifteen to nineteen cuts) and more blacks and reds. The fast pace and driving drum rhythms of these ads have a compelling, explosive quality that is often replicated by a growling announcer's voice. A Construx ad provides a good example of these production values. In it the boys are shown magically assembling their vehicles and then engaging in a rescue combat in a fantasy desert environment that clearly represents the galactic mythos of cosmic struggle. The opening sequences show the boys not so much building as manipulating the toys, which begin to move as if on their own. The vehicles smash, jump and crash through the rugged landscape in a daring rescue-mission sequence, ending on the 'product beauty shot' and logo:

Chorus (sung): Construx! You build.
Male voice: Thunder tracks.
Chorus (sung): You build.
Male voice: Skyblazer.
Male voice: Sold separately.
Chorus (sung): Action.
Male voice: Construx.
Chorus (sung): Rescue.
Male voice: Construx.
Kids' voices: Mission accomplished.
Chorus (sung): Construx.
Male voice: Construx. Thunder tracks and Skyblazer. Each sold separately (metallic sound). From Fisher-Price.
Chorus (shouted): Construx!

Although here the visual force of the sequence is missing, at least the fast-paced hypnotic rhythm, chant-like exhortations and general excitement that permeates the ad's highly condensed language give a sense of the mood. The 'dialogue' between chorus and announcer is like a ritual incantation or religious service – with a demented tone of urgency the commercial manages to repeat the product name six times. Given this format and mood, it is worth noting that Construx is a construction toy. The battle-and-rescue sequence and the mood of excitement reflect the fact that many toy marketers simply adopted stylistic elements from character-marketing as a way to address the boys' market.

Such stylistic preferences are not the result of unthinking carelessness. Attention to visual and musical detailing is essential in the children's market. The design of the commercial and the ideas conveyed by the music and graphic elements are crucial for not only communicating the 'affective' aspects of character identity but also reaching the right audience segment. Music is particularly important, not just as a background or simple theme tune but as a means of organizing the commercial's narrative dimension. Short, cute and melodic nursery songs and basic pastel colours match the caring-friendship feelings promoted by commercials destined for the younger audiences. In many commercials the music provides structure, offering in a sweet, melodic sing-song a clear sense of the narrative context. For older girls (over six) producers prefer the pop-rock female vocals, rock video special effects, and star-burst colours to convey the glamour and excitement of girls' fashion dolls.

Non-linguistic communication is the essence of children's advertising techniques. Even seemingly simple ads have this quality of compression of meaning. Children's ads, though often linguistically simple, can be rich in visual connotation. The ads have their own iconography and their own formats, which children are very adept at understanding. The visual ideas need to be fairly sophisticated because children have limited vocabularies and capacities for processing language and understanding abstract concepts, and repetition and the quality of the voices are crucial. There is little sense in having a child in a commercial explain how a toy works or what it can do, or even why he or she likes it. Such testimonials never occur in children's advertising. Rather, action speaks louder than words: it draws kids to the product and dramatizes its qualities. The art of children's advertising design might therefore be described as dramatic condensation. The product orientation is reduced to its bare essentials and communicated primarily on the visual and musical registers that resonate throughout children's culture.

Peering at Peers

As the DMB&B advised, 'Children like things that are uniquely their own ... they enjoy watching children like themselves having fun with a product.' Kids particularly like to see other children experiencing the world as they do and succeeding in becoming happy. Scenes of happy children are common in all ads. In snack, soft-drink and cereal ads, as well as within the play sequences of toy commercials, the representation of real 'kids like me' play a significant role, constituting on average 43 per cent of the scenes in our survey. Their emotional states, when they are not engaged in imaginative play are monotonal excitement and pleasure. Of the toy ads, 98 per cent had scenes depicting ordinary children in the act of play (actually shown manipulating the toys or playing the games) or sometimes watching or admiring toys (response shots). These 'play' scenes not only convey the peer world of childhood but also telegraph the emotional states associated with toys, or expressed through them in pretend play.

Advertisers know that children are drawn to toys based on their perceptions of their peers and that they possibly model their own attitudes towards the product on those depicted in the ads. That is why real children appear so regularly in children's ads. The scenes depicting real kids at imaginary play make toy-advertising stand out from the rest of television and be recognized as such, for TV commercials represent one of the few media opportunities children have to learn about what play means to their peers.[11] Ironically, it was the cheapness of animated programming that drove the voices of their peers from the rest of children's TV schedules.

The peer locus of the character toy is always exclusively child-orientated. These commercials reveal no intrusion of adults into the play or even the presence of parents in the background of play; character toys are associated with 'non adult situations and non-restrictive environments'. By contrast, 9 per cent of the commercials for non-character toys, especially board games, show children playing in a family context or with parents watching or participating in some way. Character-toy play is also more likely to be depicted in these ads as 'social play', that is, play that includes two or more real children either using or admiring the toys (76 per cent). Only 14 per cent of the character-toy ads showed children in solitary play with their toys, which contrasts with the other ads featuring solitary play (23 per cent) and, more often, large-group play.

Advertisers use these images of peer play to address the particular strata they are targeting. But, in addition, the survey showed that their conception of the peer group was highly gendered. Toys aimed at boys (vehicles and male action dolls) always show only boys as the reference group, and toys aimed at girls (fashion, baby, family, female action dolls) reveal similar exclusivity. Boys and girls are shown together at play in less than 23 per cent of the children's commercials, and these few occasions primarily involve traditional toys (pogo ball, slinky) and games. There is virtually no mixed-sex groupings in the ads for character toys. Peer play is gender play, and this tactic of targeting play by gender is emphatically communicated in the play scenes of character toys.

Table 3 Gender Differences in the Linguistic Themes of Ads (frequency %)

	Boys	*Girls*	*Both*
Fun/good time	4.5	21.3	66.7
Battle	50.7	0	3.0
Action	40.3	4.3	6.0
Power/Control domination	20.9	0	0
Nurture (domestic)	0	31.9	3.0
Nurture (friend)	0	21.3	12.1
Glamour	0	25.6	3.0
Domestic	0	12.8	0
Construction	9.0	2.1	0
Transformability	12.0	4.2	3.0
Creativity	3.0	0	3.0

Table 4 Gender and Play Styles in Toy Advertising

	Play Style (as mentioned or enacted in ad)					
	Functional	Skilled	Games	Alternate Worlds	Role	Sensory
All ads	20	17	10	39	35	13
Girls' ads	19	9	0	19	74	34
Boys' ads	27	19	0	69	13	0

The marketing logic behind this decision is clear. Children not only identify with kids they like, but they often have a negative response to the child actors in the ads, those whom they find 'unrealistic', inappropriate, or simply not someone they would 'like to play with'. If child models are not cast properly and the play situation not constructed carefully, an ad can make the child feel the product is not for her or him. Companies routinely monitor children's reactions in focus groups, and when producers use children who are too young or of the wrong sex for the target group playing with the toy, the kids complain. Despite the theories about the need for non-sexist socialization, the pragmatics of marketing lead advertisers to rely on children's strictly gendered notions of peer play: 'Boys prefer invincible action figures ... Girls prefer cuddly creatures, action figures or incline to romanticism.' Only one of the commercials in our survey, for a toy aimed at girls, showed a mixed-sex group. Poignantly, it was a drama concerning the intrusion of a little brother into girls' play. Character-marketing has resulted in a more sex-typical representation not only of themes and voice-overs but also in representations of play in advertisements.

Engaging the Imagination

The depiction of appropriate play activities and imaginative styles is a delicate matter in toy-advertising. The non-verbal dimensions of play are recognized by children and judged harshly if they don't feel or look right. But 'make believe' or 'pretend' play is a complex and varied mental activity, involving the transformation of a child's understanding, attitudes and self-concepts.[12] Parents are generally such poor observers of their children's play that they tend not to distinguish the many forms of imaginary play engaged in by their children.[13] The pretend-play capacities and styles develop as the children grow, and boys and girls seem to learn to prefer different play styles in their free-form pretending.[14] Both toy marketers and feminist psychologists agree that these distinctions are crucial – children must be taught to engage in pretend play and some forms may be more beneficial in cognitive growth and maturation than others.[15]

To engage in pretending, a child must shift perspective from the here-and-now reality of experience to an 'as-if' universe – the

249

imaginarium. When there are no rules or structures implicit in the imaginarium – that is, when imagined ideas float freely along without attempts to control or act upon them – psychologists tend to describe that process as free-fantasizing or daydreaming. Crayons and plasticine have long been regarded as excellent aids to development because they promote a form of creative expression that gives free reign to fantasy. As in dreaming, so too in art children do not consciously guide their imaginations in such exercises of 'free play'.

Social-dramatic play is a more restricted kind of fantasizing: the imagining is defined by a social field of representation in which the child imagines social situations, settings or even societies.[16] Imaginative children can become happily involved in discovering and acting out the rules and dynamics of these alternative universes, as the makers of fantasy games such as Dungeons and Dragons or Monopoly discovered. The 'as if' of social-dramatic pretending is a mental process of re-engagement in which children consciously take on new perspectives. The content of the fantasy is dependent upon their understanding of the social universe they are entering: its roles, language, characters, social forms and related behavioural repertoires. Much of children's observed play is social-dramatic role play, a kind of play in which the content is defined by the child's stock of social knowledge, i.e. roles and relations. This kind of social-dramatic play is closely associated with dolls and toy vehicles. In role play the toy is used as a prop that aids social-dramatic enactment by signifying some aspect of the imagined social world. When a girl scolds her doll for not finishing dinner, we say she is role-playing at being 'mother'. When a boy loads up his truck in the sandbox and moves sand to another pile, we say he is role-playing at being 'construction worker'. Role play with toys is interpretative: the toy's symbolic reference is interpreted and brought into a mental relationship with the child's established social cognitions. Make-believe play with toys therefore relies on a child's stored knowledge as well as experience in the act of intentional pretending.

Children can engage in these same fantasies without the aid of toys. Moreover, children can incorporate any other objects that they find into their fantasies. Children don't need toys to imagine. Children who place twigs in their belts and call themselves pirates are experiencing the 'indeterminacy' of the toy as symbol. When they engage in such 'object transformative' pretending, they ignore the appearance and form of the object in itself, viewing it only as a symbol of something imagined in the play. In the absence of their toys, children will often pick up anything handy and pretend it is 'the stethoscope' or the 'microphone' in enacting their role-based play scripts. Children will announce these object transformations to each other in attempts to synchronize their pretending in social pretend play.

Toy commercials, on the other hand, teach the child that social-dramatic pretending is much more exciting if you have the right toy and use it in the right way. For example a young boy given a doctor's black-bag set should act out a medical examination on his sister; a girl given a stroller and doll should pretend to be a mother taking the child for a walk; a doll's house should be used for the re-enactment of domestic scenes of nurturance, caring and self-maintenance. Toy play in advertising shows object-specific social fantasies in which the child must enter the field of reference of the toy and use it according to the symbols designed into it. The theme that runs through all toy-merchandising is how the toy's design and qualities will make playing more vivid and enjoyable. In advertising you don't see a baby doll used as a warrior, or a dump truck used to take baby for a walk, although you will occasionally see such play happen at home.[17]

Symbolic design is the process marketers use to narrow the representational fields of the toy (product design, advertising, programming) to depict a specific role portrayal in a specific social universe. Contemporary marketing not only tries to position the product's distinct characteristics in relation to other toys; it also promotes a specific play value through the design of the toy. The toy Baby Talk, for example, is designed as an electronic 'role-play' doll. Its selling point is that it articulates the mothering play script. The doll actually says 'hug me mummy' and 'feed me', and the smiling little girl in the commercial does so accordingly. Dino-Riders were conceived as museum quality replications of dinosaurs because boys already knew about the differences in these reptiles. For this reason, the Dino-Riders' back-story had to be historically plausible.

The Barbie doll is possibly the best example of gender-specific symbolic design. Barbie's original back-story had 'positioned' her as a fashion model, which justified the constant dressing and grooming play activities and explained the extensive wardrobe. Barbie was intentionally crafted to invoke a specific kind of imaginary role play that went beyond the mothering and family scripts that had until then defined doll play. Barbie was not only visually more sexually developed but also exuded a more sophisticated sense of self-presentation. The ads typically worked the more mature 'preteen' concerns with fashion, self-presentation and glamour into a fantasy of supposed sophistication and beauty. In one commercial, Barbie goes on a romantic outing (I wouldn't call it a date) into the star-spangled world of dream-glo glamour. The outing is an animated sequence with Barbie in various poses glowing here in the dark Manhattan-by-night settings:

> *Female voice* (sings): We girls have a romantic side. Right Barbie?
> *Chorus*: Dream-glo Barbie.
> *Female voice* (sings): ... to shade her lovely face
> *Chorus*: But when the sun is out of sight, we light up the night, we turn the stars upside down.
> *Girl watching Barbie inserts*: Wowee!
> *Female voice* (sings): And spark up the town, we girls can do anything.
> *Female voice*: They're here, Barbie, dream-glo fashions that glow in the dark. Dolls and fashions sold separately. New from Mattel.

The girl witnessing the outing does not pretend to be Barbie. Her personal involvement is signified by a rapturous 'wowee' as she watches the spectacle from a distance. Girls may be able to 'do anything', but in this case the player is not even shown manipulating the Barbie doll. Barbie is simply the releaser of the girls' established 'romantic-side' fantasies.

The increased targeting of gender segments in children's promotional toys means that television advertising depicts a gender-specific or sex-typed kind of role play.[18] The TV commercials we sampled repeated scenes where children merely 'acted out' tried and true play values associated with girls (nurturance, mothering, grooming, performing) and boys (working, building, managing, battling). When marketers are criticized for stereotyping, for being narrow and sexist – especially given children's acknowledged abilities to engage in a wider variety of social-dramatic play scenes – they respond by arguing that for marketing reasons their ads have to show the most popular and acceptable kinds of play – that is the way to attract children. Sex-stereotypic play, they point out, existed long before advertising and would not disappear if there were no advertising. In our total sample of commercials, 51 per cent of the toy ads aimed at girls depict a style of imaginary play that can be characterized as simple sex-typed role enactment. Interestingly, only 30 per cent of the boys' ads can be characterized in that same way. The play scenes depicted in the girls' commercials make little mention of imagination. Girls' play, it seems, is more like a spectacle or performance than an act of imagination. The play requires them to use established social scripts to incorporate the toys into their pretending. The commercials show girls looking at the dolls and sometimes manipulating them through simple domestic rituals. The ads portray girls' subjective mental states as a matter of awe, wonder and excitement concerning the toy. The style of play is performative role enactment; the girls are rarely personally engaged in creative make-believe.

A different quality of imagining predominates in the make-believe of boys' commercials. First, the boys are shown playing at being specific personalities rather than taking up social roles. More importantly, they are not spectators to toy-based dramas but are actively engaged. When a boy in a Rambo commercial says with gleeful pride, 'Got 'im!' his subjective participation in the victory derives from the fact that he is 'identified' with the Rambo character. In the action-toy ads the boys talk and act not like a 'typical soldier' but like their heroes. They project themselves into the toy and imagine the world from the character's subjective point of view. The challenges and triumphs of the character define the boys' affective experience in pretend play.

Indeed, the action-toy ads convey a highly emotional subjective involvement with toys. Identification demands a transformation in the child's whole sense of self, an act visualized in one Transformer commercial where a boy is shown in animation gradually becoming a robot warrior. His voice changes too. The essential act of pretending is therefore a relocation of the subject totally within the imaginarium of the toy. The child does not make reference to known social roles or even his personal history or experience. Make-believe means suspending both experience and real social knowledge. It is only through such suspension of mental ties to the real world that the players can feel for themselves the more intense fantasies of the toy. In our survey the indication of identity-transformative play occurred in 46 per cent of the boys' play scenes and 23 per cent of the girls'.

The gender and age differences of advertising are seen in both the content of the fantasy and the portrayal of imagining. It is not surprising, then, that studies of children's play indicate that boys and girls make believe differently.[19] Character-advertising has the most gendered portrayal of play, promoting its own specific form of make-believe defined by both a suspension of social experience and a projective identification with heroes. Little wonder that it is the boys who bound around their playrooms, classrooms and playgrounds announcing themselves as TV heroes while girls play quietly in the doll's house.[20]

It is worth noting, too, that character toys are more often depicted as being used in social play. Social play is distinguished from non-play interaction (when, for example, the kids just talk about the toy) by the fact that both players synchronize their make-believe – sharing a fantasy or stage-managing interactions between different toys in a way reminiscent of puppets in a puppet theatre. In real-life social-imaginary play, the children usually engage in constant dialogue about play to help define the boundaries and maintain the synchronization of the fantasy. In the character-toy ads this level of discourse is unnecessary because the players are following a predetermined script shown in the animated narrative (attack, rescue, battle, victory). In this sense, the portrayals of action-toy play seem performative rather than creative. But the lack of creativity does not diminish the need for mental activity: social performance is a demanding style of play; each child identifies with a character and interacts with other children's characters through the adoptive identities, using the appropriate voice, weapons and traits to make the fantasy come to life.

Character-marketing puts a unique emphasis on the play value of making-believe, on the toy as a tool that helps children pretend. Character-toy commercials emphasize a style of play that relies on children's active fantasizing – transforming the here-and-now world through imagining it otherwise. The representation of a link between the activity of peer play and the imaginary toy world is therefore the central structuring element of the commercials aimed at boys. The commercials reveal the imaginary link to the other world by intercutting animated scenes with more naturalistic scenes of several boys at play with their toys. The girls' commercials, on the other hand, tend to use animation differently. They often simply introduce the commercial spot with familiar animation scenes and logos and then show the toys being played with in more naturalistic set-ups or model-play situations (for example sometimes the dolls are shown moving on their own).

Character commercials in general (and increasingly ads for non-character toys have adopted the tactics and stylistics of character-marketing) often use up to one-half of the commercial's thirty seconds to portray the alternative 'imaginary world' promised by the toy. In the boys' ads these scenes are almost always battles taken from the TV animations; they are intercut to music with images of the boys playing with the toy models. A highly typical G.I. Joe commercial, for instance, shows the visual link provided between play and fantasy: a boy is shown holding a toy plane, he shrinks in size until he is able to climb into the cockpit; the plane begins to move as if it is the boy who flies off into an animated dogfight in which the enemy is vanquished:

> *Male voice*: You're looking at an incredible new plane. The G.I. Joe Conquest X-30 (model beauty shot).
> *Male voice* (sings): The G.I. Joe Conquest X-30.
> *Boy*: Wow!
> *Male singing*: Imagine being aboard it, as it takes flight (boy climbs into model).
> *Boy*: There's Cobra (in cockpit).
> *Male singing*: The G.I. Joe Conquest X-30. It's going to beat Cobra in a big dogfight. (Animation.) And Cobra's gonna know you can't beat G.I. Joe.
> *Male chorus*: G.I. Joe – a Real American Hero (model aerial battle).
> *Male voice*: Live the Adventure of G.I. Joe. G.I. Joe Conquest X-30 comes with pilot.
> *Kids*: Go Joe!

The ad itself is a polemic – a lesson in imaginary play – an instruction on how to use the toy to make access with the imaginary universe.

This kind of imaginary transition was absent from a set of twenty-two commercials recorded from Canadian television during the same season. In 1986 the guidelines for Canadian children's advertising appeared to be effectively restraining Canadian broadcasters. The code advised children's advertisers against fantasy and unrealistic uses of the product in an advertisement. Indeed, the Canadian Code of Advertising Standards prefaced their code with the warning that advertisements should not exploit the credulity, lack of experience, or imaginations of children. Advertisers should 'recognize the special characteristics of the children's audience. Children, especially the very young, live in a world that is part imaginary, part real, and sometimes do not distinguish clearly between the two. Advertisements should respect and not abuse the power of the child's imagination.'[21]

Perhaps as a result many of the Canadian ads had a somewhat

255

old-fashioned look and feel, contrasting sharply with the G.I. Joe commercials. Few showed children doing anything except happily manipulating their toys in the course of their daily lives. Many included children playing in mixed groups. Even the ads for licensed properties (Transformers, Jem, Care Bears) did not include animation sequences from the associated programmes, because this would have violated the guidelines on commercial separation. A Canadian commercial for the Slinky toy is typical of the product-demonstration formula that avoided make-believe. The Slinky commercial consists of four naturalistic scenes, starting with a normal suburban backyard where a mixed group of young children play with the toy. The children put a plank against a tree and watch the Slinky go down. The next scene moves indoors where two boys watch Slinky go down some stairs. Then a girl plays with her Slinky on a construction of books and chairs. She smiles to the boys and the image cuts to a product-beauty shot of the toy. There is no dialogue but a female voice-over sings a song:

Female voice: It's Slinky, it's Slinky,
For Fun it's a wonderful toy
What walks down stairs, alone or in pairs
And makes a slinkety sound?
A spring a spring, a marvellous thing
Everyone knows it's Slinky
It's Slinky, it's Slinky
For fun it's a wonderful toy.
It's fun for a girl and a boy.
Male voice: Slinky and Plastic Slinky – each sold separately.
A Slinky Brand toy.

This product demonstration was typical of the format found in US advertising before the 1980s. Only about 18 per cent of our 1986 sample could similarly be categorized as simply showing the toy in naturalistic use. What makes these commercials seem so odd now is that they don't tell a story. The product itself is the only link between the scenes of play; and children at play in the real (as opposed to animated) world is the only back-story.

In contrast, the G.I. Joe commercials link real children at play with the back-story by telling a little story that explains the narrative transition. The announcer says to the boy, 'Imagine being aboard', and later exhorts him to 'Live the G.I. Joe adventure'. Some 34 per cent of the character-toy ads in our sample made a similar verbal reference to pretending or imagining. This compares with 20 per cent of the commercials for other kinds of toys (for instance, games or pogo balls) in which the dominant linguistic descriptions of what play is about are related to mastery and control. But verbal instructions are unnecessary (and absent from most ads) because older children fully understand the animated references to imaginary play.

Triumph by Imagination

The advertising of action figures operates as an exhortation to the powers and pleasures of fantasy, the dynamism of dreams and the eternal qualities of myths. The hyperbole is no doubt intended to incite the boys' imaginations by accentuating and intensifying the affective dimension of imaginary play:

Chorus: Rambo.

Animated characters
Mad Dog: Nice Village.
Havoc: Yeah. We'll use it for target practice.
(Machine gun noise.)
Male villager: It's Mad Dog and Havoc – We need Rambo.
Chorus: Rambo, the force of FREEDOM.

Two boys playing
Boy with Mad Dog: Rambo's got a flame-thrower.
Boy with Havoc: The heat's on.
Boy with Mad Dog: I'll use my shotgun Havoc.
Boy with Havoc: Let's get our cycle.
Boy with Rambo: Here's your cycle. Got him!
Male voice: Get Firepower, Rambo and Mad Dog. Figures and Strike Cycle each sold separately.

The imagined play scenario of this commercial depicts two boys imitating exactly the Rambo of television. Although the storyline has been greatly reduced and the actions simplified, the boys know they are to act out the Rambo fantasy – its anger, humour and aggression – in their play. The ad retains all the narrative qualities of the Rambo television series (dialogue, characters, weapons, moral stature) and

257

children are clearly instructed to internalize these qualities into their own play scripts.

The tone, pace and excitement of these fantasy encounters convey the back-story's unique structure of feeling (excitement, awe and cynical humour). In the thirty seconds the hero courageously confronts the evil Mad Dog and Havoc and rescues the innocent jungle villagers, who had trembled before the unthinking cruelty of the villains. Although there is no verbal directive, the animated battle scene can only be interpreted as a fantasy to be recreated in play, a reading emphasized by the fact that the boys are seen to mimic exactly the ritual movements of mechanized triumph in their play. For this reason many critics see Rambo as a war toy and these ads as promoting war play.[22] Yet is the war play here all that different from the more traditional qualities of play – chase, challenge, rescue, competition – that likewise characterized what boys did with toy soldiers or cowboy and Indian figures?[23]

The Social Imaginary

The character-toy advertisements create roads down which the child's imagination travels to an alternate universe. That universe is populated by a host of characters who behave according to specific social roles, rules and interaction rituals defined in their animation programme. In fantasizing their way into the back-story, the children discover not only a new self but also a fictional sociality – a new pattern of interacting with others who inhabit the imagined realm. Character play is a form of social drama in which the intrigue of the toy depends on how attractive, exciting and compelling this imagined universe can be. The qualities of the imaginary social orders depicted in commercials are distillations of the carefully crafted product concept – artfully designed to appeal to age- and gender-specific preferences, capacities and play styles. The DMB&B guideline is clear and direct on this issue: 'Children's preferences and values show major differences according to their age and sex.' In seeking to locate their product in one of the three separate markets – preschoolers, the 'magic years' (five to eight) and the peer group (nine to twelve) – children's advertisers narrowly design the ads to reflect and communicate these characteristics promising different play values to different age groups.

Imaginary Companions:
A Gentler, Kinder America

The advertisers fully knew, of course, that children had and valued imaginary companions who proved easier to get along with than the self-willed lot they met in the world around them. By turning toys into imaginary companions, children build strong bonds of attachment to them. The toy makers know that preschoolers especially spend hours conversing with, hugging and loving their favourite cuddly creatures, and grown-ups often have strong memories of their own attachments to such transitional objects. The lesson of the teddy bear was transformed into a play value that could be strengthened by fantasy: the toy's fantasy world could express, or signify, the emotional experiences of imaginary friends and family relations. The child is drawn into the web of fictive emotions created by the animation.

Most of the character-toy commercials designed for this market segment stress this strengthening of emotional bonds with the toy. After all, as DMB&B advised, 'Children respond to emotional, non-verbal stimuli'. Attachment to a doll was an emotional state that could be connoted by a tactile relationship with the doll. It is a bond of love, expressed sensually through kissing, hugging and constant companionship. The pretend play of these commercials is a sensory play, characterized by a ritual autoerotic stimulation. The girls are shown admiring, touching, kissing and fondling the toys:

My Little Pony character: I love nuzzling up to you, Aunt Whistler. You're so Fuzzy.
Female chorus: So Soft, My Little Pony.
Female solo: My Little Pony so fuzzy to touch.
Girl: I love the way you feel My So Soft Pony.
Chorus: So Soft My Little Pony.
Female solo: My Little Pony so fuzzy to touch. So fuzzily soft, you're going to love her so much.
Girl: You're so soft.
Female voice: Feel how fuzzily soft they are. So Soft My Little Ponies from Hasbro.

The art of preschool toy design was to know how to find those visual attributes of characters and convey them in ways that accentuated their lovability. Children's unschooled affections are amazingly strong; a child with a choice between a very similar pony or rag doll can become deeply attached to one and ignore the other.

The ads for slightly older girls talk about more than an emotional bonding with animals. Imagination is a key difference, the players are more actively engaged, and the social universes they inhabit are more gendered. In a My Little Pony commercial, for instance, the girls are actively conversational – one of the few ads in which girls are talking about and not just looking at their character toys. Yet their activity is parallel play rather than interactive play in the way that boys' battle scenes are. After the opening scene, which shows the girls standing together, they are seen individually with their Ponies while they talk about living within the Paradise Estate. They visit the play set but do not move into the animation. Only the opening logo sequence of flying ponies uses animation from the TV programme, as Hasbro invites the girls to 'imagine living' in a pony land. Like Alice in Wonderland, through the magic of television the girls are shrunk so they can explore Paradise Estate. Although the ad tells a story about a girl's journey into fantasy the imaginary world inhabited by the Ponies is not topsy-turvy, confusing, or odd. The affective quality of imagination is no wonderland of surprises but simply attractive and pleasurable. It is a place where a girl wants to 'live with all My Little Ponies'.

Music. Animated Pony logo.
Girl 1: Wow, here's My Little Pony Paradise Estate. Isn't it beautiful? Imagine living there.
Girl 2: There are so many rooms. It's the perfect Pony Estate.
Girl 3: Where's Megan? Look, there's Megan by the swimming pool.
Chorus: My Little Pony, living so great.
Girl (sings solo): In the new Paradise Estate.
Girl: I'm going to live here with all My Little Ponies.
Girl: It really is paradise.
Female voice: My Little Pony Paradise Estate comes with what you see here.

On closer examination, the essence of their social interaction seems to be the sharing of their longing for the Ponies and the synchronization of their fantasizing.

The social world of the preschoolers' character toys offers a glimpse of what seems a 'gentler, kinder' social community in which feelings and friendships matter. The act of play is less a matter of active imagining than of joining in and being protected or comforted by loving friends, siblings or other children. A typical Care Bears commercial, for example, is an animated tale in which style and content merge; the message is a simple reminder of the emotional benefits of plush toys. The story unfolds in the animation, with only one awe-struck reaction shot of a child (not holding the Bear) and a product beauty shot at the end. The ad therefore makes no reference to how the toy is used in play, it shows no peer group, it has no imaginary transition. The animation is slow and simple. Such ads do not require children to be visually literate and make sense of cleverly intercut play and animation sequences. The story does not depend on understanding the character or the implied rules of the land in the clouds. The ads invoke a generalized imaginary space – albeit a sanitized artificial realm where friendship is a deep bond and caring a call to action. The animated sequence shows Braveheart 'fall over and hurt' himself. He is then swarmed by his cohorts, and they all get caught up in a small dance of emotional solidarity that looks something like a vaudeville routine:

Male voice: Travel to a mythical place in the clouds . . .
Bear: Ah found it.
Male voice: The land of Care-a-lot.
Bear: Whoaa!
Male voice: And meet the Care Bear Family.
Little Bear: Ah, Braveheart fall down and go boom. Woooo!
Male voice: They're cuddly companions, friendly defenders of feelings, caring and friendship.
Care Bears: Do the Care Bear countdown.
Male voice: Share a smile with the Care Bear Family.

The fantasy world of Care-a-lot is the same cuddly, friendly world of simple emotions and simple actions associated with character plush toys. The commercials contain no parable of play, no reference to human experience – just emotional icons drifting across the screen in a neat episodic package.

The world of preschool plush is situated in the shadow of Winnie the Pooh but lacks the wit, individuality, and subtle humour of Milne's eternal characters. The bears are neither characters nor toys but symbols of the feelings that make children want to hug something. The idea that only their toys understand how kids feel is at the heart of many of the commercials directed at preschoolers. In one

Teddy Ruxpin ad, the bear is shown climbing on to a school bus and going to one lonely child sitting sadly at the back. 'Hi, I'm Teddy Ruxpin,' he says. 'Can we be friends?' Soon the whole group of children is clustered around the isolated child, talking and playing with him and Teddy. The parable of children gaining friends through having attractive toys is undoubtedly not lost on the audience.

Fictional friendship is not a play value limited to character toys. Many different toys cultivate this same play niche equally effectively, including Cricket, a personified tape recorder that substitutes for having friends:

> *Cricket*: Hi, I'm Cricket, and welcome to my world.
> *Cricket* (sings): Let's be friends, We'll do things together.
>   We'll have a great old time.
> *Girl*: Cricket, what makes you talk?
> *Cricket*: I've got a real cassette tape player built right in. You just put
>   in any one of my special tapes and press Play.
> *Girl*: Great! But what about regular cassettes?
> *Cricket*: Oh, I can play those too.
>   Say, why don't we play my Party Time tape right now?
> *Girl*: Yeah!
> *Cricket* (sings): Let's be friends. Just you and I.
>   I'll be talking to you.

Cricket's last statement implies that imaginary friendship is an exclusionary world. And lurking beneath the sing-song exchange we can also sense a guarded reference to the desperate solitude of childhood: the commercial seems designed for a child who feels alone. Companionship toys invoke both the sense of isolation and the vulnerability of the contemporary child by celebrating the opposite: the meaningfulness of strong bonds of attachment, not with other children, but with fictional beings.

Gendered Fantasies

For the preschool girl these bonds of fictional love are often interpreted in familial and domestic terms. The commercials denote the traditional family role play of baby dolls as the social drama within which the child enters the play fantasy. It is not surprising to find that the most often repeated verbal themes in commercials for little girls refer to nurturing mother or older sibling. This social pretext for interacting with dolls is also witnessed in some ads for character dolls. My Little Pony Babies, for example, come with diaper changes and bottles. It falls to the ads to condense and articulate this highly gendered play value, and few do it as well as an animated commercial for Sylvanian Families:

Female voice (sings): Sylvanian.
Chorus: Sylvanian Families. They have come from far and near, a brand new baby is here. Sylvanian Families.
Female voice: Sylvanian Families just don't feel complete without a little baby. So they all have one, with its cradle and baby bottle. Figures and accessories sold separately.
Chorus: Sylvanian Families. To collect and love.

The fantasies of the young girls' toys are thematically adjusted to resonate with these well-known play values. 'Hair play', for example, became a much sought-after attraction in doll marketing circles because it combined grooming and nurturance and anticipated the more complex self-stylizing of the fashion doll. A narration from an ad for Corn Silk Cabbage Patches amounts to a dissertation on the perceived benefits of this play value:

Male voice: An unusual thing happened recently. Some Cabbage Patch Kids were born with beautiful Corn Silk Hair. Look, everyone said, you can wash and curl their hair. And braid it. And style it lots of ways. And they have their own brush they can hold. It seems as if they could have a different hairdo almost every day. And they always love to be loved. A lot.

An ad for Barbie also shows how important play values like hair play are in positioning even well-loved dolls like Barbie in the competition with Corn Silk Cabbage Patch dolls and the My Little Pony creations:

Woman (singing): We girls love styling our long luscious hair.
Chorus: Like Super Hair Barbie.
Woman (singing): First twist it around the secret barrette, push the tip and then the clip.
Chorus: Super Hair Barbie.
Girl: More hair.
Woman and chorus: Anyway we want to look, our magic barrette is

all it took. (sparkles around the hair and a magic sound)
We girls can do anything. Right, Barbie?
Female voice: Super Hair Barbie Doll. With magic hair barrette and
glamorous jumpsuit. New from Mattel.

The ads fantasy scene is simplicity itself: the magical barrette is what
gives Barbie her sparkling, flowing hair. The 'we girls' addressed by
the song includes a five year old spellbound by the magical
transformation of Barbie. The age of the girl, the sing-song narrative
and the narrow focusing on hair play are indications that this
particular Barbie doll is destined for the 'magic years' girls' market.

The Powers That Be

Certain narrative aspects of the animation series have to be dropped
and others accentuated to achieve the symbolic compression necessary in the character-advertising. The ads are not a faithful miniatur-
ization of the whole TV series but make selective and specific
references. For example in the Rambo ad the animated sequences
show little of the story's build-up. The villains are terrorizing the
town (but we don't know why) and the Rambo toy jumps out to
engage both Mad Dog and Havoc in battle (we don't know how he
knew). The conflict and its moral underpinnings are conveyed
through what the characters represent – their traits and dispositions
– but the context and human motivation are limited. The conflict
sequences are played out in the ad (and intercut with kids playing),
but it is conflict without build-up, planning, arraying or skill involved.
There is no subplot or light relief. Playing at Rambo seems only
peripherally concerned with the military tactics and realities of war;
the focus is on weapons and vehicle movement. In the ad there is no
real battle, no leadership and no true heroism depicted because
technological power rather than heroic personality is the central
theme. The outcome is predetermined, never in doubt. Although the
Rambo toy at first appears to be yet another invitation to induce
children to military themes, a careful look at the advertising indicates
that it is both more and less than this. The imagining that inspires
these modern lads as players is not the soldierly bravery and superior
battle tactics of the warrior but the achievements of an abstracted
technical power – the power of technology.

Action toys are often not just heroes but technologies – objects that 'come alive' in fantasy, enabling children to experience heroic triumph in their imaginary play. That is their real power. A commercial for Rock Lords – rock-like objects that magically change into 'indestructible' fighters – articulates this power dynamic concisely:

> *Chorus*:   Rock Lords! Rocks that come alive.
> Rock Lords! Fighting to survive.
> Living rocks with strength and might,
> Rising up to crash and fight.
> Rock Lords! Powerful living rocks.
> *Voice-over*: You can control their appearance, but no force in the universe can contain the power and fury of Rock Lords.
> *Chorus*: Shaking, quaking, crashing, breaking. Rock Lords, powerful living rocks.

The message about play in all these action-toy ads, then, is the same. Conflict is not about experiencing and controlling the basic human motivation of aggressiveness; it derives from an inevitable conflict of power – over survival, the control of the cosmos, freedom. The word power is used in over 50 per cent of the ads for boys revealing an almost metaphysical concern with this cosmic force. The muscle-bound heroes are themselves the personifications of power, and their weapons the embodiments of a more abstracted technological power. Indeed, in contemporary toy-advertising the more traditional thematics associated with boys' sports and toys – gamesmanship, co-ordination, tactics, skill, perseverance, practice, manipulation – seem to have all been absorbed in this singular obsession with toys as symbols of power. Even a construction toy's play values were articulated in this way, as embodiments of abstract technological power. Legions of Power announced a toy that allows boys to 'build for power' and imagine that they 'control the universe'. Boys' action toys, however, represent powers that can be realized only in an imaginary world. This is why the advertising does not dwell on the objective features of toys or portray play as the simple act of manipulating objects or following rules alone; it refers to toys as symbols and play as the act of manipulating these symbols in fantasy.

The act of make believe in action-toy ads appears not so much an act of simple pretending as a state of mind achieved through toys. Play, these ads seem to say, is an impulsive wish-driven style of thought – a suspension of judgement and rational believing where anything you want to imagine is possible. These ads seem to speak allegorically of the power of the imagination as the 'potential' to overturn the humdrum world and to share in a more exciting heroic mode of consciousness. The ads for action toys are thus celebrations of a very unique play value. As stories about play they must be read as parables in which critical consciousness is suspended and where the bonds of social impotence that bind the child's daily experience are forgotten. The action toy's primary appeal is its power to invoke and promote omnipotent fantasy.

Omnipotent fantasy play is so revered by marketers as the unique play value, that even traditional toy lines have been redesigned to appeal to the unstoppable imaginations. Of course, not all hero fantasies would do. It is a subset of very specific thematic motifs that permeates the make believe of children's advertising reflecting the convergence of the toy makers on a narrow band of widely popular cultural symbols. Ads for construction toys, trucks, board games, fashion dolls, cereals, computer games and chocolates all played during the 1980s with the iconography of the post-holocaust future wasteland world of science fantasy, because these themes were well defined in children's culture and reliably captured children's imaginations.

When a construction toy or truck is shown in these ads, it is not played with naturalistically in a child's bedroom, garden sandbox or the family room. The toy is catapulted into the imaginary future, projected into heroic vistas envisioned in sci-fi: the scope of Star Wars, with its far flung inter-galactic struggles for survival became the preferred motifs of symbolic design portrayed in toy-advertising. The following ad for Steel Monsters reads more like an ode to the future than an accounting of selling points of a remote controlled car:

Male voice: In a world gone mad, to survive you drive . . .
Steel Monsters.
Male voice: The Bomber, a motorized 4-by-4 with rugged battle armour, steel construction and evil metal face.
Hit the secret switch and shift into three forward speeds, neutral, and three speeds in reverse.
Male voice: Now you command the wasteland.
To survive you drive Steel Monsters.
Male voice: The Bomber. Games with action figures. Batteries not included. New from Tonka.

Kids understand these references because they easily make the associations with the other symbols that permeate their popular culture. But toy advertisers mined this deep repository of science fiction imagery because its mythic scope expressed the same power of fantasy they wanted to associate with their toys.

The sci-fi thematic even penetrated the imaginarium of fashion dolls. The following Spectra and Spark ad spoke of dreams of glamour and romance tainted with the newly minted space-age aesthetic:

Female voice: Look they come from outer space.
   She's landing in your town.
Chorus: Spectra.
Female voice: The most space-age girl around.
   New Spectra and Spark.
Girl 1: Shiny pink skin. Lacy space wear.
Girl 2: Spectra, I love to fix your sparkling hair, now we are ready.
Girl 1: For your welcome to earth party.
Girl 3: Sparks spinning all around. Wow!
Chorus: Spectra.
Female voice: The most space-age girl in town.
Girl: And Spark too.
Female voice: New from Mattel. Look for this free shimmering travel kit offer in every Spectra package.

Construction toys were once sold for their ability to engage kids in skills development and give them pride in what they built. But during the late 1970s as the action-toy market began to expand, Lego and Fisher-Price thematized their construction toys, including little characters in the play sets and borrowing the same sci-fi stylization and thematics. They, too, were repositioned within the play values celebrated by the action toy, '[making it] competitive not just with other construction sets, but also with models robots, action figures and puzzles'.[24] Construction-toy advertising regales children with space-age vistas and promotes a sense of mastery achieved by using the toy to express and control fantasy.

Male voice: Who puts the future in your hands?
Chorus: Robotix.
Robot: Robotix.
Male voice: Your own creation to command.
Chorus: Robotix.

Robot: Robotix.

Male voice: The amazing world of Robotix, from the smallest vehicle to the biggest robot, if you can imagine it, you can create it. Parts, motors, motion. You control it all.

Who lets you use imagination, to make any configuration?

Who puts the future in your hands?

Robot: Robotix.

Male voice: Introducing the Expansion set and three new starter sets from Milton Bradley.

Toy lines, which once were sold to enable children to learn skills and practise their eye–hand co-ordination, are here revealed as inviting the child to gain power and control over his or her own imagination.

Dreaming is the well-spring of fantasy, and advertisers tried to invoke the emotional qualities of the dream in their ads to strengthen fantasy appeal. Yet sometimes this took the advertiser into difficult cultural terrain. Hasbro's Inhumanoids used horror themes to strengthen the emotional roots of fantasy, but the product turned into a merchandising nightmare. Metlar, the evil force at the centre of the earth was a particularly nasty piece of work: the advertisement opening included a scene in which Metlar's tendril-like hands were seen emerging from the earth. His minions included Decompose, a frightful beast whose touch turned a man into a blob of melted flesh. The marketers evidently believed it was possible to promote a character toy based on the terror of a nightmare vision:

Screams.

Male character: They're not human, They're . . .

Chorus: Inhumanoids, Inhumanoids.

The evil that lies within (scream).

Male voice: Inhumanoids. Now see them every week in their own show. Can the earth core stop this evil menace?

Chorus: From down in the fiery depths of the earth, where nightmares begin (lots of screams).

Male voice: Tune in every week for the continuing adventures of . . .

Chorus: Inhumanoids (scream).

Even among the innumerable monsters created for science fantasy, the Inhumanoids were a particularly gruesome set of beasts. In fact, the Inhumanoids toy line flopped badly for Hasbro with considerable losses to their balance sheet. The programme elicited strong emotions. But the wrong ones. Inhumanoids aroused children's fear and parental anger; it had to be taken off the air, and the characters soon left the shop shelves. Although manifestations of evil and all manner of beast could be worked into children's fiction, and although horror toys (snakes, spiders, slime) have long been part of the market, the Inhumanoids revealed how difficult it was to get the emotional tone of fantasy right.

Style Wars

The power thematic which permeates the play of action toys, is to be distinguished from that which is shown in girls' character-advertising. In the following She-Ra ad, power is being replenished in what can only be described as a grooming ritual. The young female player is shown as witness and minion to this spectacle. The ads do not use the animated She-Ra of television, but only the doll luxuriating in the magical waters of Crystal Falls. But what is the secret power of the Crystal Falls play set that the children imagine? The song tells us that the waters refresh She-Ra, renewing her powers by making her feel 'pampered beautifully'.

> *Female* (singing): Magic water gently calls, refresh all powers at Crystal Falls.
> *Girls*: Wow, ooh, ah (while grooming She-Ra in her Crystal Falls play set).
> *Female* (singing): What a lovely place to be,
> Feeling pampered beautifully.
> The seashells and shower, they have secret power,
> The fate of the world is in good hands,
> At Crystal Falls, Princess of Power.

Play with She-Ra, it seems, is a devotional act in which the enraptured gaze of the child shows her captivated by the spectacle of power-bathing. Reaction shots of the girl's face convey her ecstasy. This is no empty ritual. The girl is having a mystical vision of a transformative power. It is not a power to accomplish worldly feats or fight Hordak. She-Ra is renewing her own psychic resources, her inner world. She-Ra is a symbol of the power of fantasy to transform personal experience. And no doubt little girls understand that playing with

269

She-Ra is about feeling and becoming pampered and beautiful too.

Romance and fashion circumscribe the content of the play fantasies of the girls' magic years' toys. This is why the great and splendid deeds which She-Ra, Jem or even Barbie perform in their animated series are forgotten, to be replaced by grooming, posing and costuming in the ads. Girls may be 'able to do anything', as Barbie well knows; but what their heroines in fact do in commercials is strut, preen and groom their way through the celestial sphere of fashion.

The girls also understand the ads' thesis that fashion is a social drama where popularity is the ultimate achievement, and popularity is achieved through 'the look'. Jem's eye-catching stardom is a sign that she has mastered the look. She is not just a singer and good friend, but a fashion statement – a style. Fashion dolls ultimately speak of a female world where each is judged not so much for what the dolls can do, as how they look:

Chorus: Jem goes gold, glitter and gold.
Female (singing): Truly outrageous and beautifully bold, this is the year for glitter and gold.
Chorus: No one's got moves like glitter and gold.
Song: Jem.
   The way she crosses her legs, by the look of her smile,
   Jem is a girl with incredible style.
Female (singing): Truly outrageous and beautifully bold. This is the year for Glitter and Gold. Jem.
Female voice: Glitter-and-Gold Jem, Rio fashions and accessories sold separately. Jem.

Character-marketing hasn't changed that element of fashion-doll play. If anything, it has simply made the fashion spectacle more intense, the social dynamics of glamour more specific. Indeed, character advertisements have added much detailing to this fickle and fluid world of glamour fantasies. Each doll's appeal is located in a 'taste culture' or lifestyle. Jem of the television series lives in two worlds but her life as a generic teen is ignored in the ads. From the point of view of play values, Jem is a glittering star with a very specific style. The glamorous social life of the rock star is troubled, however, by competition. Jem's performance style has rivals and is constantly under threat. Indeed, stardom is a sort of cosmic battle ground where she must constantly perform for the supreme accolades of fame,

270

admiration, and for love. The glamour battleground is described in the following little animated ad in which the typically mesmerized players become caught up in a struggle for fame and fortune. This is significant, for in choosing Jem or the Misfits, the girls are also declaring themselves – revealing their own personal style:

Chorus (over animation from series) : Jem.
Female voice: Battling the Misfits, battling, battling the Misfits.
Girl 1 (watching Jem) : Your clothes are outrageous.
Girl 2: Truly outrageous.
Misfits (singing in animation): We are the Misfits, we are better. Our music is better, and we are taking it all. Taking it, taking it, taking it all.
Girl 2: It's Jem and the Holograms.
Girl 1: The Misfits are better.
Girl 2: We'll let our fans decide.
Female voice: Flash 'n sizzle Jem, the Holograms and the Misfits, each sold separately with cassette.
Chorus: Jem.

The quest for stardom, which underlines Jem's social motivation, seems a well-chosen and appropriate allegory. Most young girls probably agree that social respect and friendship hinge on the loyalty, admiration, affection and companionship inspired among the peer group by their toys.

The Turtles' Revenge

In May 1990, Golden Harvest Films released the movie version of Teenage Mutant Ninja Turtles. The film grossed $40 million in the first ten days of its release. Ninja Turtle dolls and licensed paraphernalia have in fact amassed half a billion dollars in global sales since this strange team of unlikely heroes were adapted from an underground comic book into an animated children's series in 1988 and Playmate Toys action figure and play-set line. The merchandising success of the Turtles makes it clear that comprehensive character-marketing remains a force to be reckoned with in children's culture, even if the marketers are having to search deeper into the crannies of the social imagination for their heroes. Ninja Turtle animations have, in fact, been shown around the world, being advertised on television in Britain, France, Germany, Australia, Japan and China to mention only a few. Through satellite, they are seen in many other countries, becoming a global phenomenon of note.

An ad for a Ninja Turtle play set was recently shown on Canadian Network television. The ad was indistinguishable in many respects from most other action-figure ads. An animated sequence is intercut with a play scene in which boys (mostly hands) manipulate their dolls through the sewer play set in a mock ambush by Shredder, Be-bop and Rock Steady. The attack, of course, is roundly foiled by the Turtles martial skills and the clever traps they have laid in the play set, which includes a bucket of green slime. The closing animated scene shows Raphael talking in soliloquy to the camera. 'Reach out and crush somebody' is his final invocation to the assembled audience.

This ad differs little from many of its cohorts shown around the globe; it illustrates the conventional way that action-figure advertisers promote these toys on television. True, the Ninja Turtles are not your cloned He-Man superhero type that we are used to. True, too, that the final call to undertake violent behaviour is sharper and more direct than most ads we see on television. Yet the pattern of representation in the ad echoes all the familiar elements of the action-toy formula – an exciting dramatization of play which links the animated cartoons with an imagined play scenario. The scenes are now so familiar that most parents will not find the 'orthodoxy of play' it envisions startling. I mention it here not for its form or originality, however, but because it appeared on Canadian television and passed the review process set up to protect children against character promotions which are defined by the code as unfair and misleading advertising practices.

While American marketing practices were changing the face of children's television, Canadian policy makers blithely ignored what was happening, overlooking the new infrastructure (satellite, cable, video) which transformed the distribution of children's culture in Canada. Because cable has been excluded from both the Broadcast Act and the Advertising Council's purview, the tendency for Canadian children to watch American syndicated television went unnoticed. Yet Canadian kids, even French speakers in Quebec, became avid fans of the new animated programmes regularly shown by border stations.[25] So, in spite of mixed broadcasting, educational networks and more active regulatory structures designed to protect children from commercial manipulation, Canadian kids were able to keep up to date on all the fads and fashions in American children's culture. The waves of faddish toys swept successively through the Canadian market.

But Canada never changed its regulatory guidelines for children's advertising – guidelines which remain clear when it comes to misleading advertising and abusing children's faulty distinction between fantasy and reality. This code states in its preamble that, because children sometimes do not distinguish between fantasy and reality, 'advertisements should respect and not abuse the power of the child's imagination ... or stimulate unreasonable expectations of product or premium performance'. The code also has a number of other important provisions including the edict that advertising:

(1.b) Must not exaggerate service, product or premium character-istics such as performance, speed, size, colour durability, etc.;

(4.a) Puppets, persons and characters (including cartoon charac-ters) well known to children or featured in children's programmes, must not be used to endorse or personally promote products;

(8.a) advertising must not encourage a range of values that are inconsistent with the moral, ethical or legal standards of Canadian society.[26]

All children's ads must be pre-cleared by a standards committee which uses these guidelines. Canadian networks are supposed to reject any children's ad that depicts or urges unlawful or immoral acts, and the use in ads of characters from children's programmes is frowned on. These restrictions on children's advertising are similar to the ones developed by the FCC and used around the world. But just as in Canada, satellite networks and cable systems throughout the world are circumventing the regulatory net, while the endless exposures erode the reasons for maintaining these standards in children's marketing.[27]

I cite the Canadian example because it reveals how policy often fails to understand the broader implications of changing marketing strategies for children's advertising. Mixed broadcasting systems and self-regulation provide minimal buffers to structural forces unlea-shed by globalized toy-marketing. The public broadcasters move out of children's production because they cannot draw the children's audiences, while self-regulation drifts closer to the business position to protect the domestic industry from unfairness created by restricted marketing. The changes continue to take place as long as there is no public protest or mobilization around children's issues.

Two years earlier, an ad like the Ninja Turtles would probably have been censored or revised by request of the Canadian Advertising Standards Council. Today, with character-marketing so well established in North America, this type of ad slips through the regulatory cracks, drawing no critical notice. By 1991, the Advertising Council apparently no longer felt that the guidelines should limit the use of animated characters from television, or the intercutting of animated material with play fantasies. Moreover, when asked about the Turtles direct invitation to random assault, the Council's spokesperson stated that kids would understand that this call to action was said with humour: 'After all he has a smile on his face and irony in his voice. Children don't take these things seriously, do they?'

Deregulation of television, it must be remembered, resulted from a new attitude concerning the functioning of the market, which has altered the cultural environment of North America – including the attitudes of policy makers, regulators and parents alike. The demands we make on the cultural industries seem permanently altered – our very criteria for judging and resisting misleading and unfair advertising seem to be evaporating. As in all political vacuums, the matter rests with public opinion and the ability of those who are concerned about what the growth in children's marketing means to their children to resist. Only two complaints were received by the Canadian Advertising Council over the last two years!

Parents today seem largely unconcerned with the over-commercialization of television and the increased pressure put on their children by toy advertising. Children, most parents say, are not that influenced by the endless cartoons that television provides because they don't connect these fantasies with their real lives. 'Aren't these Turtles just a very contemporary and mildly amusing new form of entertainment?' After ten years of reiteration these promotional formula and rationales have become culturally accepted and naturalized. Our cultural amnesia makes it appear as if television-advertising and programming has always been like this – as if children have always needed the right action toys to play with their friends, the right hero on their pillowcase. Historical examination reminds us that it hasn't.

Notes

1. B. Sutton-Smith, *Toys as Culture*, New York, Gardner Press, 1986, p. 169.

2. See Brian M. Young, *Television Advertising and Children*, Oxford, Clarendon, 1990, chs 1 and 2 for a good background to the policy debates.

3. J. McNeal, *Children as Consumers: Insights and Implications*, Lexington, Lexington Books, 1987; Scott Ward and Daniel Wackman, 'Children's Information Processing of Television Advertising', in Peter Clarke, ed., *New Models for Communication Research*, Beverly Hills, Sage, 1973; Ellen Wartella, Daniel Wackman, Scott Ward, Jacob Shamir and Alison Alexander, 'The Young Child as Consumer', in Ellen Wartella, ed., *Children Communicating: Media and Development of Thought, Speech, Understanding*, Beverly Hills, Sage, 1979, pp. 251–80.

4. Ward and Wackman, 'Children's Information Processing of Television Advertising'.

5. Jane Rae, 'If You're Going to Advertise to Kids on Television Do it Right', *Stimulus*, May/June (no year given) pp. 24–5 (TVB).

6. 'CBS Moves to Divert Advertising Money Going to Animation', *Broadcasting*, 17 February 1986; B. Lowry, 'Tie-ins: Raising the Bottom Line in Kidvid', *Hollywood Reporter*, 2 June 1987.

7. Sydney Ladensohn Stern and Ted Schoenhaus, *Toyland: The High-Stakes Game of the Toy Industry*, Chicago, Contemporary Books, 1990.

8. William Wells, 'Communicating with Children', *Journal of Advertising Research*, 1966, pp. 1–14.

9. Deborah Roedder John and John C. Whitney Jr, 'The Development of Consumer Knowledge in Children: A Cognitive Structure Approach', *Journal of Consumer Research*, 12, March 1986, pp. 406–17.

10. Stephen Kline and Debra Pentecost, 'The Characterization of Play: Marketing Children's Toys', *Play and Culture*, 3 (3) 1990, pp. 234–54. A collection of 150 children's toy commercials were randomly sampled from US and Canadian television during children's viewing hours of the autumn season of 1986 and submitted to content analysis. This sample would have included over half of the toy ads shown that season on television. Just under 44 per cent of these ads were character toys (licensed properties with series or feature programmes on television) but these ads had the big budgets and enjoyed repeated showings. Where I quote data, the percentages are not expressed as proportions of exposures but of the sample.

11. Margaret Carlisle Duncan, 'Television Portrayals of Children's Play and Sport', *Play and Culture*, 2, 1989, pp. 235–52.

12. Greta Fein, 'A Transformational Analysis of Pretending', *Developmental Psychology*, 11, pp. 291–6.

13. Nancy Eisenberg, Sharlene Wochik, Robert Hernandez and Jeannette Pasternack, 'Parental Socialization of Young Children's Play', *Child Development*, 56, pp. 1506–13; Candace Schau, Lynne Kahn, John Diepold and Frances Cherry, 'The Relationships of Parental Expectations and Preschool Children's Verbal Sex Typing to their Sex-Typed Toy Play Behavior', *Child Development*, 51, 1980, pp. 266–70.

14. M.B. Liss, 'Learning Gender-Related Skills Through Play', in Marsha B. Liss, ed., *Social and Cognitive Skills: Sex Roles and Children's Play*, New York: Academic Press, 1983, pp. 147–65; M.B. Liss, 'Patterns of Toy Play: An Analysis of Sex Differences', *Sex Roles*, 7 (11), 1981, pp. 1143–50; Matthews and Matthews, 'Eliminating Operational Definitions: A Paradigm Case Approach to the Study of Fantasy Play', in D.J. Pepler and K.H. Rubin, eds, *The Play of Children: Current Theory and Research*, Basel New York, Krager, 1982; 'Analyze How They Play, Not What They Say: Projective Research Techniques Extract Valuable Market Data from Children', *Marketing News*, 21 January 1983, pp. 19–20; Elaine R. Jackowitz and Malcolm Watson, 'Development of Object

Transformations in Early Pretend Play', *Developmental Psychology*, 16, 1980, pp. 543–9; Greta Fein, 'A Transformational Analysis of Pretending', *Developmental Psychology*, 11, pp. 291–6; Jennifer Connolly, Anna-Beth Doyle and Flavia Ceschin, 'Forms and Functions of Social Fantasy Play in Preschoolers', in Marsha Liss, ed., *Social and Cognitive Skills: Sex Roles and Children's Play*, New York, Academic Press 1983.

15. Stephen Kline, 'The Limits to the Imagination: Marketing and Children's Culture', in I. Angus and S. Jhally, eds, *Cultural Politics in America*, Routledge & Kegan Paul, 1988; Marsha B. Liss, 'Girls: The Challenge to their Confidence', *Toronto Star*, 16 January 1990. Robert Fink, 'Role of Imaginative Play in Cognitive Development', *Psychological Reports*, 39, 1976, pp. 895–906.

16. Nancy Eisenberg, Sharlene Wochik, Robert Hernandez and Jeannette Pasternack, 'Parental Socialization of Young Children's Play', *Child Development*, 56, pp. 1506–13; Nancy Eisenberg, 'Sex-Typed Toy Choices: What Do They Signify?', in Liss, ed., *Social and Cognitive Skills*.

17. Vivian Gussin Paley, *Boys & Girls: Superheroes in the Doll Corner*, Chicago, University of Chicago Press, 1984.

18. Lori Swartz and William T. Markham, 'Sex Stereotyping in Children's Toy Advertisments', *Sex Roles*, 12(2), 1985, pp. 157–70; Chris A. Downs, 'Letters to Santa Claus: Elementary School Age Children's Sex-Typed toy Preferences in a Natural Setting', *Sex Roles*, 9(2), 1983, pp. 159–63.

19. Delly Karpoe and Rachel Olney, 'The Effect of Boys' or Girls' Toys on Sex-Typed Play in Preadolescents', *Sex Roles* 9(4), 1983, pp. 507–18; Janet Lever, 'Sex Differences in the Games Children Play', *Social Problems*, 23, 1976, pp. 478–87.

20. Kathy Silva, Carolyn Roy and Marjorie Cants, *Childwatching at Play Group and Nursery School*, London, Grant Macintyre, 1984; Vivian Gussin Paley, *Boys & Girls*; J. Singer and D. Singer, 'Implications of Childhood Television Viewing for Cognition, Imagination, and Emotion', in J. Bryant and D. Anderson, *Children's Understanding of Television, Research on Attention and Comprehension*, New York, Academic Press, 1983, pp. 265–95; J. Singer, D. Singer and W. Rapaczynski, 'Family Patterns and Television Viewing as Predictors of Children's Beliefs and Aggression', *Journal of Communication*, 34, 1984, pp. 3–21.

21. Canadian Association of Broadcasters, Broadcast Advertising and Children, Ottawa, 1985.

22. Wegener-Spohring, 'War Toys and Aggressive Games', *Play and Culture*, 2 1989, pp. 35–47.

23. B. Sutton-Smith, 'War Toys and Childhood Aggression', *The Journal of Play and Culture*, 1, 1988, pp. 57–69.

24. 'Construction Toys Are Solidly Building', *Chain Store Age*, January 1985, pp. 102–4.

25. M. Goldberg, 'The Effects of the Law Intended to Eliminate Advertising Directed at Children in Quebec', Office de la Protection du Consommateur, Government of Quebec, 30 March 1986.

26. Canadian Advertising Standards Council, Code for Advertising to Children, Canadian Advertising Foundation, 1981.

27. 'Satellites: Shoot 'em Sky High, Sell 'em Cheap', *Guardian*, November 1988, p. 18.

9

Technicians of the

Imagination

... but the net result of all the intellectualizing was ... Every-myth. All the original ideas and disparate approaches could be discerned, but somehow the sum of all the parts sounded strangely familiar – sort of a combination of the Iliad, Ivanhoe, and The Last of the Mohicans, plus a healthy dose of Star Wars. In other words, archetypal characters interacting in stock situations.[1]

Contemporary children's culture exists because merchandising interests are willing to invest in the production of children's television. This economic consideration provides the foundational logic of the culture industries, and always has. And there is ample evidence that the marketplace has been delivering 'what children want' better than any other contemporary agency of socialization. But many still ask whether what children choose to watch is necessarily good for them or our society in the long run.

Since television's early days, regulators at the Federal Communications Commission (FCC) have had to wrestle with the tension between television's popularity with children's audiences and concerns expressed by parents and critics. Given the economics of children's television, the preferred regulatory mechanism has been limitations on both the total commercial time on children's television and types of techniques used by children's marketing. Because regulation also involved advertising, the Federal Trade Commission (FTC) played an active role in regulating children's television.[2] Throughout the 1970s there was constant regulatory activity including hearings, research investigations and public inquiries, all aimed at discovering the optimum compromise that might establish a balance between the principles of children's special vulnerabilities, the potential impact of television, and the rights to commercial speech enjoyed by children's marketers. Deregulation of commercial television in the 1980s, therefore, marks an important shift in attitudes towards the rights of commercial interests and away from the criteria of programming quality and the developmental needs of children.

Indeed, the growing reverence for the marketplace dynamic inspired by Reaganomics had an enormous impact on US policy debates about children's television in the 1980s, tipping the previously established balance between the vulnerability of children and the rights of commercial interests. Commercial television was 'deregulated' on the singular idea that all matters of popular culture – even children's culture – are best determined through the marketplace mechanisms of consumer choice and unfettered commercial media. The FCC position was justified on the grounds that the children's cultural marketplace should only be restricted if there is proof of harm done to children, placing the burden of proof on children's researchers and advocates to demonstrate such harm.

In the meantime, children's media were granted new life and funding. No one will deny the fact that the toy marketers' enthusiasm for character promotions resulted in an enormous boom in children's television production activities in the 1980s. Television animators were allowed to innovate in the new forms of programmes appropriate within the new merchandising environment. What deregulation also achieved, therefore, was a new kind of children's programming guided more directly by merchandising interests. Long gone are the pretensions of innocence, artfulness and educational benefits. When the advertising subsidy was replaced by the total marketing infrastructure, the programming criteria were merged into the comprehensive marketing strategy of tie-ins, spin-offs and licensing. As Cy Schneider admits:

> The licensing explosion and the half-hour commercial ... have created a new source for the characters and video literature of our children's culture. What was once the sole province of children's authors, comic strip artists, and film artists ... has now become a creative outlet for toy and greeting card manufacturers. Should this phenomenon continue to grow, and it shows no sign of a slowdown, the new animation television programs will be dominated and commercially fueled by creations from toy companies.[3]

This shift in content has enormous implications not only for children's viewing, but also for those interested in the relationship between television and socialization because, in today's television business, the criterion for success is no longer entertainment value or audience size. Success in marketing terms can only be measured through the number of character licences contracted out and the profits from toy and other related merchandise sales. Toy marketers have become the major authors of children's fiction but their eyes are fixed on another set of books.

It is legitimate to ask whether the new purposes and arrangements for the production of children's television influenced either the quality or content of the programmes themselves. Cy Schneider, with years of experience in kids' television and toy-marketing, regards the boom in children's programming favourably. Schneider's view is that television producers have always had an eye for spin-offs so that merchandising opportunities were often built into TV shows or movies in the past: 'If entertainment creators anticipate a television show or movie is going to succeed with children, the show's creators almost always design elements in the entertainment that they can later license for manufacturing.'[4] This claim is no doubt true, as anyone with a Davy Crockett coonskin cap or Mickey Mouse watch can testify. But this overlooks the fact that character merchandisers favoured animation and pressured for the cheapest possible production and more selectively targeted audiences. Producing live-action drama was precluded because the costs and risks associated with programmes such as *The A-Team*, *Wonder Woman* and *Bionic Man* put them beyond the scope of the toy companies. Other programmes such as *Laser Tag Academy* and *Captain Power* quickly taught the industry to be wary of overly expensive formats in their programmes and ads. Money would flow to programming only if it had the potential to deliver the right audience cheaply.

But this lack of financial commitment isn't really new to children's television either. Schneider, therefore, doesn't think the new corporate players and their way of working have had any great impact on kids' television production, 'except for possible weaknesses in story lines and character development'. It is with this cynical shrug that most programmers cast aside the question of the quality of children's television as fiction. But if the narratives don't matter, why then do the marketers go to such pains to revise the scripts and characters?

The problem lies in the fact that producing good fiction and effective marketing are not always harmonious goals. It is for this reason that the meddling of the toy merchants and advertising agencies went beyond finance to shaping the form of children's 'programming properties' which, as Cy Schneider notes, 'are now being designed more for their merchandising potential than for their pure entertainment value'. A closer look at this new generation of children's fiction is therefore in order.

The Bottom (Story) Line

Three dimensions of marketing logistics have had a particularly important influence on the quality of the character animations' narrative: tighter production economies, product positioning strategies and the more specific targeting by age and gender. Because investment in animation and marketing was the foremost consideration in the viability of the marketing plan, the production arrangements for character television have produced ever greater pressure on the studio costs. These economic considerations pushed in two directions: keep the costs of the animation down (as close as possible to the cost of producing a commercial); and make sure the positioning and targeting are right, because the cost of failure is high. Rather than encouraging innovation, the approach drove marketing designers into derivative programming. They would prefer variations on tried and true properties that had proved themselves in the marketplace. The result was a panoply of abundantly formulaic scripts that seemed even more rigid in form and contrived than their predecessors.

Programmes such as *He-Man* and *Care Bears* are not scripted as moral parables or even innocent amusements. Character fiction must serve the marketing functions of introducing a new range of personalities into children's culture, orientating children to this product line, creating a sense of excitement about these characters, and ultimately leading children to want to use those characters in play. Most of the new children's television animations have been created explicitly for selling a new line of licensed goods. It is simply not sufficient for a programme to be popular with kids. The programme must instil in them the promise of an imaginary world that can be entered not just by watching television but also by owning and playing with a specific toy line. Children must want to have the characters and props, to own and to play with them to re-create their imaginary universes within their own play spaces.

In their account of Tyco's development of the Dyno-Riders Sydney Stern and Ted Schoenhaus give a clear sense of how marketing considerations squeeze out any possibilities for creativity and innovation in the development of new character lines and their television properties.[5] In the case of Dyno-Riders, the toy originated with the toy makers' understanding of children's fascination with dinosaurs. The dinosaurs themselves were thought to be the unique focus of this product's play value and so the characters were cast carefully as museum-quality models of real dinosaurs. But this conception was quickly revised as the exigencies of marketing an action-adventure play set were adjusted to the problems of using television-marketing exposure as the main promotional avenue. The final models were grotesquely inaccurate in colour, shape and implied behaviour. The back-story narrative about extra-terrestials who tamed dinosaurs was twisted until it became a highly formulaic composite of whatever programme themes had proved successful on television before. Quite at odds with the original conception, the dinosaurs were made to talk – 'The dinosaurs must talk for there to be a bond between the audience and the characters'. So in the back-story there must be two classes of dinosaurs – one free and one subjugated: 'Only free dinosaurs have developed personalities. Enslaved dinosaurs are no more than transformed fighting machines who are brutish and growling.' These conventions are essential because, as the experienced character marketers explain,

> There are certain idiomatic expressions, visual as well as verbal. In film, for example, a dissolve usually means time is passing. And there are some idioms in looks. A strong heroic character is typically a blond, Aryan type. You have very little time to tell your story, and you don't have time to get bogged down. You can't deal with a short, dark character as the hero without taking more time to set it up.[6]

And so the characters' names and traits were reworked with the emphasis shifting from dinosaurs and what they might be like to the wars and politics of their riders.

The Economics of Animation

Moreover, unlike earlier cartoons produced to entertain and amuse children, a producer of these new programmes could not expect a decade of repeats in children's time-slots as a means of recouping production costs. Success would be determined more by the profits of toy lines than by the residuals that accrued to the producer of much-loved cartoon animations. The producers of these tied-in animations took a shorter-term perspective for recouping their investments and they knew they had to appeal to the children of the present rather than to successive generations in the way Bugs Bunny or Fred Flintstone had done. The programme would run on TV once or twice after the toy line entered the market, and if it became popular it could enjoy some global sales. The production costs would have to be amortised over the life-cycle of the toy in the market. If the costs were kept down they could be viewed simply as promotional write-offs and tax losses. The eternal or venerable qualities sought (with economic justification) by the early cartoon producers had become unnecessary in these more mercantile productions.

Two factors that helped to reduce the production costs of animation had a further significant impact on animation design. The first factor is the introduction of computerized animation systems, which have automated camera movement, background movement and cel production. The new processes have dramatically reduced the artists' labour, which was the significant component of production costs in the work of Disney or even Hanna-Barbera. Most animation effects can now be achieved by computer programming rather than by a group of artists working out and painting in the cels in great detail. This means that animation ideas – the characters and actions that form the basis of the stories – can be all laid out in advance on story-boards and sent off to Japan, Hong Kong or Korea for production. In the past many of the animation ideas were more serendipitous, emerging as the artists and writers worked directly with the materials and discovered the potential of a character or scene. Modern animation has increasingly become the prerogative of technicians who operate the technology in conjunction with producers who work out the concepts; the influence of an artist is often limited to preliminary sketches of the characters and design stylistics for the series. Although the teams that produce a modern series are as big, if not bigger, than their predecessors, there is less scope for the interplay among artists and writers that was traditionally the creative spark in animation.

Keeping costs down is clearly a top priority in the scripting and execution of the visuals. That subtle fascination with the movement of an object in space, the humour of surprise and irony, and the emotional expressiveness of characters that dominated early animators' love of the art (and which resulted in the major costs of the Disney studios), have been sacrificed for economized suggestion and stylized displays. The social interplay between characters is staged as a series of abbreviated poses. The action, chase and battle scenes are merely contrived and jerky visual techniques. There is reduced expressiveness, beauty of movement, versatility and complexity in these new tales. Indeed, these new animators have proved that the labour-saving methods pioneered by Hanna-Barbera when they created the first programme-length cartoons could be simplified even further and still retain a child's interest.

The driving music and sound tracks (standing in for complex plot and dialogue) and the graphically produced visual effects cannot disguise the fact that the animators are stingy in their illustration of characters and backgrounds. For people who consider the design and illustration of cartoons to be a fine art, these modern offerings are a great disappointment. They don't compare, for example, to the background drawings of the house in Disney's *Lady and the Tramp*, in which the stair carpet is a beautifully detailed Persian rug that changes with the changing light conditions as Tramp runs up the stairs to save the baby; or the expressiveness of the dogs' faces, when the dinner behind the spaghetti restaurant results in a surprise first kiss. If we compare the stilted and repetitive stunts and poses of Paw-Paws, He-Man or Ninja Turtles with the masterfully fluid and precisely timed movements or the moody scenes of *Fantasia*, the price of hyper-economy in animation quality becomes clear.

The highly successful (from a merchandising point of view) *Care Bears* series reveals the extremes to which these simplifications have been taken. In the *Care Bears*, the characters are so alike that they are differentiated only by an emblem on the front of their bodies, slightly different voices, and the fact that they always respond and say things according to their character. Such simplifications don't make the storylines very interesting, but they have obvious logistic advantages. The Care Bears concept creates not just one personality but a host of cuddly characters, each associated with a different childhood feeling (Grumpy, Friendship, Hugs 'n Tugs, Sunshine Bears, Brave Heart Lion) offering greater flexibility in identification and, like all products sold as teams, motivating multiple purchase. For the writers and producers the predictability makes production straightforward: there is no need to make sure that each character is drawn according to characteristic movements, actions or expressions when all that changes is the colour of the emblem and voice.

Although some of the Japanese-produced series, most notably *Robotech*, have inspired critical acclaim by animation fan-zines,[7] most contemporary animations are circumscribed by a very limited range of social relations, emotions and themes. Although the pretext of these stories is purely fantastical, the stories do not broadly explore the spectrum of human experience. The overriding impression they generate is that of predictability. Compared with children's books, it is easy to conclude that children's television fiction has lost much of its charm, freshness, humour and individuality in favour of formula plots and plodding one-dimensional characters. Unfortunately, this has probably always been the case with children's television, for it has always been underfunded. A more judicious observation might be that putting control of scripts in the hands of marketers hasn't done much to improve the already limited quality of children's television.

Vulnerable Targets

Any account of children's culture has to recognize the increasing fragmentation of the children's market. As DMB&B advised in the advertisement (see Plate section) 'It is vital for marketers to understand the complexity of the children's market, which is not one market but three, with children's preferences and values showing major differences according to age.' Toy marketers attempt to fit their properties to the established cultural preferences of an audience, and their research showed that audiences of children differed in what they liked to watch and how they liked to play. Targeting implies the ability to break up the children's market into segments or clusters of individuals with common attributes defined by their preferences for or orientation to goods.

Target-marketing depends on the degree to which these clusters can be addressed as audiences through the available communication channels. The networks have always preferred universally popular programmes that increased their gross ratings and children's share. Whereas the Tom and Jerry, Mickey Mouse, or Woody Woodpecker presentations were intended to appeal to children of all ages and sexes, the new designed-for-syndication series would be viewed by much narrower segments of the population, at a lower cost to the advertiser. Nine year olds have little interest in Teddy Ruxpin, girls don't buy or ask for G.I. Joe dolls, nor do boys play much with Barbie. Toy-marketing campaigns are designed around much more specific appeals than were the advertising industry's earlier calls to all children. The advertising economies that accrue from a saturation process achieved within a preferred market segment and rather than with gross audiences can be significant. But the syndication of stations turns out to be a very complex arrangement in which an enormous volume of audience statistics have to be distilled to ensure coverage and exposure to the right age group.[8] For example an advertiser considering an afternoon spot might now prefer an earlier day-part or programme slot if programmers manage to attract preschoolers; such moves can have enormous consequences for reach and frequency calculations.

For marketers and their researchers, the world of afternoon children's viewing involves precise and detailed information about what goes on in the home: what children are watching, when and with whom. Watching patterns depend on sibling and parenting dynamics and on the habits children develop for the after-school period: over 65 per cent of our sample of six and seven year olds reported watching TV as the first thing they did when they got home. But when their older siblings get home, preschoolers may be forced to watch the programmes their older brothers and sisters choose. This means that younger children do get exposure to programmes that are more popular with an older age group. Marketers have to analyse these patterns. Should a company advertising preschool toys use afternoon syndicated TV, the early Saturday morning networks, or prime time – and in what proportion and intensity?

Age segmentation is a social practice that also runs deep in our educational system; we subdivide children into a sequence of graduated ability levels. Teachers and psychologists tend to believe that learning experiences delivered at the right time and at the right level – when children are ready – are the most effective. A similar philosophy of pragmatic developmentalism also provided the conceptual basis for the marketers' tactics for engaging and influencing children in their relations with goods. Children grow through a maturation cycle, which means that their preferences for toys, for heroes and for when to view television can be studied through research and then fed back to them in programmes targeted to age. If research shows that children are on average most interested in imaginary friends between the ages of two and five, or that they are unclear about what a brand name actually means until they are six years old, or that they have difficulty following a complex and involved plot before they are eight, the programming has to take these details into account. Significantly, the credits for some of these animation series (*Superfriends, He-Man, Defenders of the Earth*) include 'psychological consultants' as part of the creative team.

The most dramatic impact of age-targeting is on the placement, repetition and scheduling of advertisements. Research enterprises that provide the detailed data on children's television habits and preferences began to use more precise age and gender breaks, and media buyers came increasingly to rely on this information, especially for the scheduling of syndicated TV. The impact of targeting strategies was clearly evidenced in our study of the contemporary cartoon genre, in the narrowness of the themes when we submitted the episodes from the ten top-rated animated programmes of 1987 to detailed analysis.[9] Altogether we examined 180 animated programmes. We then selected 25 of these which we thought were typical of the subgenres we found, transcribed them and submitted them to exhaustive content analysis. The series in the top ten happily included examples from all genres: action figures (He-Man and Thundercats); plush (preschooler) (Smurfs and Care Bears) and fashion toys (My Ponies and Jem). These programmes were first analysed as a set and then separately by gender and age segments so that the stratified design of the narratives could be discussed.

Overall, there is also evidence of a generic formula emerging which, although related to the traditional Saturday morning cartoon short, is very unlike it. There are, in fact, few surprises in these stories and, considering the variety of pretexts, a disappointing convergence in theme, action and narrative structure. But the defining feature of this metagenre lies in the structure of the dramatic conflict (we didn't simply count hits on the head but took note of the situation in which conflict was expressed). The conflict in these programmes is very idiomatic and conventionalized – echoing the blended conventions of science fiction and folklore established in Star Wars so the dramatic tensions are often explained in abstract terms. The charts below reveal the percentage of all episodes which made reference to these particular explanations of why conflict occurred. It is noted here that conflict is primarily justified as a matter of species survival and expressed in the context of logistical arrangements in cosmic and moral battles that had no end.

Critics have noted that although there are fewer examples of physical aggression in these programmes, the character genre may be more violent (in terms of meaningful conflict) than other forms. This seems to be true, for the formula has replaced the short aggressive slapstick clashes of the comedy cartoon (Roadrunner, Bugs Bunny) with one or two grander confrontation sequences.

Conflicts (explanations of conflict)

Pragmatic (survival, logistics)	37
Domestic/Ingroup	17
Power or control	11
Ideological (good v. bad, progress, freedom)	6
Other	4
Origins, Race and History	3
Personal	2
Natural occurrence	1

Content	*Frequency*
Rely on and use technology (action)	85
Problem-solving, task orientation (action and discussion)	77
Maintain hierarchical structure (discussion, meetings)	72
Offensive conflict (battle sequence)	54
Race against time (action with a deadline)	50
Gathering information (reconnaissance, spying)	37
Defensive conflict	25
Competition, contest (race, skills)	21

If we combine offensive and defensive scenes of physical confrontation, battling episodes would account for about 25 per cent of the total narrative, but occurs in only 9 per cent of the episodes in our sample. It is also worth noting that the storylines pay careful attention to the equipment and accoutrements that so preoccupy the denizens of cartoon universes in the build-up to conflict – weapons, vehicles, personal ambitions and other accessories which define the preoccupation of the characters and feature prominently in the staging of conflict in the episodes. A fair bit of time is also spent in problem-solving and maintaining the hierarchical structures of the mini-worlds (most evil empires being autocratic and good aristocratic).

287

Task-orientated discussion	200
Conversations (informal)	80
Soliloquy, inner dialogue	62
Battling, fighting	61
Working with technology	57
Arguing, insulting	48

Although battles and technology are the plot pivots, it is also worth noting that when it comes to the conversation, the characters in these animations are very task-orientated and pragmatic – many of these conversations occur in the preparation for and during the conflicts. Informal conversation does occur, especially in setting the scene, but insults and arguments are also common. We occasionally get to know the inner thoughts of some of the characters in soliloquies, which is necessary because deception and spying are important themes; these inner dialogues help the viewer understand the differences between 'real' motives and 'appearances' a distinction which is crucial to many of the stories.

Since we also examined the actions, social interactions, themes, characters, conflicts and complexity of the storylines in context, the rest of this chapter tries to distil what we found in this analysis.

The broad conclusion of our review of the children's animation genre is that there is no such thing as a single formula: the series on children's television must be differentiated into narrative categories which are targeted by gender and by age. The differences in characterization, theme and story complexity reflects the fact that marketing is now a force for fragmentation in children's culture creating a more differentiated 'television' than many critics admit. This not only makes it hard to talk about children's television; it implies that children no longer share a unified field of fiction. Children of different ages may not have the same common heroes to idolize, or programmes to discuss in their recess conversations and play interactions at home. This is true not only of different age segments, but also of gender strata. As targeted marketing replaces mass marketing, the shared sense of a children's culture is challenged with a more divisive imagery of miniaturized consumption tribes.

Interviews with children show that they are fully aware of this targeting dynamic in their television schedules. Although children from about three years on will distinguish animated shows as 'for kids', they also have a clear conception of programmes that are for 'boys' or 'girls' or of programmes that they were too old or young to watch or like.[10] When asked, six and seven year olds can give consistent explanations of what makes a particular kind of show interesting for themselves or for another particular group. Although there is an overlap of audiences – with the young showing a willingness to watch 'older kids'' shows and girls willing to watch Transformers or G.I. Joe along with their male siblings – conversations with children serve to reinforce the idea that their experience of their culture is increasingly fragmented.

Themes without Variation

The improved segmentation statistics encouraged advertisers to think about kids as an age-segmented audience, which in turn intensified the thinking of programme designers. Modern marketing demanded a certain sensitivity to narrative, and although they never had to produce truly creative writing, writers did have to base their scripts on the imagery and themes that children respond to. As the DMB&B researchers urged:

> Children enjoy a plot or story. They identify with action and characters in a story, which should be simple, clear, concrete, moving quickly to completion or resolution. The pace should not be too fast, particularly for the under 6's. Story line should not be dependent on audio.... Children respond well to a variety of strategic and tactical elements.

The creators extended the role of age-targeting and the absence of aesthetic considerations to the storylines and dialogue, giving rise to a highly formulaic approach to fiction. In the name of economy, they replaced character with caricature, and substituted setting the scene and mood of a narrative with simple backdropping. They reduced the nuance and subtlety of the children's story to a 'plot-line' consisting of a sequence of actions worked out on a story-board and filled in by the animators. The overly simplified illustration and stilted dialogues of preschoolers' television are probably the worst offenders. It has become almost impossible for most parents to watch the inane dialogue and stultified animation with their children.

289

The designers obviously borrowed from *Sesame Street*'s experimentation with highly concentrated episodic form and very saleable plush creatures like Bert and Ernie, Cookie Monster, and Big Bird. Preschooler television continues to be populated by lovable fluffy animal-like creatures designed to appeal to a child's need for imaginary companions (Paw Paw Bears, My Ponies, Pound Puppies, Popples). Assuming short attention spans and a need for simple storylines, these fragmented little ads for plush toys appear to be constructed from loosely knit scenes in which characters act out their preordained traits in an 'imaginary' community that only children can understand.

Many of the character toys marketed to the preschool market seemed to mimic the Smurfs, who in 1981 set the new pace in television spin-offs for plush toys. One of NBC's concerns in creating *Smurfs* – before deregulation – was to counter the mounting criticism of network children's television by producing a non-violent pro-social cartoon series. For this reason the producers were motivated to script a cartoon series that worked with what they saw as the more acceptable elements of traditional children's culture. Following the cartoons of the Belgian cartoonist Peyo Culiford based on German folklore creatures (rather like European Shmoos), the concept was adapted to television by Hanna-Barbera. A little community of imaginary creatures live in a forest mushroom patch in a medieval landscape. The Dungeons and Dragons fad of the 1970s had alerted children's marketers to the fact that the sword, quest, magic and castles imagery of traditional heroic adventure literature was still potent stuff for the young.

The Smurfs look like neotenous blue dwarfs. Although their social organization seems to have a familial quality, there is no maternal figure. The nominal head of the community is Papa Smurf, who leavens the proceedings with wisdom and occasional bits of medicine and magic. The social relations and interactions are more fraternal than paternal, however, without much reference to hierarchy or government; precedents and personality traits define personal rights and duties. The stories usually involve one of the Smurfs getting into trouble. Although the Smurfs all look alike, each of them is attributed a name like Jokey Smurf or Brainy Smurf, implying a unique trait or disposition that is then invoked in events involving the character. Jokey Smurf is often playing jokes, for example, some of which backfire, and Brainy Smurf is handy with books when the group has to find a solution to a difficult problem such as researching a magical potion.

Cheaply animated in the style that the Hanna-Barbera studio had perfected for television, the *Smurfs* first stories exploited the humour and unusual domestic practices that could be imagined in the mushroom patch. Avoiding the standard visually exciting (and violent) cartoon humour, the jokes were banal and sloganistic. For example, the Smurfs use Smurf language: they don't eat raspberry but smurfberry pie. The dialogue that sustained the early stories tended to be somewhat flat, in keeping with the unidimensional characterizations engaged in trait-specific antics.

At first the NBC producers thought life among the Smurfs would be sufficiently intriguing to attract and hold the intended young audience, bringing youngsters back to network television. But a slow growth in ratings led the producers to change their minds about the attractions of simple folk characters. So they introduced a new character, Smurfette (the only female smurf), to the male gathering. More significantly, they brought in Gargamel, a mean warlock with a penchant for black magic, a cat, and an apprentice called Scrupple, who all lived nearby and were intent on destroying the Smurfs.[11] Now the stories hinged on the survival of the community and the personalities of the mushroom patch were mustered in a more grand struggle against mindless malevolence. The ratings immediately shot up and so did the sale of Smurf dolls. And so it was discovered that while the simplified and humble bumbling of a folk community of blue dwarfs couldn't sell toys, if you wrapped these same simple characters around a storyline motivated by conflict and magic of pure good against pure evil, the grail would come into sight.

Following *Smurfs*, the series concepts for plush toys varied; but marketers were more interested in concocting an imaginary play universe accessible to the child, unlike the world of the Smurfs. Some shows, like *Teddy Ruxpin*, were explained as toys that were brought to life by magic, but most of the new TV characters inhabited an imaginary universe of childhood that ran parallel to the child's world of experience and could be accessed only by a child's belief in such a world. This device of the parallel world was often worked into the story by a human child who gains access to these imaginary friends or guardians, or who protects them from harm.

The Care Bears, for example, live in the cloud kingdom of Care-a-lot. The Care Bear cousins (stuffed toy animals who are not bears) live on the ground in the Forest of Feelings. The Care Bears and cousins are alerted to people needing their help by a care-o-meter and care-alarm. Some go on patrol in cloud-cars. Where they can they intervene, bringing feelings to one another and to the human lives they touch. They are called on often, for the evil Noheart who lives in a storm cloud castle is bent on getting rid of caring from the world.

The Care Bear characters are clearly intended to denote a realm dominated by peer culture. The characters live in cosy communal clusters or in peer groups with traditions and social practices more like those of friends and siblings. There are no established social hierarchies or systems of government, no king or queen figures – the elements so typical of folk tales and older children's action dramas. The action centres on the preservation of the rather vulnerable group and on its defence not only from the predations of Noheart but also from the many technologies of everyday life (water fountains, kitchen equipment, lawn-mowers) that don't quite work as they should.

The episodic story structure of *Care Bears* means that the plot-lines tend to be capers or escapades rather than adventures or quests. The scenes seem designed to resonate with children's feelings – the site of imaginary friendships. The social relations within these tales play upon the fluid peer interactions and impotence the preschooler experiences within the world at large. The simple plots hinge on the problems of social and emotional adaptation, and none of the Bears is really capable of taking charge. There is, in fact, no whole personality among them, for they are emotional icons, acting according to simple psychological laws. They are scripted as allegorical narratives that consciously attempt to treat the experiences of childhood on a fantasy plane: the scripts focus on the loneliness, fear, clumsiness, foolishness, egotism, frustration and social misunderstanding typical of childhood.

The situations are so contrived and abstracted from the child's experience that it remains difficult to know how children can actually connect them to real experiences in their own lives. These stories seem to reduce the moral problems that children face to bland banalities. The problems and their solutions have little relation to the difficulties of growing up that many children face. Themes of abandonment, separation, incompetence and helplessness are all there, but there is little of the social context of real life, and there is no room in the tales for issues such as divorce, child brutality, poverty or negligence. The *Care Bears* story is not an allegory to help children make sense of their feelings, the characters are emotional symbols employed to further the child's identification with and bonding to a toy.

An episode of *Care Bears*:[12]

While Proudheart is supervising work on her garden and Tenderheart is admiring it, Proudheart receives a gift from a 'secret admirer'. Beastly watches in anticipation from a hiding spot. Ignoring caution, Proudheart unveils the gift. Meanwhile, Playfulheart is showing off with the lawn-mower and loses control of it. The cousins are chased around the garden by the lawn-mower, which ruins the garden. Playfulheart turns on the fountain and Proudheart turns the water up, ignoring advice to turn it down until the water sprays her head. However, the fountain will not turn off. The cousins come up with the idea of plugging the fountain with mud but Proudheart won't let them. The fountain begins to flood the Forest of Feelings. Tenderheart signals the Care Bears for help. They rescue the cousins and bring them up to Care-a-lot.

Noheart explains how flooding the Forest of Feelings will keep Care-a-lot overcrowded and cause the Care Bear family to fall apart.

Back in Care-a-lot conflicts begin to arise due to the crowding. Beastly, as he spies, comments on how living together is turning them all into grumpy bears and the more they forget about caring the lower the Caring Meter goes. The Care Bear family is too caught up in their own problems to stop Noheart from getting rid of all the feelings in the world. Finally, the cousins begin to ask questions about the fountain and to link it to Noheart. Noheart and his Shadows set out to destroy the feelings of the world.

Tenderheart and Proudheart realize that the water must be coming from Noheart's storm cloud and that once it is all out the cloud will disappear and there will be nowhere to return the water to. Tenderheart designs a subdirigible to pump water back to Noheart's storm cloud. They must work together to build it. Tenderheart points out that they are forgetting to care for each other and they are able to finish the work.

Proudheart and Playfulheart enter Noheart's castle while others take the subdirigible to the fountain. Proudheart and Playfulheart confront Beastly and inform him that the storm cloud will run out of rainwater and persuade him to show them the control valve to the fountain.

The other Care Bears hook up the pump to the storm cloud and begin to pump the water back in.

The Forest of Feelings is returned to normal. Proudheart says she has learned that if you've got something nice, don't try to change it.

Prologue: two kids about to go on stage in a school play share their feelings about stage fright and help each other.

Toys as Heroes

While both age- and gender-targeting have influenced the design of the product concept in TV animation, it has had a particular effect on the play values woven into the narratives. The hair play of the My Little Ponies, the fashion and grooming of Barbie, the bedside imaginary friendship of the Pound Puppies, or even the technologized militarism of G.I. Joe are all part of these marketing plans. Language, colour, movement, music and every detail of production have been thoroughly considered in these terms, making the product concept and its appeal a projection directed to a particular stratum and niche in children's peer culture and the toy market.

A quick glance at the oft-repeated glamour and popularity themes of Jem, or at the militarism of Rambo and G.I. Joe, provides tempting evidence to anyone who wishes to write contemporary children's television off as simply more capitalist realism promoting aggressiveness in boys and vapid sexism in girls.[13] Tempting as such generalizations are, a more systematic study shows these stories do not flow from a single ideological position or follow a rigid pattern of characterization. Far from simpering Doris Day types, many of the female characters in children's television are endowed with amazing powers and a strong sense of themselves. They are formidable foes and important components in competent teams. Moreover, a close inspection of the futuristic militarism of many of the programmes reveals that the heroic forces are motivated by anti-fascist and anti-racist attitudes in strong defence of democracy.[14] Indeed, it is not uncommon to find that the foe of freedom is a megalomaniacal capitalist who is attempting to corner the market on energy crystals.

Ideology in narrative is never easy to unmask. As Celia Anderson perceptively notes, Saturday morning television does not offer up a dogmatic ideology to the observer so much as a mythology that takes the form of superhero fantasy. 'We already have a set of new myths. We have simply been slow in identifying them as such because, unlike the old models which were creation myths or explanations of the psyche, the new are survival myths,' Anderson writes. 'As prime agents in disseminating these new myths to the young, science fiction cartoons deserve serious investigation.'[15] Anderson sees the superhero cycle as a reworking of traditional images of nature and technology within the context of a struggle for ultimate power. The survivalism theme she notes is particularly significant for children, whose lives clearly lack a sense of power over their environment.

But it is also an important part of marketing strategy.

Marketers have long understood the relationship between heroic personality and sales. As Cy Schneider states:

> Easy and correct definition of the character is most important. The character must be – or become – an essential part of the American popular culture mainstream. While the character can relate to or be reminiscent of characters which have come before, he or she must be unique in some important way. Uniqueness is usually achieved by a difference in personality, design, graphic execution, story line, or identity.... These characters are usually larger than life. They are super special and can often perform extraordinary feats.[16]

The universe of play has been best stimulated by the heroic imagination of children. Their quest for heroic identities for their toys brought them increasingly to the threshold of legend and myth. So marketers devised narratives 'potentized' by conscious reference to the heroes of literature and history – narratives which stood out in the marketplace and commanded children's attention. Often the opening sequences of a show retell the origin story and put the characters in perspective, a pattern laid out by the adventurous and formidable director–producer George Lucas, who in his *Star Wars* trilogy consciously set out to produce new children's myths in the cinema by pilfering images, characters, ideas and scenes from old stories and classic films.

Alienated Heroes

Knowing that 'omnipotent' characters and heroic deeds were appealing to children (especially to boys), character designers explored the older recesses of fiction and folklore to find new inspiration for television. One source is particularly noticeable: Superman, that comic-book model of the omnipotent hero, was not only a true innovation in narrative but also a beacon for the attempt to modernize children's myths. The Superman storyline was in essence a combination of modernized Greek legends distilled in visual narrative form that was compatible with the mediums of comic books, television and the cinema. The Superman character has earned its place in the pantheon of legendary stories by inspiring three generations of children.

Superman, like the heroes of Greek myth, is an alien. His special powers and abilities do not spring from human history – from either scientific advancement or the human potential perfected – but are simply attributes of his identity. He has his strength, his impervious skin, his X-ray vision and freezing breath, for example, only because he comes from the world of Krypton. This dislocation of origins in the superhero narrative paralleled the fact that as an image of heroism, Superman did not emerge from the mists of history and the depths of accumulated cultural experience. Superman was a conscious myth: an archetype of the hero created by the unitary consciousness of writers. The achievement of its authors lay not in their abilities to fabricate a profoundly resonant piece of folklore but to inspire a genre of children's tales that concerned themselves with incredible deeds of an otherworldly being – the primary objectives of Superman's creators were, after all, the sale of comics to kids.

On television Superman inspired a number of comic-book hero sequels, each of them helping to fill out the notion of a modern superhero: Batman and Wonder Woman found their way to television in the 1960s and 1970s and into the animations of the 1980s. Their long-term appeal lay in the compelling and careful way heroic narrative was reduced to a set of basic ingredients: amazing powers, triumph by force, secret identity and moral righteousness defined the superhero genre. Basing their work on more or less the same ingredients, toy marketers further refined this narrative lineage in their heroic characterizations. Following the consciously mythic paths cultivated by the superhero narratives, the companies introduced Defenders of the Earth, the Superfriends and He-Man into the action-toy market.

Superman wasn't heroic, but superheroic. In superhero stories, deeds override motives and formative experience as the basic elements of the tale. Scenes of maturation, of practice, of training and of the emergence of heroic traits are rare: Superman's power lay with his alien origins, with his genetically bestowed potency. This was one of the most important ways in which the superheroes' tales reduced the narrative. Even his childhood experience with the Kents – those important civilizing moments with the typical American family – are much reduced and fragmentary. They certainly don't explain Superman's extraordinary deeds or his unswerving commitment to 'truth, justice and the American way', as the TV programme of the cold war 1950s put it. Not that understanding the inner workings of the personality matters in superhero narratives, for the story is a tale of deeds and actions writ in graphic detail. There are many scenes of great deeds and heroic rescues, but there are few indications of the tempering of the heroic personality.

Superman, it must also be remembered, acquired unique powers because he no longer lived within his time and space. His origins lay in a mysterious other world. What this narrative device achieved for Superman's writers was the possibility to disengage his heroism from the bonds of realism and credulity about human powers, to explore them in the abstract. Classic heroes of myth and literature, like any real personality, have human frailties as well as divine inspiration. The comic version of heroism reduced the problem of hubris to a single weakness – in Superman's case, kryptonite. Fragments of his former world float into the stories to provide a weapon for his arch-enemies and a threat to his omnipotence. In superhero tales, hubris is substituted by a power thematic and its relation to the alien origins of the hero.

However mythic in reference, the superhero does not prove to be as psychologically portentous as the more vulnerable Greek heroes, who like Theseus and Narcissus turn out to be subject to the whims of the Gods and the Fates. Greek heroes are potent images of human personality because they struggle on a metaphoric level with those cosmic forces and represent them within the human psyche, in a way that helped to make unconscious forces and human frailties easier to appreciate and resolve. Superheroes, on the other hand, are consciously designed around a power thematic. They are in the guise of myth but do not emerge from the same cultural and historical processes of incubation. Like Superman they gain power only by being freed from their own world. They are liberated by fantasy.

Rather like Claude Lévi-Strauss's handyman (*bricoleur*) who takes old bits of leftover objects and remakes a new and functioning device, George Lucas's myth-making process drew upon the widely known 'heroic' traditions of history and film as widely divergent as Samurai costumery and cowboy bar scenes. His ambitious undertaking was to infuse character narrative with cosmological pretensions and moral underpinnings. Indeed, if by myth we simply mean a system of signs that makes reference to other myths, then, following Lucas's work, all the elements of mythology are present in the newly minted pantheon of demigods for children, often in a seemingly kaleidoscopic pot-pourri. Some of the programming concepts were directly taken from known legends and updated for the modern child: Jayce and the Wheeled Warriors were space age Trojans; Bravestarr (a cosmic sheriff); He-Man (a medieval Conan); others, such as the Super-friends, Defenders of the Earth, Wonder Woman, Batman and the Ninja Turtles, were lifted from comic books and given new life in animation.

Possibly Lucas's greatest contribution to modern narrative was the character Darth Vader, for in this technomorphic antagonist he blended the fantasy and science fiction genres into a formidable imaginary being. In so doing he also showed how to mine an enormously rich cultural vein of heroic fantasy. The Silverhawks, for example, like many of the character series derived from *Star Wars*, were fusions of technology and human life-forms. This line of cybernetic cowboy birds attempted to brave the marketplace using a blend of Western characterization and space age settings, as the following trailer indicates:

> Take off with the daring super-androids, with the minds of men and the muscles of machines. The mighty Silverhawks. Let's move Silverhawks. They are ready to clean up the galaxy of Limbo, and put the evil Munstar and his gang of spacebums behind bars. You've got your work cut out for you. So soar with the superheroes. With wings of silver and nerves of steel. The Silverhawks. Don't miss them. Weekday mornings at 7:30.

Lucas knew that mythic narrative blurs the lines between the realms of legend and reality, man and technology, life and death, good and evil, gods and man, nature and culture, and between the familiar and the mysterious. And with little credit to Lucas's creative insight, these traditional distinctions have become the symbolic reservoir of children's narrative. Series such as *Voltron, Transformers, Robotech, Gobots* and *Ewoks* are all direct descendants of the *Star Wars* imagination; but many more of these animated series also bear the signs of the genre elements that Lucas helped to implant at the core of children's popular culture.

Children's television now presents a confusing spectacle of magic and technology: swords, wizardry, spells and curses, illusions, ancient chants, religious ritual, spiritual projection and horrible monsters and apparitions mix with robots, cybers, ray guns, computers, laser beams, mind rays, star ships and space travel. The unfamiliar scope of fantastic literature makes the thematic patterns difficult to analyse, yet there is one certainty in the scripts: the opposition of mystical and technological power is always resolved in the heroic struggle for survival. As Celia Anderson notes:

The cumulative message of the series is that these superfriends somehow combine the forces of nature, the machine and the mind of man; they are our jets and radio waves and laser beams and computers personified. Through their human shapes they contribute to a dubious modern myth that identifies us with the power of the machine and discounts our fragility and mortality ... resolution after resolution of plot encourages the notion that some suprahuman power will save modern civilization in its last extremity.[17]

He-Man, Mattel's first series-length production after deregulation, was not conceived as a parable but as a new mythology for childhood. Billed as the most powerful man in the universe, He-Man is indeed the archetypical new male superhero. The stories are set in the distant future, and He-Man is the child of an American woman astronaut (now Queen Marlena) and King Miro of Eternia. His secret identity is the cowardly and meek Prince Adam. He is accompanied on his exploits by his female warrior friend Teela (no romantic interest) and her father, Man-at-Arms, whose job it is to train him as a warrior prince. But Adam is no ordinary prince, for Falcon the sorceress had bestowed upon him the secret powers of the Castle Greyskull, a miraculous sword and a mission to use his powers for good and to oppose the evil Skeletor who aspires to be the sole master of the universe. When trouble arises – as it inevitably does due to the unceasing plotting of Skeletor – cowardly Prince Adam and his feeble battle-cat Cringer disappear in fright, transformed by the magic oath of Greyskull into the mightiest warrior, who will confront with humour and courage the most awesome new weaponry and beasts that Skeletor can throw against Eternia. With a feat of arms, determination, teamwork and occasionally intelligence, He-Man's forces always defeat the enemy without ever killing a living being. He-Man shows great forbearance, pulverizing only insentient things and machines and preferring to send the failed minions back to the Master of Doom for their punishment.

The *He-Man* series brilliantly blended advanced technology, medieval magic and bulging muscles into a postmodern heroic that is meaningful only as a pastiche of modern mythologies. The hero has, of course, a dual identity and a team of supporters who aid his struggles against the ultimate incarnation of evil, Skeletor. Skeletor is a rather well-muscled, skull-headed devil character who projects himself through space at will, commands an enormous arsenal of magical technologies, and bullies his minions into constant attacks on Eternia. He is clever and powerful and not above laying traps by magic and deception: a mirror that captures the reflected, or a gun that transforms rocks into warriors. This unique blending of past and future, magic and technology, came to define the basic thematic structure of most character narratives.

Postmodern Morality

Mythic narrative must not only pose symbolic oppositions; it must resolve them through conflict. Although the preferred imagery of children's television was borrowed from myth, and the characters were borrowed from legend and literature, the plots came from action-adventure series. After all, it is through great deeds that heroes become known: through triumphant struggles, quests of daring, rescues of the innocent and nobility of spirit. Heroic narrative celebrated adventure using plots structured around action. As Gina Marchetti noted, a deep-seated tendency in television narrative is to resolve conflict through physical confrontation: 'Within the action-adventure genre, narrative takes a back seat to spectacle. The emphasis is not on plot or characterization but on action, on the visual display of violence.... The main pleasure of the text revolves around spectacular fights, gun play, torture, and battles.'[18]

Yet in bringing their first character series to television, the producers were clearly worried about the regulators and the criticisms of the fantasy adventure narrative. To forestall and cushion themselves against the charge that they induce aggressiveness in children who watch a lot of television, the producers decided to avoid the wanton violence of cartoons by changing both the nature and the narrative context of children's television, by introducing new kinds of programming that would make it more difficult to point to a causal relationship between viewing and behaviour.[19] In doing this they had two narrative devices in their arsenal of justifications. First, they reasoned that aggression that is either realistic or mindless is likely to arouse the wrath of regulators. Second, by choosing to root their stories in a mythic guise, producers and marketers presented a narrative form that would serve to divert the accusations that television stimulated aggressive mimicry.

Indeed, if there is one striking common feature that came to define character narrative as a genre and distinguish it from cartoons, sit-coms or the action drama shown on children's TV, it is the presence of rather heavy-handed moralizing. The producers of children's television began to morally circumscribe the action sequences, so the struggles of their heroes could be explained away as parables rather than as wanton violence.

Mattel, concerned that He-Man's combats should be justified in the narrative, produced mini-morality plays, rather like eighteenth-century folk tales. After each triumph of the hero, there is a moral summing up that articulates the social lesson being exemplified (and, the producers hope, blunts any possible criticism of the violence). In one episode, for example, He-Man's defensive actions are interpreted as an indication of the need for the TV watchers to 'take the responsibility to care about your fellow man'.

Subsequent action series didn't bother with restating the lessons, preferring to justify the action in American values. Hasbro's success with transforming its G.I. Joe action toys into 'A Great American Hero' provides a classic case of the way character narratives wove their tales into the fabric of American mythology. Hasbro brought G.I. Joe into the market in the 1960s, basing the series on a moderately successful comic book set in the Second World War. For the 1985 television series, Hasbro remoulded and remechanized the G.I. Joe character as a futuristic anti-terrorist guerrilla team led by a paramilitary type named Duke: 'America's daring, highly trained, special mission force'. The same mood of post-Vietnam rejuvenation of US pride that sparked a series of films about Vietnam was coupled with a never-ending sequence of hi-tech weaponry and mobile equipment in a conscious attempt to weave an American folk hero into action-doll lines. The guerrilla force pretext was a proven spinner of action and conflict that could feature the vehicles and underpin the hero worship; G.I. Joe announced clearly that – at least within children's imaginations – 'America was back'.

The guerrilla theme became the most repeated idea in action-toy programming, combined with greater or lesser evidence of a civilian social order. In some programmes the military squads provide a kind of household guard for a benevolent (but weak) imperial order (*Voltron, He-Man, Rambo, Thundercats, Silverhawks, Centurions*). In others the paramilitary organizations dominate the narrative more completely in a future world caught up in total war against an unstoppable evil force *Robotech, Inhumanoids, Transformers*). The wars fought on children's television are always wars of survival and self-defence. The action focuses on the deeds of teams (which means, not coincidentally, there are more purchases necessary for play). These teams adopt a defensive posture, fighting for freedom against the

301

ceaseless onslaughts of the megalomaniacal incarnations of an evil empire – always ruthlessly led by one clever megalomaniac (Crang, Skeletor, Mum-Ra, Cobra).

The world portrayed in children's fiction is predominantly a bifurcated universe where implacable good is arrayed against unfathomable evil in an eternal and seemingly losing struggle. The minions of evil – the host of servile and unquestioning foot soldiers of doom – are always subhumans who combine the worst traits of automata – mechanical thinking and awesome power – with the salacious, greedy and self-serving attributes of degraded humanity. This subhuman dimension of the enemy is most often signified in the cartoons by a blending of evil sorcerer and reptilian animal (toads, serpents, alligators), many of whom come equipped with modern weaponry and endless magical powers. The megalomaniac rules by ruthless fear and despotic command.

It is always a tightly knit democratic force that scrimmages against these autocracies. The command structure of the good guys contrasts sharply with the practices of the empire of evil. Good teams work as a kind of skill-specific co-operative (not unlike the A-Team), a meritocracy, or a standard military command hierarchy based on loyalty, morale and team commitment. Although each member of the team offers a special skill, they are led by an alpha male character (Liono, He-Man, Sergeant Slaughter, Rambo) whose leadership is rarely questioned because he is both rarely wrong in his judgement and remarkably strong and skilled in his personal abilities. The leader's musculature is as well defined as plastic moulding will allow, and although groups always include an 'egg head' or technological whiz, the man of action is the real leader. A single female warrior figure (Cheetara, Teela, Scarlet) and some child characters might be included.

With two militarized organizations thus arrayed for action, the storylines consist of a pretext for combat: a new technological innovation, the entrapment or capture of a team member, destabilizations, carefully planned invasions, the search for new resources, spying and information-gathering, trials, tests, quests and training missions. Occasionally duplicity, mind control, disinformation and uprisings inspire the inevitable final combat sequence in the form of rescue, pre-emptive attack or defence. But the texture of these stories is provided by the technology. Each character comes equipped with a line of weapons and vehicles, and much of the plot revolves around the characters planning, maintaining, preparing, practising with, explaining or repairing the weapons, energy sources, star ships and magical powers used in the exploits.

The G.I. Joe television show exhibits all the above qualities. The exploits are based on an anti-terrorist commando squad composed of a flexible group of specialists including Sergeant Slaughter, General Hawk, Wetsuit, Leatherneck, Mainframe, Sci-Fi and Scarlet. Other characters were added when the series went into its second year of production. They are all locked in combat with the 'ruthless' terrorist organization Cobra, led initially by Cobra Commander and later by Serpentor (genetically recombined from all the Earth's bad guys), and consisting of a few henchmen like Dr Mindbender or Destro and an array of nameless troopers and machines. Cobra's goal is to eliminate the Joes and rule the world. Technology ranging from secret explosives, deadly rays, and cloned copies of new super-weapons – always plays a crucial role in Cobra plans.

In contemporary children's television the dialogue hinges on discussions of military hardware, battle tactics and long-term strategy. Tactics and logistics feature in the dialogue and provide a central thematic focus of the narrative. Discussions about counter-intelligence, firepower or the destruction of command centres are as common in She-Ra as in Rambo. Many of the problems facing the heroes depend upon the invention of a weapon, or on spying, or on a new trap that the hero must analyse and counteract. The action is the culmination of these tactics, counter-tactics and battle engagements, with little sense that either force does anything but fight. Scenes of civilian life do occur, as the good guys' mission tries to keep the bad guys' forces from intruding into the peaceful lives of ordinary people. Negotiations between the sides are rare indeed, and casual conversations between characters, or images of them at leisure, are fragmentary and soon disrupted. The most important part of the script is always the battle sequence itself, which can include some five to six minutes of animated fast-action pyrotechnics.

G.I. JOE
Programme: SYNTHOID CONSPIRACY[20]

The Joes prepare to participate in war games while the top Pentagon brass watches.

Meanwhile a Cobra submarine hides within the area, observing. Zartan and Cobra Commander have a plan to humiliate the Joes, destroy their spirit and then lead them to their doom. Cobra jams the Joes' missiles and then attacks.

Meanwhile the Pentagon officers are put to sleep by Zartan (who has been on board their ship in disguise); and, while a smoke-screen is created outside, Cobra brings in 'synthoids' to replace the officers. Synthoids are artificial humans who follow Cobra's orders without question. The next step in Cobra's plan is to destroy the Joes from within by creating a synthoid Joe. Cobra Commander and Zartan warn Destro against putting on airs and not obeying orders, because even he can be replaced.

The synthoid Pentagon officers cut the Joes' funding, so that the Joes are unable to get new supplies. Cobras then attack the Joe base. Duke is taken prisoner and replaced by a synthoid. The synthoid general blames the Joes for the equipment and property destroyed in the attack, and orders the Joes disbanded. Mutt's dog, Junkyard, growls at the fake Duke and General, and attacks the General. The General orders the dog destroyed and Mutt and the dog run. The General attempts to shoot them, but another Joe knocks the gun aside. Mutt is pursued.

Prologue: boy attempts to pet a dog, the dog growls and Mutt appears to warn the boy not to run, and not to pet strange dogs.

The Rites of Marketing

The reason no simple ideological structure dominates children's narrative is because the scripting of children's television is mediated by business objectives. As Cy Schneider so aptly pointed out, the limits of television narrative can be defined by three basic rules: keeping the costs down, keeping the regulators out, and moving the product off the shelf. It is the interplay of these script limitations that points the way to heroic fantasy as the genre of choice for character-marketing.

First, unlike the amoral and anarchic tales of classic cartoons (was Bugs Bunny really a good guy?), the newer animations clearly situate characters within a moral universe – where good and bad are clearly denoted by more than the colour of hats. To ban G.I. Joe would be to censor democracy itself. Moreover, even the young cannot confuse these tales with reality, because their form is folkloric parables projected into cosmic struggles. But unlike the literary efforts of the eighteenth-century moralizers, these parables of good and evil arise from the pragmatism of the toy merchandisers, who found that the use of mythology was a successful means of promoting toys.

The marketers found that production economy and mythic texture can be neatly intertwined within the fantasy adventure formula. The stylized plot structures and highly contrived story-telling methods contrast markedly with the free form and zany antics of the more traditional cartoon, where anything seemed possible and everything that could go wrong was likely to do so. In contrast, the adventure fantasy is structured around a single conflict and its resolution. In general, the story-telling takes place through actions that succeed each other in predictable order: challenge, search, accident, capture, release, resolution. In the name of economy and recognizability, character development and carefully crafted dialogue are likewise dropped as production values. Each of the look-alike Ninja Turtles, for example, has a characteristic set of phrases, scarves and weapons. But the characters are in little danger of ever learning anything substantial about themselves or of changing their pizza-gorging, TV-watching way of life.

Narrative in children's animation is, in fact, a sequence of scenes strung together like a moving story-board: the various encounters may cut back and forth between different aspects or perspectives of an event, but they rarely involve a weave of subplots, character backgrounders or visual jokes – which might confuse the viewers or develop the motivation of the characters. Narrative is a direct line between a problem and its resolution. Neither is in doubt: the problem initiated at the beginning of the show by a protagonist's foolishness or by the intrusion of a new threat, whether from a rival's plot, technology or weaponry, will be neatly resolved in a climax involving a visually dynamic and musically excited confrontation scene followed by a happy debriefing where the world, now set right, is once more reaffirmed.

The heavy hand of positioning and targeting is witnessed in every scene of these action adventures. Not only is the structure predictable and repetitious, but the actual visual sequences also tend to be highly repetitive, both within a single programme and throughout a series. Often the plots are intended to feature a new character in the toy line, or a new weapon or technology associated with a character. A typical *Transformers* confrontation sequence can focus a minute's animation on a battle sequence that contains very few different drawings but lots of brandishing of weapons. It is not at all demanding to script these kinds of scenes and it is not expensive to put them together.

Some of these animations also reuse a known sequence in every programme, which along with headers and titles helps to reduce the actual new animation done for each episode by two to three minutes. For example the 'arming sequence' in *Centurions*, the 'call-up' sequence in *Mask*, the 'transformation' sequences in *Voltron*, or even the 'performance' sequences in *Jem* all use the same animation. Because the clothing of the characters never changes, many sequences can be taken from standard 'cels'. Similarly, conversations between characters using full frontals or head and shoulders (with limited facial expression or movement) are a cheap alternative to more complex dialogues in which characters move and talk in a more elaborate way, in which they might use facial and body gesture to add layers to the interaction. Without methods and production values, the costs of animation would be much higher than action drama. In fact, many of the current series are more cheaply produced than a sitcom, soap opera or even a game show, and so they are able to charge far less to advertisers.

Targeting Gender

The Smurfs were targeted at the preschool audience and proved, like *Sesame Street*, to appeal to both sexes. Yet the characters are considerably more male, more like bumbling brothers. Marketers saw the need for a kind of animation stylistic that could promote girls' toy lines too and reflect little girls' fantasies and play values. Indeed, as Tom Englehardt has noted, this targeting motive led to the origination of *Strawberry Shortcake*, possibly the first comprehensively marketed character animation to define a distinctively feminine animation stylistic: its feel, looks, voice and colour were crafted with a narrower market niche in mind. Its female strawberry-sweet protagonist became a standard motif in children's television and the inspiration for many animation sequels. Very different from her superhero cousins of the action adventure, this loving heroine mediated between the fantasized community of caring, natural creatures and a harsh and uncaring reality. She was superfriend, the companion of imaginary friends.

This motif, which infuses the preschool plush animations, is exemplified by *My Little Pony*, a series whose self-conscious rendering of folkloric innocence gained prominence in narratives directed at young girls. The fantasies were clearly sex-typed in two directions, one stylistic and one symbolic. The Flutter Ponies live in the realm of

306

Flutter Valley. Other ponies live outside the valley in Paradise Estate. Both of these imaginary kingdoms were granted to them in replacement for their lost 'dream' castle. The dream theme is continued in the ponies' ability to fly over the rainbow and seek the help of their friend Megan, a little girl, whose life outside the exploits with the ponies remains obscure. The connection between a female protagonist and the fantasy creatures is what most often characterizes these stories.

The ponies have baby ponies who live in lullaby nursery and their world is populated with other creatures, such as Stone Backs, bees, Fur Bobs and bushwoolies, who can all get caught up in the adventures. This dream world would be more or less trouble-free if it were not for the witches who live on the Volcano of Doom. These witches not only like to produce mischief; they also particularly hate happiness and happy endings – so they are constantly being mean to the ponies and trying to ruin their fun, if not banish their happy and friendly ways altogether. Melodic lilting songs or dance routines that provide a simple break or explanatory interlude make these stories more like musicals than moral tales. The structure is so episodic that the scenes in the following two programme epics could be described as a loosely structured series of capers.

MY LITTLE PONY

Programme: THE END OF FLUTTER VALLEY[21]

Bees are after Megan, the Flutter Ponies, a Fur Bob, Sting (a bee), and three Stone Backs in order to get the Sun Stone.

The witches have taken over Flutter Valley. The ponies in Flutter Valley have been taken prisoner. (Fur Bob remembers suddenly to report this news?)

Sting takes Fur Bob to FurBobbia to get the help of other Fur Bobs. Witch Hidia gives Og, a giant 'spider' a potion to drink which makes him not ticklish, and he blocks the way to Flutter Valley.

It is a race against sunset to get the Sun Stone back to Flutter Valley.

When confronted with Og, Megan suggests they tickle him to get by, but it doesn't work. They fear they won't make it to Flutter Valley before sunset.

Second episode:

Using utter flutter the Flutter Ponies cooled the Sun Stone so it could be carried back to Flutter Valley. Racing the setting sun, Megan took the Sun Stone back to the home of the Flutter Ponies, unaware of the danger that awaited her there. Og blocks the way, and is no longer diverted by tickling. The end of Flutter Valley seems at hand.

307

Megan, six Flutter Ponies and three Stone Backs stand blocked from passing through the mountain by Og and his web. One of the Flutter Ponies, Earthdust, cries and says this never would have happened if they had done something about the witches in the first place. The Stone Backs snort and paw the ground. Megan comes up with the idea of, with the Stone Backs' help, tunneling under Og. Out of Og's sight, the Stone Backs begin to dig with the Flutter Ponies helping them.

Meanwhile, in Flutter Valley, the sun is near setting. The witches drink to the end of Flutter Valley. The ponies trapped in a net hanging from a tree say that they are out of ideas for something to do, and lament that if Megan were here she'd know what to do.

Megan pauses in her digging to wish they had more help. Just then Baby Cuddles's pony, Sting, and some Fur Bobs arrive. The Fur Bobs don't want to work with the Stone Backs, but Megan says they must make friends right now, because they all have to work together.

They dig through together, and run (and fly) to the valley.

When the witches see the Flutter Ponies coming they know that they have lost. The lead witch cries out that Flutter Valley was almost hers, and her daughters have to help her away.

The Flutter Ponies free the ponies from the net, using utter flutter to break the ropes. Together they all bring the Sun Stone back to where it belongs. Using simple rope-and-pulley technology they raise the Sun Stone back into its place on top a stone temple-like structure. They succeed just in time. Then Bumble and her bees arrive.

Sting and Bumble grab hold of the Sun Stone and struggle over it. Sting tells Bumble to leave it for the Flutter Ponies, who it belongs to, but she wants it because it makes flowers grow with delicious nectar. Sting tells her that she is fat, greedy and selfish, and only wants to think of herself. Rosedust flies up and says that if Bumble promises to leave them alone she can come to Flutter Valley for the flowers any time. Bumble doesn't know what to say over this kindness. Sting tells her to say she'll be nice and maybe he'll come back to Bumbleland. Bumble thanks Rosedust, saying she'll be nice. Bumble says 'Oh what a wonderful day' and leaves with Sting. Everyone says goodbye to the bees.

The Sun Stone is returning to normal. Morning Glory says she(?) guesses Honeysuckle was right when he(?) said there were some bad things they had to be careful of, and Honeysuckle says Morning Glory was right too – that even bad things can turn out good.

Suddenly a cloud appears, seemingly magically. Without more sunlight the Sun Stone will fade forever. The witches appear on a cliff-top and say they have come to claim Flutter Valley for their own. 'In a matter of minutes it will be dark, dank and dreary forever.'

The Flutter Ponies fly up and try to blow the cloud away with utter flutter. It begins to work, and Hidia counters with an incantation from a book. The flowers and trees begin to droop, but the sun appears and they rise again.

The witches run and the Flutter Ponies chase them, blowing them so that they tumble away.

Megan and the others sing and dance through the valley: 'From the sun comes life. From the sun comes power.'

The Great Divide: Style Wars

Strawberry Shortcake and *My Little Pony* showed that the programme preferences and viewing habits of young girls could be productively differentiated from those of boys, whose stories continued to hinge on heroic narratives where action and physical confrontation defined the action-adventure narrative. Mattel wondered if a similarly gender-targeted approach might also work in the action-doll market. The company tested this idea out by bringing out *She-Ra*, whose series was twinned with *He-Man*, combining the same admixture of science fiction (ray guns, space and time travel, advanced technology) with medieval fantasy (swords, sorcery, castles) elements. Yet these elements were symbolically adjusted for known appeals, most notably in the kinds of problem She-Ra confronted and in the technology she used. Indeed, magic often substituted for technology in She-Ra, and although she is powerful her solutions often demand greater skill in problem-solving so she can avoid direct confrontation with Hordak and his Horde.

She-Ra, the twin sister of He-Man, was kidnapped by Hordak and brought through another dimension to a world called Etheria. From childhood she had been trained to be captain in Hordak's Evil Horde. But she managed to overcome Hordak's magic spell, which had bound her to evil, and came to lead the rebels in their struggles for freedom from Hordak's brutal rule. She rides a flying unicorn called Spirit, and along with Glimmer, Madame Razz, and Kowl she does battle with the Horde's many beastly creatures. She too has a secret identity, as Princess Adora who lives among the splendours and seeming ease of Etherian life (cleverly providing a fashion interest) until the evil spells, plots and traps of Catra, Hordak's cat-like, evil female companion, intrudes into the idylls of the Etherian royal house. Like Prince Adam in *He-Man*, Princess Adora has a magic sword that she uses to the 'honour' of Greyskull to transform herself into a woman with considerable fighting prowess. But her inevitable victories result from the use of her wits, her co-operation with friends, and her many other talents, rather than her strength. When the going gets really tough, He-Man and She-Ra can come to each other's aid by maintaining contact through the gem on her magic sword.

AN EPISODE OF SHE-RA:

While Adora is thanking Prince Orwall for delivering supplies for the rebellion, Catra and robots attempt to ambush and capture them. Orwall escapes on Spirit, and Adora changes into She-Ra to fight.

She-Ra and Catra both fall through a crack in the earth and end up outside an underground city (each not yet knowing the other is there). Catra, in cat mode, is mistaken by the cat people of the city to be their missing queen, and she is happy to deceive them. When She-Ra arrives Catra orders her to be imprisoned. When She-Ra and a cat person attempt to expose Catra as an impostor, Catra is asked to fight She-Ra by herself to prove she is the Queen. Catra loses and attempts to escape.

Using magic the cats send Catra back to Hordak, but with her memory of them lost. She-Ra suggests that one of the cats use Catra's dropped communicator to impersonate Hordak through illusion in order to have their real Queen, who is a Hordak prisoner, returned. The Queen is reunited with her men. In payment for She-Ra's help the Magi-cats create an illusion which will hide Prince Orwall's supply wagons from Hordak.

Given the similar structures and rationales of these programmes, the subtle guidance of gender-targeting intrudes primarily into the characterization of the dolls. He-Man is a muscle-studded medieval warrior. There are no clothing changes to accompany his transformation from Prince Adam. Indeed, it is hard to figure out how his identity remains a secret. She-Ra dolls, however, all have multiple clothes, long, flowing hair and bathing-beauty looks. To meet the needs of girls' preferred play forms, the fantastic settings and costumes of Etheria play a more important part in the She-Ra narrative, as do her cleverness and her association with friends.

These gender differences in play became accentuated in subsequent attempts to install girls' action dolls on television. While the boys' superheroes drifted increasingly into the realm of mechanized warriordom (always accompanied by separately purchaseable weaponry and transportation technology), the girls' lines followed the exigencies of known play values into the fashion, hair play and performance domain. Character-marketing always implied that play values remained deeply rooted in the narrative.

The military premisses of the G.I. Joe and Rambo characters

contrast sharply, then, with the performance wars of Jem, the action doll that rocked the domination of Barbie with a very modishly styled television animation. Jem's universe is not a distant planet but the more familiar teenage terrain of 'style wars'. The stories are structured around a different set of mythic conflicts – conflicts of musical taste, media stardom and meaningful friendship.

Jem is really Jerrica Benton, who inherited her father's music company, the Starlight Home for Girls, and a computer that is only known to her and her rock group, the Holograms. Jerrica communicates with the computer via her ear-ring. This computer 'synergy' not only transforms Jerrica into the band's lead vocalist, Jem, but also projects images and costumes on to the other band members as required. Other than this there is no reference to magic or implausible technology. Jem otherwise has the contours of an animated teen drama focusing on the life of stars – a sort of female-orientated rewrite of *The Monkeys* with a touch of Japanese 'wasai pops'.

The stories feature the performance exploits of the band, following the trials of the dual characters of Jem and Jerrica (not even her boyfriend Rio knows they are the same), caught as they are between the home for orphaned girls and a dazzling music career. The home for girls is constantly under financial pressure or experiencing an emotional upset because of a particular problem with one of the girls; friendship, loyalty and honesty are constantly being tested. But the conflicts are often ultimately traced to the nasty (rather than evil) interventions of a rival rock group called the Misfits, managed by the greedy Erik Raymond. The Misfits' lead singer, Pizzazz, is especially jealous and competitive, wanting to oust the Holograms from their top-billed popularity in the music world and ruin Jerrica's music business. Pizzazz will go to unusual lengths to upset Jem and the Holograms.

In *Jem*, differences in musical style clearly connote broader divisions in values, lifestyles and personality. The Misfits are a blend of heavy metal and punk, which, in contrast to Jem's more mainstream and straight rock, condemns them to losing out in the style wars. But the costume possibilities of the rock world offered a brilliant back-story for glamour dolls and a very up-to-the-minute stylization for little girls' fantasy play.

AN EPISODE OF JEM

Pizzazz throws darts at the Misfits' manager's photo and complains about

311

not going to a party that night. Their manager walks in the door and tells them why they can't go to the party, promising that they will play at the Indy 500 victory party.

Later that night, at the party, the Misfits' manager, Erik Raymon, discusses a deal with two other men to attempt to fix the race. He places a bet on car 007.

Jem appears to christen a race car that Starlite Music will be sponsoring.

The Misfits plot to get into the party. They steal the Holograms' car and crash the party. They wreck the party and are thrown out along with their manager.

A man sabotages the Starlite car. The race qualifier starts. Rio takes photos from a platform. The car goes out of control, crashing into the platform.

Both Rio and Martino, the race-car driver, are in hospital. Jerrica visits Rio.

The car is wrecked and Martino can't race. The Holograms, with the help of Synergy, attempt to fix the car in time for the race. They finish with a few hours to spare, but both Martino and Rio are still disabled. Jem becomes the driver.

Erik Raymon changes his bet from car 007 to Jem's car.

Pizzazz berates the driver of 007, and takes over the car at the pit-stop. She pulls into the lead through dirty driving. Jem crashes while attempting to pass Pizzazz. It looks like she is out of the race. Raymon changes his bet again. Jem pulls back into the race and regains the number 2 position. She calls on Synergy to distract Pizzazz and pulls ahead, but still has one lap to make up. Jem makes it over the finish line ahead, but as one of her tyres comes off. She is pulled from the car before it explodes.

Pizzazz drives into the garage to get mad at Raymon just as he is about to be beaten up by the two men he made the deal with. They leave him to Pizzazz.

Jem becomes the first rock 'n roll star to win the Indy 500.

Epilogue: A girl gives up playing guitar, but Jem shows up to tell her to keep on trying.

Criticizing the Myth

How do these changes in the structure, tone and texture of children's television narrative influence the critique of children's culture? Is there reason to believe that the stilted moralizing of character-marketing business makes a significant difference to children's understanding of the world? Does the simple moral structure of the narratives transform symbolic conflict into useful lessons? Are the producers correct when they point to the deathless conflicts of He-Man and the Transformers and the clearly whimsical antics of Care-a-lot or Paradise Estates as an improvement in the level of violence and quality of television? Have these new imaginative animations in fact introduced a more judicious yet innocent mixture of fantasy, nurturance and emotional salience to children's programming, as an alternative to the 'adultifying' sitcoms and action adventures? Can the toy-makers claim credit for producing a popular and highly imaginative new folklore for children?

To answer these questions we would need a theoretical yardstick concerning folk tales and mythology and their role in the maturation of a child. Unfortunately, there are no such existing models of aesthetics and literary quality, of the role of allegory in child development, or even of the way children absorb and use the parables, models, actions and stories that television produces. Nor is it likely that any particular model will soon be at hand. The empirical research finds it difficult if not impossible to prove that young children are intellectually stimulated by or even understand what they watch on television. All we know is that they do watch and like these programmes.

Armed with ambiguous evidence about the deleterious social effects of television in general, it is tempting for critics to concur that, maybe, and after all, we have seen a tangible improvement in children's TV, given these morally contextualized conflicts, the new highly stylized violence and the preschooler programmes dealing with the young's fears and feelings. The problem, however, is this: a researcher who manages to watch hundreds of hours of children's television soon finds that the multiple desire – to tell a great and meaningful story, to arm and educate children with perspectives and knowledge that will help them understand the world around them, or to give them parables with which to judge and talk about their own experiences and emotions – is barely detectable. The alterations on the surface of children's animations soon become transparent. At their heart, the stories reveal themselves as the empty exemplars of postmodern sentiment for which the limits to criticism are an untranscendent history. As Fredric Jameson put it:

> The breakdown of temporality suddenly releases its present of time from all the activities and intentionalities that might focus it and make it a space of praxis; thereby isolated, that present suddenly engulfs the subject

313

with indescribable vividness, a materiality of perception properly over-whelming, which effectively dramatizes the power of the material – or better still, the literal – signifier in isolation.[22]

Although children's television appears to be filled with heroes and folk stories, somehow the programming does not capture the psychological depth or intrigue of the original tales. The pro-grammes are stylistically mythic, but the self-conscious attempts to deal with emotions appear stilted and hollow. Each character is only an emblem or fragment of experience and not meant to represent someone struggling with conflicted real-life problems and ambig-uous emotions. The inability of these stories to deal adequately with feelings and experience usefully has its roots in these truncated characterizations: the imaginary feelings, experiences and social life of a robot warrior, a pony tribe and a rock star offer few opportunities to create useful parables for the young. The stylized narratives provide ample representations of feelings – of excitement, venge-ance, embarrassment and fear – but do so in a fantastic collage that has no focus or grounded resolution of conflict.

Animation is a denaturalized fiction, and in the course of produc-ing it character-marketing has undercut the production of a tele-vision drama that would deal authentically with real children and their struggles to accommodate to modern social life. Live drama has been all but banished from children's television. Whereas drama once provided paths to the understanding of personal experience, fiction now only digs deeper channels to fantasy. It is this unbalanced quality in children's television that in the end must engage our attention. The imaginary cast of character narrative in fact reveals its deeper and primary purpose, which is to convey the protocols of fantasy play.

Notes

1. S.L. Stern and T. Schoenhaus, *Toyland*, 1990, p. 180.
2. Brian M. Young, *Television Advertising and Children*, Oxford, Clarendon Press, 1990.
3. C. Schneider, *Children's Television: The Art, the Business and How it Works*, Illinois, NTC Business Books, 1987, p. 157.
4. Ibid. p. 113.
5. Stern and Schoenhaus, *Toyland*, ch. 7.
6. Ibid., p. 179.
7. See T. Smith, S. Johnson and M. Graham, *Japanese Animation Program Guide*,

Sunnyvale, California, BayCon, 1986; Bill Wilson, 'There's No Business Like Cho Business', *C/FO The Magazine*, 4, 1983, pp. 3–5.

8. ARF, *Everything You Should Know About Children's Research*, Transcript Proceedings, New York Hilton, 28 April 1986.

9. Rather than bog the book down in the details of research I have only outlined a rather complex and exhaustive research process. The content analysis involved a team of coders working with three protocols – one for each level of coherence that exists in any series. The levels we found necessary for genre analysis are similar to parallel work done by Hodge and Tripp (1986): series, programme and episode. We examined 180 of the programmes to give the impressions of the genre and its sub-genres. This number was necessary to understand the origins and limits to the characters defined in each series. Then 25 typical examples were coded using the programme protocol which allowed us to understand how stories were structured. Neither of these two analyses produced numerical data, but they did ensure that the episode analysis would be better understood in the context of the overall fictional universe created by the series. The episode analysis which followed was based on scenes or interactions taken at random (by random footage counter within each programme) from the 25 programmes included in the programme analysis. This method, when coupled with the measured duration of the episode, allows us to estimate the percentage of any story that has the theme or action category. This sample taken in 1987 exemplifies the patterns of programming in that period. It is likely that there are some changes in emphasis (for example fewer explicitly paramilitary series) in the last five years.

10. Our survey included children in grades two and three in rural and urban communities. The schools were selected to ensure middle-class and working-class respondents. Overall about 250 children were interviewed, watched at play, and included in media literacy exercises during this project.

11. Jube Shiver, 'Child's Play', *Black Enterprise*, August 1986, pp. 31–4.

12. Care Bears – Programme: Home Sweet Homeless.

13. A. Dorfman and A. Mattelart, *How to Read Donald Duck: Imperialist Ideology in the Disney Comic*, New York, International General Editions, 1975.

14. N. Carlsson-Paige and D. Levin, *The War Play Dilemma: Children's Needs and Society's Future*, Columbia University, New York, Teachers College Press, 1987.

15. C. Anderson, 'The Saturday Morning Survival Kit', *Journal of Popular Culture*, Spring 1974, p. 155.

16. Schneider, *Children's Television*, p. 124.

17. Anderson, 'Saturday Morning', p. 156.

18. Gina Marchetti, 'Action-Adventure as Ideology', in Ian Angus and Sut Jhally, *Cultural Politics in Contemporary America*, New York, Routledge, 1988, pp. 196–7.

19. See 'Television at the Crossroads: Education and Violence' *Social Science and Modern Society*, 21(6), Sept./Oct. 1984.

20. G.I. Joe – Programme: Synthoid Conspiracy, Part One.

21. My Little Pony – Programme: The End of Flutter Valley.

22. Fredric Jameson, 'Postmodernism, or, the Cultural Logic of Late Capitalism, *New Left Review*, 146, 1984, p. 73.

10

Conclusion

Playing with Culture

They are not usually the toys parents would choose for their children. They are the toys children choose for themselves. Children want the products they see on television and if their friends have them, they want them even more. The urgency with which their children insist that they 'need' these heavily pro- moted products is one of the reasons parents dislike them. And when as is often the case, the products do not do very much and their appeal quickly fades, the children soon focus on the next exciting product they see on television. The toys' lack of play value thus encourages an acquisitive, throwaway mentality, which earns them further parent enmity.[1]

After forty years of research academics and critics mostly agree that television has helped to diminish the value of certain experiences in children's lives, such as reading books, rhyming games, street play and extended family meals – all of which seem to be among the activities abandoned for the easy pleasures of the box.[2] But few critics have noticed that the one thing television didn't displace from children's culture was story-telling. Nor did television completely banish those traditional literary themes from modern childhood. Indeed, one of contemporary television's singular achievements has been the rearticulation of those traditional patterns of fiction within a future mythic framework – a process in which the basic narrative forms have been refashioned to harmonize them with the task of gathering kids to the box and interesting them in the appropriate merchandise. Television similarly didn't eliminate the peer group or peer interaction either: rather, it discovered that the peer acceptance was a value that could be added to the motivation to purchase goods. Nor did television eliminate the traditional images of innocence and play; it simply made watching television a prerequisite for children's experience of that charmed realm. In short, it is not what television has displaced from children's lives that fuels the public's criticisms and discomfort with this medium, but the way it continues to promote particular patterns of social understanding, attitudes and self-expression.

Arguing that television's content should never be written off as trivial and superfluous just because it is fictional in form, Raymond Williams noted that television's power lies in the way it has adopted drama as the preferred modality of social representation: 'It is clearly one of the unique characteristics of advanced industrial societies that drama as an experience is now an intrinsic part of everyday life, at a quantitative level which is so very much greater than any precedent as to seem a fundamental qualitative change.'[3] Television could have been institutionalized in other ways that might have given emphasis to alternative social purposes and cultural forms, such as news, documentaries, state propaganda, education or religion. But, as Williams argues, the commercial structure of television entrenched a specialization in entertainment: and what most people found entertaining was to watch representations of their social world in the form of dramatic narrative or fiction. Commercial television's main cultural impact therefore is connected with the way it privileges fiction as a cultural form and the fantasy mode of consciousness and expression. And nowhere is this tendency to amplify the dominion of fiction more evident than in the new approach to communication resulting from the link forged between children's television and toy industries.

Deregulation of television clearly resulted in a new promotional infrastructure more narrowly and purposively focused on promoting toys and other merchandise. Children's toy merchandisers enhanced their role in children's culture by renovating their use of television's story-telling potential and making their advertisements have ever greater peer appeal. In the process they left behind the innocent garden world of literature for a cosmic battleground of mock-heroic adventure. They probably never thought much about the impacts they were having on children's culture. The narrative motifs that they favoured were simply the ones that first and foremost promoted their products. But there was a cumulative impact to their pragmatism – their efforts implicitly emphasized a consumerist framework and privileged particular styles of self-expression in imaginary play.

317

The Crisis of Criticism

The critical discussion of television's impact on childhood, however, has reached an impasse. Although critics have launched many assaults, researchers have been unable to demonstrate clear and consistent behavioural 'effects' of television. Even the much-researched issue of violence and children's aggression has only produced equivocal scientific evidence. And now it would be harder to secure such evidence because in response to the debates about violence children's television producers have a better argument against the accusations that they contribute to children's aggression: the animated genre so popular on television today reduces the frequency of violent acts while providing a narrative veneer of myth, moral correctness, unreality and humour to the cartoon.[4] The producers can legitimately argue that children appreciate these animations as simply entertainment – a fantasy realm distinguished from their daily lives so that there is little likelihood that they will imitate the behaviours. And the matter may rest there just so long as the public doesn't ask programmers to explain why animated fantasy is almost the only form of fiction offered to children by television.

It is now clear that television's influence on children is not likely to be discovered through direct correlations of specific contents and behaviours, however complex and well designed the effect's studies may be. Children's audiences are not homogeneous; there is still a matter of choice in what they watch and who watches with them; so that picking up cultural values from television is a complex social process determined in part by the parental, sibling and peer relationships that govern viewing.[5] Besides, the origins of most critics' discomfort with children's television lie hidden in the commercial structure and dynamics of our media system in which adventure fantasy animations have become the norm: simply put, there is no commercial impetus to produce any other kind of fiction; nor can one expect the marketers who favour and commission this programming to be concerned about the aesthetic and social objectives that once piqued the consciences of previous generations of children's producers. And so, although most researchers would concede that television has accentuated the competitive, militaristic and aggressive dimension of our culture by repeating and legitimating these themes on the screen, there is very little research into how these fantasies affect children or what these repeated patterns of fictional representation mean to children's attitudes and maturation in the long run.[6]

Children, we now realize, are also more culturally sophisticated than the original 'hypodermic' models implied. They are 'active decoders' capable of understanding the fictional nature of television cartoons; after six years of age they do not generally confuse cartoon violence with real acts of violence such as they see on the news.[7] So the effects of television violence or any other repeated motif on children remain difficult to trace because such 'effects' depend on how children 'interpret' fiction – that is, how they make sense of the context of the violent act within the narrative framework that explains and justifies it.[8] After all, a violent youth culture does not just derive from the repetition of violence scenes on television, but gains force through children's internalization of acceptable social behaviour appropriate for their daily interactions with others. Astutely commenting on the failure of 'effects research' to explain any important aspects of television's influence on children, Cedric Cullingford has called for researchers to pay more attention to the way children internalize the contents and use television's fictions and heroes in their general production of social knowledge or, as he phrases it, 'in the formation of general attitudes and in styles of interpretation'.[9]

As children will readily tell anyone who asks, even though the characters and situations are not 'real', this does not imply that children don't try to make sense of television's tales and relate them to their own motivation, quests or aspirations. Children clearly identify with their heroes, and this means they internalize in some difficult-to-describe way the inherent ideas of these narratives. We should not be surprised, therefore, when researchers report that contemporary children now spend about 80 per cent of their spare time engaged in social fantasies – either while watching television or playing with their toys, or both simultaneously. For boys, many of these fantasies are focused on violent confrontations. More significantly, children often express these fantasy themes in their play – both verbally or implicitly in the structure and pattern of play activities. Yet because these expressive acts are difficult to fix or isolate, behavioural researchers will continue to find it difficult to document these partial and uncertain influences because it is difficult to anticipate whether, how or when a specific child will use scenes from television's imaginary worlds. They may see them as allegories or as templates or models for understanding their own lives; they may make them the basis of their play and social interactions with peers and family; but we cannot know unless we live with the children for extended periods of time. It is unlikely therefore that researchers will be able to prove or document the potential for specific contents and motifs of television fiction to frame children's thinking, shape their peer culture or inflect their self-expression and learning.[10] That doesn't mean that there is no influence on children, however.

For this reason we can resist the argument that children's television is simply fun; that whatever its aesthetic shortcomings, television at least offers children a harmless diversion or entertainment. To see television as harmless just because its effects are on broad and vague aspects of children's attitudes and play expressions diminishes the significance of children's active social imaginations – the objective so carefully sought by children's merchandisers and celebrated by play researchers. We have seen how by harnessing the magic of animation, television captured children's attention and became the pre-eminent channel through which children's merchandisers could project their designs into children's culture. The vistas of contemporary children's television emerge from successive experiments in programming, most recently guided by toy marketers, who sought marketing advantage from every new technique which could engage young consumers' active imaginations in their product lines. To understand fully the impact of television, therefore, we must try to figure out what is at stake in this direct link between the merchants and imaginative play.

Even a casual observer will have witnessed the impact of television on childhood in the structure and content of play. Though the G.I. Joe and He-Man may or may not have led to an increase of aggression on the playgrounds, they did unequivocally strengthen the role that television programmes have in children's play. Studies of children's home life have documented the propensity of play outside the schools to be social-dramatic or symbolic in style.[11] Play researchers Jerome and Dorothy Singer were among the first psychologists to investigate the mental processes which underwrite young children's identification with their television characters. They noted that television, even before deregulation, was altering the protocols and actions of children's play. Observing the way children take on identities in rough-and-tumble play or announce loudly that they are playing something in a manner inspired by television, the Singers concluded that 'television is also providing in its way, a new cultural

320

background – a host of archetypes, identification and stereotype figures around which children can organize their imaginative experience'.[12] Television permeates children's daily activities and conversations: when we observe them arguing about G.I. Joe's firepower, or simulating World Wrestling Federation bouts, or staging mock battles based on Ninja Turtle heroics, or even when they tell us that they can't fall asleep without their Care Bears or that they want to grow up to be as beautiful as Barbie, synergy between television and children's wants and play fantasies is abundantly evident.

Television, Socialization and Play

The most obvious impact of toy-marketing on children's culture is that it makes children want more toys, particularly the ones that are promoted on television. As James McNeal in his review of the literature on the influence of children's marketing on children suggests, 'It certainly appears that television advertising is a major contributor to children's attitudes towards brands of products and towards product categories. These are the exact results that marketers want and expect.'[13] Though their design and communication methods were far from foolproof, the cumulative effect of the application of marketing principles, creativity and careful research (augmented by a set of social and demographic factors) was to produce a major boom in toy sales.

On this question of cultural impact at least the evidence is clear. The cumulative weight of television promotions did help increase the demand for specific toys. Toy makers have had ample 'bottom-line' evidence of the impact of television from the dramatically expanding sales of licensed toys, which have risen from 20 per cent of the US market in 1977 to almost 70 per cent in 1987. Character-marketing emphasized new forms of social-dramatic play that grew from the willingness of children in the USA to identify with television characterizations and want more and more of those toys as 'seen on television'. In Britain, by way of contrast, where advertising codes and public-interest television prevented the saturation of children's television with character-programming, only 30 per cent of the toy market consisted of 'licensed toys' by 1987. In Quebec, Sweden and Norway, where policies and public service television have likewise strictly limited children's marketing efforts, promotional toys do not dominate children's expressed preferences and wish lists.

This relationship between television and toy preferences was documented in a study we conducted of 300 letters to Santa which were collected in Southern Ontario during December 1986. Southern Ontario provided an excellent site for such an experiment in the impact of toy promotion because, in 1986, the advertising regulation by the Canadian Advertising Standard's Council restricted the commercials for these toys to US stations which could be seen only by cable. However, within the Toronto region about 80 per cent of children live in cabled households which are regularly exposed to syndicated US stations (particularly WUTV from Buffalo).

However, children in many rural Ontario communities live outside the cable networks and are neither exposed to character programmes nor to promotional toy advertisements, which their cabled cousins watch regularly. The comparison between the wish lists of these two groups of children confirmed that the absence of intense marketing influenced what they wanted from Santa. Fifty-three per cent of the children in the cabled region included a request for at least one promotional toy while only 25 per cent of the uncabled children's letters made such specific requests.

Indeed, there is clear evidence of the displacement effect, for the children not exposed to these toy promotions tended to ask for more traditional types of presents: bikes, sleds, skates and games. Interviews with children later revealed that television promotion is only one factor which shapes what children want from Santa. Family size and parental attitudes, television-viewing patterns, as well as other demographic variables (ethnic background, rural lifestyle) all contribute to the way children learn their preferences for playthings, including the number of toys they would ask for and the role of 'peer acceptance' as a criterion for wanting a toy. Boys, particularly the younger ones, were most likely to report being influenced by toy promotions. Girls and older children in general (aged ten or over) were more likely to want unlicensed toys and presents other than toys (records, books, clothes). For this reason it is impossible to calibrate precisely how much these new marketing techniques have changed children's play activities.

It has already been noted how much television has in common with play. Like narrative, our instinct for play has been expressed in many thematic guises: ritual, religion, drama, guessing games, sports, role play and pretending all continue to engage children to various degrees. But in the contemporary generation, the extreme popularity of animated fantasy adventure and character toys hints at a conjunction in the specific way these activities harness the common dynamic of the social imagination. Examining this synergy created between fiction and play by character-marketing may help us recognize that character-toy play is a particular style of play which induces a unique mode of consciousness. It demands mental structures and the cultural knowledge for expression which parallel those same skills of 'interpretation' the child uses for making sense of television fiction. These interpretive skills include how to understand the narrative order of events, how to understand why characters act in the ways they do and, most importantly, how to identify with or position one's own subjectivity within the fantasy. Watching television has therefore become a primer for learning the particular mental prerequisites of character play. Television advertising promotes this play style over others by repeatedly modelling this type of peer play and modelling the interpretive protocols which activate it.

In character play the mental processes of 'expression' (entailed in the creative encoding which takes place in a child's play enactments) and 'interpretation' (the application of social knowledge and media grammar which allows a child to understand television fiction) must be brought into alignment. The activities of watching television and playing with toys have thus become mutually reinforcing: television feeds the child's social imagination with knowledge about fictive social universes which only a particular toy can make available for simulated play enactment. The synergy created between television and toys through their merger within a single narrative universe links these separate domains of expressive and interpretive experience through a common structure of fantasy. However, marketers do this in a targeted way: they address individual children within a narrow social stratum accentuating differences in the content of fantasies. It is the implications of this new synergy of fantasy in children's culture which demands that we develop a critical understanding of this modality of character play which the marketers so energetically promote.

Intensified Identification

Can we be more precise in our observations of how the growth in character-marketing influences children's play? In this respect, we can notice that much of the evidence of television's influence is exhibited in behaviour that expresses children's identification and

323

involvement with the personae projected through the box. Researchers have begun to recognize that forms of children's pretend play in the home use television's dramatis personae as a prime reference in their play expression:

> Various fantasy person characters were enacted by a number of children. Their portrayal was stylised. Children usually announce they are going to play the particular character. Batman and Robin were depicted by running head down and with arms outstretched behind; Daleks extended stiff arms and growled in monotone: exterminate, exterminate; Bionic man or Steve Austin ran in slow motion with massive strides. Kung Fu gave a karate-type kick.... While children were never questioned about the identities of these roles, it was as though the small pieces of action which defined the character had become emancipated from the character itself.[14]

In this light it is worth noting that identification with toys was the psychological process promoters relied on to increase the child's attachment to a particular toy: character marketers sought to accentuate the child's emotional investment with the toy's identity by crafting more lovable, attractive and heroic character universes. Preschoolers nuzzling attachments to soft toys, the admiration they developed for the fashion prowess of Barbie or potency of the Rambo – marketers realized from this that they could sell their toys only if they got children to increase their emotional investment in them.

The Singers' research found an interesting positive relationship between intense television-viewing and imaginativeness among the children. For this reason the Singers speculate that if television promotes and increases children's 'active' imaginary play whatever its form, then such creative fantasy activity might mediate the effects of television and in fact make a positive contribution to the child's development. As they argue, 'The stuff of fantasy, the character names or play situations might be heavily influenced by TV but the structure, complexity or richness of imaginative play might be either un-related to viewing frequency or perhaps even negatively associated with it.'

The Singers hypothesize that a child's capacity to imagine is the main contributory factor in their maturational employment of play – the more imaginary play the better the child is able to adjust to and master a disturbing situation. They assume that emotional maturation relies on the child's exercise of a cognitive process of mental representation when they state that 'an important feature of pretend play is that it again provides opportunities for expression and control of affect and the representation in miniaturized form of conflictual or frightening scenes or encounters'. In this view, playing with character toys may be beneficial because it encourages children to fantasize those emotive scenes from TV until they experience in play their control over those situations. Noting that, even among heavy TV viewers, the more imaginative children – especially those who lived in households that encourage a rich fantasy life – showed less aggressive behaviour at school, they speculate that imaginative play might even reduce the likelihood of aggressive responses to violent cartoon programmes because children can express conflicted feelings through their fantasy play. The Singers note too that children also use plush toys as 'imaginary friends' which may help them adjust to loneliness and fear. This is why they claim television personae can be useful in children's lives, for in their assimilation in play they can provide the templates for socio-emotional adjustment and help kids overcome the uncertainties and vagaries of childhood – just so long as the child works through these conflictual schemes in their play. For the Singers, imaginative play is the best remedy for limiting the effects of television violence. As they explain: 'If television stimulates make-believe play then the child can engage in rehearsal processes, and can gain a sense of efficacy that permits a very different mode of storage of the material than is possible only from the gross viewing experience.'[15]

Social-dramatic play with fictional characters engages far more profound psychological processes than theories of behavioural modelling and imitation admit. Identification is itself a mental process which implies both an emotional investment (cathexis) with the toy and some internalization of traits, motivations and attitudes exhibited by the character into the child's sense of self. Bruno Bettelheim, for example, recommends that parents don't interfere with or impose too many rules on children's play: 'When there is no immediate danger it is best to approve of the child's play without interfering, just because he is so engrossed in it. Efforts to assist him in his struggles, while well intentioned, may divert him from seeking and eventually finding the solution that will serve him best.'[16] In this respect the observations of psychiatric theorist and therapist Erik Erikson provide some useful clues about these more subtle ramifications of children's identifications with toys. Erikson recognizes that symbolically toys can serve the child as 'transitional objects'. He points out that children use their dolls and play sets as a way of 'acting out' and 'working through' the emotional difficulties which they experience at different stages in their development. As Erikson goes on to observe, the dramatization that takes place in play can be a crucial dynamic in the maturational process: 'Utilizing his mastery over objects, the child can arrange them in such a way that they permit him to imagine that he is master of his life predicament as well.'[17] This is why clinicians of various schools use play in their therapy – through the identification process children learn to express and control some of the emotional content of the identification experience – their loneliness, powerlessness and feelings of inadequacy. But in therapy the process is guided: maturation depends on the specific fantasies children express through their play gradually working their way into consciousness and self-identity.

The direct impact of programmes on the play activities of heavy television viewers, however, does not appear to be lessened by the imaginative capacity of the child. In this respect it is worth noting that the Singers found in their study

> that television has a major influence on the content of the imaginative play of our children ... a careful thematic analysis of the specific features of play in the protocols of extreme high and low television viewers suggest that frequent reference to TV characters in the course of play is indeed linked to high TV viewing and also to the involvement in more action-adventure play.[18]

Yet like many psychologists, the Singers have great faith in the autonomy and usefulness of all pretend play. They believe that children will inherently fantasize in play in ways that always serve their immediate maturational and emotional needs. Their data, however, does not entirely support this faith in the assimilative capacity of fantasy play. Commenting on some of their own evidence, they also observe that emotional mastery through fantasy is absent from the play styles of heavy viewers of TV violence: 'Clearly the heavier viewers seem to be more uncomfortable, aggressive or impulsive in their play styles.'[19] The emotions or problems that children can explore through character-toy play are specific to the opportunities that action-adventure (and we should now add fashion) play provides. Having reviewed the content of character-toy television, we must ask what kind of opportunities for emotional mastery are promoted and what kind of imaginary emotional universes are our kids mastering through the fantasies they produce while manipulating these plastic heroes. The mimicry of television characters could as easily be a factor for ritualizing the expression of very restricted socio-emotional conflicts – and without resolution – as a force leading to emotional mastery and maturation.

Orthodoxy and Agency

All learning, in psychologist Jean Piaget's terms, is a balance between creative discovery (in his more technical language 'assimilation') and imitation (in which the child 'accommodates' and internalizes the meaning imposed from outside the self). This is why the question of what children learn in their character play is related to whether promotional toy-marketing imposes limitations on children's play. Although it is difficult to prove that kids are more isolated, consumer-conscious or less creative than they were, say, ten years ago, it is hard to deny evidence of an emergent pattern or 'orthodoxy' of play being promoted through television. Brian Sutton-Smith explains this notion of orthodoxy by suggesting that children 'will not be over determined by the particular commercial, but the range of what they (parent and child) will think about is increasingly influenced, even confined by what they see on television'.[20] Sutton-Smith worries that through repeated exposure to television commercials the child comes to accept the marketer's definitions of what the toy 'means'. In this respect television could narrow the framework of play because the possibilities for pretending are confined to the actions and situations associated with the particular toys.

The case for such limitations imposed on imaginative play depends upon the question of who has 'agency' over the imaginary ideas children employ in play. On the one hand, the modelling of character play in commercials seems to be a force for rigidifying and consolidating particular play 'scripts' – sequential patterns of action and meaning – which children replicate in their play. If this were the case, then it is likely that children are simply accommodating their pretending to the possibilities of the toys. Acknowledging the tremendous pressures of toy-marketing on children, Sutton-Smith still believes, however, that

> despite the apparent hegemony of toys in much of today's world, a real case can also be made that usually the child players control the toys rather than the other way around. This is what we have meant by the toys as agency. They are the agencies of the players. They are controlled rather than controlling.[21]

Sutton-Smith believes that however sophisticated the television marketing, children will be pushed by the play instinct and their own imaginativeness to use their toys creatively – to play rather than simply mimic and imitate what they have seen on television. This is his statement of faith in the power of assimilative play. Yet the question of agency can only be settled by a close examination of the structure and content of pretend play.

Since military conflict was one of the most prominent thematics introduced into television by the marketers of action toys, it was two researchers interested in war-toy play who offered a different picture of how kids learned in play. Critics argued that fantasy play is not always a creative force for learning, that in pretend play children also schematize the particular social and emotional conflicts depicted in television, 'mastering them' as scripts for play and thus building specific models or schema for social actions, motivations, behaviour and feelings.[22] Rather than contributing to emotional mastery, some teachers felt that these war toys stimulate and ritualize conflict into a compulsive and repetitive game – one which they call 'war play'.

War play, Carlson-Paige and Levin argue, does not exhibit the characteristics of an open-ended exploration and creative elaboration of an imaginary world. Rather, entrenched in strong character identification, the play seems to stress the internalization of television's predefined scripts because 'children assume the roles of characters they have seen on TV and play out scenes which resemble television scripts. Children's play scenarios often use simple static schemes and a lot of aimless running around with aggressive, Macho and stylized actions. Many children no longer seem to be in full charge of their play.'[23] They go on to explain the dangers of war play as contingent on what children are actually learning therein. With so little evidence of the assimilative aspect of play 'the political ideas children use in their play are more likely to be imitations of what they have seen rather than understandings of their own construction. In such a situation children are likely to be mimicking the militaristic ideas they have been exposed to without constructing a foundation for their own political ideas and understanding.'[24] Play, they believe, only intensifies and consolidates the social learning of television's justificatory structure for violence implicit in fiction; and their argument about war play could be applied equally to the ritualized behaviour of play with fashion dolls.

Clearly, modern character toys are not designed to enhance children's creativity and meet their emotional needs; rather, they are

fashioned around carefully researched and positioned play niches –
cosy defenders of feelings, omnipotent heroes and glamorous
superstars – symbolic representations of characters which children
like to manipulate in their play. In light of these new trends in toy
design, it may be necessary to reassess Piaget's definition of play as a
creative and assimilative form of learning. This might have been true
of play with the simple toys before television but the play activities
exhibited with contemporary toys reveals evidence of imitative
learning in which children accommodate their mental schema to
prevailing attitudes and norms in society. Two aspects of toy-
marketing seem to stress these imitative aspects of pretend. The first
is the narrow scripting of the associated television animations to elicit
carefully targeted play values. The second is the way most toy
advertisements model repeatedly a style of play which replicates the
television scripts in the depiction of children's play behaviour.

We interviewed, observed and studied the drawings of over 200
children between the ages of six and eight in order to assess whether
television helps to tip the balance between discovery and mimicry in
children's play. In discussing these drawings 15 per cent of children
volunteered the fact that they were structuring their play to be 'just
like on television' or to be repeating a script they recently 'saw on
TV'. Another group (53 per cent) depicted themselves using television characters or script structures in their play, if not directly
imitating scenes, at least visibly incorporating elements from the
programmes into their fantasies. To some extent, the play activities
often take the general form of long-established games such as chase,
search and rescue, singing, grooming, disguise, fondling which have
been part of children's culture for a long time;[25] but these general
forms are narrated by the child in very specific ways. Children may
say in the middle of a game of tag, for example, that their
'transformer's energy source is running out' or in a dress-up game
that 'Jem is getting dressed for the singing contest'. The dialogue
children use in and around their games gives a strong indication of
how television is being used as a source of ideas which give structure
and rationale to their play. Moreover, there is equally strong evidence
that the affective component of the play experience is highly gender-
stereotyped: boys repeatedly used their action dolls in conflicts of
strength and power, and girls to fantasize about glamour, friendship
and love.

It is clear from talking to children over six years of age that the
nature of their identifications are not a wholesale internalization of

the hero character or a result of confusion about reality and fantasy. Indeed, character-toy play may be a vital part of children's learning about the relationship between fiction and reality. If you ask 'Do Inhumanoids exist?' or 'Could you go and see Barbie at a rock concert?' they think you are being stupid and laugh (though, in fact, you *can* now see Barbie at a concert). Some of the children will even give you a protracted discussion of the naturalistic fallacy. They will go on to explain that imaginary beings are essential to their forms of play. In this sense they are not just playing Cabbage Patch or Transformers, but with imaginary beings like Julia or Ultra-Magnus: 'I like to be Ultra-Magnus . . . he's the leader of City Complex.' They exhibit clear affective preferences and happily annunciate a hierarchy among their toys: 'Mostly I play with my Jem dolls, but sometimes I take out my Cabbage Patch.' Their preferences were expressed as specific reasons or attributes of the doll: 'she's beautiful'; 'he's the strongest'; 'I like her hair'; 'she's nicest', 'I like the way she sings'; 'he's the fastest'; 'he can fly'.

Children's preferences for toys and play activities were often expressed as a liking for a specific toy within a product range: 'When I play with my Barbies I mostly play with Beach Barbie.' Even in elaborate play set-ups, it was the characters' individuality, their particular personalities that orientated the child to a particular view of what play was about. These children could give equally strong reasons why they didn't like a particular toy, and many of the girls responded in horror when we asked them to dress Jem in a Misfits outfit; the boys were equally shocked when we asked if they would ever use He-Man to attack Cobra. Play talk often involves detailed comparisons of these different characters, their attributes, their technologies or abilities. The girls' discussions of styling, comportment and music are sophisticated. Children also can be heard discussing the nature of their laser guns, or how their magic claw deflected the thought-beams. Playing with these toys in part means playing with the identities – the technologies they use, the cars they drive, the magic powers they possess. But it rarely involves their subjectivity – the feelings, philosophies, wishes or hopes that these pretend characters experience. It is rare in our observations of these children at play to see them use these characters to explore the inner experience of human desire and feeling in a simulated play situation.

We cannot pretend to answer the very difficult questions concerning the role of identification with character toys in the emotional maturation of children with such simple observations. It will take extensive research on very different kinds of children, before we properly understand how children use their emotional investment with these toy personalities in their maturational projects. We can, however, say that character identities, attributes and accessories provided by toy-marketing give structure to children's play. Play seems to be mediated by the identification process, but we must exercise caution in interpreting this idea. Playing at being He-Man is not the same as wanting to be He-Man. When asked they might say 'I'd like to be strong like He-Man. I'd like a magic sword. I would like to be in a rock group.' There were few signs that children ever considered emulating these fictional heroes. When asked if she wanted to grow up to be like Barbie, one girl thoughtfully corrected us, 'Only to be beautiful like Barbie'. Having a favourite is not the acceptance of a personality type which serves to guide their experience or to model their social interactions. One boy distinguished between the fact that he often play wrestled as Ricky the Dragon Steamboat but not if he got in a real fight. Yet we can't help feeling as we watch these children at play that their activities are sex-typed, stereotypic and predictable.

Surrogate Fantasies

The Singers' research indicated that the imaginativeness of play depends a lot on the family environment. A family that encourages and supports children in their assimilative use of play may provide the child with a kind of guidance or framework for using fantasy to deal with everyday emotional issues – with separation, moving house, ostracism, failure, lack of emotional control and feelings of jealousy. In a healthy family context imaginative play could be an important means of emotional adjustment. But commenting on how the young child makes his mother disappear in a fantasy game, Freud argued that play can be a kind of ritualized wishing. Play, like all fantasy, shifts attention from the here and now on to the less restrictive plane of the possible. Erik Erikson notes that 'the game alone, as reported by Freud, could have become the beginning of an increasing tendency on the child's part to take life experiences into a solitary corner and to rectify them in fantasy, and only in fantasy'.[26]

There is the possibility that these fantasized resolutions of socio-emotional conflict are substituting for opportunities to work on the

331

real source and roots of these conflicts. If, as Bruno Bettelheim, states, 'the most important function of play and games for the well being of the child is to offer him a chance to work through unresolved problems of the past, to deal with pressures of the moment and to experiment with various roles and forms of social interaction in order to determine their suitability for himself', then we need to ask how character-marketing influences the social context of fantasy.[27] The child who engages excessively in solitary fantasy play may not be learning the social skills and emotional adjustments necessary to maturation. Brian Sutton-Smith, in particular, has noted that the play forms of the modern child are very different from the highly social street play and collective games of earlier generations which often mixed conversation, role enactment, tag, sports and competition and rules into a polyglot and fluid play activity.

Like the observations of children at home, most of the children's drawings of play reflected their sense of an isolated pretending – a world of child and toy, or of the child within the toy's universe. This kind of pretending was commonest in their drawings of character toys. Very few of our subjects (12 per cent) drew other children playing, and in over 200 drawings only one adult appeared. To the child play connotes a private action with a favourite toy – an intense moment of doing or pretending in which the child is personally engaged by the toy.

The absence of parents in the children's pictures and discussions was striking. Some children's response to our probe: 'Do you ever play ... with your parents' was laughter; others just looked at us in amazement. It was clear from discussions that they rarely played with their parents, and thought parents couldn't play with character toys. When we probed this common observation, we got a variety of responses: 'they're too busy'; 'they work'; 'they're not interested'; 'they watch too much TV'; 'they don't know how to play with Barbie'; 'they don't like My Little Pony'. When asked what they did play with their parents, the occasional child said, 'Cards, Scrabble, games'. From the children's accounts, parents seem to have little interest in their imaginations and still less in character toys. It is very likely that parents, who don't watch these programmes on television, are not really capable of intervening in imaginative play or in helping children use their play fantasization with character toys in a more useful and less thematically constricted way (G.I. Joe the loving father, Barbie defender of the Amazon rainforest). Bathed in the exclusivity of children's culture, character toys make it more difficult for parents (often ignorant of that culture) to guide imaginative play or make it relevant to their experience.

Limited Scripts

Indeed, even in peer play with character toys, the kinds of opportunities for learning are minimized because of the 'high definition' backstories associated with character toys. As the Russian psychologist Lev Vygotsky argued: 'The imaginary situation already contains rules of behaviour, although it is not a game with formulated rules laid down in advance.'[28] The act of creative pretend play involves the discovery of implicit rules of the make-believe situation through the discussion of narrative possibilities of social pretending. This makes the discourse children have around and in play one of the most interesting aspects of pretending, and possibly one of the most developmentally useful.[29] How children negotiate with others their understanding of the implicit rules and definition of the play situation constitutes a tremendous potential to learn from play. In fact, listening to the play conversations reveals that children often alternate between discussion of the general definition of the play or set-up (What do you want to play? Have you got Beach Barbie's ear-rings?); play narration (Here comes Liono to the rescue! Watch out for Hordak!); character vocalization (Vrrm vrmm, You're trapped Slaughter!); and play adjudication (Mumra lost his power, Jem sang better).[30] Some of the most useful social and emotional transactions take place during these play conversations because not only are the children laying out the rules of a pretend situation and adjudicating them, but because it is in these verbal accompaniments to play that children articulate and apply their social cognitions and schema.

It is the discovery aspect of such play-negotiating that is threatened by character-marketing or any other factor that makes play less social and less verbal. The concern is that the play performance may be limited because the TV narratives have strictly defined the rules and outcomes of play. Character play, in our observation, seemed to invoke little rule-breaking or rule transformation. Much of the dialogue was simply the articulation of rules and the actions were rule-following. The most typical negotiations seem to involve what a character should wear or do: what's possible within the game structure as defined by the child's understanding of the TV character or a story they watched. This script bias is evidenced by the fact that we only rarely observed children mix characters from different imaginary universes – G.I. Joe rarely gets to fight Transformers and Barbie rarely has to sing with My Ponies. Such mixtures might be the occasion for rather elaborate discussions of the possibilities of interaction between two sets of rules. But they rarely happened. The children clearly understand the implicit rules and traits which govern the toy – their powers, weapons, moral dispositions and voices. If a violation of these attributes occurs a child may well dispute them: 'Moto can't fly, he's a motorcycle' or 'Gem always goes on stage last'.

It is also of concern that it is difficult for children playing with character toys to change the perceived structure laid down by the toys' universe. In one dyad of boys playing with transformers battling as flying machines, the smaller boy was obviously receiving some nasty blows as the toys flew around and then repeatedly engaged in battle. The smaller one was being frustrated by the damage both his character and his fingers were sustaining and complained repeatedly. These complaints were ignored by the older child, who felt his more powerful robot had the right to win. Finally the littler fellow struck upon an idea: 'Look, we're both aerobots, we should be flying in formation. I'll fly here and guard your wing.' The other looked at him, trying to figure out the legitimacy of the new game. Playing transformers for him always meant combat. Quickly the little one added, 'See that box over there, that's the enemy base.' With no further thought they flew off in perfect formation, making appropriate noises and flying about the room in tandem and dive-bombing the base. The little one was able to redefine the game, but not the narrative structure.

A Flight of Fancy

Early children's television was, at least partially, viewed by writers as a way of helping children make sense of their experiences within the family, the peer group, the schools and society at large. But contemporary marketers target imaginary play rather than entertainment and enlightenment. They developed a preference for stories which didn't have to 'work' as education, mythology or folklore. To work as product promotions, the narratives had to make children want to use particular toys in their fantasy play. Because character-toy back-stories became more fantastic for promotional purposes, the narrative register of children's play has also shifted

334

further from realism. Such toys provide few opportunities for children to mesh their lived experience with their fantasies in play.

The educationist John Holt has expressed his concern that television fantasies can commandeer the fantasy process by supplanting or displacing the social imaginings that children would otherwise produce in their play activity:

> Of course, children these days are very early hooked by the mass media. We are seeing something new in human history, a generation or two of children who have most of their daydreams made for them ... when I first began to pay attention to children, the pretend games they played with each other were more likely to be games like house, in which someone would be the mommy and someone daddy and someone the baby, or maybe school or doctor. They didn't run around pretending to be superman. Such fantasies must be learned from the adults who invent and sell them.[31]

To understand Holt's comments about fantasy we cannot conceive of fantasizing as simply a matter of Freudian wish-fulfilment or the mental release of unbidden images. Fantasizing is also a modality of consciousness, a process by which children organize perception and interpretation to build social knowledge. Holt's fears are tied to the pattern and content of fantasy that commercial television favours, for they rob social-dramatic play of the reference to experience: 'If we try to make children fantasize these fake fantasies, like the ready-made fantasies of TV, we will in time drive out most of their true fantasies, the ones that come from their experience in the world and their need to make sense of it and become at home in it.'

The abstract and alienated thematics of character fiction means that children are unlikely to play out with these toys fantasy scenes of going to school, being ill or waking up frightened, still less peer rejection, family break-up, isolation anxiety, parental rejection or the death of a pet. It's not impossible, of course, but they simply don't interpret their toys in that way. And this means that the potential to schematize and master in play a whole range of difficult emotional material is also absent in their lives. Children will have confronted stage fright, star flight, cosmic holocaust, beauty pageants and scheming witches in their daily play, but will rarely avail themselves of the chance to anticipate and rehearse for a new sibling, a dying parent or a runaway pet.

A few of the children's play drawings revealed very disturbing signs of a deeper layer of emotionality that can be engaged by toys:

Sargeant Slaughter with a huge phallus and a child victim of Metlar with eyes dripping blood. In interviews, too, several young children's description of their fears associated with some of the toys were striking. A few of the children reported having trouble going to sleep because they imagined being attacked by these toys or imaginary monsters they associated with them. Others cleverly avoided watching any programmes which they thought too scary. But overall, these examples of emotional disturbance were exceptional cases. Our concern is only for disturbed or troubled children who may experience the powerful images without adequate opportunity for resolving them.

Yet overall, play with character toys should not be described as a profoundly emotional activity. From what the children said it is experienced as an energetic and pleasurable 'activity' that mingles fantasy with manipulating objects. The children's descriptions of their play fantasies seemed at times off-hand, as if they were engaged in a simple exercise of the imagination. This is not to say that play fantasies are free of conflict: 'Rodimus Prime is going to kill me but I am going to kill him back' says one. 'G.I. Joe is waiting for the twins. It's a trap. He's going to blast them,' says another. Although these children are describing conflicted and highly charged situations, they don't necessarily seem emotionally engaged or involved in meaningful emotional experiences. Play is, generally speaking, just a happy time with their favourite toys. Children's accounts of the feelings that are simulated or enacted in the play seemed similarly limited: 'The Misfits want to win' or 'Skeletor got scared'. Often, these emotional terms apply more to the child's feelings than those of the characters. One child, for example, when asked about the picture he had drawn of a Transformer waiting for its enemy said he 'felt happy so he can destroy them [the enemy]'. When asked about why they play, children typically say ''cos it's fun'. When asked how they feel when they are playing, they respond equally simply, 'happy'. It is difficult, therefore, to generalize about the deeper emotional implications of character toys given such truncated reports, but these interviews provided little evidence that character toys were being meaningfully assimilated to children's daily experiences or helped them to resolve personal emotional struggles.

From the kid's point of view, action toys are often most enjoyed in the having. They take pride in a complete set or the possession of a prized or faddish toy. The toys, when used, are exercises in remembering and imagining; they are only rarely representations in miniature of deep socio-dramatic conflicts. Play, then, like the fantasizing that goes on while viewing television, is undertaken not so much to escape harsh reality, but as a fun pastime or leisure preoccupation. Play is a desirable form of entertainment which, like television, taps children's imaginations.

The Complexities of Play

The issue of the developmental benefits of character toys comes down to a matter of the style of imaginative activity that children undertake when playing with them. It's possible, of course, to play creatively with these toys, to extend and consolidate schemata, to build new cognitive structures, to dramatize elaborate stories, to break rules, to learn new attitudes and skills. These are the kind of activities which lead psychologists to put great faith in play. Such creativity, unfortunately, is not the kind of play activity depicted repeatedly in the toy commercials. In these snapshots of play, the child is shown simply manipulating plastic characters in accord with the highly stereotypic patterns of narrative assigned to the particular characterization. In this respect, advertising and life can be said to reflect each other very accurately.

Developmental psychologist Jerome Bruner has long argued that the cognitive developmental benefits of fantasy play depend on the complexity of pretending. Bruner and his co-workers believe that free-form and unguided pretend play is particularly lacking in cognitive benefits because this kind of play tends to be cognitively unstructured.[32] In their extensive study of nursery-school play Silva and her colleagues tested out Bruner's ideas by calibrating play activities to discover which play styles mentally stretch the child.[33] Two particular results are of interest. First, they note that certain kinds of imaginative toys encouraged social interaction (including object play, pretend play) and thus might optimize the learning of social and verbal skills. They also note that 'too many of the freer, low yield activities must mean diminished opportunity for planning and elaborating' – the mental schema they consider most conducive to conceptual learning. From their observations, most pretend play seems both absorbing and simplistic when judged by their combined criteria of commitment and concentration, and this reduced complexity leads them to doubt its usefulness for the child. They also argue that the absorption and concentration exemplified by pretending can be explained by the dramatic structure: 'It seems to us that children are committed to two kinds of activities, those with clear goals and those with dramatic force.' The supposed benefits of pretend play have always been assumed because of the 'dramatic force' associated with role play. Role play does keep kids interested and engaged in their toys; but in these researchers' evidence children don't learn very much about complex self-generated thinking through socio-dramatic free-play activities.

It was the simplicity of the play activities associated with war toys that also led Carlson-Paige and Levin to see such toys as unsuitable for the classroom. They observed that 'Many children get stuck and repeat the same play behavior over and over as if by rote rather than elaborate their play over time.'[34] Similarly Davie and his British colleagues observed in relationship to the free play of the home that

> A great deal of the fantasy play observed was highly repetitive and stereotyped. The same play was performed repeatedly by individual children on different occasions and also different children would engage in very similar fantasization. This was particularly true of representational fantasy play, where the boys spend long periods parking and reparking toy cars and the girls arranging and rearranging domestic replica objects.[35]

Pretend play can be a complex and sophisticated mental process consolidating social and perceptual schema and demanding anticipatory planning and negotiation. Dolls and action toys in particular can encourage complex linguistic structures (as the child shifts between the perspectives of character, player, narrator and self); role cognition (as the child adopts the perspective of a character or decides what the character can and should do); rule definition (as the child negotiates the action with others); sequencing (as children co-ordinate events within a scene); and empathic understanding (as the children synchronize their enjoyment with other players through interaction). Social drama enacted between two or more children playing with several imaginary characters could be one of the most profound encouragements to complex social cognition possible. Hence group social-dramatic play is regarded by educators as one of the best ways for children to learn social skills because it combines the mental activities of scripting with role enactment. Even children playing alone with their toys at imaginary scenarios confront the task of thinking about motivations, enacting multiple points of view, co-ordinating multiple actions and ultimately solving problems of conflicts in social relations.

But in watching children playing with their character toys one also notices that another voice is sometimes used in the vocalizations. In this voice the child expresses the perspective of the play narrative. For a moment he or she is the announcer at the mike, the story teller. The addition of television's narrative voice to children's play may be one of the most troubling aspects of television's influence on play. The child playing hockey for example, may announce 'And it's the great Gretsky making fools of the opposition' as he stick handles down the ice. Similarly, the child with an action toy announces 'Who knows what dangers lurk in the cave for Liono?'. Both these examples remind us of the linkage that exists between pretend play and television. The linguistic and cognitive skills involved in constructing narrative in play are precisely those that children need to understand television and to transfer its tales to their play. In one sense, there is evidence of a potential new complexity in play: the child is a playwrite devising a script, a director staging the dramatic event, and the actor making appropriate voices, gestures and noises – all at the same time. On the other hand, the child as play programmer also has an easier option. Like the jaded Hollywood producer he or she can choose to use simple-minded, off-the-rack scripts and trite actors to serve up mediocre and shallow entertainments.

It is against this backdrop of enormous 'potential' for learning, that what kids actually do with their character toys seems so ritualistic and impoverished. Occasionally children perform highly transformative and assimilative playlets – a game of hockey played by Gobots; a Barbie detective murder mystery; a cosmic courtroom drama with Skeletor as its judge. But sadly these were the exceptions. The dialogues and dramatic imaginings we heard repeated in children's play vocalizations seemed thin and repetitious. They rarely used comic or ironic narrative (so much a part of children's peer culture), preferring to stick to the prevailing mood of action drama and fashion pretension. Instead of elaborate scenes of improvisational toy theatre, we see in children's play only the repeated spectacles of combat and fashion, narrated with the same TV slogans interspersed with TV's theme music and sound effects. It is possible that children have very elaborate internal fantasies and interior dialogues during their play; but these are not in evidence in character play or in the descriptions children give of the play.

The stories most children tell in their character-toy play are highly episodic. In fact this form of play rarely has an overriding structure linking the various actions together into a more complex story. When boys are given vehicles, they pretend to race or go through obstacles or do tricks. When two enemies meet they engage in a mock battle. With Cabbage Patch dolls or My Little Ponies, girls play at happy families; with Jem and Barbie they dress and groom for fashionable outings or occasionally musical performances. Children also exhibit little resourcefulness in their incorporation of other objects or features of their play spaces into the imaginary situation – using, for example, a desk as a space ship or a pillow for a Pony nest. The narrowness of the play scripts they follow calls for appropriately designed objects used in appropriate ways.

The most cognitively elaborated features of character play that we observed were the sophisticated discussion of tactics which guides the deployment and interaction of these toy figures. Among boys in particular, the building of bases and arraying of battle groups is a major feature of their play. When asked to explain particular outcomes in their play scenes, boys happily announce tactical wisdoms such as attacking from the blind side, disguising themselves for sabotage, and the impact of surprise, as if they were young cadets. When pushed, one finds their tactical knowledge can be supplemented by a detailed discussion of weapons' capacity, mobility or strategic advantages of the characters and their accessories. The girls are equally adept in the discussion of the pragmatics of grooming and performance. Their explanations are equally grounded in ideas of matching accoutrement colour schemes, what makes a song a success, or how to get a baby to eat its supper. The rehearsal and practice of tactical thinking is the only evidence we saw of complex cognitions being employed in children's character-toy play.

A Many Gendered Thing

Researchers studying the sex differences in children's fantasy play have long complained about the divergent content and play styles they find in the classroom and home.[36] Even when boys and girls are playing with the same toys, they are often employing them in very different imaginary contexts and interacting differently with their playmates. Some kinds of toys promote social interaction, more discussion and more transformative thought than others. Boys, it seems, tend to transform the objects around them through make-believe, while girls accommodate their play routines to the groups' given or established definitions. Boys also seem to spend a lot more time arguing about the rules of the imaginary games they are playing.

Several commentators therefore have argued that girls should be encouraged to adopt more object-transformative play styles because they believe these may be more developmentally beneficial.[37] Other researchers have thought it advisable to enhance girls' social-dramatic play because in it they create and co-ordinate complex narratives and social cognitions.[38] Still others have argued that girls' disposition towards social-relational play themes has advantages, for in this kind of role play they are developing their social skills while boys are simply manipulating objects and arguing.[39] But what all researchers agree on is the fact that sex-typing of toys is an important force for separating the sexes in terms of the cognitive, emotional and social skills that children acquire therein.

It is agonizing to see how sex-exclusive children's advertising is[40] and how sex-stereotypical children's play is.[41] Although boys now play with dolls and girls do have powerful female role models in their television, these changes seem strangely limited. Targeting in the toy market, after all, had two important consequences: it gendered the themes of children's television programming and it created a markedly sex-typed image of peer play in the commercials. Television before deregulation strove for large audiences so producers designed programmes for a homogeneous children's audience. Whereas the cartoon characters of the 1950s were either asexual or balanced in their gender appeal, the action-figure animations specifically use characterization and storyline to accommodate known gender preferences and play values.[42]

It is not surprising, then, that when children are asked what they like on television, they respond by explaining their preferences in gender terms. Boys and girls claim that they rarely watch and do not like the same TV shows. When pushed to explain what they don't like on TV they often responded with the idea that they avoid a particular show because 'that's meant for girls' or 'for boys'. This same attitude extends through most goods from books to shoes, but is especially noticeable in their expressed preferences for character toys. Preferences, however, are not defined through rigid same-sex identity rules. For example Cheetara (a female member of the Thundercats) is a suitable toy for a boy to play with because she is part of the Thundercat team; Ken is fine for girls because he is integrated into the Barbie universe.

Children feel that the eyes of their peers are always upon them.

School yards are notoriously gender cliqued from kindergarten on and most children prefer to play socially with members of their own gender, although most can adjust their play in order to fit in with mixed-sex groups when required. When interviewed about this, both genders reported that outside the family they rarely played with the opposite sex. Their explanations of why this was the case were particularly interesting: most frequently the reason was because they liked doing different things and playing with different toys. Goods, especially toys, were definitional to their conception of the suitability of their playmates. Indeed, of the self-portraits of play we examined, only two included members of the opposite sex in the play group.

Children like to play with others who share their interest in particular toys ('Jill plays with Cabbage Patch too. We like to bring them together and play family'). The mutual admiration for particular toys is often the pretext for same sex get-togethers ('I like Janet to come because we both play Barbie'). A much-repeated and strongly expressed view from all children was that boys didn't play with fashion dolls. Some girls, we discovered, watched programmes like He-Man and Transformers and reported playing with 'their brothers' toys' occasionally. Few boys did the same with a sister's fashion dolls. This division was not based on some sense of genetic differences between the sexes. The children explained that it was 'all right' for boys to play with My Little Ponies and for girls to play with G.I. Joe; but they just 'preferred not to'. It is the implicit rules defined through notions of gendered preference and not perceived differences in capacity which lie at the root of this divide between the sexes.

Every child understands the unspoken rules of catch or tag and so they can convene these games at any time. But to play with Thundercats or Barbie assumes a substantial amount of knowledge that only aficionados of the television programmes can hope to acquire. Because of the gender differences in television-viewing, boys and girls, however, no longer share a common mythology – a defined set of heroes and feats that they can make reference to in their conversations and their social-dramatic play. For this reason character toys can become the source of difficulties for children in mixed groups. When children of the opposite sex (family friends, cousins, classmates) come into their playrooms children reported having trouble finding common toys with which to play. If Zoe likes to play with Cabbage Patch dolls and Luke with his Dino-Riders then an imaginary play universe which can accommodate both of their

342

fascinations is hard to negotiate. After several failed forays into pretend, in this situation children will often revert to cards, games, computers or videos, or end up in parallel play. The kids explained why this happens so frequently: 'They [the opposite sex] don't know how to play with these [character] toys.' Without the sense of common bonding to toys and without a shared knowledge about characters, play scripts and appropriate game structures, boys and girls now seem to find it harder to mesh their make-believe play than ever before.

Transient Objections

Studies of children's bedrooms conducted in the 1970s revealed the astonishing number of toys the middle-class child possesses. Of the ninety separate playthings found there, the majority were sex-typical.[43] It is not hard to imagine that by now this figure may have doubled and the proportion of sex-typed objects increased. The clutter of kids' bedrooms often leads exasperated parents to declare that children have too many toys and to wonder if, distracted by this abundance, children are not getting as much out of their play. This concern with the quality of children's attachment to their playthings echoes an objection expressed by John Locke well before industrialization. Locke believed that children should have playthings of 'divers sorts' but have only 'one at once' to play with because 'This teaches them betimes to be careful of not losing or spoiling Things they have whereas Plenty and Variety in their own keeping makes them wanton and careless and teaches them from the beginning to be Squanderers and Wasters.' Locke warns parents not to buy playthings for the child because 'this will hinder that great Variety they are often overcharded with, which serves only to teach the Mind to wander after Change and Superfluity, to be unquiet, and perpetually stretching itself after something more still, though it knows not what, and never to be satisfied with what it hath.' He goes on to tell of one child 'so accostumed to Abundance, that he never thought he had enough, but was always asking, What more? What more? What new Thing shall I have?' Locke's solution to the dilemma is to allow children to have all the toys they want just so long as they make them themselves.

Roland Barthes has argued that a child's experience of toys mirrors the alienated position of consumers to all manufactured things:

Faced with this world of faithful and complicated toys the child can only identify himself as owner, as user, never as creator; he does not invent the world, he uses it; they are prepared for him, actions without adventure, without wonder, without joy ... they are supplied to him ready-made; he has only to help himself, he is never allowed to discover anything from start to finish.[44]

The profusion of toys, he implies, lessens the depth of involvement with any particular toy and the social bonds constructed through using and sharing them. Every parent knows that a toy which a child desperately needs one day can be abandoned the next. Some toys do become meaningful and treasured objects that are remembered for a lifetime, but most follow a faddish cycle of transient fashions. When the fad dies, the toys lose their play-appeal. To some degree, through the attitudes to objects they establish in play, toys teach children about consumerism – their relationship with all things.[45]

On examining the social skills and attitudes expressed through the use of toys in the family, the psychologist Lita Furby argued that experiences with and interactions around toys may provide important foundations for many of our society's attitudes to possessions.[46] Through play, children learn sharing, receiving, giving and lending, anticipating, waiting and reciprocating, planning and organizing their use of things to give pleasure. Often the parent and older sibling play a crucial role in adjudicating and explaining the social basis of these formative experiences: 'Johnny gets a bike because he's older' or 'Now it's Lorrie's turn to wash Barbie's hair'. Furby noted that parents rely on toys as rewards or tools with which to instruct children in some important social protocols, particularly those concerning property rights, exchanges and the significance of possessions.

At a very early age children understand and express in language the ideas of property rights: 'It's mine, don't touch, you get it next.' Because of their strong attachment to and positive regard for their playthings, the child's first articulation of the rights of possession concerns toys. Whereas clothes may often be hand-me-downs, or simply regarded by parents as necessities (no room for choice or expressions of preference granted), toys are given to children because of the child's assumed enjoyment and interest in them. Parents equate the strength of attachment to toys with rights of control over use. These rights vary from family to family but can include the limitations on friends' and siblings' use, as well as priorities, order and duration of control. Parents will enforce these rights in disputes and articulate the various principles of property which apply to the child's use of toys.

Furby's work helped to develop a way of thinking about toys which recognized how important the patterning of children's use and treatment of objects can be in modern childrearing. Toys, she observes, also play a very critical part in communicating the parents' attitudes about the importance of self-expression, individuality and the way the child should judge others. The patterning of play also communicates to children important abstract notions such as their ideas of fairness, their understanding of unequal distribution of wealth, and about the general social standing that accompanies owning or having things – in short the social relations of property.

To account for the significance of acquisitiveness within the modern cultural framework, Furby's research traced the various functions that key possessions have at various stages of the life-cycle. Her analysis of early childhood pinpoints three important social constructs primarily learned through play which she regards as contributing to the modern child's regard for their possessions:

1. an owner's use and right to control an object;
2. the positive affect or regard for what is owned;
3. the owner's ability to effect the surrounding environment and gain personal control of it and others through objects.

Furby calls this third aspect of play 'effectance', highlighting it as the most important because as children use their toys to feel and express control over their own physical skills, their environment and others they gain their first experience of the potential of objects to communicate broader social and economic ideas. Toys are not simply objects for personal use. They are also used in social play and therefore children quickly learn social ramifications: taking a toy away from a younger sibling, for example, produces crying; bragging about a present is a way of taunting siblings; showing off a new bike on the playground attracts friends and attention. Children clearly understand the role that toys play in social communication, formulating their judgements of their peers upon their toys.

The theoretical implications of Furby's analysis broadens our view of what can be learned in play. For her, play is crucial to the development of the very foundations of the modern economy because toys help children establish a fluid relationship to property.

Toys have this paradoxical quality. They are vital tools of childhood development and cognitive maturation, but at the same time, as Brian Sutton-Smith states they are 'the possessions with which children can learn the materialistic cultural habits of late twentieth century, American civilization'. Parents consciously employ toys in the consumer socialization of their children. At birth, the child is inundated with a host of soft objects and distracting mobiles in a festive welcome to the sensory delights of a material world. These simple pleasures are supplemented quickly with rattles, teething and manipulation objects which are the first manipulable tools with which all children are expected to acquaint themselves, for these toys must familiarize the child with skills necessary for manipulating and controlling objects.

As children get older, symbolic play supplants manipulation and children learn to express their own preferences for playthings as they negotiate with adults for things they want. Realizing children's attachments to toys, parents too use them as rewards – to please and encourage the child and to celebrate important occasions such as visits, returns and birthdays. As children begin to gain a disposable income from monetary gifts and allowances, the toy can also become the vehicle parents chose to teach children to save or at least to choose products carefully by encouraging children to make their first autonomous consumer decision in the toy shop. Christmas has become a seasonal consumption rite in which toys not only provide the emotional fuel but the central interpretation of spiritual experience for the child. The approach of this season always guarantees intense consumer socialization as children forage through catalogues, watch ads on TV and write lists to Santa in their attempts to impose order on their desires and guile their parents into appropriate acquisitions. Families therefore play an important part in the emerging consumer attitudes of the child. Toys therefore bear many messages for the child on top of the ones communicated on television.

A parent's supervision of their children's emerging ability to translate pleasure into purchase, however, does not take place in a vacuum.[47] From a very young age, children use television commercials to help integrate their expanding knowledge of the consumer market with their personal dilemmas of friendship, desire, and choice.[48] Indeed as Roy Moore and George Moochis state in their review of consumer socialization, recent research indicates 'that family and other socialization agents such as school may be inadequate in teaching relevant consumer skills, knowledge and attitudes leaving room for the mass media to serve as substitutes in the socialization process.'[49] They believe that 'young people may acquire from the mass media the expressive aspects of consumption'. The evidence from their research indicates that television ads not only directly influence product knowledge, but commercials help to consolidate the broader economic knowledge and problems of choice in a consumer society. Researchers have shown in detail how television helps children form the attitudes and skills of consumerism, starting from the child's ability to recognize and understand advertising – its intent and forms – and link this to their requests and purchases.[50]

Contemporary family television provides an extremely bourgeois image of familial roles and attitudes to modern life. This same concern with fads and fashion in toys confirms the instability of children's wants; the dolls are not only consumer objects; they induce the anticipation of consumer styles in social-dramatic form. Indeed, in playing with her fashion dolls, a girl quickly discovers she can exercise and express some of the most important social attitudes and judgements of her consumer lifestyle – ideas which she can barely express in language and rarely talk about with either friends or parents – as a style, aesthetic or look associated with clothes. The imaginative manipulation of toy symbols is the defining feature of social-dramatic play. Character toys are particularly potent artefacts because as fantasies condensed into objects, they afford the child a chance to express attitudes and practise behaviours in the protected realm of play that usually remain incommunicable. It is not surprising, then, that children express bourgeois sentiments and social judgements not only about their toys but in their play. In this sense toys not only communicate parents' attitudes to the child and rights of ownership but function as prototypical commodities of a consumer culture because they invite children to understand the meaning of objects as the potential to transform the material experience of goods through the act of fantasy.

In this respect, the broad social vistas of character programmes may be less influential to the child's view of his or her world than the more explicit information about toys and why they want them, that children derive from watching advertising. Advertisements acquaint children with the basic framework of consumer behaviour – with the need for money to purchase things they want in the stores. Toys themselves not only mirror in miniature the essential elements of the ideology of consumerism (cars, boats, playhouses) but acquaint

347

children with the social dynamics of a consumer market – social judgement by others depends on meshing individual desires with those of specific peer groups by a common agreement on objects and how they should be used.

Of the social cognitions communicated in play, class and gender are probably the concepts most deeply associated with distinctions children make between the implicit social relations of play. Children will distinguish in their play a range of roles, characters traits and ways of playing as appropriate to boys and girls. These judgements are informed by the specific interest each gender expresses in particular toys and their features. Gender status and orientation are likewise defined by the different ways that boys and girls think about, feel and use their toys. Children also willingly judge other children by the toys they own, by the number and cost of the toys, and rank them based on their possessions in terms of who is 'luckier or richer'. By five children have come to understand that some families have more wealth, even if they have only the vaguest ideas about work and the economy.[51] They can conclude this because that child has more toys, or toys of a more desirable sort. Children understand their position within the social structure largely through their perception of consumption styles expressed in play. Wealth and status are ascribed to those children with more of the 'right' things. Children also learn that things are bought in shops and become quite adept at influencing their parents in subtle ways to get what toys they want.

Television commercials may also guide children in their formation of mental representation of their aspirations. As Cedric Cullingford concludes based on his interviews with children:

> When asked to state their three wishes it is interesting to note how often children mix up the world that is offered by television with the real one. Television not only becomes a part of their fantasies, providing material for their natural tendency to have fantasies, but seems to suggest an attitude in which the pragmatic and the glamorous are very closely related.[52]

Although the children we interviewed did not often identify their toy heroes with their own personal identities it seems that many of their aspirations are connected with products either directly – 'to have all the Thundercats', 'to take Barbie on my holiday' – or indirectly – 'to have a Magic Sword', 'to be a rock star like Jem' when they grow up. However unrealistic such goals may seem, it is clear that toys help children to schematize and consolidate their wants and goals on a cognitive level.

Traditionally toy play has been valued for its release of energy, for offering children a suspended realm in which they could make emotional adjustments, for its helpful rehearsal of valued social roles, for its laying down of schemata for cognitive development, for its teaching of social skills and rule structures, and as an aid to sensori-motor development. Toys offer these many opportunities to the maturing child, and parents have supported children's expanding desire for toys for these reasons. But we can hardly be surprised that the intensification of children's marketing, especially the television promotions of character toys, is beginning to change what children actually learn in the realm of play. In the age of marketing, toys also serve a new function: they are the templates through which children are being introduced into the attitudes and social relations of consumerism.

Coda

Though their sights are set on simply selling their products, the situation of modern merchandising demands that marketers manage their communication with children in order to increase sales. In the current context this means using television as the primary channel of communication with the children's market. As long as no 'harm' to children is proven, public policy makers have acceded to the marketers' view that television should now be governed by the principle of commercial speech and so this medium has become the market's primary vehicle for consolidating and amplifying children's fascination with toys and sweets. Surely nobody can feign surprise anymore that commercial television fails to educate, inform or inspire our children. Nor should we be startled when we find that children become jaded with their toys and mimic in their play what they have seen on television. Children are simply finding their place within our consumer culture. But does this constitute a harm to children or diminish or interfere with their maturation? Clearly not, for these children are simply being socialized into the way of life of our consumer culture.

But parents and teachers who must bear the consequences of this shift in children's cultural environment are put on the defensive by this framing of the issue. What the issue of proven harm obscures is

349

the fact that we have granted to marketers enormous powers to meddle in the key realms of children's culture – the peer group, fantasy, stories and play. The key question we must pose is why the marketplace must be given so much influence within the matrix of socialization. Parents who are concerned or who resist the cultural thrust of the market are told they have the choice to control their child's television-viewing, to read, talk and play with their kids and, if they are really radical, to support media literacy programmes in the schools. In the USA they have been recently granted the right to get information from their local television stations concerning whether they meet 'pro-social programming' and advertising practices. And so, as Peggy Charren states, it's still 'going to be up to the parents to let the broadcasters know they're looking'.[53] In Canada and Britain, as in many other countries in Europe they are told self-regulatory watchdogs are guarding their children. Only in Quebec and Sweden are there clear limitations on commercial control of children's culture, and both these are easily circumvented by cable and satellite technologies.

The rationale for all of this supposed protection of the vulnerability of children rests on the assumption that marketing is an economic and not a cultural activity – that the advertising of goods plays no part in the formation of children's culture. This book has tried to show that this is an inaccurate if not ridiculous assumption. The problems that have been identified in children's marketing are the same as in all marketplaces – it is not a question of 'harm done' but, rather, of our failure to find ways to make the marketplace a positive cultural force in contemporary society. For this reason the debates about the limits on children's advertising, the banality and violence in children's programming, and the maintenance of creativity in children's play can all be reduced to the same root issue. The marketplace will never inspire children with high ideals or positive images of the personality, provide stories which help them adjust to life's tribulations or promote play activities that are most help to their maturation. Business interests trying to maximize profits cannot be expected to worry about cultural values or social objectives beyond the consumerist cultural vector that underwrites commercial media. If we value a cultural dimension beyond the domain of the commodity, we must first establish a new framework for the culture industries which recognizes this limitation and ensures that quality and excellence remain criteria for the production of children's culture.

Notes

1. Sydney Ladensohn Stern and Ted Schoenhaus, *Toyland: The High-Stakes Games of the Toy Industry*, Chicago, Contemporary Books, 1990, p. 29.

2. Tannis MacBeth Williams, *Impact of Television: A Natural Experiment in Three Communities*, Orlando, Academic Press, 1986.

3. Raymond Williams, *Television: Technology and Cultural Form*, London, Fontana, 1974, p. 59.

4. 'New Kids' Shows Marketed to Pass FCC Muster', *Broadcasting*, 28 Jan. 1991, pp. 27–8.

5. Bradley Greenberg, 'Television and Role Socialization: An Overview', in D. Pearl et al., *Television and Behaviour: Ten Years of Scientific Progress and Implications for the Eighties*, vol. 2, *Technical Reviews*, National Institute of Mental Health, Washington, US Government Printing Office, 1982, p. 179; Robert Hawkins and Suzanne Pingree, 'Television's Influence on Social Reality', in Pearl et al., *Television and Behaviour*, p. 224.

6. Guy Lometti and Alan Wurtzel, 'Researching Television Violence', *Society*, 21(6), 1984, pp. 22–8; David Pearl, 'Violence and Aggression', *Society*, 21(6), 1984, pp. 17–22; D. Pearl et al., *Television and Behaviour*.

7. Richard Haynes, 'Children's Perceptions of "Comic" and "Authentic" Cartoon Violence', *Journal of Broadcasting*, Winter 1978, 22/1, pp. 63–70; Bradley Greenberg, and Byron Reeves, 'Children and the Perceived Reality of Television', *Journal of Social Issues*, 32(4) 1976, pp. 86–97.

8. Albert Bandura, 'Social Learning Theory of Aggression', *Journal of Communication*, Summer 1978, 28(3), pp. 12–29.

9. Cedric Cullingford, *Children and Television*, Gower, Aldershot, 1984, p. 180.

10. Leonard N. Reid, and Charles F. Frazer, 'Television and Play', *Journal of Communication*, 30(4), 1980, pp. 66–73; James Navita Cummings and Thomas McCain, 'Television Games Preschool Children Play: Patterns, Themes and Uses', *Journal of Broadcasting*, 26(4), 1982, pp. 783–800.

11. Barbara Tizard, J. Philips and I. Plewis, 'Play in Pre-School Centres – The Effects on Play of the Child's Social Class and of the Educational Orientation of the Centre', *Child Psychology*, 17, 1976, pp. 265–74; B. Tizard, Janet Philips, and Ian Plewis, 'Play in Pre-school Centres: I Play Measures and their Relation to Age, Sex and I.Q.', *Journal of Child Psychology & Psychiatry & Allied Disciplines*, 17(4), 1976, pp. 251–64.

12. Jerome L. Singer and Dorothy G. Singer, *Television, Imagination, and Aggression: A study of preschoolers*, New Jersey, LEA Publishing, 1981, p. 13.

13. J. McNeal, *Children as Consumers: Insights and Implications*, Lexington, Lexington Books, 1987, p. 80.

14. C.E. Davie et al., *The Young Child at Home*, Windsor, NFER-Nelson, 1984, pp. 112–13.

15. Jerome L. Singer, *The Child's World of Make-Believe*, New York, Academic Press, 1973, p. 13.

16. Bruno Bettelheim, 'The Importance of Play', *Atlantic Monthly*, March 1987, p. 36.

17. Erik H. Erikson, *Childhood and Society*, New York, W.W. Norton, 1963, p. 217.

18. Singer and Singer, *Television*, p. 37.

19. Ibid., p. 82.

20. B. Sutton-Smith, *Toys as Culture*, New York, Gardner Press, 1986, p. 190.

21. Ibid., p. 205.

22. A. Beresin, 'Toy War Games and the Illusion of Two-Sided Rhetoric', *Play and Culture*, 2(3), 1989, pp. 218–24.

23. N. Carlson-Paige and D. Levin, *The War Play Dilemma: Children's Needs and Society's Future*, New York, Columbia University, Teachers College Press, 1987, p. 44.

24. Ibid.

25. B. Sutton-Smith, 'War Toys and Childhood Aggression', *The Journal of Play and Culture*, 1, 1988, pp. 57–69.

26. Erikson *Childhood*, p. 214.

27. Bettelheim, 'The Importance of Play', p. 38.

28. L.S. Vygotsky, 'Play and its Role in the Mental Development of the Child', in J.S. Bruner, A. Jolly and K. Sylva, *Play: Its Role in Development and Evolution*, Harmondsworth, Penguin, 1976, p. 541.

29. Helen B. Schwartzman, *Transformations: The Anthropology of Children's Play*, New York, Plenum Press, 1979; Mary Ann Magee, 'Social Play as Performance', *Play and Culture*, 2, 1989, pp. 193–6; Corinne Hutt, Exploration and Play in Children', in J.S. Bruner, A. Jolly and K. Sylva, *Play: Its Role in Development and Evolution*, Harmondsworth, Penguin, 1976.

30. Catherine Garvey, 'Some Properties of Social Play', in Bruner et al., *Play*.

31. John Holt, *How Children Learn*, Harmondsworth, Penguin, 1967, p. 239.

32. Kathy Sylva, Carolyn Roy and Marjorie Cants, *Childwatching at Play Group and Nursery School*, London, Grant Macintyre, 1984; K. Sylva, J.S. Bruner and P. Genova, 'The Role of Play in the Problem-Solving of Children 3–5 Years Old', in Bruner et al., *Play*.

33. Beverly I. Fagot and Mary Driver Leinbach, 'Play Styles in Early Childhood: Social Consequences for Boys and Girls', in Marsha Liss, ed., *Social and Cognitive Skills: Sex Roles and Children's Play*, New York, Academic Press, 1983.

34. Carlson-Paige and Levin, *The War Play*.

35. Davie et al., *The Young Child*.

36. Marsha B. Liss, 'Patterns of Toy Play: An Analysis of Sex Differences', *Sex Roles*, 7(11), 1981, pp. 1143–50; Vivian Gussin Paley, *Boys & Girls: Superheroes in the Doll Corner*, Chicago, University of Chicago Press, 1984; Janet Lever, 'Sex Differences in the Games Children Play', *Social Problems*, 23, 1976, pp. 478–87.

37. C. Jan Carpenter, 'Activity Structure and Play: Implications for Socialization', in Marsha Liss, ed., *Social and Cognitive Skills*.

38. Lorrain Nicholich and Carol Bruskin, 'Combinatorial Competency in Symbolic Play and Language-Importance for Language and Play', in D. Pepler and K. Rubin, eds, *The Play of Children: Current Theory and Research*, Basel, S. Krager, 1982.

39. Beverly I. Fagot and Mary Driver Leinbach, 'Play Styles in Early Childhood: Social Consequences for Boys and Girls', in Marsha Liss, ed., *Social and Cognitive Skills*; Asther Blank Greif, 'Sex Role Playing in Pre-School Children', in Bruner et al., *Play*; M.B. Liss, 'Learning Gender-Related Skills through Play', in Liss, ed., *Social and Cognitive Skills*, pp. 147–65.

40. Renate Welch, Aletha Huston-Stein, John Wright and Robert Plehal, 'Subtle Sex-Role Cues in Children's Commercials', *Journal of Communication*, Summer, 1979; Mary E. Verna, 'The Female Image on Children's TV Commercials', *Journal of Broadcasting*, 19, 1975, pp. 301–8; Stephen Kline and Debra Pentecost, 'The Characterization of Play: Marketing Children's Toys', *Play and Culture*, 3(3) 1990, pp. 235–54; Lori A. Schwartz and William T. Markham, 'Sex Stereotyping in Children's Toy Advertisements', *Sex Roles*, 12(1/2), 1985, pp. 157–70.

41. Candace Schau, Lynne Kahn, John Diepold and Frances Cherry, 'The Relationships of Parental Expectations and Preschool Children's Verbal Sex Typing to their Sex-Typed Toy Play Behavior', *Child Development*, 51, 1980, pp. 266–70; Vivian Gussin Paley, *Boys & Girls: Superheroes in the Doll Corner*, Chicago, University of Chicago Press, 1984; Francine Prose, 'Girls: The Challenge to their Confidence', *Toronto Star*, 16 Jan. 1990.

42. S. Kline, 'The Limits to the Imagination: Children's Play in the Age of Marketing', in I. Angus, and S. Jhally, eds, *Cultural Politics in America*, New York, Routledge & Kegan Paul, 1988.

43. Burton L. White, *The First Three Years of Life*, New York, Prentice-Hall, 1975.

44. Roland Barthes, *Mythologies*, London, Paladin, 1957, pp. 53–4.

45. John Locke, *Some Thoughts Concerning Education*, 14th edn, London, J. Whiston, pp. 192–3.

46. Lita Furby and Mary Wilke, 'Some Characteristics of Infants' Preferred Toys', *Journal of Genetic Psychology*, 4(2), 1982, pp. 207–19; Lita Furby, 'The Origins and Early Development of Possessive Behavior', *Political Psychology*, 2(1), 1980, pp. 3–42.

47. David Reisman and H. Rosenborough, 'Careers in Consumer Behavior', in Lincoln Clark, ed., *Consumer Behavior II: The Life Cycle and Consumer Behavior*, New York University Press, 1955.

48. Brian M. Young, *Television Advertising and Children*, Oxford, Clarendon Press, 1990.

49. Roy Moore, and George Moschis, 'Role of Mass Media and the Family in Development of Consumption Norms', *Journalism Quarterly*, 60, pp. 67–73.

50. Thomas E. Barry, 'Children's Television Advertising', *American Marketing Association, Monograph Series 8*, 1977; James, McNeal, *Children as Consumers*, Austin, University of Texas, Bureau of Business Research, 1964; Daniel B. Wackman, Ellen Wartella and Scott Ward, 'How TV Sells Children/Learning to be Consumers', *Journal of Communication*, Winter 1977, pp. 138–57; Scott Ward, and Daniel B. Wackman, 'Children's Information Processing of Television Advertising', in Peter Clarke, ed., *New Models for Communication Research*, Beverly Hills, Sage, 1973; Ellen Wartella, ed., *Children Communicating: Media and Development of Thought, Speech, Understanding*, Beverly Hills, Sage, 1979; Ellen Wartella, Daniel Wackman, Scott Ward, Jacob Shamir and Alison Alexander, 'The Young Child as Consumer', in Wartella, ed., *Children Communicating*, pp. 251–80.

51. Hans G. Furth, *The World of Grown-ups: Children's Conceptions of Society*, New York, Elsevier, 1980.

52. Cedric Cullingford, *Children and Television*, Aldershot, Gower, 1984, p. 53.

53. 'Some Kids' TV Shows Deemed Commercials: FCC Ruling Doesn't Go Far Enough, Say Children's Advocacy Groups', *The Globe and Mail*, 10 April 1991.

Appendix

Questions about Development

1. What would you say about your interest in the way your children play?

Very interested	58%
Somewhat interested	31%
A little interested	10%
Not interested at all	0%

2. Comparing the experience of your children with your own experience, do you think the *general situation* of children is better or worse, the same or different?

Somewhat better	29%
Much better	21%
About the same	15%
Somewhat worse	14%
Different	13%
Much worse	7%

3. Why do you think it is (better or worse) for children today?

   No response:

No or little change	7%
Don't know/not sure	5%

   Positive:

More opportunities/advantages/benefits	20%

More/better toys/amusements	8%
Other positive (e.g. more money to spend on kids)	7%
Children better understood/taken seriously/respected	5%
Better schooling/healthcare	4%
Negative:	
Moral breakdown/unclear rules/families less close	6%
Grow up too fast/life too competitive/ pressure on kids	6%
Uncertain world future	6%
Other negative (e.g. TV, single parenthood, complex society, consumer culture)	4%

4. There are many different aspects to the *full development* of a child. How important do you consider each of the following to be in your child's development:
   a) Learning to make moral judgements:
Top priority	52%
Very important	39%
Somewhat important	7%
Not very important	0%
   b) Learning to read and write:
Top priority	78%
Very important	17%
Somewhat important	3%
Not very important	0%
   c) Learning to be an imaginative and expressive individual:
Top priority	43%
Very important	39%
Somewhat important	15%
Not very important	3%
   d) Learning to get along with other children:
Top priority	51%
Very important	41%
Somewhat important	7%
Not very important	0%
   e) Learning to fit in with society:
Top priority	44%

Very important	38%
Somewhat important	13%
Not very important	3%

Questions about Toys

5. Do you buy your children toys as presents?

Sometimes	57%
Often	22%
Rarely	18%
Never	3%

6. Children have too many toys these days:

Agree	52%
Strongly agree	27%
Disagree	17%
Strongly disagree	0%

7. When you give presents to your children which types of presents do you like to give?

   a) Toys:

Sometimes	57%
Often	25%
Rarely	15%
Never	2%

   b) Clothes:

Sometimes	54%
Often	25%
Rarely	17%
Never	4%

   c) Books:

Often	42%
Sometimes	41%
Rarely	13%
Never	3%

   d) Games:

Sometimes	47%
Often	24%
Rarely	22%
Never	5%

8. Do you feel that if your children do not have popular toys they will experience difficulties in playing with other children?
   Will have:

Some difficulties	35%
No difficulties	32%
Few difficulties	25%
Many difficulties	5%

9. Do your children have any toys that you would regard as war toys?

None	43%
Some	27%
Few	25%
Many	4%

   a) If yes, have you ever bought these toys for your children?

Yes	41%
No	22%

   b) Do you agree with those people who say that children who play with war toys show *more aggressive behaviour* when they play with other children?

Agree	43%
Disagree	32%
Strongly agree	12%
Strongly disagree	3%

10. Would you agree with those who say that there are some toys that boys should play with, and some toys that girls should play with?

Agree	42%
Disagree	32%
Strongly disagree	10%
Strongly agree	3%

    a) Do you ever notice that your children ask for or play with toys that seem more suitable for the opposite sex?

Never	33%
Sometimes	32%
Rarely	32%
Often	0%

b) If yes, do you worry about this?

Not at all	47%
A little	8%
Sometimes	1%

c) Why do you worry about the fact that you notice your own children playing with or asking for toys that seem more suitable for the opposite sex?

Other (e.g. doesn't occur enough to be concerned, matter of degree)	9%
Gender confusion/peer problem	4%
They're only toys/harmless	3%

11. Do you have any concerns about the way your children play with modern toys? What are they?

No response	70%
Other (e.g. confuse reality, not durable, good v. bad)	12%
Tendency to fight/argue with toys/be violent	8%
We don't have these toys	4%
Toys are poor role models/ exaggerated/silly	2%
Kids saturated with character toys/too many toys	1%
Toys are fads	1%

12. Some of the new toys imitate characters that are not very realistic. Can you name any of these?

Don't know/not sure	13%
Other (e.g. Sesame Street, ET):	13%
Transformers	11%
He-Man	9%
Alf	4%
Cabbage Patch Kids	3%
She-Ra	3%
Smurfs	3%
Thundercats	3%
Wrestlers	3%
Robot toys	3%
G.I. Joe	2%
Real Ghostbusters	2%

13. Some of the new toys resemble robots, machines and computer-like toys.

    a) Can you name any of these toys?

Transformers	32%
Don't know/not sure	28%
Most toys	8%
Other (e.g. Masters of the Universe, Jayce and the Wheeled Warriors)	6%
Star Wars	4%
No response	4%
Robot toys	4%
Computer/video games/toys	3%
Thundercats	2%
He-Man	1%
Teddy Ruxpin	1%

    b) Do you think these toys help your child to *prepare for life* in a high-tech society?

A little	29%
Not at all	28%
Somewhat	22%
A lot	4%

    c) In what ways do you think these toys help prepare your child for life in a high-tech society?

No response	40%
Socializes/familiarizes children with machines/high-tech/computers	27%
Don't know/not sure	12%
Develops mechanical skills	6%
Doesn't prepare for life	3%
Educational	3%
Other (e.g. life training, not educational)	3%
Encourages imagination	2%
Illustrates adult roles	2%

14. Do you play with any toys with your children?

Sometimes	62%
Often	21%
Rarely	12%
Never	3%

15. What toys do you and your children play with together?
    Other (e.g. race cars/train sets,
        cops/robbers, bicycles)   14%
    No response   11%
    Board games/cards   10%
    Computer/electronic games   7%
    Air Raiders   6%
    Construction toys   4%
    Arts and crafts   4%
    Puzzles   4%
    Sports   4%
    Transformers   4%

Questions about Television

16. Would you say your children watch television?
    Sometimes   44%
    Often   38%
    Rarely   15%
    Never   1%

17. How many hours a day do your children watch television?
    3 hours   32%
    4 hours   22%
    2 hours   20%
    5 hours   7%

18. Do you know what kind of shows your children are watching?
    Know most   50%
    Know some   40%
    Know very few   5%

19. Do you watch television with your children?
    Sometimes   65%
    A lot of the time   17%
    Rarely   13%
    Never   2%
    a) How many hours a week do you watch TV with your children?
    5 hours   15%
    6 hours   13%

4 hours	9%
8 hours	7%
2 hours	7%
3 hours	6%
10 hours	6%
11 hours	6%
7 hours	6%
no response	6%
9 hours	5%
Don't know/not sure	4%

b) Do you encourage your children to watch particular shows?

Yes	65%
No	33%

c) Do you prevent your children from watching any particular shows?

Yes	54%
No	43%

d) What types of shows do you encourage them to watch?

No response	35%
Educational	15%
Sesame Street	10%
Children's shows	6%
Situation comedy	6%
Other (e.g. Kids' World, TV Ontario, Mr Dressup)	28%

e) Which specific shows or kinds of shows do you prevent your children from watching?

No response	44%
Adult theme	12%
Violent	11%
Sexually explicit	6%
Other	5%
Crime drama	4%
Horror thriller	3%

20. Some recent television programmes have character toys which you can also buy in stores. What are some names of character toys associated with recent television programmes?

No response	15%

Character toys:

He-Man	7%
Jem	6%
ALF	5%
G.I. Joe	2%
Care Bears	2%

Programme titles:

Transformers	17%
Sesame Street	6%
Smurfs	4%
Pound Puppies	3%
Real Ghostbusters	3%
Thundercats	3%
Jem	2%
My Little Pony	2%

a) Does your child watch any of these programmes?

Sometimes	50%
Often	25%
Rarely	9%
Never	6%

b) Does your child ask for any of these toys?

Sometimes	46%
Often	18%
Never	13%
Rarely	12%

c) If your child has any of these toys, do you have any concerns about them?

No	62%
Yes	21%

d) If your child has one of these toys, what are your concerns, if any, regarding them?

No response	78%
Expense	4%
Toys cause rougher, more aggressive play/fighting	3%
Other (e.g. violent imagery, too many 'accessories')	3%
Not creative	2%

21. Do you have any concerns about the quality of children's
    television programmes?

    No   53%
    Yes   45%

    a) What are your concerns regarding the quality of children's
       television programmes?

    No response   46%
    Other (e.g. gender stereotyped, too
        much sex, shows designed to sell
        toys, adult-orientated)   12%
    Too violent/too many war themes   11%
    Lack of educational shows   7%
    There are many good children's
        programmes   5%
    Poor animation/music/plot   4%
    Characters/shows too unrealistic   3%

22. One concern about children's television programmes is that they
    mix up and confuse fantasy and reality, and then *children* have
    trouble telling the difference.

    a) Thinking about modern cartoon programmes do you
       think . . .

    Too much   32%
    Would be happy. . .   1%
    Indifferent/some good/some bad   3%
    No variety   3%

    b) Do children's television programmes cause children to have
       difficulty telling the difference between fantasy and reality?

    No response   54%
    Other (e.g. child gets confused,
        good/evil overemphasized)   14%
    Don't know: 6%
    Yes, never show true picture of the real
        world   6%
    Children easily distinguish difference   4%
    Only a problem for the young   4%
    No   3%
    Parent's job to explain difference   3%
    Yes, children become obsessed with
        war shows and violence   3%

23. Would you say that you are concerned about the amount of violence on children's television shows?

Somewhat concerned	37%
Not very concerned	32%
Very concerned	16%
Not concerned at all	8%

a) What programmes would you single out for concern, in terms of the amount of violence on children's television?

No response	45%
Don't know	6%
Cartoons	6%
Crime drama	4%
Shows:	
G.I. Joe	9%
Transformers	6%
Rambo	6%
He-Man	3%
Inhumanoids	3%

24. Do you think the *government* should influence television programming for children?

Somewhat	48%
To a large extent	29%
A little	15%
Not at all	5%

a) How should the government influence television?

No response	39%
Don't know	13%
Produce children's programmes more/better/quality	13%
Regulate children's TV/set guideline standards	10%
Other (e.g. input but not govern, opinion polls on subject	11%
Restrict violence/conflict on children's TV	7%
Fund quality children's programmes	4%
Monitor/ongoing review of commercial television	3%

25. Do you think *parents* should influence television programming for children?

Somewhat	48%
To a large extent	29%
A little	15%
Not at all	5%

   a) How should parents influence television viewing for children?

Guide/monitor viewing	24%
Restrict viewing	23%
No response	11%
Write to broadcasters/government/ sponsors	10%
Other (e.g. boycott sponsors)	8%
Create/join lobby groups	7%
Don't know	7%
Watch with child	4%

26. Do you have any concerns about *advertising* either directed at children or shown on children's television?

Yes	69%
No	29%

   a) What are your concerns about advertising directed at children or shown on children's television?

No response	30%
Too much advertising to children	14%
Children are manipulated/vulnerable	14%
Ads pressure children to be materialist/consumers	9%
Other (e.g. over-priced toys, toy tie-in shows)	8%

Ads force parents to say no to many
   unhealthy products advertised
   (junk food)
	6%

Product glamorized/distorted by ads	5%
Children's wants	3%
Ads create false wants	3%
Don't know	3%

27. Do you agree that toy-advertising directed at children makes it more difficult for parents to 'instruct their children in the way that they should go'?

Agree	54%
Disagree	23%
Strongly agree	11%
Strongly disagree	3%

Content Analysis of Toy Advertisements

Data for content study of 150 toy ads expressed as percentage of each type of product advertisement which includes behaviour code.

Behaviour Code	Character Toys	Other Toys
Verbal References to Play:		
imagine/pretend	34	20
power to build/control/master	6	29
Voice-Over:		
describes play	14	29
product info	38	21
Parents in Play:	0	9
Play Activities Involve:*		
laughing	0	10
talking	30	20
manipulating toy	24	8
competing	4	12
fighting	10	2
building	6	15
Play Elements:		
care for toy	20	9
skills/operate/assembly	8	23
role play	0	6
objects imitate real objects	0	17
games	0	13
narrative	16	0
manipulative/hold product	14	15

Play Sociality:

alone	14	23
two s/s	46	33
familial	6	15

Play Styles:*

functional	12	33
skills/construction	4	21
sensory	18	9
role-taking	26	45
fantasy play	92	32
game play	0	15

Imaginative style:*

Interactive	10	11
Enactive	32	8
Relational Enactive	24	11
Appendage	4	8

*indicates multiple coding option was used

Thematic Bibliography

1 Media

1.1 *General Studies and Surveys*

Himmelweit, Hilde, B. Swift, M.J. Biberian. 1977. *The Audience as Critic: An Approach to the Study of Entertainment.* London: London School of Economics.

Innis, Harold Adams. 1964, *The Bias of Communication.* Toronto: University of Toronto Press.

Mander, Jerry. 1978. *Four Arguments for the Elimination of Television.* New York: William Morrow.

McDonald, Dwight. 1957. 'A Theory of Mass Culture', in Bernard Rosenberg and David White, eds, *Mass Culture, The Popular Arts in America.* New York: Free Press, pp. 59–73.

McLuhan, Marshall. 1962. *The Gutenberg Galaxy.* London: Routledge & Kegan Paul.

Mendelsohn, Harold. 1966. *Mass Entertainment.* New Haven: College and University Press.

Meyrowitz, Joshua. 1985. 'Where Have We Been, Where Are We Going?'. In *No Sense of Place: The Impact of Electronic Media on Social Behaviour.* New York: Oxford University Press, pp. 301–29.

Rosenberg, Bernard and David Manning White, eds. 1957. *Mass Culture: The Popular Arts in America.* New York: Free Press.

Rosenberg, Bernard. 1957. 'Mass Culture in America', in Bernard Rosenberg and David Manning White, eds, *Mass Culture: The Popular Arts in America.* New York: Free Press.

Schiller, Herbert. 1973. *The Mind Managers: How the Master Puppeteers of Politics, Advertising and Mass Communication Pull the Strings of Public Opinion.* Boston: Beacon Press.

Seldes, Gilbert. 1957. 'The People and the Arts', in Bernard Rosenberg and

David White, eds, *Mass Culture, The Popular Arts in America*. New York: Free Press, pp. 74–96.

Skornia, Harry. 1965. *Television and Society: An Inquest and Agenda for Improvement*. New York: McGraw-Hill.

Smythe, Dallas. 1977. 'Communications: Blindspot of Western Marxism'. *Can. J. of Political and Social Theory*, vol. 1 (3), pp. 1–27

Williams, Frederick. 1983. *The Communication's Revolution*. New York: Mentor.

Williams, Raymond. (1962) 1980. 'Advertising: The Magic System'. *Problems in Materialism and Culture*. London: New Left Books.

Williams, Raymond. 1974. *TV: Technology and Cultural Form*. London: Fontana.

Williams, Raymond. 1974. 'Communications as Cultural Science'. *Journal of Communication*, summer, pp. 17–21.

Williams, Raymond. 1961. *The Long Revolution*. New York: Columbia University Press.

1.2 *Studies of Television and Learning*

Anderson, Daniel and Patricia Collins. 1988. *The Impact on Children's Education: Television's Impact on Cognitive Development*, Working Paper 2. Washington: US Dept of Education.

Collins, W. André. 1979. 'Children's Comprehension of Television Content', pp. 21–52 in Ellen Wartella, ed., *Children Communicating: Media and Development of Thought, Speech, Understanding*. Beverly Hills: Sage Publications.

Comstock, George, S. Chaffee, N. Katzman, M. McCombs and D. Roberts. 1978. *Television and Human Behaviour*. New York: Columbia University Press.

Gavriel, Salomon. 1979. 'Shape, Not Only Content: How Media Symbols Partake in the Development of Abilities', pp. 53–82 in Ellen Wartella, ed., *Children Communicating: Media and Development of Thought, Speech, Understanding*. Beverly Hills: Sage Publications.

Singer, J. and D. Singer. 1983. 'Implications of Childhood Television Viewing for Cognition, Imagination, and Emotion', pp. 265–95 in J. Bryant and D. Anderson, eds, *Children's Understanding of Television, Research on Attention and Comprehension*. New York: Academic Press.

Singer, Jerome, Dorothy Singer and Wanda Rapaczynski. 1984. 'Family Patterns and Television Viewing as Predictors of Children's Beliefs and Aggression'. *Journal of Communication*, vol. 34, pp. 3–21.

1.3 *Television and Socialization*

Bantman, Beatrice. 1989. 'Children's TV Survey Is a Real Eye-Opener'. *Manchester Guardian Weekly,* 13 August, p. 15.

Barcus, Dr. F. Earle. 1975. *Television in the Afternoon Hours.* Newtonville, Mass.: Action for Children's Television.

BBM Survey (television). 1985. *U.S. Television viewing in Canada,* fall.

Brown, Ray, ed. 1976. *Children and Television.* Beverly Hills: Sage Publications.

Burton, Sydney, James Calonico and Dennes McSeveney. 1979. 'Effects of Preschool Television Watching on First-Grade Children'. *Journal of Communication,* summer, pp. 164–70.

'Children and Media Conference Focuses on TV'. 1985. *Broadcasting,* 13 May, p. 98.

Collins, Andrew. 1983. *Children's Understanding of Television.* New York: Academic Press.

Cullingford, Cedric. 1984. *Children and Television.* Aldershot: Gower.

Dunphy, Cathy. 1989. '10 Steps to Better Family TV Viewing'. *Toronto Star,* 28 April.

Gardner, Howard, with Leona Jaglom. 1981. 'Decoding the Worlds of Television'. *Studies in Visual Communication,* vol. 7 (1), pp. 133–47.

Gardner, Howard. 'Cracking the Codes of Television: The Child as Anthropologist'. *Transmission,* pp. 93–102.

Glennon, Lynda M. and Richard Butsch. 1983. 'Social Class: Frequency Trends in Domestic Situation Comedy 1946–1978'. *Journal of Broadcasting,* vol. 27 (1), pp. 77–81.

Goldberg, M. and J. Gorn. 1979. 'Television's Impact on Preferences for Non-White Playmates: Canadian "Sesame Street" Inserts'. *Journal of Broadcasting,* vol. 23 (1), pp. 27–32.

Greenberg, Bradley S. and Byron Reeves. 1976. 'Children and the Perceived Reality of Television'. *The Journal of Social Issues,* vol. 32 (4), pp. 86–97.

Greenberg, Bradley. 1982. 'Television and Role Socialization: An Overview', pp. 179 in Pearl, D. et al., *Television and Behaviour: 10 Years of Scientific Progress and Implications for the Eighties,* vol. 2, *Technical Reviews.* National Institute of Mental Health, Washington: US Government Printing Office.

Hawkins, Robert and Suzanne Pingree. 1982. 'Television's Influence on Social Reality', pp. 224 in *Technical Reports from Violence and TV,* in Pearl, D. et al., *Television and Behaviour: 10 Years of Scientific progress and Implications for the Eighties,* vol. 2, *Technical Reviews.* National Institute of Mental Health, Washington: US Government Printing Office.

Himmelweit, Hilde T. 1958. *Television and Children: An Empirical Study of the Effect of Television on the Young.* London: Oxford University Press.

Himmelweit, Hilde T. 1977. *Yesterday's and Tomorrow's Television Research on Children.* London: London School of Economics.

Lindlof, Thomas, Milton Shatzer and Daniel Wilkinson. 1988. 'Accommodation of Video and Television in the American Family'. pp. 158–92 in James Lull, ed., *World Families Watch Television*. Newbury Park: Sage.

Lonial, Subhash C. and Stuart Van Auken. 1986. 'Wishful Identification with Fictional Characters: An Assessment of the Implications of Gender in Message Dissemination to Children'. *Journal of Advertising*, vol. 15 (4), p. 4.

Lyle, J., and H.R. Hoffman. 1972. 'Children's Use of Television and Other Media', in E.A. Rubinstein, G.A. Comstock and J.P. Murray, eds, *Television and Social Behaviour*, vol. 4, *Television in Day-to-Day Patterns of Use*. Washington DC: US Government Printing Office.

Maccoby, Eleanor. 1954. 'Why Do Children Watch Television?'. *Public Opinion Quarterly*, vol. 8 (3).

Marchetti, Gina. 1988. 'Action-Adventure as Ideology, pp. 182–97 in Ian Angus and Sut Jhally, eds, *Cultural Politics in Contemporary America*. New York: Routledge.

Medrich, Elliott A. 1989. 'Constant Television: A Background to Daily Life'. *Journal of Communication*, summer, pp. 171–6.

Melody, William. 1973. *Children's Television: The Economics of Exploitation*. New Haven: Yale University Press.

Melody, William and W. Ehrlich. 1974. 'Children's TV commercials: The Vanishing Policy Options. *Journal of Communication* 24: pp. 113–25.

Miller, M. Mark and Byron Reeves. 1978. 'A Multidimensional Measure of Children's Identification with Television Characters'. *Journal of Broadcasting*, vol. 22 (1), pp. 71–86.

Morley, David. 1988. 'Domestic Relations: The Framework of Family Viewing in Great Britain', pp. 22–48 in James Lull, ed., *World Families Watch Television*. Newbury Park: Sage.

Ordovensky, P. 1989. 'Parents Must Restrict TV, Aid Studying'. *USA Today*, 24–26 February.

Quanforth, Joanne. M. 1979. 'Children's Understanding of the Nature of Television Characters'. *Journal of Communication*, vol. 29 (1), pp. 210–18.

Reeves, Byron. 1979. 'Children's Understanding of Television People', pp. 115–56 in Ellen Wartella, ed., *Children Communicating: Media and Development of Thought, Speech, Understanding*. Beverly Hills: Sage Publications.

Reid, Leonard N. and Charles F. Frazer. 1980. 'Television and Play'. *Journal of Communication*, vol. 30 (4), pp. 66–73.

Roberts, Elizabeth J. 1982. 'Children's Sexual Learning: An Examination of the Influence of Parents, Television and Community Service Providers'. *Dissertation Abstracts International*, vol. 43 (5-A), pp. 1400–01.

Rosenblatt, Paul C. and Michael R. Cunningham. 1976. 'Television Watching and Family Tensions'. *Journal of Marriage and the Family*, February, pp. 105–11.

Schramm, Wilbur Lang. 1961. *Television in the Lives of our Children*. Stanford:

Stanford University Press.

Taragan, Robert J. 1986. 'Trends in Children's TV Viewing Behaviour'. Paper presented to Advertising Research Foundation (Children's Research Workshop, New York Hilton), 28 April.

Wartella, Ellen and Byron Reeves. 1985. 'Historical Trends in Research on Children and the Media: 1900–1960'. *Journal of Communication*, spring, pp. 6–21.

Waters, Harry F. 1990. 'Watch What Kids Watch'. *Newsweek*, 8 January, pp. 51–2.

Williams, Tannis MacBeth. 1986. *Impact of Television: A Natural Experiment in Three Communities*. Orlando: Academic Press.

1.4 *Television Industry*

Associated Press. 1990. 'Disney Drops out of Hour Long Drama. Shows Too Costly to Produce, Studio Executives Conclude'. *Vancouver Sun*, 22 September, p. B13.

BBM Bureau of Measurement. 1984, 1986 and 1987. *Television Statistics for Toronto*. Toronto: Bureau of Broadcast Measurement.

'Board games: New License Vehicle'. 1985. *Chain Store Age (General Merchandising Trends)*, February, pp. 145–8.

Boden, Ann. 1991. 'TV Gives Best Access to Junior Marketplace'. *Marketing*, p. 17.

Bogart, Leo. 1958. *The Age of Television*. New York: Unger Publishing.

Boyer, P. 1988. 'NBC Considers Risk of Killing Saturday Morning Cartoons'. *The Globe and Mail*, 20 September, p. A23.

'CBS Moves to Divert Advertising Money Going to Animation'. 1986. *Broadcasting*, 17 February.

CRTC. 1977. *CBC Television: Programming and Audiences: The English Language Service*. Ottawa.

Englehardt, T. 1986. 'The Strawberry Shortcake Strategy', pp. 68–110 in T. Gitlin, ed., *Watching Television*. New York: Pantheon Books.

'Film Animation Making Forays into TV'. 1987. *The Globe and Mail*, 8 January, p. B15.

Hanna Barbera Productions Inc. *News: History of Hanna Barbera Productions*. Hollywood, California.

Kastner, Susan. 1987. 'Lovable Little Smurfs Have a Hidden Darker Side When They're Crossed'. *Starweek*, 18 July.

Lowry, B. 1987. 'Tie-ins: Raising the Bottom Line in Kidvid'. *Hollywood Reporter*, 2 June.

McCollum/Spielman Topline Report, vol. 2 (2) 1983. New York.

McCollum-Spielman Topline Report. 1985. 'Star Power 2: Understanding Kids and their Stars'. *Topline*, vol. 4 (2).

McGill, Douglas, C. 1989. 'They haven't even started on Huey, Dewey and

Louie'. *The Globe and Mail*, 26 May, p. C3.

Mediaweek. 1991. 'Daylight Spending Time', 15 April, pp. 30–31.

Miller, Mark Crispin, 'Hollywood: The Ad'. *Atlantic Monthly*, April 1990, pp. 41–68.

'More Animation from Telepictures'. 1985. *Broadcasting*, 7 October, pp. 44–6.

'New Kids in the Animation Blocks'. 1985. *Broadcasting*, 4 November, pp. 44–5.

Palmer, Edward. 1988. *Television and America's Children: A Crisis of Neglect*. New York: Oxford University Press.

Projecting the Size of the U.S. Licensing Industry in 1985: A Methodological Study and Benchmark. 1986. Study prepared for the Licensing Industry Merchandisers' Association, summer.

Playthings. 1991. 'Viewpoints: How Will the New Regulations Governing Children's Television Affect Toy Advertising?', January, p. 52.

'Robots from TV'. 1987. *Fortune*, 2 February, pp. 8–9.

Schneider, Cy. 1987. *Children's Television: The Art, the Business and How it Works*. Lincolnwood, Illinois: NTC Business Books.

Shiver, Jube. 1986. 'Child's Play'. *Black Enterprise*, August, pp. 31–4.

Special Issue: Licensing and Merchandising (including focus on Product Placement). 1987. *The Hollywood Reporter*, 2 June.

'Two Faces of Kids' Television'. 1987. *Broadcast Week*, 28 November, pp. 8–9.

1.5 *Semiotics, Content Analysis, Studies of Programming*

Anderson, Celia. 1974. 'The Saturday Morning Survival Kit'. *Journal of Popular Culture*, spring, pp. 155–64.

'Advertising and Marketing: CBS Moves to Divert Advertising Money Going to Animation'. 1986. *Broadcasting*, 17 February.

Barcus, F. Earle. 1977. *Children's Television: An Analysis of Programming and Advertising*. New York: Praegar.

Fischer, Stuart. 1983. *Kid's TV: The First 25 Years*. Faction File Publications.

Grossman, Gary. 1981. *Saturday Morning TV*. New York: Dell.

Henry III, William A. 1989. 'The Big Turnoff, The Rise and Fall of Network Television'. *Lears*, November, pp. 97–108, 164.

Hill, Dave. 1989. 'Angry Young Defenders of the Faith'. *Independent*, 8 July, p. 29.

Hodge, Robert and David Tripp. 1988. *Children and Television: A Semiotic Approach*. New York: Polity Press.

Mayes, Sandra and K.B. Valentine. 1979. 'Sex Role Stereotyping in Saturday Morning Cartoon Shows'. *Journal of Broadcasting*, vol. 23 (1).

O'Connor, John J. 1990. 'Hidden Dangers Seen in 'Toon Time'. *Vancouver Sun*, 3 March, p. E1.

'Research Tunes in to Kids' TV'. 1988. *The Globe and Mail*, 12 December.

Rense, Rip. 1990. 'Groening's Odyssey (Simpsons)'. *The Vancouver Sun*, 3 March, pp. E1, E6.

Siegel, Mark. 1985. 'Foreigner as Alien in Japanese Science Fantasy'. *Science Fiction Studies*, vol. 12, pp. 252–63.

1.6 *Television and Aggression*

Bandura, Albert. 1978. 'Social Learning Theory of Aggression'. *Journal of Communication*, vol. 28 (3), pp. 12–28.

Collins, W. Andrew, B.L. Sobol and S. Westby. 1981. 'Effects of Adult Commentary on Children's Comprehension and Inferences about a Televised Aggressive Portrayal'. *Child Development*, vol. 52, pp. 158–73.

Drabman, Ronald S. and Margaret Hanratty Thomas. 1977. 'Effects of Television/Children's Imitation of Aggressive and Prosocial Behavior When Viewing Alone and in Pairs'. *Journal of Communication*, summer, pp. 199–205.

Etaugh, Claire and A. Happach. 1979. 'Effect of Aggressive Play on Children's Subsequent Aggressive Behavior'. *Psychological Report*, vol. 45, pp. 656–8.

Haynes, Richard B. 1978. 'Children's Perceptions of "Comic" and "Authentic" Cartoon Violence'. *Journal of Broadcasting*, vol. 22 (1), pp. 63–70.

Huston-Stein, Aletha and John C. Wright. 1979. 'Children and Television: Effects of the Medium, its Content and its Form'. *Journal of Research and Development in Education*, vol. 13 (1) pp. 19–31.

Lometti, Guy and Alan Wurtzel. 1984. 'Researching Television Violence'. *Society* (Television at the Crossroads: Education and Violence), vol. 21 (6), pp. 22–8.

Meringoff, Laurence. 1980. 'Influence of the Medium on Children's Story Apprehension'. *Journal of Educational Psychology*, vol. 72 (2) pp. 240–49.

National Coalition on Television Violence. 1988. 'Bestseller Books Issue', vol. 9 (5).

Pearl, D., L. Bouthilet and J. Lazar, eds. 1982. *Television and Behaviour: Ten Years of Scientific Progress and Implications for the Eighties*, vol. 2, *Technical Reviews*. National Institute of Mental Health, Washington: US Government Printing Office.

Pearl, David. 1984. 'Violence and Aggression'. *Society*, vol. 21 (6), pp. 17–22.

Potts, Richard, Aletha Juston and John Wright. 1986. 'The Effects of Television Form and Violent Content on Boys' Attention and Social Behavior'. *Journal of Experimental Child Psychology*, vol. 41, pp. 1–17.

Signorielli, Nancy, Larry Gross and Michael Morgan. 1982. 'Violence in Television Programs: Ten Years Later', pp. 158–73 in Pearl, D. et al., eds, *Television and Behaviour: Ten Years of Scientific Progress and Implications for the Eighties*, vol. 2, *Technical Reviews*. National Institute of Mental Health, Washington: US Government Printing Office.

Singer, Jerome L. and Dorothy G. Singer. 1981. *Television, Imagination, and Aggression: A study of Preschoolers.* New Jersey: LEA Publishing.

Van der Voort, T.H.A. 1986. *Television Violence: A Child's Eye View.* Amsterdam: North Holland.

Wakshlag, Jacob J., L. Bart, J. Dudley, G. Groth, J. McCutcheon and C. Rolla. 1983. 'Viewer Apprehension about Victimization and Crime Drama Programs'. *Communication Research*, vol. 10 (2), pp. 195–217.

1.7 *Television and Society*

Bower, Robert. 1985. *The Changing Television Audience in America.* New York: Columbia University Press.

'Captain Power'. 1988. *Cave News*, vol. 6 (1).

Comstock, G. 1980. *Television in America.* Beverley Hills: Sage.

Comstock, George. 1982. 'Television and American Social Institutions', in Pearl. D., L. Bouthilet, and J. Lazar, eds, *Television and Behaviour: Ten Years of Scientific Progress and Implications for the Eighties*, vol. 2, *Technical Reviews.* National Institute of Mental Health, Washington: US Government Printing Office.

CRTC. 1986. *Role Stereotyping in the Broadcast Media: A Report on Industry Self-Regulation.* Ottawa.

Kunkel, Dale. 1990. 'Child and Family Television Regulatory Policy', in J. Bryant, ed., *Television and the American Family.* Hillsdale, New Jersey: Lawrence Erlbaum.

Kunkel, Dale. 1988. 'From a Raised Eyebrow to a Turned Back: The FCC and Children's Product-Related Programming'. *Journal of Communication*, vol. 38 (4), pp. 90–108.

Lull, James. 1980. 'The Social Uses of Television'. *Human Communication*, vol. 6 (3), pp. 197–209.

'Magazine Explores Television Values'. 1988. *Cave News*, vol. 6 (1).

Postman, Neil. 1985. *Amusing Ourselves to Death: Public Discourse in the Age of Show Business.* New York: Viking Penguin.

Ruston, Phillipe. 1982. 'Television and Pro-Social Behaviour', pp. 248 in Pearl. D. et al., *Television and Behaviour: Ten Years of Scientific Progress and implications for the Eighties*, vol. 2, *Technical Reviews.* National Institute of Mental Health, Washington: US Government Printing Office.

'Satellites: Shoot 'em Sky High, Sell 'em Cheap'. 1988. *Guardian*, November, p. 18.

Steiner, G. 1963. *The People Look at Television.* New York: Knopf.

Winn, Marie. 1977. *The Plug-In Drug.* New York: Penguin.

2 Childhood: Play, Toys and Culture

2.1 *Studies of Socialization in General*

Adams, Paul. 1972. 'The Infant, the Family and Society', pp. 51–90 in Adams, Paul, Leila Berg, Nan Berger, Michael Duane, A.S. Neil and Robert Ollendorff. 1971. *Children's Rights: Towards the Liberation of the Child.* Wellingborough: Elek Books.

Ariès, Philippe. 1962. *Centuries of Childhood: A Social History of Family Life.* New York: Alfred Knopf.

Cayley, David. 1986. *The World of the Child.* CBC Ideas Radio.

DeMause, L. 1974. 'The Evolution of Childhood', in L. DeMause, ed., *The History of Childhood.* New York: Harper Torchbooks.

Engel, Brenda. 1984. 'Between Feeling and Fact: Listening to Children'. *Harvard Educational Review,* vol. 54(3), pp. 304–13.

Erikson, Erik H. 1963. *Childhood and Society.* New York: W.W. Norton.

Feshback, Norma D. and Kiki Roe. 1968. 'Empathy in Six and Seven Year Olds'. *Child Development,* vol. 39(1), pp. 133–46.

Fortino, Michael. 1988. BBC Radio 4, broadcast 23 June.

Furth, Hans G. 1980. *The World of Grown-ups: Children's Conceptions of Society.* New York: Elsevier.

Helper, Malcolm M. and Mary Jean Quinlivan. 1973. 'Age and Reinforcement Value of Sex Role Labels in Girls'. *Developmental Psychology,* vol. 8(1), p. 142.

Holt, John. 1967. *How Children Learn.* Harmondsworth: Penguin.

Illick, Joseph E. 1975. Child-Rearing in Seventeenth Century England and America, pp. 303–50 in L. DeMause, ed., *The History of Childhood.* New York: Harper Torchbooks.

Isaacs, Susan. 1963. *Intellectual Growth in Young Children.* London: Routledge & Kegan Paul.

Isaacs, Susan. 1964. *Social Development in Young Children: A Study of Beginnings.* London: Routledge & Kegan Paul.

Jordan, Thomas E. 1987. *Victorian Childhood: Themes and Variations.* Albany: State University of New York Press.

Locke, John. 1773. *Some Thoughts Concerning Education.* 14th edition. London: J. Whiston et. al publishers (reprint).

Maital. S. 1982. 'From Pleasure to Reality: Learning to Wait Begins in Childhood', in *Minds, Markets and Money.* New York: Basic Books.

Pollock, Linda A. 1983. *Forgotten Children: Parent–Child Relations from 1500 to 1900.* New York: Cambridge University Press.

Postman, Neil. 1982. *The Disappearance of Childhood.* New York: Dell Publishing.

Rheingold H. and K.V. Cook. 1975. 'The Content of Boys' and Girls' Rooms as an Index of Parents' Behavior'. *Child Development,* vol. 46, pp. 459–63.

The Gene Reilly Group. 1973. *The Child.* Darien, T: The Gene Reilly Group

Incorporated, vols. 1,2,3,4, December.

Spock, Benjamin. [1946] 1979. *Baby and Child Care.* New York: Pocket Books.

Smith, Vivian. 1990. 'Laissez-faire Parenting Concerns Psychologists'. *Globe and Mail,* 8 May, pp. 1, 9.

Sutton-Smith, Brian and May Ann Magee. 1989. 'Reversible Childhood'. *Play and Culture,* vol. 2 (1), pp. 52–63.

Tucker, M.J. 1974. 'The Child as Beginning and End: Fifteenth and Sixteenth Century English Childhood', pp. 229–58 in Lloyd deMause, ed., *The History of Childhood.* New York: Harper.

White, Burton L. 1975. *The First Three Years of Life.* New York: Prentice-Hall.

Winnicott, D.W. 1969. *The Child, the Family and the Outside World.* Harmondsworth: Penguin.

2.2 *Play and/in Learning or Education*

Bettelheim, Bruno. 1987. 'The Importance of Play', *Atlantic Monthly,* March, pp. 35–43.

Bruner, J.S. and V. Sherwood. 1975. 'Peekaboo and the Learning of Rule Structures', in J.S. Bruner, A. Jolly and K. Sylva. 1976. *Play: Its Role in Development and Evolution.* Harmondsworth: Penguin.

Carpenter, C. Jan. 1983. 'Activity Structure and Play: Implications for Socialization', in Marsha Liss, ed., *Social and Cognitive Skills: Sex Roles and Children's Play.* New York: Academic Press.

Erikson, Erik H. 1976. 'Play and Actuality', pp. 210–28 in J.S. Bruner, A. Jolly and K. Sylva, eds, *Play: Its Role in Development and Evolution.* Harmondsworth: Penguin.

Johnson, James E. and Joan Ershler. 1980. 'Developmental Trends in Preschool Play as a Function of Classroom Program and Child Gender'. *Child Development,* vol. 52, pp. 995–1004.

Knight, Jane. 1984. 'Television: Plague or Play Partner?' *I.P.A.,* vol. 8 (7), pp. 5–6.

Lancy, David F. and B. Allan Tindall, eds. 1977. *The Study of Play: Problems and Prospects: Proceedings of the First Annual Meeting of the Association for the Anthropological Study of Play (Detroit, 1975).* West Point, New York: Leisure Press.

Liss, Marsha B. 1983. 'Learning Gender-Related Skills through Play', in Marsha Liss, ed., *Social and Cognitive Skills: Sex Roles and Children's Play.* New York: Academic Press.

Manning, Kathleen and Ann Sharp. 1977. *Structuring Play at the Early Years at School.* London: Ward Lock.

Matterson, Elizabeth M. 1965. *Play with a Purpose for Under-Sevens.* Harmondsworth: Penguin.

Matthews and Matthews. 1982. 'Eliminating Operational Definitions: A Paradigm Case Approach to the Study of Fantasy Play', in Pepler, D.J. and

K.H. Rubin, eds, *The Play of Children: Current Theory and Research*, Basel/
New York: Krager.

Nicholich, Lorrain and Carol Bruskin. 1982. 'Combinatorial Competency in
Symbolic Play and Language-Importance for Language and Play', in
Pepler, D., and K. Rubin, eds, *The Play of Children: Current Theory and
Research*. Basel: S. Krager.

Norbeck, Edward. 1977. 'The Study of Play – Johan Huizinga and Modern
Anthropology', pp. 13–22 in David Lancy and B. Allan Tindall, eds, *The
Study of Play: Problems and Prospects*. New York: Leisure Press.

Pepler, D.J. and K.H. Rubin, eds. 1982. *The Play of Children: Current Theory and
Research*. Basel/New York: Krager.

Piaget, Jean. 1976 'Symbolic Play', in J.S. Bruner, A. Jolly and K. Sylva. eds,
Play: Its Role in Development and Evolution. Harmondsworth: Penguin.

Piaget, Jean. 1976. 'Mastery Play', in J.S. Bruner, A. Jolly and K. Sylva, eds,
Play: Its Role in Development and Evolution. Harmondsworth: Penguin.

Rubin, Kenneth, Terrence Maioni and Margaret Hornung. 1976. 'Free Play
Behaviors in Middle and Lower Class Preschoolers: Parten and Piaget
Revisited'. *Child Development*, vol. 47, pp. 414–19.

Rubin, K. 1982. 'Introduction' and 'Early Play Theories Revisited: Contributions to Contemporary Research and Theory', in Pepler, D. and K. Rubin,
eds, *The Play of Children: Current Theory and Research*. Basel New York:
Krager.

Smith, Peter and Ralph Vollstedt. 1985. 'On Defining Play: An Empirical
Study of the Relationship between Play and Various Play Criteria'. *Child
Development*, vol. 56, pp. 1042–50.

Smith, Peter K. and Kevin K. Connolly. 1980. *Ecology of Preschool Behaviour.*
Cambridge: Cambridge University Press.

Smith, Peter K. and Susan Dutton. 1979. 'Play and Training in Direct and
Innovative Problem Solving'. *Child Development*, vol. 50, pp. 830–6.

Sylva, K., J.S. Bruner and P. Genova. 1976. 'The Role of Play in the Problem-
Solving of Children 3–5 Years Old', in J.S. Bruner, A. Jolly and K. Sylva,
eds, *Play: Its Role in Development and Evolution*. Harmondsworth: Penguin.

Sylva, Kathy, Carolyn Roy and Marjorie Cants. 1984. *Childwatching at Play
Group and Nursery School.* London: Grant Macintyre.

Tizard, Barbara, J. Philips and I. Plewis. 1976. 'Play in Pre-School Centres –
The Effects on Play of the Child's Social Class and of the Educational
Orientation of the Centre'. *Child Psychology,* vol. 17, pp. 265–74.

Tizard, B., Janet Philips and Ian Plewis. 1976. 'Play in Pre-school Centres: I.
Play Measures and their Relation to Age, Sex and I.Q.'. *Journal of Child
Psychology & Psychiatry & Allied Disciplines*, vol. 17 (4), pp. 251–64.

Vandenburg. 1982. 'Play Is a Clown in the Realm of Psychological Phenomenon', p. 18 in Pepler, D. and K. Rubin, eds, *The Play of Children: Current
Theory and Research*. Basel: S. Krager.

Vygotsky, L.S. 1976. 'Play and its Role in the Mental Development of the
Child', in J.S. Bruner, A. Jolly and K. Sylva, eds, *Play: Its Role in Development*

and Evolution. Harmondsworth: Penguin.

2.3 *Toys: History, Industry, Production, Analysis of Toys*

Berry, Jon. 1990. 'Hello Dolly. An All-Time Favorite Makes a Comeback'. *Vancouver Sun,* 10 March, p. B9.

'Board Games: New License Vehicle'. 1985. *Chain Store Age,* February, pp. 145–8.

'Bumper Crop of Ethnic Kids'. 1985. *Chain Store Age,* January, pp. 106–9.

Chase, Richard. A. 1984. 'Research in the Toy Industry'. *Children's Environmental Quarterly,* vol. 1 (2), pp. 9–14.

'Dolls, Toys, Games, and Children's Vehicles'. 1987. *U.S. Industrial Outlook 1987 (Toys & Games).*

Dorman, Scott. 1987. 'Focus on Product Placement: Bridging Hollywood & the Corporate World'. *The Hollywood Reporter,* 2 June, p. S-15.

Ferri, John. 1987. 'Revolution in Toyland'. *The Sunday Star* (Toronto), 29 November, p. A16.

Fisher-Price Canada. 1987. *Fisher-Price Corporate History.* Mississauga, Ontario: Fisher-Price Canada.

Frank, Allan Dodds. 1987. 'Leisure and Recreation'. *Forbes,* 12 January, pp. 158–9.

Fraser, Antonia. 1966. *A History of Toys.* London: Weidenfeld & Nicolson.

Hasbro, Inc. Annual Report 1986. 1987. Hasbro Canada Inc., 12 August.

'History of the American International Toy Fair'. 1988. *Immediate Release: American International Toy Fair,* 8–17 February.

Information and Public Relations, LEGO System A/S. 1987. *Facts and Figures, Lego.* Denmark.

Lewis, Beatrice. 1984. 'Antique Toys: Vestiges of Childhoods Past'. *Children's Environments Quarterly,* vol. 1 (1), pp. 3–6.

Medley Pamphlets. 'Toys Are for Fun' and 'Cooperative Games FUN for Kids'.

National Statistics Program: Shipments 1985 vs. 1986. 1987. Toy Manufacturers of America, Inc., February.

'Radio-Control Toys Zooming'. 1987. *Chain Store Age,* April, p. 67.

Smith, Peter and Sue Bennett. 1990. 'Here Come the Steel Monsters!' *Changes,* vol. 8 (2), pp. 97–105.

Spinks, C.W. 1987. *Tools and Toys: Objects, Numbers, Signs.* Paper presented to the Assn for the Study of Play. Montreal, 25–28 March.

Statistics Canada. 1985. *Special Industry Survey of Selected Statistics of the Toy and Decorations Manufacturing Industry (as defined by CTMA).* Statistics Canada, November.

Sutton-Smith, Brian. 1984. 'A Toy Semiotics'. *Children's Environments Quarterly,* vol. 1 (1), pp. 19–21.

Sutton-Smith, B. 1986. *Toys as Culture.* New York: Gardner Press.

The Canadian Toy Manufacturers Association. 1979. *Mixing Business and Pleasure: An Outline of the Canadian Toy and Decoration Industry.*

The Toy Industry Fact Book. 1987 edition. Toy Manufacturers of America.

'Toy Industry Holds its Own with Stable Retail Sales Growth in 1986'. 1987. *Immediate Release: News from TMA*, 9 February.

'Toy Industry Enjoys Banner Year in 1984'. 1984. *Children's Environments Quarterly*, vol. 1 (3), pp. 63–4.

Whittle, Fran. 1985. 'British Toy and Hobby Fair: A Question of Images'. *IPA Newsletter*, vol. 9 (2), pp. 16–18.

2.4 *Social Play or Play at Home:*
Socio-linguistics of Play, Gender Roles and Learning, Play Interactions, Group Play, Toys and Consumerism

Balaban, Terry, Joel Cooper and Diane Ruble. 1981. 'Gender Constancy and the Effects of Sex-Typed Televised Toy Commercials'. *Child Development*, vol. 52, pp. 667–73.

Cummins, James Navita and Thomas McCain. 1982. 'Television Games Preschool Children Play: Patterns, Themes and Uses'. *Journal of Broadcasting*, vol. 26 (4), pp. 783–800.

Davie, C.E., S.J. Hutt, E. Vincent and M. Mason. 1984. *The Young Child at Home.* Windsor: NFER-Nelson.

Downs, Chris A. 1983. 'Letters to Santa Claus: Elementary School Age Children's Sex-Typed Toy Preferences in a Natural Setting'. *Sex Roles*, vol. 9 (2), pp. 159–63.

Eisenberg, Nancy, Sharlene Wochik, Robert Hernandez and Jeannette Pasternack. 1985. 'Parental Socialization of Young Children's Play'. *Child Development*, vol. 56, pp. 1506–13.

Eisenberg, Nancy. 1983. 'Sex-Typed Toy Choices: What Do They Signify?', in Marsha Liss, ed., *Social and Cognitive Skills: Sex Roles and Children's Play.* New York: Academic Press.

Fagot, Beverly I. and Mary Driver Leinbach. 1983. 'Play Styles in Early Childhood: Social Consequences for Boys and Girls', in Marsha Liss, ed., *Social and Cognitive skills: Sex Roles and Children's Play.* New York: Academic Press.

Furby, Lita and Mary Wilke. 1982. 'Some Characteristics of Infants' Preferred Toys'. *Journal of Genetic Psychology*, vol. 4 (2), pp. 207–19.

Furby, Lita. 1980. 'The Origins and Early Development of Possessive Behavior'. *Political Psychology*, vol. 2 (1), pp. 3–42.

Garvey, Catherine. 1977. *Play.* Cambridge, MA: Harvard University Press.

Garvey, Catherine. 1976. 'Some Properties of Social Play', in J.S. Bruner, A. Jolly and K. Sylva, eds, *Play: Its Role in Development and Evolution.* Harmondsworth: Penguin.

Greif, Asther Blank. 1976. 'Sex Role Playing in Pre-School Children', in J.S.

Bruner, A. Jolly and K. Sylva, eds, *Play: Its Role in Development and Evolution.* Harmondsworth: Penguin.

Hughes, Bob and Hank Williams. 1984. 'Looking at Play – A Biological Model'. *IPA*, vol. 8 (7), pp. 7–13.

Huizinga, Johan. 1976. *Play and Contest as Civilizing Functions*, in J.S. Bruner, A. Jolly and K. Sylva, eds, *Play: Its Role in Development and Evolution.* Harmondsworth: Penguin.

Huizinga, Johan. 1950. *Homo Ludens: A Study of the Play Element in Culture.* Boston: Beacon Press.

Hutt, Corinne. 1976. 'Exploration and Play in Children', in J.S. Bruner, A. Jolly and K. Sylva, eds, *Play: Its Role in Development and Evolution.* Harmondsworth: Penguin.

Karpoe, Delly and Rachel Olney. 1983. 'The Effect of Boys' or Girls' Toys on Sex-typed Play in Preadolescents'. *Sex Roles*, vol. 9 (4) pp. 507–18.

Lever, Janet. 1976. 'Sex Differences in the Games Children Play'. *Social Problems*, vol. 23, pp. 478–87.

Liss, Marsha B. 1981. 'Patterns of Toy Play: An Analysis of Sex Differences'. *Sex Roles*, vol. 7 (11), pp. 1143–50.

Liss, M., ed. 1983. *Social and Cognitive Skills: Sex Roles and Children's Play.* New York: Academic Press.

Liss, M.B. 1983. 'Learning Gender-Related Skills through Play', pp. 147–65 in Marsha B. Liss, ed., *Social and Cognitive Skills: Sex Roles and Children's Play.* New York: Academic Press.

Magee, Mary Ann. 1989. 'Social Play as Performance'. *Play and Culture*, vol. 2, pp. 193–6.

Moore, Nancy, C.M. Evertson and J.E. Brophy. 1974. ' "Solitary Play": Some Functional Reconsiderations'. *Developmental Psychology*, vol. 10 (6), pp. 830–4.

Paley, Vivian Gussin. 1984. *Boys & Girls: Superheroes in the Doll Corner.* Chicago: University of Chicago Press.

Prose, Francine. 1990. 'Girls: The Challenge to their Confidence'. *Toronto Star*, 16 Jan. 1990, pp. B1, B4.

Romatowski, Jane A. and Mary L. Trepanier. 1985. 'Attributes and Roles Assigned to Characters in Children's Writing: Sex Differences and Sex-Role Perceptions'. *Sex Roles*, vol. 13 (5/6), pp. 263–72.

Roopnarine, Jaipaul. 1986. 'Mothers' and Fathers' Behaviors Toward the Toy Play of their Infant Sons and Daughters'. *Sex Roles*, vol. 14 (1/2), pp. 59–68.

Schau, Candace, Lynne Kahn, John Diepold and Frances Cherry. 1980. 'The Relationships of Parental Expectations and Preschool Children's Verbal Sex Typing to their Sex-Typed Toy Play Behavior'. *Child Development*, vol. 51, pp. 266–70.

Schwartz, Lori and William T. Markham. 1985. 'Sex Stereotyping in Children's Toy Advertisements'. *Sex Roles*, vol. 12 (2) pp. 157–70.

Schwartzman, Helen B. 1979. *Transformations: The Anthropology of Children's*

Play. New York: Plenum Press.

Sprafkin, Carol, Lisa A. Serbin, Carol Denier and Jane M. Connor. 1983. 'Sex-Differentiated Play: Cognitive Consequences and Early Interventions', in Marsha Liss, ed., *Social Roles and Cognitive Skills: Sex Roles and Children's Play.* New York: Academic Press.

Van der Kooij, Rimmert. 1989. 'Research on Children's Play'. *Play and Culture,* vol. 2, pp. 20–34.

Van der Kooij, Rimmert and Wilma Slaats-van den Hurk. 1991. 'Relations between Parental Opinions and Attitudes about Child Rearing and Play'. *Play and Culture,* vol. 4, pp. 108–23.

Weir Ruth. 1976. 'Playing with Language', in J.S. Bruner, A. Jolly and K. Sylva, eds, *Play: Its Role in Development and Evolution.* Harmondsworth: Penguin.

2.5 *Imagination and Play, Pretend and Performance:*
Studies of Socio-Dramatic and General Role Play
– Contents, Effects and Style

Fein, Greta. 'A Transformational Analysis of Pretending'. *Developmental Psychology,* vol. 11, pp. 291–6.

Connolly, Jennifer, Anna-Beth Doyle and Flavia Ceschin. 1983. 'Forms and Functions of Social Fantasy Play in Preschoolers', in Marsha Liss, ed., *Social and Cognitive Skills: Sex Roles and Children's Play.* New York: Academic Press.

Fink, Robert. 1976. 'Role of Imaginative Play in Cognitive Development'. *Psychological Reports,* vol. 39, pp. 895–906.

Gardner, Howard. 1985. *Artful Scribbles: The Significance of Children's Drawing.* New York: Basic Books, pp. 100–115.

Jackowitz, Elaine R. and Malcolm Watson. 1980. 'Development of Object Transformations in Early Pretend Play'. *Developmental Psychology,* vol. 16, pp. 543–9.

Kline, Stephen. 1988. 'The Limits to the Imagination: Children's Play in the Age of Marketing', in I. Angus and S. Jhally, eds, *Cultural Politics in America.* New York: Routledge & Kegan Paul.

Kline, Stephen and Debra Pentecost. 1990. 'The Characterization of Play: Marketing Children's Toys'. *Play and Culture,* vol. 3 (3), pp. 235–54.

Kline, Stephen. 1991. 'Lets Make a Deal: Merchandising im US-Kinderfernsehen'. *Media Perspektiven.* vol. 4, pp. 220–34.

Kline, Stephen and Peter Smith. 1992. 'A Global Play?: Comparing British, Canadian, American and Japanese Toy Advertisements'. *Ethnografica.*

Singer, Jerome L. 1973. *The Child's World of Make-Believe.* New York: Academic Press.

Singer, Jerome. 1977. 'Imagination and Make Believe Play in Early Childhood: Some Educational Implications', vol. 1 (1), pp. 127–44.

Wolf, Dennie and Sharon Grollman. 1982. 'Ways of Playing: Individual Differences in Imaginative Style', in D. Pepler and K. Rubin, eds, *The Play of Children: Current Theory and Research.* Basel: S. Krager.

Yawkey, Thomas. 1980. 'An Investigation of Imaginative Play and Aural Language Development in Young Children, Five, Six and Seven', in Paul Wilkinson, ed., *Celebration of Play.* London: Croom Helm.

2.6 *Toy-Marketing: Distribution, Licensing, Sales*

'A Kids' Craze Could Start with a Pillow'. 1987. *Chain Store Age,* March, pp. 52–3.

ARF. 1986. *Everything You Should Know about Children's Research.* Transcript Proceedings. New York Hilton, 28 April.

'Barbie Fights Off Rivals'. 1987. *Chain Store Age,* February, pp. 101–3.

British Toy and Hobby Manufacturers Association. 1987. 'Advertising Toys to Children – A Members' Guide', September.

Canadian Toy Manufacturers Association. 1986. *Annual Report.*

'Can Baby Talk Match Cabbage Patch'. 1986. *Chain Store Age,* September, p. 68.

'Can Retailers Afford to Grin and Bear It (Plush Add-on Sale Programs)'. 1987. *Chain Store Age,* November, pp. 29–31.

'Construction Toys are Solidly Building'. 1985. *Chain Store Age,* January, pp. 102–4.

'Deck the Aisles with Lots of Basics'. 1986. *Chain Store Age,* September, pp. 67–9.

DiManno, Rosie. 1987. 'Barbie Lives! And She's, Well, She's a Doll!' *The Sunday Star,* 13 September, p. A6.

'Every Kid is an Adult at Heart'. 1987. *Chain Store Age,* September, p. 65.

'Firms See Strengths in Partnerships (Toy/Entertainment)'. 1987. *Chain Store Age,* June, p. 67.

'G.I. Joe, the American Retailing Hero'. 1986. *Chain Store Age,* October, pp. 80–1.

Gilligan, Eugene. 1989. 'Imports Help Retailers Find their Niche', *Playthings,* November, pp. 34, 35, 57.

Harmetz, Aljean. 1989. 'But Will Buyers go Batty?'. *The Globe and Mail,* 16 June, p. C1.

Hartnett, Michael. 1986. Toys/Licensing: Rise of Licensed Plush: Where Are Profits?'. *Chain Store Age (General Merchandising Trends),* February, pp. 87–9.

'Headed for "The Last Wound-Up"'. 1987. *Chain Store Age,* August, p. 59.

'High Prices Put Retailers in a Quandary'. 1987. *Chain Store Age,* May, p. 80.

Hyatt, Carol. 1986. 'Learning the Child Research Ropes'. *Everything You Should Know about Child Research (Proceedings of the ARF Key Issues Seminar).* New York, April, p. 101.

'Infant Product Sales Flattening'. 1987. *Chain Store Age*, October, p. 52.

'Interactive Video Toys Seem Likely To Be Hot Items despite Dispute about Effects'. 1987. *Globe and Mail*, 10 February.

Is There Life after Trivial Pursuit?' 1985. *Chain Store Age*, February, pp. 114–23.

Jereski, Laura. 1983. 'Advertisers Woo Kids with a Different Game'. *Marketing and Media Decisions*. September, pp. 72–3, 126–8.

Leccese, Donna. 'Toy Manufacturers, Retailers Battle Profit Squeeze'. *Playthings*, June pp. 30–4, 75.

'LEGO Leglocks Construction Category'. 1985. *Chain Store Age*, January, pp. 104–6.

'Licensed Games: More than a Name'. 1985. *Chain Store Age*, February, pp. 123–4.

'New Toys May Boost Summer Programs'. 1986. *Chain Store Age*, January, pp. 75–7.

'No Clear Winner Emerges in Toys'. 1987. *Chain Store Age*, July, p. 30.

'No Playing Around in Toyland'. 1987. *Chain Store Age*, September, pp. 39,40,42.

'OAA Expands Distribution Horizons'. 1986. *Chain Store Age*, November, p. 58. (Cabb. Kid co.)

'Parker Bros. Plays the Game'. 1985. *Chain Store Age*, February, pp. 124–8.

'Playskool Brand Name Opens Doors'. 1987. *Chain Store Age*, February, pp. 96–101.

'Profits Still Tough on Characters'. 1986. *Chain Store Age*, February, pp. 93–4.

Reysen, Frank. 1991. 'Industry Reports Slight Gains in 1990 Toy Sales. *Playthings*, March, p. 29.

'Retailers Predict Slimmer Margins'. 1987. *Chain Store Age*, July, p. 28.

'Sears & Spielberg'. 1986. *Chain Store Age*, June, pp. 59–60.

'Shoppers Rate Toy Specialty Stores Tops'. 1986. *Chain Store Age*, February, pp. 123–7.

'Shoppers Seek Quality at Best Price'. 1985. *Chain Store Age*, February, pp. 130–43.

Stavro, Barry. 1985. 'The Making of a Popple', *Forbes*, 16/12, pp. 174–6.

'Streamlined Lionel Seeks Stability'. 1986. *Chain Store Age*, February, pp. 112, 114.

'TCFC Are at it Again'. 1986. *Chain Store Age*, November, pp. 57–8.

'Technology Rocks the Cradle for Babies'. 1987. *Chain Store Age*, October, pp. 50–1.

'The Year of the Bear in Plush Toys'. 1985. *Chain Store Age*, February, pp. 109–11.

'Toys/Licensing: Profits Still Tough on Characters'. 1986. *Chain Store Age (General Merchandising Trends)*, February, pp. 93–4.

'Toys New Products'. 1987. *Chain Store Age*, April, p. 68.

'Toys "R" Us Reaps Muppet Bonanza'. 1985. *Chain Store Age*, February, p. 113.

'Trivia Breathes Life into Board Games'. 1985. *Chain Store Age*, February, p. 113.

Sydney Ladensohn Stern and Ted Schoenhaus. 1990. *Toyland: The High-Stakes Game of the Toy Industry.* Chicago: Contemporary Books.

Turner, Janice. 1987. 'It's Back to Basics Christmas for Toys'. *The Sunday Star,* 29 November, p. A17.

Vescovo, Rosemarie Del. 1988. 'Foreign-Made Toys Broaden Retailer Mix'. *Playthings,* November pp. 40–1.

'When Two Stores Are Better than One'. 1987. *Chain Store Age*, February, pp. 93–6.

'Will Superman Fly?'. 1987. *Chain Store Age,* June, p. 69.

2.7 *Aggressive Play and War Toys:*
Television and Play Content and Form, Critical Studies or Commentary on Play

Beresin, A. 1989. 'Toy War Games and the Illusion of Two-Sided Rhetoric'. *Play and Culture,* vol. 2 (3), pp. 218–24.

Brody, Jane E. 1987. 'Stranger in the House'. *Victoria Times Colonist,* 24 February, p. C3.

Carlson-Paige, N. and D. Levin. 1987. *The War Play Dilemma: Children's Needs and Society's Future.* Columbia University, New York: Teachers College Press.

Costabile, Angela, P.K. Smith, L. Matheson, J. Aston, T. Hunter and M. Boulton. 1989. 'A Cross-National Comparison of How Children Distinguish Serious and Playful Fighting', 12 December.

Duncan, Margaret Carlisle. 1989. 'Television Portrayals of Children's Play and Sport'. *Play and Culture,* vol. 2, pp. 235–52.

'Electronic Guns Stun Retailers'. 1987. *Chain Store Age,* March, pp. 54–6.

Feinburg, Sylvia G. 1976. 'Combat in Child Art', in J.S. Bruner, A. Jolly and K. Sylva, eds, *Play: Its Role in Development and Evolution.* Harmondsworth: Penguin.

Feshback, Seymour. 1956. 'The Catharsis Hypothesis and some Consequences of Interaction with Aggressive and Neutral Play Objects'. *Journal of Personality,* vol. 24E, pp. 449–62.

Green, Rick and Andrew. 1986. 'Toys that Turn Violent Are Preparation for Later Life'. *The Globe and Mail,* 2 December, p. A7.

'March of the Toy Soldier Retreats'. 1986. *Chain Store Age,* July, p. 34.

Nilsson, Nic (IPA President). 1982. 'Campaign against War Toys: Progress in Europe'. *IPA Newsletter,* vol. 8 (3), pp. 3–4.

Radkewycz, Alexandra. 1986. 'Toy Robots Linked to More Violence in Student Essays'. *The Globe and Mail,* 22 April.

'Retailers say "Yo Joe!"'. 1986. *Chain Store Age,* June, p. 63.

Sutton-Smith, B. 1988. 'War Toys and Childhood Aggression'. *The Journal of*

Play and Culture, vol. 1, pp. 57–69.

Valpy, Michael. 1990. 'Finesse Absent in Turtles' Model'. *Globe and Mail,* 8 May.

Wegener-Spohring. 1989. 'War Toys and Aggressive Games'. *Play and Culture*, vol. 2, pp. 35–47.

3 Consumption

3.1 *Consumer Literacy and Education:*
How Children Learn to Become Consumers

Gallagher, John E. 1989. 'Wooing a Captive Audience: A Controversial Plan to Beam News – and Ads – into Classrooms'. *Time*, 20 February, p. 41.

3.2 *Children and Consumption:*
Advertising, Marketing, Children's Understanding and Responses

'Analyze How They Play, Not What They Say: Projective Research Techniques Extract Valuable Market Data from Children'. 1983. *Marketing News*, 21 January, pp. 19–20.

Atkin, Charles. 1982. 'Television Advertising and Socialization to Consumer Roles', pp. 191 in D. Pearl. et al., eds, *Television and Behaviour: Ten Years of Scientific Progress and Implications for the Eighties,* vol. 2, *Technical Reviews.* National Institute of Mental Health, Washington: US Government Printing Office.

Atkin, Charles. 1975. 'Observation of Parent–Child Interaction in Supermarket Decision-Making'. *Journal of Marketing,* vol. 42, pp. 41–5.

Atkin, Charles and Gary Heald. 1977. 'The Content of Children's Toy and Food Commercials'. *Journal of Communication,* vol. 27, pp. 107–14.

Bahn, Kenneth D. 1986. 'How and When Do Brand Perceptions and Preferences First Form? A Cognitive Developmental Investigation'. *Journal of Consumer Research,* vol. 13, December, pp. 382–7.

Barry, Thomas E. 1977. 'Children's Television Advertising'. *American Marketing Association, Monograph Series* 8. USA.

Bloome, David and Danielle Ripich. 1979. 'Language in Children's Television Commercials: A Sociolinguistic Perspective'. *Theory into Practice,* vol. 18 (4), pp. 220–25.

Caron, Andre, and Scott Ward. 1975. 'Gift Decisions by Kids and Parents'. *Journal of Advertising Research,* 15 August, pp. 15–20.

Daily, Brenda (Manager Product Testing at Milton Bradley) in *Communicating to the Youth Market: A Child's Perspective.* Research report circulated by TVB. pp. RC-7.

Doolittle, John and Robert Pepper. 1975. 'Children's TV AD Content: 1974'.

Journal of Broadcasting, vol. 19 (2), pp. 131–42.

Fitch, E. 1985. 'Marketing Youth'. *Advertising Age*, 14 February.

Francese, Peter. 1985. *American Demographic Trends and Opportunities in the Children's Market*. Ithaca, New York.

Francese, Peter. 1986. 'People Patterns – an Expensive Season for Parents'. *Advertising Age*, 9 January (TVB).

Friderres, James. 1973. 'Advertising, Buying Patterns and Children'. *Journal of Advertising Research*, vol. 13, pp. 34–6.

Goldberg, Marvin and Gerald Gorn (1974). 'Some Unintended Consequences of TV Advertising to Children', *Journal of Consumer Research*, 5 (June), pp. 22–9.

Hall, Jane. 1987. 'TV's New Toys Send Critics Scrambling for their Guns', *People*, vol. 27 (12), pp. 34–5.

Hawkins, Del and K.A. Coney. 1974. 'Peer Group Influences on Children's Product Preferences'. *Journal of Academy of Marketing Science*, 2 (spring), pp. 322–31.

John, Deborah Roedder and John C. Whitney Jr. 1986. 'The Development of Consumer Knowledge in Children: A Cognitive Structure Approach'. *Journal of Consumer Research*, vol. 12, March, pp. 406–17.

'Kids Will Talk When They're Having Fun'. 1986. *Marketing News*, 12 September.

Kunkel, Dale. 1991. 'Young Minds and Marketplace Values: Issues in Children's Television Advertising'. *Journal of Social Issues*, vol. 47 (1), pp. 57–72.

Levin, Stephen R., T.V. Petros and F.W. Petrella. 1982. 'Preschoolers' Awareness of Television Advertising'. *Child Development*, vol. 53, pp. 933–7.

Liebert, Diane E., Joyce N. Sprafkin, Robert M. Liebert and Eli A. Rubinstein. 1977. 'How TV Sells Children/Television Disclaimers'. *Journal of Communication*, winter, pp. 118–24.

Liebert, Diane, J. Sprafkin, R. Liebert and E. Rubenstein. 1977. 'Effects of Television Commercial Disclaimers on the Product Expectations of Children'. *Journal of Communication*, vol. 27 (1), p. 118.

Lonial, Subhash C. and Stuart Van Auken. 1985. 'Children's Perceptions of Characters: Human versus Animate, Assessing Implications for Children's Advertising'. *Journal of Advertising*, vol. 14 (2), pp. 13–22.

Lutz, Kathy A. and Richard J. Lutz. 1977. 'Effects of Interactive Imagery on Learning: Application to Advertising'. *Journal of Applied Psychology*, vol. 62 (4), pp. 493–8.

Marney, Jo. 1983. 'The Importance of the Children's Market'. *Marketing (Advertising Research)*, 27 June (TVB).

Marney, Jo. 'Catch Them While They're Young'. *Marketing (Advertising Research)*, 15 November (TVB).

'Matchbox Bows to Consumer Groups, Won't Market Doll Based on Film Friend'. 1989. *The Toronto Star*, 21 October, p. C2.

Morgenstein, Elaine and Marvin Schoenwald. 1986. 'Success in the Children's Market Rests with Showing the Familiar'. *Marketing News*, 12 September, p. 48.

'Now Billy, Age 6, Picks Brands'. 1983. *Marketing and Media Decisions*, March, pp. 68–9 (TVB).

Rae, Jane. 'If You're Going to Advertise to Kids on Television Do it Right'. *Stimulus*, May/June, pp. 24–5 (TVB).

Reid, Leonard. 1979. 'Viewing Rules as Mediating Factors of Children's Responses to Commercials'. *Journal of Broadcasting*, vol. 23 (1), pp. 12–26.

Reid, L.N. and Charles Frazer. 1980. 'Children's Use of Television Commercials to Initiate Social Interaction in Family Viewing Situations'. *Journal of Broadcasting*, vol. 24, pp. 149–158.

Roberts, D. 1983. 'Children and Commercials: Issues, Evidence, Interventions', pp. 19–35. in J. Sprafkin, C. Swift and R. Hess, eds, *Rx Television: Enhancing the Preventive Impact of TV*. New York: Haworth Press.

Robertson, Thomas S. and John R. Rossiter. 1977. 'Children's Responsiveness to Commercials'. *Journal of Communication*, vol. 27 (1), pp. 101–6.

Ross, Rhonda, Toni Campbell, Altetha Huston-Stein and John C. Wright. 1981. 'Nutritional Misinformation of Children: A Developmental and Experimental Analysis of the Effects of Televised Food Commercials'. *Journal of Applied Psychology*, vol. 1 (4), pp. 329–47.

Rust, L. 1986. 'Children's Advertising: How it Works, How to Do it, How to Know If it Works', in *Everything You Should Know About Children's Research* (Proceedings of ARF Key Issues Workshop). New York, April.

Schuetz, Stephen and Joyce Sprafkin. 1979. 'Portrayal of Prosocial and Aggressive Behaviours in Children's TV Commercials'. *Journal of Broadcasting*, vol. 23 (1).

Schwartz, Lori A. and William T. Markham. 1985. 'Sex Stereotyping in Children's Toy Advertisements'. *Sex Roles*, vol. 12 (1/2), pp. 157–70.

'Shoppers Seek Quality at Best Price'. 1985. *Chain Store Age (General Merchandising Trends)*, February, pp. 130–43.

Television Bureau of Advertising. 1986. *Target Selling the Children's Market*.

The Children's Market. 1986. Toronto: Television Bureau of Canada.

Van Auken, Stuart and S.C. Lonial. 1985. 'Children's Perceptions of Characters: Human versus Animate Assessing Implications for Children's Advertising'. *Journal of Advertising*, vol. 14 (2), pp. 13–22, 61.

Verna, Mary E. 1975. 'The Female Image on Children's TV Commercials'. *Journal of Broadcasting*, vol. 19, pp. 301–8.

Wackman, Daniel B., Ellen Wartella and Scott Ward. 1977. 'How TV Sells Children/Learning to be Consumers'. *Journal of Communication*, winter, pp. 138–57.

Ward, Scott and Daniel B. Wackman. 1973. 'Children's Information Processing of Television Advertising', in Peter Clarke, ed., *New Models for Communication Research*. Beverly Hills: Sage.

Wartella, Ellen, ed. 1979. *Children Communicating: Media and Development of*

Thought, Speech, Understanding. Beverly Hills: Sage Publications.

Wartella, Ellen, Daniel Wackman, Scott Ward, Jacob Shamir and Alison Alexander. 1979. 'The Young Child as Consumer', pp. 251–80, in Ellen Wartella, ed., *Children Communicating: Media and Development of Thought, Speech, Understanding*. Beverly Hills: Sage Publications.

Welch, Renate, Aletha Huston-Stein, John Wright and Robert Plehal. 1979. 'Subtle Sex-Role Cues in Children's Commercials'. *Journal of Communication*, summer.

Wells, William. 1965. 'Communicating with Children'. *Journal of Advertising Research*, March, pp. 1–14.

Young, Brian M. 1990. *Television Advertising and Children*. Oxford: Clarendon Press.

3.3 *General Theory and Critiques of Consumption*

Ashman, Roy, John Hasenjaeger and H. Keith Hunt. 1979. *Advertising and Government Regulation: A Report by the Advertising and Government Panel of the American Academy of Advertising*. April, pp. 79–106.

'Battle of Brands: The Day Mass Marketing Was Born'. 1990. *The Vancouver Sun*, 24 February, p. H5.

Bell, Daniel. 1973. *The Coming of Post-Industrial Society: A Venture in Social Forecasting*. New York: Basic Books.

Corbiel, Carole. 1987. 'The Advertised Infant: Ivan's Adventures in Babyland'. *This Magazine*. vol. 21 (2), p. 26.

Csikszentmihalyi, M. and Rochberg-Halton, E. 1981. *The Meaning of Things*. Cambridge: Cambridge University Press.

Douglas, Mary and Isherwood, Baron. 1978. *The World of Goods*. Harmondsworth: Penguin.

Ewen, Stuart. 1976. *Captains of Consciousness*. New York: McGraw-Hill.

Evernden, Neil. 1985. *The Natural Alien, Humankind and Environment*. Toronto: University of Toronto Press.

Evernden, Neil. 1988. 'Nature in Industrial Society', in Angus, I. and S. Jhally, *Cultural Politics in America*. New York: Routledge & Kegan Paul.

Frank, Allan Dodds. 1987. 'Leisure and Recreation'. *Forbes*, 12 January, pp. 158–9.

Frazer, James George. 1966. *The Golden Bough: A study of Magic and Religion*. New York: St. Martin's Press.

Furby, Lita. 1978. 'Possessions in Humans: An Exploratory Study of its Meaning and Motivation'. *Social Behaviour and Personality*, vol. 6(1), pp. 49–65.

Furby, Lita. 'Possessions: Toward a Theory of their Meaning and Function Throughout the Life Cycle'.

Galbraith, John Kenneth. 1990. 'Who's Afraid of Adam Smith'. *Observer*, London, 15 July, p. 18.

Galbraith, John Kenneth, 1958. *The Affluent Society.* Boston: Houghton Mifflin.

Goffman, E. 1976. *Gender Advertisements.* New York: Harper & Row.

Greyser, Stephen. 1972. 'Advertising: Attacks and Counters'. *Harvard Business Review,* March–April, pp. 1–9.

Hirsch, Fred. 1976. *The Social Limits to Growth.* Cambridge: Cambridge University Press.

Jhally, Sut. 1987. *The Codes of Advertising.* New York: St. Martin's Press.

Kavanaugh, John F. 1981. *Following Christ in a Consumer Society: The Spirituality of Cultural Resistance.* Maryknoll, New York: Orbis Books.

Lasch, Christopher. 1979. *The Culture of Narcissism.* New York: Norton.

Leiss, W., S. Kline, and S. Jhally. 1986. *Social Communication in Advertising.* Toronto: Methuen.

Leiss, William. 1976. *The Limits to Satisfaction.* Toronto: University of Toronto Press.

Levy, Sydney. 1969. 'Symbols by which We Buy', in L.H. Stockman, ed., *Advancing Marketing Efficiency.* Chicago: American Marketing Association.

Linder, Steffan. 1970. *The Harried Leisure Class.* New York: Columbia University Press.

McCraken, Grant. 1988. *The Culture of Consumption.* Illinois: University of Illinois Press.

Marchand, Roland. 1985. *Advertising the American Dream: Making Way for Modernity, 1920–1940.* Berkeley: University of California Press.

Mittelstaedt, Martin. 1989. 'The Billion-Dollar Cure'. *Report on Business,* June, pp. 19–21.

Penz, Peter. 1986. *Consumer Sovereignty and Human Interests.* Cambridge: Cambridge University Press.

Perry, J.M. 1979. 'To Raise a Politician to the Heights, Try a Helicopter and Music.' *Wall Street Journal,* 24 July.

Pope, Daniel. 1983. *The Making of Modern Advertising.* New York: Basic Books.

Ray, Michael. 1982. *Advertising and Communication Management.* Englewood Cliffs, NJ: Prentice-Hall.

Ray, Michael L. et al. 1973. 'Marketing Communication and the Hierarchy-of-Effects', in Peter Clarke, ed., *New Models for Communication Research.* Beverly Hills: Sage.

Reisman, David, N. Glazer, and R. Denny. 1956. *The Lonely Crowd: A Study of Changing American Character.* New York: Doubleday.

Sahlins, Marshall. 1976. *Culture and Practical Reason.* Chicago: University of Chicago Press.

Smith, Adam. 1937. *An Inquiry into the Nature and Causes of the Wealth of Nations.* Edwin Cannon, ed. New York: The Modern Library.

Snyder, Richard. 1972. 'Trends in the Sporting Goods Market', pp. 423–44 in M. Marie Hart, ed., *Sport in the Socio-cultural Process.* Dubuque: Wm. C. Brown.

Touchek, Gary. 1987. 'Beams of Power Are Pointed at the Kids'. *Globe and*

Mail Broadcast Week Magazine, 29 November, p. 9.

Twedt, Dik Warren, ed. 1978. *1978 Survey of Marketing Research,* pp. 41, 44.

3.4 *Children, Families and Consumerism*

Almqvist, Birgitta. 1989. 'Age and Gender Differences in Children's Christmas Requests'. *Play and Culture,* vol. 2, pp. 2–19.

Blankenship, A.B, Chakrapani, Chuck and Poole, W. *A History of Marketing Research in Canada,* Profession Marketing Research Society, Toronto.

Berey, Lewis and R. Pollay. 1968. 'The Influencing Role of the Child in Family Decision Making'. *Journal of Marketing Research,* vol. 5, pp. 70–2.

Feldman, Shel, Abraham Wolf and Doris Warmouth. 1977. 'How TV Sells Children/Parental Concern about Child-Directed Commercials'. *Journal of Communication,* winter, pp. 125–37.

Francese, Peter (American Demographics). 1985. 'Trends and Opportunities in the Children's Market'. *People Patterns.*

Galst, Joann P. and M.A. White. 1976. 'The Unhealthy Persuader: The Reinforcing Value of Children's Purchase-Influencing Attempts at the Super-Market'. *Child Development,* vol. 47, pp. 1089–96.

Guest, Lester P. 1942. 'The Genesis of Brand Awareness'. *Journal of Applied Psychology,* 26 December, pp. 800–8.

Guest, Lester P. 1964. 'Brand Loyalty Revised: A Twenty Year Report'. *Journal of Applied Psychology,* vol. 48, pp. 93–7.

Holbrook, Morris. 1987. Mirror, Mirror, on the Wall, What's Unfair in the Reflections on Advertising, *Journal of Marketing,* vol. 51 (July) pp. 95–103.

Jones, John P. 1990. *What's in a Name? Advertising & the Concept of Brands.* Lexington, MA: Lexington Books.

Lea, Stephen, R.M. Tarpy and P. Webley. 1987. 'Growing up in the Economy', in *The Individual in the 2.4 Economy: A Textbook of Economic Psychology.* New York: Cambridge University Press.

McNeal, J. 1987. *Children as Consumers: Insights and Implications.* Lexington: Lexington Books.

McNeal, James. 1964. *Children as Consumers.* Austin, Tex.: University of Texas, Bureau of Business Research.

Moore, Roy and George Moschis. 'Role of Mass Media and the Family in Development of Consumption Norms'. *Journalism Quarterly,* vol. 60, pp. 67–73.

Morgenstein, Elaine and Marvin Schoenwald. 1986. 'Success in the Children's Market Rests with Showing the Familiar'. *Marketing News,* 12 September, p. 48.

Pollay, Rick. 1989. 'On the Value of Reflections on the Values in the "Distorted Mirror"'. *Journal of Marketing,* vol. 51, July, pp. 104–9.

Reisman, David and H. Roseborough. 1955. 'Careers in Consumer Behavior', in Lincoln Clark, ed., *Consumer Behavior II: The Life Cycle and Consumer*

Behavior. New York: New York University Press.

Sheikh, Anees and L. Moleski. 1977. 'Conflict in the Family over Commercials'. *Journal of Communication*, winter, pp. 152–7.

Schudson, Michael. 1984. *Advertising: the Uneasy Persuasion.* New York: Basic Books.

Stacey, Barry G. 1987. 'Economic Socialization', pp. 1–33 in S. Long, ed., *Annual Review of Political Science*, vol. 2. Norwood: Ablex Publishing.

Stacey, Barrie G. 1982. 'Economic Socialization in the Pre-adult years'. *British Journal of Social Psychology*, vol. 21, pp. 159–73.

Wackman, Daniel, E. Wartella and Scott Ward. 1977. 'Learning to Be Consumers: The Role of the Family', *Journal of Communication*, pp. 138–51.

Ward, S. and D. Wackman. 1972. 'Television Advertising and Intrafamily Influence: Children's Purchase Influence Attempts and Parental Yielding', in E.A. Rubenstein, G.A. Comstock and J.P. Murray, eds, *Television and Social Behavior*, vol. 4, *Television in Day-to-Day Life: Patterns of Use.* Washington DC: US Printing Office.

Ward, Scott. 1974. 'Consumer Socialization'. *Journal of Consumer Research*, 1 September, pp. 1–14.

3.5 *Critiques of Childhood Consumerism, Policy, Advocacy*

Ashman, Roy, John Hasenjaeger and H. Keith Hunt. 1979. *Advertising and Government Regulation: A Report by the Advertising and Government Panel of the American Academy of Advertising*, April, p. 47.

Berger, Nan 1971. 'The Child, the Law and the State', pp. 153–79 in Adams, Paul, Leila Berg, Nan Berger, Michael Duane, A.S. Neil and Robert Ollendorff, *Children's Rights: Towards the Liberation of the Child.* Wellingborough: Elek Books.

Duane, Michael. 'Freedom and the State System of Education', pp. 180–239 in Adams, Paul, Leila Berg, Nan Berger, Michael Duane, A.S. Neil and Robert Ollendorff. 1971. *Children's Rights: Towards the Liberation of the Child.* Wellingborough: Elek Books.

Armstrong, B. and M. Brucks. 1989. 'Dealing with Children's Advertising: Public Policy Issues and Alternatives'. *Journal of Public Policy and Management*, vol. 7, pp. 98–113.

Federal Trade Commission. 1978. *FTC Staff Report on Television Advertising to Children*, February, Washington, DC.

Feldman, Shel and A. Wolf. 1974. 'What's Wrong with Children's Commercials?' *Journal of Advertising Research*, vol. 14, pp. 39–43.

Globe and Mail. 'Some Kids' TV Shows Deemed Commercials: FCC Ruling Doesn't Go Far Enough, Say Children's Advocacy Groups', 12 April 1991. Arts Section.

Goldberg, M. 1986. 'The Effects of the Law Intended to Eliminate Advertising Directed at Children in Quebec'. Office de la Protection du Consommateur, Government of Quebec, 30 March.

Grass, Jennifer. 1979. 'Quebec Banning Ads to Children'. *Financial Times*, 19 February, p. 35.

Wertham, Frederic. 1954. *The Seduction of the Innocent.* New York: Rinehart.

Supreme Court of Canada. 1989. Attorney General of Quebec versus Irwin Toy Ltd.

4 Books, Comics and Literacy

4.1 *History and Commentary on Children's Books, Literacy, Studies and Reading and its Effects*

Avery, Gillian Ellis. 1975. *Childhood's Pattern: A study of Heroes and Heroines of Children's Fiction 1770–1950.* London: Hodder & Stoughton.

Barry, Florence V. 1922. *A Century of Children's Books.* London: Methuen.

Bettelheim, Bruno. 1977. *The Uses of Enchantment: The Meaning and Importance of Fairytales.* New York: Vintage Books.

Darton, F.J. Harvey. 1970. *Children's Books in England, Five Centuries of Social Life.* New York: Cambridge University Press.

Hildick, Wallace. 1970. *Children and Fiction: A Critical Study in Depth of the Artistic and Psychological Factors Involved in Writing Fiction for and about Children.* London: Evans.

Jones, Philip. 1976. *Children's Books of Yesterday.* London: The Studio.

Moses, Montrose J. 1975. *Children's Books and Reading.* Detroit: Gale Research.

Newbery, S. Roscoe and Carnan Power. *A Provisional Check List of Books for the Entertainment Instruction and Education of Children and Young People Issued under the Imprints of John Newbery and his Family in 1774–1802.* London: Library Association.

Opie, Iona and Peter Opie, eds. 1951. *The Oxford Dictionary of Nursery Rhymes.* Oxford: Clarendon Press.

Quayle, Eric. 1971. *The Collector's Book of Children's Books.* London: Studio Vista.

Thwaite, M.F. 1963. *From Primer to Pleasure, An Introduction to the History of Children's Books in England from the Invention of Printing to 1900.* London: Library Association.

Whalley, Joyce Irene. 1974. *Cobwebs to Catch Flies: Illustrated Books for the Nursery and Schoolroom 1700–1900.* London: Elek Books.

Wolfenstein, Martha. 1947. 'The Impact of a Children's Story on Mothers and Children'. *Monographs for the Society for Research in Child Development,* vol. 9 (42). Washington DC: National Research Council.

4.2 *The Book Industry, Children's Publishing, the Market*

'Book Sales Rise 8.3% to $9.88 Billion in 1985'. 1986. *Publishers' Weekly*, 18 July, p. 18.

'Cultural Statistics'. 1986–87.

Grannis, Chandler B. 1987. 'U.S. Book Title Output and Average Prices, Final 1986 Figures'. *Publishers' Weekly*, 2 October, pp. 45–52.

'No Affront to the Children – Why is Britain's Children's Book Business the Best in the World?'. 1986. *The Economist*, 13 December, pp. 99–100.

'Printing, Publishing and Allied Industries'. 1986.

Quayle, Eric. 1971. *The Collector's Book of Children's Books*. London: Studio Vista.

Slopen, Beverley. 1986. 'Straddling the Cultures'. *Publishers' Weekly*, 12 September, pp. 54–7.

Schneider, George A. 1972. 'Millions of Moral Little Books: Sunday School Books in their Popular Context', Russel Nye, ed., pp. 1–15 in *New Dimensions in Popular Culture*. Bowling Green: Bowling Green Popular Press.

Smith, Anthony. 1979. *The Newspaper: An International History*. London: Thames & Hudson.

Taylor, Jennifer. 1986. 'U.K. Children's Publishing: Growing Up'. *Publishers' Weekly*, 12 September, pp. 50–3.

Taylor, Jennifer. 1987. *Drive in U.K. to Push Children's Books'. Publishers' Weekly*, 20 March, p. 38.

'U.S. Book Title Output and Average Prices, 1983–1985'. 1986. *Publishers' Weekly*, 3 October, pp. 89–92.

Wishinsky, Frieda. 1987. 'A New Era in Canadian Children's Books'. *Publishers' Weekly*, 20 March, p. 36.

4.3 *The Comic Book: History, Content, Analysis*

Barker, Martin. 1984. *A Haunt of Fears: The Strange History of the British Horror Comics Campaign*. London: Pluto Press.

Berger, Arthur Asa. 1973. *The Comic Stripped American*. Baltimore: Penguin.

Bogart, Leo. 1957. 'Comic Strips and their Adult Readers', in Bernard Rosenberg and David Manning White, eds, *Mass Culture: The Popular Arts in America*. New York: Free Press.

Brodbeck, Arthur and David M. White. 1957. 'How to Read Li'l Abner Intelligently', pp. 218–24 in Bernard Rosenberg and David White, eds, *Mass Culture, The Popular Arts in America*. New York: Free Press.

Crafton, Donald. 1982. *Before Mickey: The Animated Film 1889–1928*. Cambridge, MA: MIT Press.

Daniels, Les. 1971. *Comix: A History of Comic Books in America*. New York: Outerbridge and Dienstfrey.

Feiffer, Jules. 1975. *The Great Comic Book Heroes.* New York: Bonanza Books.

Finch, Christopher. 1975. *The Art of Walt Disney: From Mickey Mouse to the Magic Kingdoms.* Walt Disney Productions.

Lupoff, Dick and Don Thompson. 1970. *All in Colour for a Dime.* New York: Ace Books.

Perry, George and Alan Aldridge. 1971. *The Penguin Book of Comics.* London: Penguin.

Reitberger, Reinhold and Wolfgang Fuchs. 1972. *Comics, Anatomy of a Mass Medium.* London: Studio Vista.

Smith, T., S. Johnson and M. Graham. 1986. *Japanese Animation Program Guide.* Sunnyvale, California: BayCon.

Streicher, Helen White. 1974. 'The Girls in the Cartoons'. *Journal of Communication,* spring, pp. 126–37.

Warshow, Robert. 1957. 'Paul, and Horror Comics, and Dr. Wertham', pp. 199–211 in Bernard Rosenberg and David White, eds, *Mass Culture: The Popular Arts in America.* New York: Free Press.

White, David Manning and Walter Abel, eds. 1963. *The Funnies: An American Idiom.* Glencoe, New York.

Wilson, Bill. 1983. *There's No Business Like Cho Business'. C/FO The Magazine,* vol. 4, pp. 3–5.

Index

Index